PUBLIC PERSONNEL
ADMINISTRATION

——————•——————

Second Edition

RONALD D. SYLVIA
C. KENNETH MEYER

HARCOURT COLLEGE PUBLISHERS

Fort Worth   Philadelphia   San Diego   New York   Orlando   Austin   San Antonio
Toronto   Montreal   London   Sydney   Tokyo

PUBLISHER	Earl McPeek
EXECUTIVE EDITOR	David Tatom
MARKETING STRATEGIST	Laura Brennan
PROJECT MANAGER	Angela Williams Urquhart

Cover design by Jane Tenenbaum Design, Inc.
Cover image provided by Photodisc © 2002.

ISBN: 0-15-506268-9
Library of Congress Catalog Card Number: 00-111491

Address for Domestic Orders
Harcourt College Publishers, 6277 Sea Harbor Drive, Orlando, FL 32887–6777
800–782–4479

Address for International Orders
International Customer Service
Harcourt College Publishers, 6277 Sea Harbor Drive, Orlando, FL 32887–6777
407–345–3800
(fax) 407–345–4060
(e-mail) hbintl@harcourtbrace.com

Address for Editorial Correspondence
Harcourt College Publishers, 301 Commerce Street, Suite 3700, Fort Worth, TX 76102

Web Site Address
http://www.harcourtcollege.com

Printed in the United States of America

1 2 3 4 5 6 7 8 9 0   066   9 8 7 6 5 4 3 2 1

Harcourt College Publishers

CONTENTS

PREFACE IX

ACKNOWLEDGMENTS XIII

CHAPTER 1: THE EVOLUTION OF PERSONNEL MANAGEMENT 1

The Early Period 1

1820 to the Present 3

State and Local Patronage 6

The Development of the Federal Merit Systems: 1883–1978 10

The 1978 Civil Service Reform Act 18

The Office of Personnel Management 19

The Senior Executive Service 22

The Merit System Protection Board 24

The Office of Special Counsel and the Whistleblower Protection Act of 1989 25

The Equal Employment Opportunity Commission 26

The Federal Labor Relations Authority 27

Merit Pay 28

Summary and Conclusion 29

Case: Patronage or Cronyism? 30

Case: Keep Your Stick on the Ice or Your Views to Yourself 33

Notes and Resources 36

CHAPTER 2: TRENDS IN STATE AND LOCAL GOVERNMENT HUMAN RESOURCES SYSTEMS 43

State-Level Trends 43

Evolution in Local Government 50

Summary and Conclusion 53

Case: Promises Real or Implied 54

Notes and Resources 55

CHAPTER 3: EQUAL EMPLOYMENT OPPORTUNITY IN THE UNITED STATES 57

The Civil Rights Movement 57

The Evolution of Affirmative Action 58

Federal Implementation of Proactive Affirmative Action 62

Equal Employment Opportunity, Affirmative Action, and the Courts 73

Remedial Affirmative Action 78

Summary and Conclusion 86

Case: A Proud Tradition of Affirmative Action 87

Case: AIDS in the Public Workplace 89

Notes and Resources 90

CHAPTER 4: WOMEN AT WORK 95

History of Women at Work 95

Sexual Harassment 99

Summary and Conclusion 101

Case: Trust and Commitment 101

Notes and Resources 104

CHAPTER 5: WORKFORCE DIVERSITY AND FAMILY ISSUES 105

Domestic Partners 105

Day Care 106

Eldercare 107

Flexible Scheduling 108

Summary and Conclusion 111

Case: Betting on Family Life 111

Case: Leave It to the Bereavement Policy 112

Case: Time and Time Again 115

Notes and Resources 119

CHAPTER 6: HUMAN RESOURCE PLANNING 121

The Planning Context 121

The Human Component in Agency Planning 122

The Technology of Human Resource Planning 126

Summary and Conclusion 131
Notes and Resources 131

CHAPTER 7: RECRUITMENT 135

Recruitment under Patronage 135
Recruitment under Merit Systems 137
Merit Recruitment and Social Equity 146
Personnel Management under the Merit System 149
Summary and Conclusion 151
Recruitment Exercise 151
Notes and Resources 155

CHAPTER 8: CLASSIFICATION SYSTEMS 159

Types of Classification Systems 159
Classification in the Federal Civilian Service 163
The Techniques of Classification 166
Constructing a Pay Scale 170
Ongoing Applications and Issues 174
Summary and Conclusion 175
A Classification Exercise 176
Notes and Resources 192

CHAPTER 9: COMPENSATION 195

Comparability 195
Motivation 196
Summary and Conclusion 203
Notes and Resources 204

CHAPTER 10: PERFORMANCE APPRAISAL SYSTEMS 207

Appraisal Systems and Organization Outcomes 207
Instruments of Evaluation 215
Summary and Conclusion 223
Case: Boundary Limits and Employee Counseling 223
Notes and Resources 225

CHAPTER 11: EMPLOYEE TRAINING AND DEVELOPMENT 227

Training in the Public Sector 227
The Professionalization of Public Service 229
An Organizational Perspective on Types of Training 230
Summary and Conclusion 236
Case: Madison County's Zero-Tolerance for Harassment and Discrimination
    Directive 237
Notes and Resources 239

CHAPTER 12: PUBLIC-SECTOR COLLECTIVE BARGAINING 243

The Historical Context of Labor Relations in the United States 243
Unionization in the Public Sector 246
Collective Bargaining at the State and Local Level 249
Collective Bargaining at the Federal Level 256
Strikes 261
Alternatives to Strikes 263
Arbitration 264
Summary and Conclusion 271
Notes and Resources 272

CHAPTER 13: MANAGEMENT IN A UNION ENVIRONMENT 275

Union Contracts as Constraints on Management 275
Preparing for Negotiations 280
Developing a Positive Approach 281
Summary and Conclusion 288
Notes and Resources 288

CHAPTER 14: EMPLOYEE DISCIPLINE AND CONFLICT RESOLUTION SYSTEMS 291

EEO Constraints 291
EEO Grievance Systems 292
Merit System Constraints 294
Disciplinary Systems 296

Job Rights of Classified Employees 300
Sexual Behavior and the Rights of Public Employees 307
Guidelines for Off-Duty Conduct Public Employees 308
Drug Testing and the Rights of Public Employees 311
Summary and Conclusion 316
Case: Teacher Discipline 316
Case: Opossums and Other Excuses 319
Case: Supervising God 321
Case: The Sweet Smell of a Good Appearance Policy 323
Notes and Resources 324

POSTSCRIPT 329

APPENDIX 333

For Richard, Kathleen-Grace,
Lauren, and Sidney

This text starts from the fundamental premise that the management of human resources is critical to the successful implementation of government programs. Most public managers recognize that the effective management of their human resources is the primary method whereby they achieved agency goals. Setting clear and realistic expectations for employees, providing them with necessary mission-relevant training, and providing them a work environment free from harassment and discrimination should be priorities for all line managers.

For years human resource management was viewed as a Byzantine labyrinth that only the intrepid dared to challenge. The rules for hiring were elaborate and largely created and enforced by a central department whose word was law and whose motives were suspect. Public employees traded certain rights to full participation in the political process for a measure of job security that was much greater than is normally found in the private sector. Removing an unsatisfactory employee was deemed impossible by some and not worth the effort and frustration by others. The system was overlaid by a web of labor contracts that further limited managerial discretion. The limitations of the classification system, moreover, often made it as difficult to reward employees as it was to discipline them.

A number of reforms have occurred since civil service systems first began to replace patronage towards the end of the nineteenth century. Each time a flaw was detected, a new policy was generated to correct it. Each time a new management theory came along, government operating systems were adapted to include it. Very often the new system was an add-on rather than a replacement. The farthest reaching change in the federal personnel system occurred in 1978. The Civil Service Reform Act (CSRA) of that year replaced the Civil Service Commission with an alphabet soup of agencies to oversee one or more personnel functions. The CSRA had four major goals. The first was the reaffirmation and expansion of the principles of merit. Second, the CSRA sought to reassert the authority of political executives over the policy process. Third, the act attempted to enhance agency autonomy over the personnel process. Finally, the act consolidated equal opportunity and labor relations oversight into single autonomous agencies.

The first edition of this text focused on this history and the legal framework of human resources management in the public sector and the functional components of personnel management: planning, recruitment, classification, appraisal, collective bargaining, and employee discipline.

Since the first edition of this text, many changes have occurred at all levels of government that directly impact the way personnel management operates. The National Performance Review (NPR), for example, was the centerpiece of the Clinton administration's efforts to streamline the operations of the federal government. In addition to simplifying the procurement process and reducing paperwork, the NPR focused on the government's personnel system. The role of the Office of Personnel Management was overhauled and given a new mission: to facilitate innovation and enable agencies to run their own human resource functions as they see fit. The results of the NPR have been dramatic, as we shall see. The Merit System Protection Board (MSPB) has come full circle in its view of recruitment. The MSPB now advocates a return to a system of written examinations for ranking qualified candidates for federal employment.

In many state and local governments, managing in the context of collective-bargaining agreements is a reality of governing. Public-sector unions have moved from being an awkward stepchild of the labor movement to being the most organized of any sector of the American economy. The federal government and many state laws have also granted public employees substantially the same political participation rights as those enjoyed by nongovernment workers. Public employees still must resign their positions before seeking partisan political office. That said, they have become a major force in the political process, from serving as a source of funds for political campaigns to serving as officers at various levels in the Democratic Party.

Virtually every aspect of public personnel management has been impacted by the technology revolution that has taken place in the last decade. Employment information and applications, for example, are available on-line. Some cities have contracted their employee screening process to private vendors who collect, screen, and rank resumes electronically. These services can present the agency with a list of certified candidates and a list of ranked eligibles within minutes of the job listing's closing. Electronic databases also facilitate the human resource planning process and the administration of benefits.

This second edition addresses current issues and procedures in 14 reorganized and updated chapters. Where appropriate, we provide case studies for discussion and hands-on exercises designed to introduce students to the various aspects of personnel management. The first five chapters cover the political, historical, and policy context of human resources management. Chapter 1 deals with the evolution of public personnel systems from the advent of patronage through the emergence of civil service systems. The chapter has been expanded to include a discussion of the political and free speech rights of public employees.

Chapter 2 addresses current trends in state and local government from Georgia's decision to abolish its merit system to the advances in electronic technology as applied to personnel systems.

Chapter 3 deals with equal employment opportunity and affirmative action in government. The chapter provides extensive updates on court decisions regarding affirmative action and state-level initiatives such as California's decision to outlaw the practice in hiring, contracting by state and local governments, and university admissions.

Gender issues have become so important in the workplace that we have added a separate chapter on women at work. Chapter 4 documents women's struggle against disparate opportunity based on gender, such as perceived pay inequities and promotional opportunities. By far the largest section of the chapter deals with sexual harassment in the workplace and the most recent court decisions on the topic.

Chapter 5 deals with workforce diversity and family issues. From the family leave act, to day care, flextime, and maternity leave, government employers find themselves providing a range of services and benefits to employees that recognize the need to balance work and family.

Chapters 6 through 14 deal with various functions associated with personnel management, from human resources (HR) planning to employee discipline and conflict management systems in government. Chapter 6, Human Resource Planning, makes the point that effective HR planning is entirely dependent on strategic planning systems of the larger organizations. We also discuss the issue of succession planning. Many agencies have determined that their most vital senior managers are due to retire within five years. The organization must therefore immediately begin to identify, train, and retain the successors to the current crop of executives. Thus, human resource planning has become the number one priority of the agency.

Chapter 7, Recruitment Systems, treats the function most often associated with personnel. From job analysis to interview techniques, nothing a line manager does will have a more lasting impact on the organization than the people he or she hires. The chapter discusses traditional personnel systems and then moves to innovations in recruiting, including alternative referral sources, the extensive use of internships, and electronic recruitment. The chapter concludes with a recruitment exercise designed to introduce students to the various steps in the process, from identifying critical qualifications to conducting a successful interview.

In the previous edition, classification and compensation were combined into a single chapter. Here they are separated and expanded. Chapter 8, Classification Systems, reviews the various classification systems that exist from rank in the corps to rank in the job. A special emphasis is placed on benchmark factor classification systems that assign point values to various duties, responsibilities, and qualifications associated with a position. The chapter explains how to create a pay scale based on organization, contribution, and market forces. Students are then asked to apply the benchmark factor system used by the federal government to two sample positions.

Chapter 9, Compensation, discusses the various rewards systems used in government, from performance pay to incentive to longevity pay, and their relative values for motivating employees. The failed merit pay experiment of the federal government is presented along with the reasons for its failure. The pros and cons of individual and group rewards are discussed along with the various benefit packages governments are using to compete for the best employees in the current tight labor market.

Performance appraisal is the subject of Chapter 10. Here we discuss the purpose and form of various appraisal systems. In some agencies, the appraisal system is part and parcel of their program management system. For others, it is a chore foisted on unsuspecting and unwilling managers by a personnel division that does not have enough to do. The pros and cons of various systems are discussed, including the latest techniques of subordinate appraisal of supervisors and 360 evaluations designed to measure performance in the context of the position. The chapter concludes with an exercise in constructive criticism.

In Chapter 11, training and development are discussed. Training is the first thing touted when managers want change and the first thing cut when funds get tight. The chapter examines training as it relates to the critical organization functions of production, adaptation, socialization, and coordination. Also treated are the relevance to training of organization development and total quality management. Students are then asked to consider the complexities of designing a training program.

Chapter 12 reviews the history and development of collective bargaining in the public sector and the evolution of impasse resolution procedures that state and local governments have developed to allow collective bargaining without fear of strikes.

Chapter 13 deals with managing in a union environment. The chapter treats such factors as preparing for negotiations, developing working relationships with union leaders, and establishing a grievance process that is both expeditious and fair to all involved.

Chapter 14 addresses employee rights and conflict resolution systems in government. The range of behaviors that are subject to management scrutiny extend well beyond the workplace. They include recreational drug use and such other lifestyle issues as sexual orientation or the way a person conducts a private business. The chapter details the tests of a grievance that are commonly used by labor arbitrators and civil service examiners. The chapter concludes with several case studies in which students are asked to apply the principles they learned in the chapter to real-world incidents.

ACKNOWLEDGMENTS

Many people contribute to the production of a book. First and foremost are patient family members who so graciously surrender family time to the necessities of writing and editing. The authors especially want to thank Dona Hightower, our freelance developmental editor, whose good humor and useful comments eased the chore considerably. Thanks also to our Harcourt book team: David Tatom, Glenna Stanfield, and Angela Urquhart.

We also wish to thank our thoughtful reviewers:

Lawrence Downey of University of Baltimore

Richard Kearney at East Carolina University

Lana Stein of University of Missouri–St. Louis

Joseph Cayer of Arizona State University

David Hamilton of Roosevelt University

William Eimicke of Columbia University

Myron Mast of Grand Valley State University

Their gentle critiques of the first edition led to most of the changes that are included here. We believe that the collective effort has resulted in a tighter, more readable book with much more of an applied focus than the first edition.

As textbook writers, we are also deeply indebted to our colleagues whose articles in professional journals shaped and guided this study. Similarly, no serious public personnel scholar could begin to address the topic without the work of hundreds of career bureaucrats, who analyze and report on the policies, practices, and overall status of public personnel systems. Lastly, as teachers, we want to acknowledge the learning we have experienced from our students; they may not have kept us young, but they certainly kept us on our toes.

THE EVOLUTION OF PERSONNEL MANAGEMENT

American political institutions were born of a revolution. The constitutional covenant into which the revolutionaries entered reflected the values of the Enlightenment, but it was also shaped by their distrust of centralized government and of executive authority. Early in the life of the nation, nonetheless, the covenant was redrafted, strengthening central governmental authority and laying the groundwork for what was to become a "presidential nation."[1]

The intent of the founding fathers was to design a set of political structures that would guarantee the continuation of a representative democracy. The Constitution therefore established a separation of powers among the legislative, executive, and judicial branches of the federal government and carefully prescribed how political offices were to be gained and how policies were to be enacted. Legislation dealing with money, for example, was to be initiated in the House of Representatives because it was the institution believed to be closest to the people. Clearly, the emphasis was on Enlightenment concerns for the proper relations among the branches of government and the investment of sovereignty in the electorate. For all its political precision, however, the document overlooked some important features of government. How policies were to be administered once they were enacted was scarcely mentioned. How administrative offices of the government were to be organized and how administrators were to be selected were likewise completely ignored in the fundamental document.[2]

THE EARLY PERIOD

TRUSTEES OR REVOLUTIONARY FUNCTIONARIES?

Modern scholars have designated the Constitutional era as the "trustee period" of public personnel policy because the persons who first staffed the government could be characterized as the elite of the society that produced them.[3] These early American bureaucrats were recruited from the mercantile class and the landed gentry. As a prerequisite to gaining a government post, a candidate had to be of good character and had to be sponsored by somebody with access to the system. The composition of Washington's cabinet provides evidence to support this trustee thesis. For example, Alexander Hamilton and Thomas Jefferson, both aristocrats and intellectuals, were secretary of the treasury and secretary of state, respectively.

Although higher social status and education were common characteristics of America's first functionaries, another contributing factor in their selection was undoubtedly their role in the Revolution. It is common in successful revolutions for the revolutionary leaders to seize control of government institutions in order to complete their agenda. Thus, Washington, the revolutionary general, became president; Adams, with his northern power base, became first vice-president and then president; Jefferson, who drafted the Declaration of Independence, became secretary of state, then president; Alexander Hamilton, Washington's aide-de-camp, became his secretary of the treasury.[4] The point here is that the government was staffed by active members of the Revolution; that they were educated merely speaks to the class origins of the revolutionary leaders. Whether they were the most qualified and deserving of their positions on the basis of their knowledge of administration is open to debate. For example, one might legitimately question whether the members of Hamilton's Treasury Department were objectively more qualified than the bureaucrats who formerly collected the king's taxes.

But whether we classify the period as one of trusteeship or of revolutionary functionaries, the period was short-lived. Competition between political factions soon came to dominate most aspects of national government, including the staffing and administration of public bureaucracies. President Washington felt it necessary, in fact, to warn the nation in his farewell address that factionalism could undermine all that the Revolution had achieved.[5]

FACTIONALISM

In reality, factions were at work from the beginning of the nation, accounting for many of the compromises that were necessary to bring the Constitution of 1789 into being. The original formulas for determining representation in the two houses of Congress, the three-fifths rule for counting slaves, and the appointment by each state legislature of two senators who would vote as equals to their colleagues regardless of population are examples of factional compromises. The three-fifths rule allowed a proportion of the slave population to be counted in the census for allocating representatives, without enfranchising them politically. The equal representation of states in the Senate balanced the population advantage of large states in the House of Representatives, and the appointment of senators by state legislatures was a recognition of the special interest of each state in the national political process.[6]

Factionalism also played a role in the selection of administrative officials early in the nation's history. Leaders of the first political parties (Federalist and Democratic-Republican) recognized the advantages of staffing the instrumentalities of government with persons favorable to their particular political worldview.[7] A celebrated case in point is *Marbury* v. *Madison* (1803), in which the behind-the-scenes protagonists were the second and third presidents of the United States.[8] Marbury was denied an appointment as a federal justice of the peace when incoming President Jefferson failed to deliver a number of last-minute appointments of his predecessor, John Adams. Marbury filed suit before the Supreme Court to obtain his appointment but lost on what may be America's most famous legal technicality. Writing for the Court, Chief Justice Marshall noted that Marbury was entitled to the appointment but that the Court would not order its delivery because the act giving the Supreme Court jurisdiction was unconstitutional. In denying Marbury's complaint, Marshall took for the Court the power of judicial review. The factional intensity of the controversy is evidenced by the fact that Marshall was secretary of state under Adams at the time of Marbury's appointment. In other words, factionalism in federal appointments can be traced to the first election in which there was a change in political parties.

1820 TO THE PRESENT

POLITICAL PARTISANSHIP AND GOVERNMENT APPOINTMENTS

The practice of using federal jobs to reward the politically faithful became critically important with the advent of universal white male suffrage.[9] In the beginning, the franchise was normally confined to property owners of sufficient standing in the community to warrant the voting privilege. These early voters closely identified their economic and political self-interest with one or the other political party. In short, mobilizing support for the party position and getting out the vote did not require complex political organizations.

By the 1820s, however, virtually any white male could exercise the franchise by presenting himself at the polls on election day. This was the era of so-called beard politics, when industrious political partisans would grow full beards prior to the election, present themselves at a number of polling places to vote, then shave off all but a mustache and repeat their rounds. The process could be repeated a third time clean-shaven. At a dollar per vote, an enterprising fellow could collect a handsome profit, limited only by the distance between polling places and whether he had a horse.[10] Clearly, getting out the vote and regulating it in these mass-based elections required considerably more organization than before. Thus, the political machine was born of necessity. Staffing the machine required rewards for the faithful in the form of government jobs. During its heyday, the patronage system was standard operating procedure at all levels of government.

THE ADVANTAGES OF PATRONAGE. Patronage systems have been praised for promoting direct political accountability on the part of program administrators, who serve at the will and pleasure of their political bosses. Some early patronage advocates even believed that the system would take government out of the hands of the elite and make it accountable to the people, because a change of elected leaders could result in a complete replacement of administrative staff who would have insufficient time to entrench their power. Patronage advocates, such as Andrew Jackson, also argued that the long-ballot aspects of the system made government officials more accountable to the public for their actions. The long-ballot system assumes that anybody of average ability is capable of running the government; therefore, making the maximum number of officials stand for election guarantees their accountability to the public. If these officials conduct themselves inappropriately or dishonestly, they can be swept from office by an aroused electorate in the next election or, in some states, by a special recall election. The long ballot survives today even in some states that use merit systems to select rank-and-file bureaucrats. The virtues of bureaucratic accountability notwithstanding, patronage has a dark side that eventually led to its demise at the federal level.

The Dark Side of Patronage. On the negative side, patronage increases the chances for corruption with the knowledge and consent of public managers. Businesspeople who wish to acquire government contracts can do so through participation in the political process. Politicians, in turn, intervene in the administrative process on behalf of those contractors. The abuse of patronage reached its zenith during the Civil War, when fortunes were made on the basis of access to the procurement processes of the federal government.

LINCOLN AND THE PATRONAGE SYSTEM

The early days of the Lincoln administration found the new president besieged by office seekers. Lincoln himself believed that the patronage system of appointment was as great a threat to the nation as the war.[11]

Lincoln had difficulty controlling patronage abuses throughout his term. His War Department is reported to have engaged in questionable contracting practices under its first secretary, Simon Cameron. The president, reluctant to act decisively for fear of alienating radical members of his coalition, finally resolved the issue by appointing Cameron ambassador to Russia.[12]

On the other hand, some observers contend that patronage gave Lincoln a useful tool for assuring the loyalty of the northern party bosses, which was necessary to preserve the fragile Republican coalition that made it possible for him to govern.[13] The coalition-building potential of patronage can hardly be overestimated. Of course, if the United States had moved to install a merit system at the federal level in 1840 (twenty years before the Civil War), as did England,[14] efficient systems of procurement might have been in operation at the outset of the war. Had they been, the South could hardly have lasted as long as it did in the face of a rapid and efficient Union mobilization.

Corruption at the federal level continued in the postwar era, with administration after administration being rocked by scandals involving bribery, collusion, and outright corruption on the part of public officials who, with a little effort, could feather their personal financial nests for life during a short tenure of government service. Instances of outright corruption are well documented in the literature.[15] A more subtle form of corruption involved the use of government positions and the inside knowledge gained from them to further one's own financial interest. (One nineteenth-century politician termed this practice "honest graft.")[16] If, for example, a new federal office building were to be built, partisans could inform their friends of the proposed site so the latter could buy property in the area in anticipation of a rise in property values. Of course, there was nothing to prevent a public official from owning shares in a company that speculated in real estate acquisitions and making use of this sort of knowledge more directly. Even in the twenty-first century, honest graft is possible at all levels of government. The mayor of a large city could, for example, steer the choice of locations for a new airport to a site owned by the mayor's family and friends.

THE CIVIL SERVICE ACT OF 1883

Abuses of the patronage system eventually so enraged some constituents and legislators that they mobilized to change it. Senator Pendleton of Ohio introduced the bill that eventually resulted in the Civil Service Act of 1883.[17] Supporters of reform were unable to secure passage of the bill, however, until a confluence of events brought together the necessary legislative coalition.

The most important factor contributing to final passage of the bill was the grassroots reform movement itself.[18] The second factor was the assassination of President James Garfield by a disappointed office seeker. What legislator up for reelection could afford to publicly oppose reforming a system that was so corrupt as to lead to the murder of a president? Finally, the majority Republican party was facing a probable loss of power to the Democrats in the upcoming election of 1884. (In fact, Grover Cleveland became the first Democratic president in the post–Civil War era.) A law that would insulate government officials from appointment and removal for partisan reasons no doubt made sense to some Republican partisans in the legislature. In any event, the act did pass, creating the United States Civil Service Commission that was to protect government recruiting practices from partisan interference. Although the 1883 act covered only a small percentage of federal employees, today virtually all are covered by one or another government merit system of recruitment and promotion.

American presidents retain the authority to appoint their cabinet officers, the administrators of noncabinet agencies (such as the National Aeronautics and Space Administration [NASA]), some deputy administrators, and some high-level program administrators. Increasingly, presidents have been able to appoint lower-level workers (government service [GS] pay rates 13 to 15) using Schedule C (reserved for policy-sensitive or personal-service positions), temporary appointments, and other tactics, because the professional entry exam known as PACE (Professional Administrative Career Exam) was suspended as part of a consent decree in a civil rights suit.[19] Lamentably, during the 1980s, an extraordinary number of appointed officials used their authority, positions, or access to other top officials to advance their private interests or those of their family, friends, and associates at public expense.[20]

Despite the potential for abuse, the principle of administrative accountability is of such paramount importance to American-style democracy that no move has been made to expand upward the use of career administrators. The National Commission on the Public Service, however, has called for limiting presidential appointments to 2,000, with substantial administrator control of appointments below the highest echelons.[21] To date, Congress has chosen to counter the threat of official corruption by expanding the protections afforded to whistleblowers in the career service.

STATE AND LOCAL PATRONAGE

METHODOLOGY OF PATRONAGE

The long-ballot system of open candidacy is still prevalent at the state and local level, where many positions not usually associated with partisan politics are elective. In many places, officials such as the county clerk and treasurer are elected; even the county engineer, whose only function is road repair, is sometimes an elected official, though prequalified on the basis of having appropriate experience and degrees. Although these positions are by and large administrative, gaining and holding them requires a political support base. Members of that base are rewarded for their contribution to the campaign with positions in county government. The public has no assurance that such appointees are the most qualified for the positions or even that they possess the necessary minimum qualifications for them. In such a patronage system, government jobs can be a source of long-term stable employment if the party to which one owes loyalty can maintain itself in office.

Proponents of the system point out that the rank-and-file bureaucrats as well as the elected administrative officer are directly accountable to the electorate. A greater public-service orientation is believed to follow from this accountability, because rudeness or insensitivity to client concerns can result in losing office in the next election.

Public accountability notwithstanding, the wholesale replacement of bureaucrats through the election of new officials at the top of the administrative ladder may ill serve the public, because each wave of incoming officials must spend time learning the bureaucratic routines, not to mention the laws and regulations that govern their behavior. More important, however, as patronage systems frequently operate in one-party, noncompetitive districts, elected officials and their subordinates often continue in office until retirement. In the worst cases, when career elected administrators staff their offices on the basis of partisan or personal loyalty, the public may be saddled with marginally qualified cronies and ne'er-do-well family members and friends of elected officers.[22]

Of course, state and local agencies are also subject to the sorts of corrupt practices that befell the federal government in the nineteenth century. For example, when the Kansas City Civic Center had to be rebuilt after a fire, "Boss" Pendergast is said to have ordered a new facility constructed completely of concrete, thus benefiting his brother, who operated the only concrete plant in the city at the time.[23] The limitations of modern patronage systems can perhaps be best illustrated by looking at county government.

PATRONAGE AT THE COUNTY LEVEL

County commissioners or supervisors stand for election in every region except New England, where counties do not exist. In some states, the commissioners act much as a city council does, exercising legislative authority by passing ordinances allocating tax resources to such administrative offices as the county sheriff, the district attorney, the clerk's office, and so forth. They also oversee the activities of an appointed administrative officer, who controls the routine operation of the county bureaucracy. In many other states, county commissioners act as both legislators and administrative officers. Frequently the county is divided into districts, often three, with each commissioner being elected by the citizens of a single district.

Road repair is the locus of much of the patronage that still operates at the county level. Upon assuming office, commissioners get a share of the county budget for the repair and construction of roads and bridges in their districts. Each one decides which roads are to be repaired and in what order. Often these decisions are based on campaign contributions of constituents rather than on actual road conditions. Each commissioner is also responsible for the purchase and maintenance of road-repair equipment and materials, the hiring of equipment operators, and in some cases, the awarding of road-building contracts to private companies. This antiquated system is full of potential for inefficiency, waste, and outright fraud.

The first potential source of inefficiency and corruption is the district-by-district purchase of equipment and materials. Also district by district, individual commissioners must assign priorities to their repair schedules, allocate human and equipment resources, and plan for the replacement of worn-out or obsolete equipment. At the very least, discounts are lost that might have been gained from suppliers if larger, countywide purchases were made. The actual number of pieces of equipment that need replacing might also be reduced if resources were allocated on a countywide basis. At worst, commissioners can enter into "blue sky" agreements with dishonest contractors, in which no equipment or supplies change hands. The commissioner issues a purchase order, then authorizes payment to a contractor, who later splits the money with the commissioner.[24]

Inefficiency also occurs when well-meaning commissioners lack basic administrative skills.[25] As do all organizations, counties possess funds that need not be expended until later in the fiscal year. Commissioners may allow these funds to languish in non-interest-bearing checking accounts. At a higher level of sophistication, the commissioners may keep the money in interest-bearing checking accounts at local banks, reasoning that because local taxpayers generate the revenues, they should be deposited locally to be available for the community's home mortgages, business loans, or credit purchases such as automobiles. The taxpaying public, however, might be better served by a professionally trained county financial officer making high-yield and secure investments in the larger investment arena beyond the county line. At the very least, local bankers could be pressured to provide better rates of return on county deposits, which may amount to millions of dollars. These higher interest rates, in turn, would reduce the need to raise taxes to pay for services.

POSSIBLE SOLUTIONS

Breaking this cycle of inefficiency and waste in county government is no small task. The reality is that individual commissioners are only accountable to the voters, who have no method of checking into their efficiency or honesty. Law enforcement agencies at the county level offer little help, because both the sheriff and the district attorney are dependent on the commissioners for their budgets.

State attorneys general could provide a nonbiased monitor, but their offices usually lack sufficient resources to conduct a statewide investigation and prosecution of corrupt commissioners. An investigation of that magnitude would need a special appropriation from the legislature, whose members are sensitive to political concerns at the local level and might be reluctant to make waves for those whose political power bases overlap their own.

One realistic solution to patronage abuses at the county level is the formation of grassroots reform groups. These groups could alter state and county laws by means of pressure on political parties and the election of reform-minded candidates to county commissions and the state legislature. In some states, reformers also can attack corruption by use of the referendum petition. The referendum makes it possible to place on a statewide ballot a proposal for legislation requiring a professional county administrator who would function much like a city manager. A referendum might also require the use of a central purchasing system for all county acquisitions and the establishment of a state-level auditing mechanism to investigate fraud, waste, and abuse.

RECENT COURT DECISIONS LIMITING PATRONAGE

The Supreme Court effectively neutralized the patronage system as a mechanism for rewarding the faithful in the cases of *Elrod* v. *Burns* (1976)[26] and *Branti* v. *Finkel* (1980).[27] Patronage systems may no longer be used to appoint partisan supporters if the appointment requires the removal of otherwise satisfactory employees not loyal to the incoming party. Such removals have been ruled violations of the incumbents' First Amendment rights to freedom of association.

In the *Elrod* case, the Sheriff's Department of Cook County, Illinois, contained some positions that were appointed on the basis of merit and some on the basis of partisanship. Newly elected Sheriff Elrod notified partisan employees that they would be dismissed unless they could provide him with a letter of support from a member of the central committee of the Cook County Democratic Party. In other words, to maintain their positions, the affected employees would have to demonstrate their partisan affiliation with the Democratic party. A number of employees sued, and the case eventually made its way to the Supreme Court. The Court ruled that elected officials, such as sheriffs and county treasurers, could no longer dismiss employees solely to make room for their own partisan supporters. The Court did allow for the removal of confidential employees (such as personal secretaries) and policy-making employees.

In the *Branti* case, the court defined what it meant by policy-making employees. At issue was whether or not attorneys appointed by the public defender's office fell under the rubric of policymakers as defined by the Court in *Elrod*. The Court chose to define policymaking narrowly, limiting it to those who make partisan policy, and ruled that even though public defenders exercise considerable autonomy over their caseloads, the decisions they make are not partisan in nature. The Court illustrated the partisan distinction with the example of a football coach at a state university who makes critical policy decisions that significantly affect the success or failure of a football program but are not partisan. The Court contrasted the role of the coach with that of an assistant to the governor who contributes to the formulation of partisan policy.

The Supreme Court extended the First Amendment protections to include partisan personnel actions short of discharge in *Rutan* v. *Republican Party of Illinois* (1990).[28] The Republican governor, by executive order, had frozen all personnel activities in Illinois unless they had direct approval by the governor. He operated this system through a Governor's Office of Personnel Management, thereby taking control of the employee dispositions of 60,000 state jobs. Rutan was a rehabilitation counselor who claimed that she had been denied promotion to supervisor because she lacked Republican party sponsorship. Others in the suit claimed that partisanship had affected their transfers and recalls after layoff. The Supreme Court agreed in a 5-to-4 decision, stating that "'the preservation of the democratic process' is no more furthered by the patronage promotions, transfers and rehires at issue here than it is by patronage dismissals."[29]

In dissent, Justice Scalia argued that patronage is a time-honored tradition and that the middling approach of leaving some jobs political while others are not invites litigation from disappointed office seekers. More important, the dissenters considered the disposition of patronage to be a political question more appropriate for the legislatures of the various states: "The appropriate 'mix' of party-based employment is a political question if there ever was one, and we should give it back to the voters of the various units to decide, through civil service legislation crafted to suit the time and place, which mix is best."[30]

In 1996 the Supreme Court extended the First Amendment protections set out in *Elrod* to independent contractors in *O'Hare et al.* v. *City of Northlake*. O'Hare was a towing contractor who had been on the city's rotation list since 1965. The O'Hare Company supported the opponent of the incumbent mayor, including posting a sign supporting the challenger. When the incumbent won, O'Hare was removed from the city's rotation list. By a margin of 7–2 the court ruled the removal a violation of the contractor's First Amendment rights of free association.[31]

As noted earlier, partisan administrators at the federal level have used temporary appointments to circumvent the civil service system. Temporary appointments were also a popular device of state and local politicos. The U.S. Court of Appeals for the Seventh Circuit (whose jurisdiction includes Illinois) ruled that temporary state employees were not exempt from the Supreme Court's earlier *Rutan* prohibition against patronage appointment in *Vickery* v. *Jones* (1996).[32]

Continuing the patronage system makes little sense in light of its potential for corruption and mismanagement and the loss of the job reappointment advantage that the system formerly rendered to victorious political parties. Indeed, the wholesale replacement of rank-and-file bureaucrats on the basis of partisan politics is part of a bygone era of rough-and-tumble politics.

THE DEVELOPMENT OF THE FEDERAL MERIT SYSTEM: 1883–1978

Reformers mark the advent of the merit system in the federal service by the passage of the Civil Service Act of 1883, but in reality, the act was the result of years of grassroots efforts to clean up government. Further evolution of the federal merit system resulted in the 1978 Civil Service Reform Act, which fundamentally altered the structure of federal personnel agencies and relocated the merit protection function in an independent agency. Many of the reforms were aimed at insulating rank-and-file bureaucrats from partisan interference in agency personnel processes. Much of the success of this approach came at the expense of employees' rights to participate in the political process and their rights to speak out on issues of general concern. Most recently, Congress has enacted legislation to protect employees who report fraud, waste, and abuse, and it has moved to restore many of their rights to political participation.

The 1883 reform of the federal personnel system reflected the dominant political values of the time in the United States. Just as patronage grew out of the movement for universal suffrage, civil service reform grew out of a broad-based discontent with corruption in government.

EARLY EMPHASIS: INSULATING PUBLIC EMPLOYEES FROM POLITICS

The Civil Service Act of 1883, known as the Pendleton Act, established the first Civil Service Commission of the United States. The commission was composed of three persons who were appointed for overlapping seven-year terms. The act further provided that no more than two members of the commission could be members of the same political party. This prohibition was supposed to ensure that patronage could not be reintroduced in collusion with a friendly commission.

The act provided for the insulation of the employee selection process from interference by politicians. The commission was to conduct the recruitment and selection of federal employees, utilizing principles of merit. That is, the government was thenceforth to be staffed with the best possible employees, selected on the basis of their qualifications to perform the jobs in question. Eventually, this merit system came to use elaborate testing and screening procedures to rank members of the applicant pool.

The commission initially exercised hegemony over only a small percentage of federal workers. Its limited scope might lead some to believe that Congress was less than fully committed to the notion of civil service reform. But an agency can also be judged, in part, by the persons chosen to lead it. The first commissioners were dedicated to merit reform; in fact, one early commissioner was Theodore Roosevelt. Anybody who believed Roosevelt would do less than push vigorously for reform of the entire government was either naive or did not know Commissioner Roosevelt. Over the years, coverage was extended to virtually all ranks of the federal service, with the exception of a few agencies, such as the State Department and the Postal Service, covered by other legislation. These agencies, however, also use merit selection procedures.

A second dimension of merit protection was introduced in 1897 with the passage of the second civil service act. This legislation guaranteed that an employee could not be removed except for "cause." It was not until the 1913 passage of the Lloyd-Lafollette Act, however, that adequate protection measures were created in the form of a postdischarge appeals process for those who believed themselves to have been wrongfully discharged. (The rights of discharged employees were incorporated intact into the 1978 Civil Service Reform Act.) Prior to enactment of these safeguards, a politically motivated administrator could replace otherwise satisfactory employees with his or her partisans for any reason except politics.

The protection of federal employees from partisan-motivated removal was granted at the expense of certain political rights—rights definitively lost via the Hatch Act of 1939. This act prohibited federal employees from participation in partisan political activities. Federal employees could not seek partisan office without first resigning their positions, hold office in a political party, or contribute to political campaigns. These prohibitions were believed necessary to prevent politically appointed administrators from coercing their employees to contribute to campaigns or give other assistance in an administration's reelection efforts.

Congress passed the 1939 Hatch Act partially out of a fear that Franklin Roosevelt would convert the federal civilian workforce into his personal political electoral machine. Over 400,000 of these employees had been hired during the first two Roosevelt terms. The New Deal agencies were being created so quickly that the administration believed it expedient to hire outside the civil service process. Virtually all of them, however, were subsequently grandfathered into the civil service as their employing programs became permanent features of the federal government.

In more recent times, Hatch Act critics have decried the loss of citizenship rights of federal employees. Efforts to restore employee rights were spearheaded by powerful public sector unions representing rank-and-file civil servants and postal employees who rights were also inhibited by the Hatch Act. During the Bush presidency, Congress tried to restore the political rights of federal employees, but President Bush used his veto power. Then, in 1993, President Clinton signed the Federal Employees Political Activities Act. The act allows federal employees and postal workers, on their own time, to manage campaigns, raise funds, and hold office in political parties. They still may not run for partisan political office without resigning; nor may they engage in political activities at work (such as soliciting contributions or wearing campaign buttons).[33]

Even though it has been deemed necessary to limit the rights of public employees to participate in partisan politics, they still possess First Amendment rights to speak out on matters of general concern to them as citizens. When those matters involve the operations of the agencies in which they are employed, however, the courts have indicated that the right to speak must be tempered by the needs of the entire polity for an efficient government.

FREEDOM OF SPEECH LIMITATIONS

PICKERING V. BOARD OF EDUCATION.   In this 1968 case, the Supreme Court recognized the right of classified public employees to speak out on matters of general public interest.[34] Pickering, a schoolteacher, wrote a letter to the editor criticizing a policy of the school district in which he was employed and was discharged as a result. The Supreme Court ruled in his favor, stating, "The problem in any case is to arrive at a balance between the interests of the teacher, as citizen, in commenting upon matters of public concern, and the interests of the State, as an employer, in promoting the efficiency of the public services it performs through its employees."[35]

The key to all such cases is balancing the employee's right of free speech against the government's rights as an employer. The nature of the system is such, however, that no matter how straightforward the language used in a court opinion, it must be interpreted by lower courts seeking to apply the ruling to other cases with different facts and circumstances.

CHURCHILL V. WATERS.   In 1994, the court distinguished between the powers of the government as sovereign and the government as employer.[36] At issue was whether a conversation that took place during a workplace break that criticized a supervisor and a hospital policy was protected by the First Amendment. The court concluded that government is much less powerful as sovereign, because it is regulating the speech of the citizenry at large. In such an arena, virtually any speech is permitted. On the other hand, government as an employer has the right to limit employee speech that is disruptive. In *Churchill,* the court decided that an employer must use good judgment to protect the free speech rights of employees and to ascertain if the disruptive speech in question actually occurred. The standard governing managers' latitude in such matters is to be interpreted broadly. The manager must weigh reports of what was said and the credibility of those alleging the disruptive speech against that of the accused.

FISHER V. WALKER.   In 1972, the U.S. Court of Appeals upheld the disciplining of a union official who criticized city policies in an in-house union newsletter.[37] In his defense, the employee argued that his criticism could not be considered insubordination, because he was exercising his right of free speech under the *Pickering* guidelines. Fisher further noted that he was acting in his capacity as a union official and, therefore, might have been accorded more protection than that given to rank-and-file employees. Finally, because the remarks were published in a union newsletter, they should have been protected as an exercise of freedom of the press under the First Amendment. The court rejected all of these arguments and upheld the disciplining, suggesting that the *Pickering* rule may be most applicable when a public employee's views are expressed in a forum outside of the agency.

JEFFRIES V. HARLESTON.   In a 1995 case, the chairperson of African-American Studies at City College of New York alleged that he was disciplined for remarks he made before an off-campus group.[38] He lost his position as chair and was not promoted. He won a judgment in the trial court that the Supreme Court vacated saying he had a right to free speech but that his tenure as a department chair was at the pleasure of school officials.

The following list summarizes these essential components of the federal merit system policy under the various acts:

SELECTION (PENDLETON ACT OF 1883)

1. Selection of federal employees must be based on qualifications and the ability to perform the job, without regard to political affiliation.
2. A three-member commission is created, designed to insulate the selection process from political interference.

SEPARATION (LLOYD-LAFOLLETTE ACT OF 1913)

1. Nonprobationary employees may only be discharged for cause. Cause is defined as nonfeasance, misfeasance, or malfeasance—that is, not performing the duties of the position, performing the duties incorrectly or incompetently, or performing the duties in a way that violates public law or agency policy.
2. Federal employees are entitled to a thirty days' written notice of the charges against them and an opportunity to respond to the charges, orally or in writing, prior to discharge.
3. Persons believing themselves to have been wrongfully discharged are entitled to a postdischarge hearing before an impartial hearing examiner. Demotions and suspensions may also be appealed to an impartial examiner.

PROHIBITIONS FROM POLITICAL PARTICIPATION (HATCH ACT OF 1939 AS AMENDED IN 1993)

1. Federal employees may not run for or hold partisan political office while employed by the federal government.
2. Federal employees may hold office in a political party.
3. Federal employees may contribute to political campaigns financially and may work in them.
4. Federal employees may not engage in political activities at work.

LATER EMPHASIS: SEEKING TO IMPROVE THE QUALITY OF EMPLOYEES

MERIT AS MANAGEMENT. The principles of a merit system quickly came to mean more than selecting employees who could do the job. Members of the reform movement further believed that the people were entitled to the best government possible. Good government, as they defined it, meant applying the principles of business management to government enterprise. This meant that the goals of the organization could best be achieved by applying its resources in the most efficient and effective manner. Thus, beginning in the nineteenth century, the values of a business-oriented culture began to be manifested in the operations of its government.

In the case of personnel management, the most obvious manifestation was the notion that through testing and other screening devices it was possible to arrive at the one best candidate to perform every job. This idea was an extension of the scientific management canon that there exists one best way to do every job.[39]

Even in the current era, candidates for government jobs continue to be ranked against objective, preestablished criteria to determine their relative qualifications. Often a candidate's performance on a written examination is a substantial portion of his or her overall ranking. In some cases, however, raters have to utilize decimal numbers to distinguish among candidates. There is potential unfairness in a system that relies overmuch on test performance and mechanical rankings. For example, one woman in Dallas, Texas, had the highest score on the air controller's exam; however, when veterans' preference points were added to her rivals' scores, she dropped more than 150 places on the list of eligible candidates.[40]

The federal government came to rely increasingly on written exams to screen and to rank candidates for a wide range of government jobs. These tests measured general intellectual capacity. The PACE exam was used to test entry-level college graduates for over 100 positions. A score of 70 was necessary to be placed on an eligibility list. In reality, candidates for employment had to score much higher than 70. The PACE exam was challenged by minority applicants who successfully demonstrated a disparity in exam performance between White applicants and those of African American and Latino applicants. The case resulted in a consent decree that suspended use of the PACE exam in 1981. As part of the decree, two hiring authorities, the outstanding scholar program and the bilingual/bicultural program, were authorized. The decree remains in force at this writing.[41]

To replace exams, federal agencies began to evaluate candidates on the basis of a review of their education, experience, and general fitness for the job. The broadening of selection criteria permitted considerable latitude for hiring authorities. It did not necessarily result in increased merit selection. Since the decree, hiring and testing has been greatly decentralized. In 1990, the Office of Personnel Management provided agencies with a nonbiased exam titled Administrative Careers With America (ACWA). Agencies can use the ACWA or develop their own exams. Some agencies came to rely on the outstanding scholar program that allows immediate selection of persons with 3.5 grade point averages in all college work. The Merit System Protection Board (MSPB) criticized this program because its studies could not link scholastic and job performance. Thus, by relying on the scholar program, agencies unfairly screened out many qualified candidates.

The MSPB notes that African-American and Latino representation in agencies is at or above their percentage in the population. The MSPB, therefore, has recommended that the Attorney General petition the court to set aside the consent decree. Once the decree is set aside, the MSPB recommends the use of the ACWA or that agencies develop alternative exams. It also recommends an expanded use of cooperative programs that allow agencies to view potentially permanent employees on the actual job before offering them permanent employment.[42]

Current testing systems do recognize that it is not always possible to identify the one best candidate for a position. The "rule of three" used by federal agencies recognizes that testing and measurement can go only so far in assessing a candidate's ability. Those involved in the selection process, therefore, are allowed to choose from among the top three candidates, as determined by objective measures that combine their test scores with their training and experience. At the state and local levels, the list may be expanded to as many as seven or, in extreme cases, fifteen.[43]

CLASSIFICATION SYSTEMS AND EMPLOYEE COMPENSATION. According to the Classification Act of 1923, the pay of government workers is to be determined within uniform classification systems. Not all federal employees, however, are covered by the act. The Postal Service (a public corporation) operates its own personnel system. The Department of State and various intelligence agencies also have their own systems, and employees of Congress, the federal judiciary, and the president's personal staff are exempt. Finally, the armed forces are not covered by the act.

Rank-and-file employees in the remaining federal agencies are covered by a single classification system that uses eighteen pay grades. Each position is analyzed and assigned an appropriate grade based on the qualifications, duties, and responsibilities associated with the position. Thus, a government service (GS) 9 rating might be appropriate for a contracting officer on a military base, a beginning aerospace engineer at NASA, or a classification specialist in the Office of Personnel Management. The federal grade system and the compensation assigned to each grade are displayed in Table 1.1. Notice that each pay grade shows a range of salaries; each grade is divided into ten steps to provide pay raises for satisfactory or superior performers without a change of grade. A change of grade normally means a change of responsibilities.

In classification, as in recruitment and testing, the tendency has been to be as scientific as possible. Classification decisions, therefore, have been made on the basis of the duties, responsibilities, and qualifications required by the position. The operative phrase here is *required by the position*. The compensation level depends on the position, not the jobholder. If, for example, a clerk typist had a doctoral degree, he or she would receive no extra compensation for education beyond that necessary to perform the duties of a clerk.

Initially, the classification function was performed only by the Civil Service Commission, but the Classification Act of 1949 delegated this function to the agencies. This transfer of authority was justified on the basis of the size and complexity of government, which curtailed the effectiveness of centralized classification operations. Decentralization also allowed for quick decisions that took into account local circumstances not common to other agencies.[44] Along with allowing for diversity, decentralization made it possible for agency managers to exercise a good deal of discretion in classifying positions. Discretion, in turn, may lead to grade inflation in order to reward employees that the administrator finds worthy. Grade

■ TABLE 1-1

Grade	Salary Range	2000 Executive Schedule	
GS 1	$13,870–17,351	Level 5	114,500
GS 2	$15,594–19,622	Level 4	122,400
GS 3	$17,015–22,118	Level 3	130,200
GS 4	$19,100–24,833	Level 2	141,300
GS 5	$21,370–27,778	Level 1	157,000
GS 6	$23,820–30,966		
GS 7	$26,470–34,408		
GS 8	$29,315–38,108		
GS 9	$32,380–42,091		
GS 10	$35,658–46,359		
GS 11	$39,178–50,932		
GS 12	$46,955–61,040		
GS 13	$55,837–72,586		
GS 14	$65,983–85,774		
GS 15	$77,614–100,897		

Salaries reflect 3.8 percent increase January 2000

SOURCE: Compiled from U.S. Office of Personnel Management, General Schedule and Executive Schedule Tables at <http://www.opm.gov/oca/2000tbls/> updated December 1999. The table does not reflect the regional cost of living adjustments that range from a low of 6.79 percent in Orlando, Florida, to a high of 15.01 percent for the San Jose–San Francisco region of California.

inflation, or overclassification, refers to agency executives' encouraging their classifiers to be generous when assessing the responsibilities of a given position.

The federal government now allows managers to decide how positions under their authority should be allocated and structured. Managers can thus alter the duties and responsibilities of productive and talented workers, which should result in greater efficiency and improved performance. By the same token, the duties of nonproductive workers can also be restructured, which could result in downgrading their pay.

CONFLICT IN THE MERIT SYSTEM: THE BEST EMPLOYEES, OR PROTECTION OF THE EMPLOYEES AND THE SYSTEM?

The Civil Service Commission's personnel management role changed over the years. These changes, however, did not entail the exchange of one function for another or the replacement of one task with another. Instead, the commission was assigned more and more responsibilities as the personnel function was expanded and public values were modified. Its mandate eventually included recruitment, testing and measurement, classification, human resource planning, administration of the federal retirement system, and policing the system for violations of both the principles of merit and equal employment opportunity. It was also responsible for conducting appeals hearings for aggrieved employees.

Essentially, the commission came to perform contradictory roles. On the one hand, it was asked to operate an effective and efficient personnel system; on the other hand, it was supposed to be a watchdog of itself and other federal agencies. The untenable nature of this contradiction was pointed out by a series of presidential commissions, beginning with the President's Commission on Administrative Management in 1935 (sometimes called the Brownlow Commission) and ending with the Civil Service Reform Committee of 1978.

Another responsibility of the commission was the protection of equal employment opportunity (EEO) in the federal service. Part of the federal EEO program involves affirmative action programs to increase opportunities for women and minorities in the federal service. Affirmative action, however, was viewed by some as directly conflicting with the principles of the merit system. Beginning with President Kennedy's Executive Order 10925, the Civil Service Commission and federal agencies in general were charged with developing and administering special programs to attract, retain, and promote minority persons in the federal service. As in the merit system, the commission had the responsibility for providing leadership to develop these programs and for policing its own and other agencies' actions for compliance with the policy.

The dual roles of administering and policing policies only compounded the problems of the commission, already overloaded with functions that its creators never envisioned. Clearly, additional reforms of the system were in order. As in 1882, the political coalition necessary for reform was slow to cohere. Ironically, the revelations of the Watergate scandal in 1973 demonstrated that the system as then constituted was incapable of carrying out the original mandate of the commission: to operate a merit system of recruitment free from partisan political interference.

BEATING THE SYSTEM

Despite the careful design for a commission that could not be dominated by any one political party, it became possible to make appointments for protected positions based upon partisanship. The Watergate investigations revealed the existence of what came to be known as the Malek Manual.[45] Malek was an official in Nixon's Office of Management and Budget who prepared a set of instructions for Republican administrators on how to circumvent the civil service system and place Republican partisans in mid-level management positions. The first step was to write the position description so that a preferred candidate for the position would appear near the top of the list when it was sent over from the commission. For example, suppose that an administrator in the Department of Defense wished to hire a GS 13 procurement officer and preferred to hire a Republican. The administrator would review the qualifications of the preferred candidate and match the position description to those qualifications. Thus, if the preferred candidate had a background in real estate, the position description might require a college education, *x* years of increasing responsibility as a manager in government or business, a knowledge of procurement procedures, and a background in real estate. Circumventing the system involved the cooperation of a friendly reviewer at the commission who was willing to certify the real estate criterion as a bona fide occupation qualification (BFOQ).

The designers of the commission could not have anticipated the unprecedented growth of government, nor envisioned the eventual complexity of the commission's role. The sheer numbers involved in recruiting for government service made careful monitoring for partisan collusion difficult. When the complexity of the commission's mission is taken into account, moreover, the monitoring task bordered on the impossible. Congressional reformers came to realize the need for change and President Carter made reform of the system a priority.

THE 1978 CIVIL SERVICE REFORM ACT

From a policy point of view, the 1978 Civil Service Reform Act represents a complete redefinition of merit. The act's centerpiece, however, was the separation of the administrative functions of personnel management (now carried out by the Office of Personnel Management) from the merit protection and enforcement function (now embodied in the Merit System Protection Board and the Office of Special Counsel). Other features of the act that have received less attention in the literature but will have a long-term impact on the operations of the federal bureaucracy include shifting the equal employment opportunity function to the Equal Employment Opportunity Commission, the creation of a Federal Labor Relations Authority, the creation of a Senior Executive Service, and the introduction of merit pay in the federal service.

The 1978 Civil Service Reform Act enumerated nine principles of merit:

1. Recruitment should be from qualified individuals from appropriate sources in an endeavor to achieve a work force from all segments of society, and selection and advancement should be determined solely on the basis of relative ability, knowledge, and skills after fair and open competition which assures that all receive equal opportunity.

2. All employees and applicants for employment should receive fair and equitable treatment in all aspects of personnel management without regard to political affiliation, race, color, religion, national origin, sex, marital status, age or handicapping condition, and with proper regard for their privacy and constitutional rights.

3. Equal pay should be provided for work of equal value, with appropriate consideration of both national and local rates paid by employers in the private sector, and appropriate incentives and recognition should be provided for excellence in performance.

4. All employees should maintain high standards of integrity, conduct, and concern for the public interest.

5. The federal work force should be used efficiently and effectively.

6. Employees should be retained on the basis of the adequacy of their performance, inadequate performance should be corrected, and employees

should be separated who cannot or will not improve their performance to meet required standards.

7. Employees should be provided effective education and training in cases in which education and training would result in better organization and individual performance.

8. Employees should be (a) protected against arbitrary action, personnel favoritism, or coercion for partisan political purposes, and (b) prohibited from using their official authority or influence for the purpose of interfering with or affecting the result of an election or nomination for election.

9. Employees should be protected against reprisal for Lawful disclosure of information which the employees reasonably believe evidences (a) a violation of any law, rule or regulation, or (b) mismanagement, a gross waste of funds, an abuse of authority, or a substantial and specific danger to public health or safety.[46]

The principles reaffirm a commitment to selection based on merit (Principle 1) and removal for cause (Principle 6), but they changed the meaning of merit. The principles redefined merit to include a federal government commitment to affirmative action and equal employment opportunity (Principle 2) and further expanded it to include equal pay for equal work (Principle 3). Other noteworthy features of the principles included making government employees responsible for protecting the public interest (Principle 4) and defining merit as a commitment to efficiency and effectiveness (Principle 5). Finally, Principle 9 protects public employees from reprisals for reporting fraud, waste, or abuse. The remaining sections of the act specify the structures in which these principles are to be embodied.

THE OFFICE OF PERSONNEL MANAGEMENT

The administrative responsibilities associated with human resource management in the federal service since 1978 have been carried out by the Office of Personnel Management (OPM). The office's role has changed significantly with regard to the functions it performs and the policy role it is expected to play, the most interesting change being a new relationship between the president and the office.

The functional responsibilities of the OPM include setting personnel policies, administering the federal retirement system, running classification audits, coordinating human resource planning, and providing agencies with needed training. The most significant change in the role of the OPM has been in the area of recruitment.

The Civil Service Commission originally performed virtually all of the recruitment and selection chores for the federal government. Under the provisions of the 1978 Civil Service Reform Act (CSRA), recruitment responsibilities now ultimately fall to the personnel offices of the individual agencies.[47] The only exception to this new pattern is recruitment for positions needed by all agencies, so that economies of scale can be achieved in the selection and testing process. For example, all agencies employ clerk typists; maintaining separate lists of applicants in each agency would involve considerable overlap that would limit both the agencies and the applicants. The agencies would be limited in the range of potential applicants, and the applicants would be limited in the number of jobs for which they could apply by the simple fact that they would have to visit each agency individually and repeat the application and testing procedures. Now the OPM maintains a list of qualified eligibles, who may be referred to various agencies as necessary.

For more specialized positions, a system of decentralized recruitment has the advantage of shortening the time between when a need to create a position or fill a vacancy is recognized and a new recruit actually begins work. Persons interested in increasing the representation of women and minorities in the federal service also favored decentralization of recruitment. Under the old system of centralized lists, career bureaucrats with years of experience could passively seek advancement in the federal service merely by keeping their names on the list of eligibles maintained at the Civil Service Commission. With their experience and, in many cases, their veterans' preference points, they would automatically be near the top of the list for referral to agencies seeking recruits. These automatic referrals would occur even if the bureaucrat was not seriously seeking a new position.

Under the decentralized system, candidates seeking government employment must "pound the pavement," or in the current era, search the web and file applications regardless of whether they are currently employed in the federal service. Thus, the only persons disadvantaged by the new system are those not serious enough about seeking federal employment to engage in an active search.

In the main, the reorganization of the personnel function has not impeded OPM's ability to perform its proper functions. Shedding the merit protection function and decentralizing the recruitment function left it with an opportunity to define its mission in light of the new relationship that the office has with the presidency.

PRESIDENTIAL RELATIONS WITH AGENCIES

Under the old civil service system, Congress took pains to interpose a nonpartisan board between the political executive and federal personnel policies in order to overcome the problems of patronage. Under the CSRA, the three-member commission has been replaced by a single OPM director who serves at the pleasure of the president. As a result, the director and the agency gain the potential for being significant instruments of presidential power. Through the OPM, the president can make and implement sweeping policies that can affect day-to-day management in all agencies covered by the act.

Giving the president control of personnel policies and apparatus implies that the president not only can but should use that power to manage government. Traditionally, little attention has been given to the role of the president as the nation's chief administrative officer.[48] The notion that presidents can or should concern themselves with administrative matters is not universally endorsed.

Some scholars argue that presidents should not concern themselves with the administration of domestic policies because of other pressing presidential duties.[49] Others argue that presidential management efforts involving change may be frustrated by alliances between agencies, their constituencies, and friendly members of Congress.[50] Finally, critics of the president-as-manager concept argue that the emphasis on the president as administrator has resulted in a proliferation of White House staff that, in turn, takes more and more of the president's time.[51]

Others believe that, far from being managerially powerless, modern presidents who wish to influence the administration of domestic policies possess the mechanisms for doing so. Much like executives of large corporations, presidents possess a number of managerial control systems for imposing their will on the organizations that they lead. The principal difference in presidential responsibilities is in the size and complexity of government operations.

STAFFING POWERS AS A CONTROL SYSTEM. In areas such as personnel management, presidents are more likely to prescribe broad policy guidelines and staff policy positions with persons of sympathetic ideological philosophies. Presidential approval of a policy may be no more than pro forma; however, assuming that a president can appoint energetic persons to exercise broad policy mandates, he or she can affect the basic operations of agencies as surely as the president of General Motors Corporation can influence the operations and managerial systems of that organization. Critics of the OPM during the Reagan administration point to the infusion of noncareer executives who then made governmentwide policies without consulting their career counterparts.[52]

OPM AS A PRESIDENTIAL MANAGEMENT CONTROL SYSTEM. The 1978 reforms enhanced the president's ability to use personnel policy to achieve broad policy objectives and to use OPM as a managerial control system. Managerially active presidents who view government as a positive instrument will use OPM differently from those who believe in the inherent incompetence of bureaucracy.

The Reagan administration's use of the OPM to question and seek to reformulate federal retirement policy illustrates the policy uses of the agency.[53] According to the administration, federal retirement benefits were out of line with comparable positions in the private sector. The Reagan OPM maintained that the retirement benefits of federal employees as a function of their salaries significantly exceeded the benefits of private-sector employees with comparable incomes.

The retirement package of federal employees, however, could also be viewed in the context of the total pay and benefits that they receive for the responsibilities they assume and the duties they perform relative to their private-sector counterparts. When viewed in the context of their responsibilities, the pay and benefits of federal employees, especially of senior-level managers, is considerably below that of their private-sector counterparts.

The Federal Employee Retirement System (FERS) that emerged in 1986 allowed current employees to convert to the new system or remain under the old; the vast majority chose coverage under the old system. The new system does allow employees to take their benefits with them if they decide to leave government service and to make individual contributions to an annuity. In addition, movement in and out of government service is enhanced by including federal employees under the Social Security System.

A decade after the passage of the 1978 CSRA, scholars and others concluded that the reforms were as yet incomplete. The CSRA envisioned an OPM that was an instrument of presidential policy and a support system for enlightened changes in human resource management. OPM was to have reversed the process of centralization of human resource management that had evolved under the Civil Service Commission. OPM was to provide training and support for agency innovation and to authorize experimentation to upgrade the system. The critics noted that in 1989 conforming to the current merit rules meant adhering to 6,000 pages of rules and regulations.[54] By 1993, the figure had risen to 10,000 pages.[55]

President Bush recognized a crisis in federal personnel systems and set about reversing the antigovernment policies of his two predecessors. President Bush established the National Commission on the Public Service (sometimes called the Volker Commission) to recommend changes to reinvigorate the public service.[56] OPM under Bush began a reversal of the politicization by involving the federal human resources community in the formulation of policies. These included unions, agency personnel, and representatives of management associations.[57]

Decentralization and streamlining the federal personnel system was a major component of the Clinton administration's National Performance Review (NPR). Led by Vice President Gore, the goal of the NPR was to reduce red tape by decentralizing purchasing and human resource authority and to change the culture of the federal bureaucracy to a public-service orientation. Executives are to stimulate innovation in technology and service delivery and to measure subordinates' performances against agency performance. OPM now encourages agency innovations in agency appraisal and reward systems.[58] The Director of OPM chairs the taskforce on improving employee development and empowerment. OPM provides training and training materials and conducts periodic studies to measure the impacts of the initiatives.[59]

THE SENIOR EXECUTIVE SERVICE

The old civil service was criticized because it shielded senior-level career officials from direct accountability for their performance to their politically appointed superiors.[60] It was also criticized for its inflexibility in the assignment and reward of upper-level managers.

The establishment of the new Senior Executive Service (SES) is possibly the single most significant feature of the 1978 act, because it makes senior career officials directly accountable for the consequences of the performance or nonperformance of their duties. The SES comprises the GS 16 to 18 positions, which in 1978 were converted to a Senior Executive Service. Persons in those ranks had the choice of being "grandfathered in"; that is, they could decline participation in the SES. When a grandfathered employee retired, however, his or her successor had to accept membership in the SES. (Reform act planners calculated that the transition to SES would take five years at most, given the number of years of service that members of the senior grades had accumulated at the time of the act's passage.)

No more than 10 percent of the SES can be politically appointed; the other 90 percent must be promoted from within the ranks of the career service. Through this requirement, the law ensures the staffing of senior positions with persons knowledgeable about the operations of national government.

POWER OF SENIOR EXECUTIVES

Persons occupying these positions supervise whole programs that account for billions of dollars and thousands of employees. Positioned at the top of the career civil service hierarchy, these executives enjoy the protections of the civil service system but exercise considerable power in determining the content and implementation of policy. Obviously, only persons of exceptional abilities can be expected to rise to the ranks of these so-called supergrades.

ACCOUNTABILITY OF SENIOR EXECUTIVES

Prior to the 1978 act, senior career officials were able to resist initiatives with which they disagreed, because of job security. Resistance never meant that they could directly refuse to carry out policies, but they could take an inordinate amount of time studying a problem or only halfheartedly implement a policy.[61] Now, an incoming administration may not take action against such executives for the first 180 days of the administration, during which time members of the SES can demonstrate their willingness to carry out the policies of the new administration. However, if they refuse to perform or are overly slow in implementing policies, they can then be transferred from their current positions. Such a transfer may mean a mere reformulation of duties, or may entail relegation to an obscure post where the official can have little impact upon agency policies. In the face of a short-notice transfer from cosmopolitan Washington to a remote post, it is not unrealistic to expect that the senior executive would opt for retirement. Thus, senior administrators can no longer frustrate the policy initiatives of political appointees with impunity.

The accountability provisions of the act may have worked too well. By 1985, fully 52 percent of senior executives who were eligible had opted to retire.[62] In fact, the National Commission on the Public Service (citing a 1987 Government Accounting Office [GAO] report) indicated that many of these departures were premature. A survey of those who were leaving found that their reasons included differences with top management, dissatisfaction with political appointees, and the way rewards were being distributed.

Apparently, the Bush administration efforts to reinvigorate the public service achieved its goals with regard to the SES. According to the NPR, by 1992 the Office of Personnel Management had authorized the creation of 8,800 SES positions. Of these, 8,200 were filled for an occupancy rate of 93 percent. Political appointees occupied 700 of the positions.

The report, however, was critical of the allocation of SES positions within agencies. The original intent of the CSRA was to create a cadre of management generalists who could be moved about to provide leadership and innovation. "The majority of senior executives, however, now serve in the SES because of their technical expertise, often as key advisors and managers of support staff or as operational managers responsible for part of line (legislative) programs rather than as agency-level leaders and program executives."[63] The suggested remedy was a redistribution of SES positions as current executives retire rather than an authorization of additional positions.

Members of the Senior Executive Service are responsible for the development of innovative policies and programs and for faithfully executing administration policy. The intent of the 1978 act was to reward executives who performed exceptionally well through a system of pay increases based on performance and one-time bonuses for major contributions to the achievement of the agency's mission. Beginning in 1982, however, reports indicate that there is inadequate funding of the bonus system to reward all who are deserving. Empirical investigations in the 1980s of employee satisfaction with the rewards have reported mixed attitudes; even those reports favorable to the bonus system report less than complete satisfaction with the adequacy of their funding.[64] A 1992 survey of federal employees reported that 81 percent of SES employees were satisfied with their pay and less than 14 percent planned on looking for work outside of government in the foreseeable future.[65]

THE MERIT SYSTEM PROTECTION BOARD

The direct accountability of senior-level executives to their politically appointed bosses and the direct accountability of the director of the OPM to the president, taken in tandem, were a cause of concern for observers who feared that the two might lead back to the abuses of the era prior to civil service protections. To guard against such potential abuses, the act created two entities that were supposed to perform the merit protection and enforcement functions of the old Civil Service Commission. The first of these is the Merit System Protection Board (MSPB).

The MSPB is a three-member board that now performs the merit system oversight functions. The board promulgates and oversees the merit rules, as provided for in the 1978 act. The board also oversees the activities of the administrative judges who hear the appeals of employees who believe themselves to have been wronged by a federal agency. The MSPB will review the decision of an administrative judge only when the employee presents significant new evidence that was not available earlier or when the judge may have made a mistake interpreting a law or regulation.[66] If an employee is not satisfied with the ruling by the MSPB, he or she has sixty days to appeal to the U.S. Court of Appeals.

A 1995 GAO review of the MSPB found that it was accomplishing its mission of protecting employees from adverse actions by agencies within the provisions of its statutory authority. The assessment was based on the positive rate at which the U.S. Circuit Court of Appeals affirmed MSPB decisions.[67]

Finally, the MSPB conducts research on issues ranging from day care in government facilities to sexual harassment.

THE OFFICE OF SPECIAL COUNSEL AND THE WHISTLEBLOWER PROTECTION ACT OF 1989

Conducting investigations into charges of violation of the merit rules is the responsibility of the Office of Special Counsel (OSC). Counsels are appointed by the president for five-year terms. In addition to investigating violations of the merit principle, the special counsel may investigate charges of fraud, waste, and abuse brought by current or former employees or by applicants for government employment. The investigation may be initiated by the counsel if he or she has probable cause to believe that fraud, waste, abuse, or gross mismanagement has occurred. In other words, the Office of Special Counsel was intended to act as an ombudsperson for federal employees. The personal initiative option of the special counsel's mandate is part and parcel of the whistleblower protection aspects of the 1978 reform act.[68] The authors of the act meant to provide federal employees with a mechanism whereby they could report with impunity acts by officials that were counter to the public interest.

In theory, when a special counsel's investigation discovers merit violations, the agency can be compelled to appear before the Merit System Protection Board to defend its actions. Instances of fraud, waste, and abuse are to be reported to higher authorities within the agency, to the president, and to oversight committees of the Congress. Where criminal activity is suspected, the findings are also to be reported to the U.S. Attorney General's office.

The intended protections for employees did not work out in practice, however, because the role envisioned by the first two special counsels was that of attorney for the merit system rather than ombudsperson for federal employees. OSC attorneys, therefore, were highly selective in the cases they were willing to take before the Merit System Protection Board.

A 1984 GAO audit of the Office of Special Counsel found that the OSC had substantially failed to carry out its mandate.[69] Congress reacted by unanimously passing the Whistleblower Protection Act of 1988, which was pocket-vetoed by President Reagan. A slightly modified version of the act was passed in 1989 and signed into law by a supportive President Bush. The 1989 statute separated the Office of Special Counsel from the Merit System Protection Board, while still permitting the OSC to bring adverse actions against agencies before the board. The principal intent of the act, however, was specifically to charge the Office of Special Counsel with the protection of whistleblowers.

Two significant features of the act were a change in the standard of proof for substantiating a claim of whistleblower retaliation and enhanced access to the MSPB by aggrieved employees unable to obtain satisfaction from the Office of Special Counsel.

STANDARD OF PROOF

Prior to 1989, an employee had to be able to demonstrate that the agency's adverse action against her or him was motivated by retaliation for blowing the whistle. The employee had to demonstrate that retaliation was a substantial, motivating, or predominant factor in the agency's action. For its part, the agency merely had to demonstrate with a preponderance of the evidence that it was not acting out of retaliation.

Under the 1989 act, the employee need only demonstrate by a preponderance of the evidence that retaliation was a contributing factor in the adverse action taken against him or her. The agency must now provide clear and convincing evidence that the adverse action would have been taken even if the whistleblowing incident had not occurred. In a very real sense, the 1989 act shifts the burden of proof from the employee to the agency.

EMPLOYEE ACCESS

The 1989 act still provides that an employee must initiate a complaint through the Office of Special Counsel.[70] But if the OSC proves unsatisfactory, the employee retains the right to appeal directly to the MSPB. The act further provides for the payment of attorneys' fees and other legal costs if the complaining employee prevails. Finally, the 1989 act prohibits the OSC from intervening against an employee in his or her hearing before the MSPB.

Congress is clearly intent on protecting the rights of whistleblowers. The support of the Bush administration for this position sent a clear signal to program administrators that, as a matter of public policy, merit protection means:

> Employees should be protected against reprisal for lawful disclosure of information which the employees reasonably believe evidences (a) a violation of any law, rule or regulation, or (b) mismanagement, a gross waste of funds, an abuse of authority, or substantial and specific danger to public health or safety. (Principle 9 of the 1978 Civil Service Reform Act)

The 1989 act provides the wherewithal to achieve this end.

The courts, however, have narrowly interpreted the protection to which an employee is entitled. An employee is entitled to whistleblower protection when he or she reports fraud, waste, and abuse or gross mismanagement outside the chain of command. They are not entitled to protection if they directly confront the person engaged in the practice.[71] Critics of the ruling find such narrowness unsettling. An SES employee, for example, would not be protected from the retaliation of a political appointee for saying that a policy he or she wished to pursue was illegal. Critics would also protect employees for internally reporting problems.[72]

THE EQUAL EMPLOYMENT OPPORTUNITY COMMISSION

A detailed history of federal equal employment opportunity policy is presented in Chapter 3 of this text. What is of interest here are the personnel implications of moving the enforcement function for this policy from the Civil Service Commission to an advocacy agency, the Equal Employment Opportunity Commission (EEOC). Beginning with President Kennedy's Executive Order 10925, federal agencies were required to review their policies regarding equal employment opportunity and to take "affirmative action" to correct flaws in the system.

By 1965 virtually complete responsibility for federal affirmative action policy—including policy formulation, investigation of abuses, and general enforcement responsibilities—rested with the Civil Service Commission. The system was flawed from the outset because of its conflicting tasks of merit enforcement and affirmative action advocacy. No examination for all entry-level management positions in government could be expected to meet the job-relevance criterion set by the Supreme Court in *Griggs* v. *Duke Power* (1971).[73] In the *Griggs* case, the Court ruled that the primary determinant of an examination's validity was its capacity to predict the ability to perform the job in question. The Civil Service Commission never questioned whether its own test met that criterion.

The 1978 reforms gave the EEOC both leadership responsibility for governmentwide affirmative action policies and enforcement authority. Of course, the principals in the implementation of affirmative action policies are the agencies. EEOC hegemony over federal agencies represented a significant policy shift, because the EEOC is an advocacy agency whose purpose is specifically to ensure equal employment opportunity; unlike the old Civil Service Commission, it is not charged with providing a full range of personnel services. When the EEOC addresses a grievance, it will not reflect negatively on another unit of its own operation, as was potentially the case when equal employment enforcement was one of the many duties of the Civil Service Commission.

THE FEDERAL LABOR RELATIONS AUTHORITY

The creation of the Federal Labor Relations Authority (FLRA)[74] is important from both a policy and an administrative perspective. As a matter of policy, the right of federal employees to bargain collectively was established by law for the first time by the 1978 Civil Service Reform Act. Prior to 1978, bargaining rights existed only by executive order, the first of which was Executive Order 10988, issued by President Kennedy. Under that initial order, bargaining rights were severely circumscribed: federal employees were not allowed to bargain over wages and salaries, nor were they permitted to strike. The 1978 act did little to broaden those rights, but it did institutionalize the legitimacy of federal-level collective bargaining with a legislative act. Prior to 1978, if a president had chosen to undo the Kennedy order, another executive order alone would have sufficed. Revoking the right now would require a positive act on the part of both houses of Congress as well as the president.

Administratively, the FLRA is important because it establishes a formalized administrative structure to oversee public employee union elections and formulate federal labor relations policy. The FLRA also houses the Impasse Panel, which can provide mediation services to agencies and employee groups who find themselves at an impasse.

A detailed history of labor relations in the federal government is presented in Chapter 13. What is important to note here is that the 1978 act is the most significant legislative achievement of federal employee groups since the Lloyd-LaFollette Act of 1913 granted federal employees the right to organize for purposes of articulating their collective interests to the Congress.

MERIT PAY

As noted previously, one of the principles of merit enumerated in the 1978 act was to make the federal service more efficient and effective. The authors of the act believed that federal managers could be motivated toward that end by a system of merit pay.

The 1978 act originally provided for a system of merit pay for all managers above the GS 9 level in the federal service. This plan met strong opposition from employee groups, however, and a compromise was reached that allowed merit pay only to managers above the GS 12 level. The original merit pay system also provided that in years when the president and Congress declared a raise for federal employees, managers eligible for merit pay would receive only half the increase; the other half, plus monies that would be used for step increases within the eligible grades, would be distributed on the basis of merit alone. For example, if government employees were to receive a 6 percent cost-of-living raise, persons eligible for merit pay would receive only 3 percent automatically. Satisfactory performers could expect a little less than 6 percent, because money to reward exceptional performers had to come from the 3 percent remaining after the cost-of-living raise. Therefore, unless a significant portion of government supervisors performed unsatisfactorily, there simply was not enough money to significantly reward the superior performer without injuring the satisfactory performer. Such problems in the system led to its revision in 1985.

The 1985 reforms created a merit pay review system called the Performance Management and Recognition System (PMRS). The PMRS provided for a five-level rating system used to determine basic salary increases and merit increases. Level 1 indicated unacceptable performance; level 2, minimally successful; level 3 meant fully successful; a level 4 rating indicated that the employee exceeded the requirements for fully successful; and level 5 ratings were reserved for employees whose performance was outstanding. If a general pay raise is declared, level 1 employees receive nothing, level 2 employees receive half the general increase, and levels 3, 4, and 5 receive the total amount.

The PMRS system was an improvement over the original system. Nevertheless it came under criticism by the National Performance Review for its narrow focus and inflexibility. Authorization for the PMRS expired in 1993. In 1995 OPM issued the final regulations abolishing the PMRS.[75] Agencies are now encouraged to be innovative in their incentive systems and to use bonuses and one-time awards rather than incentives that are built into the employee's base. Nonmonetary rewards such as time off are also possible, as are group awards known as gainsharing. In gainsharing, all employees are rewarded when a particular agency goal is reached, such as reduction in production cost or the costs associated with on-the-job injuries (see Chapter 9).

SUMMARY AND CONCLUSION

American public personnel systems have evolved from a time of revolutionary fervor, to a period of partisan appointments, and into a system of intense patronage in which government staffing was an integral part of the operations of victorious political parties. The patronage benefits of bureaucratic accountability came at the price of corruption and inefficiencies that were unacceptable. The ensuing reforms were rooted in selection of government employees on the basis of their qualifications, and otherwise satisfactory employees were protected from removal for partisan reasons. Protection against removal except for cause soon followed.

The advent of a career civil service engendered a number of agencies, laws, and procedural rules that are collectively known as the civil service system. The twentieth century saw a number of revisions and reforms that where add-ons rather than replacements of cumbersome systems. Then, in 1978, the federal government undertook a reform of the merit system that altered its fundamental principles and resulted in a proliferation of agencies whose missions is largely human resources management.

Bureaucratic accountability to elected and appointed officials was reinvigorated with the creation of the Senior Executive Service. Rank-and-file federal employees were extended protection from retaliation for reporting fraud, waste, and abuse and gross mismanagement. This whistleblower protection was found lacking by the Congress in 1985 and 1989, and the extent of protection to which employees are entitled continues to evolve.

The distribution of the duties of the old Civil Service Commission among several agencies continues to evolve as new challenges emerge. The Office of Personnel Management underwent the most change as a result of its role as an instrument of administration authority. Most recently, it has been at the center of the Clinton administration's National Performance Review. It continues to set personnel policies. Not until very recently, however, did OPM begin to delegate to the agencies the significant control over their personnel systems envisioned in 1978.

The Merit System Protection Board and the Equal Employment Opportunity Commission have overlapping jurisdictions, and the potential exists for conflicting rulings. A 1996 recommendation of the General Accounting Office strongly suggests that the MSPB have jurisdiction over matters that have systemic implications (for example, if a test discriminated against an entire class). The GAO recommends that the EEOC have authority over cases of discrimination brought by individuals.[76]

The role of the Federal Labor Relations Authority will no doubt continue to evolve, especially if the federal employee unions ever acquire the right to negotiate over wages and benefits. Currently, the FLRA spends a great deal of its time hearing appeals regarding contract issues dealing with working conditions.

The merit pay provisions of the acts sought to provide an incentive system to reward highly productive federal employees. A flaw in the system, as implemented, was inadequate funding to reward all deserving employees. OPM has authorized agencies to experiment with a variety of reward systems that include group and individual monetary rewards and nonmonetary forms of recognition.

When combined with innovations in the methods agencies use to assess performance, the system may yet devise a reward system that motivates and that is seen as fair by management and workers alike.

PATRONAGE OR CRONYISM?*

On January 4, two-year-old Kaitlin Dalby died after being beaten to death while in the care of her mother and mother's boyfriend. It appeared she had suffered weeks of abuse before her death. Area residents claimed they had made numerous calls to the Department of Human Services (DHS) to report the abuse before Kaitlin died. One call was made on December 12, less than a month before Kaitlin's death. Another call was made just four days later. The department's internal review had no record of the December 12 call, nor had DHS employees mentioned such a call. Under closer inspection, however, the department records revealed that a call had been received, but the case had fallen through the cracks after an inconclusive preliminary visit from a social worker.

DHS director Debra Foster felt department workers followed all procedures in the Dalby case but also stated that she had "grave concerns" about whether her employees responded properly to allegations that Kaitlin Dalby was being abused in the weeks before she died. The governor's office was notified about the incident and began an investigation. The investigation was barely underway when criticism from another quarter overshadowed the Dalby case almost entirely.

The state's largest newspaper ran the story under the headline "State Squanders Millions on Consultants." The story reported that the state spent $430 million on service contracts in the last budget year, compared to $161 million it had budgeted for contracts 10 years earlier. Indeed, last year, one-third of the state's total budget went to private contractors. Governor Jack Bartlett said previous leaders might have created the reliance on outside help by reducing the number of state workers. "The workload remained the same, and the state hired consultants to fill in for full-time employee," he said.

Upon examining the increase in contractors, a special state audit was conducted on two consultants in the DHS: Kathy Kramer and Matt Schilling. Foster had hired Kramer. She was a professional acquaintance of Foster when she worked as director of the human services department in a neighboring state. State auditors discovered Kramer was paid nearly $22,000 for a month's worth of work in the previous year. Three days after her consulting contract ended, Kramer was hired full time as the department's chief deputy director of policy. Her salary was fixed at $89,544 a year. As a state employee, her pay was $1,700 a week, compared with the $5,500 a week she made as a consultant.

The auditor's office found little evidence of what Kramer did during her month of consulting. In response to the auditor's request for evidence of Kramer's work, the department turned over four typewritten pages, including an informal and fragmented summary. The following excerpts are illustrative of the material pre-

*Prepared by Mary Beth Mellick and C. Kenneth Meyer, Drake University

sented in Kramer's "Summary of Responses" after she had worked in the DHS for a month as a consultant. By nearly any standard, some of the state politicians judged them to be little more than trite phrases or simple statements and many members of the department felt strongly that the consultant was paid for one month nearly what they would receive in an entire year. Taken from Kramer's report were the following representative statements:

- "Most would say that communication has come a long way in the last few years, but will also say there is still a ways to go."
- "Teamwork has another theme throughout the responses. Teamwork including line staff, field staff, central office, between divisions, at every level. 'Lead by example' and 'walk the talk' were expressions noted."
- "Contracting out was mentioned in several papers. Feeling is this should be discontinued and the funding be used for additional staff to do the work."

The following are additional excerpts from a one-page report by Kramer titled "Specific Areas of Focus":

- "Establish partnerships based on shared decision making, shared responsibilities, and shared accountability. . . ."
- "Establish a human service system founded in quality, i.e., best/promising practice, customer satisfaction, continuous improvement. . . ."

Representative Dennis Newman (R), speaker of the House of Representatives, said the arrangement with Kramer "smacks of cronyism" and appeared to be a "misappropriation" of state money.

The second case involved Texas consultant Matt Schilling, who was hired by the state to explore a new payment system for service providers that would link pay to performance for companies, counselors, child-welfare workers, and others who did business with the DHS. Like Kramer, Schilling had a previous relationship with Foster stemming from the consulting he previously provided for an agency that she directed in another state. Upon close examination, state auditors were surprised to learn that under Schilling's contract with the state, he was "paid $380,000 over 22 months."

Under Schilling's new payment system, social-service providers would be made more accountable. For example, under the old system, the DHS would pay providers for work produced, not results. A counselor under the existing system would receive payments based on the number of sessions with a troubled teen. Under Schilling's system, pay would hinge, at least in part, on changes in the teen's life—getting a job, staying in school, avoiding drug use. Providers disagreed with Schilling's system, stating that they didn't think their payments should depend on progress. However, Lutheran Social Services, the state's largest nonprofit social service agency, was "supportive of the direction of Schilling's recommendations," said Ron Green, the agency's president and chief executive officer. He also said that the public demands that payments be linked to results.

Whether Schilling's payment system would be successful, in the final analysis, was a contentious issue. Some lawmakers wondered publicly in the interviews they gave and the letters they wrote to the editor of the state's major newspaper, whether he was "worth the astronomical salary he received for his work." Some legislators were questioning Schilling's work even before his expenses became an issue. They stated that Schilling's idea of holding providers accountable sounds great. But for $380,000, he had failed to answer the question: How?

State Senator Marcia Bergman, a Democrat, said Schilling's proposals are heavy on jargon and light on "ordinary common sense" solutions. In his defense, Foster said Schilling was not expected to provide details on how to make his concepts work. "The answers for 'how to' are going to come from our front lines, not from in here," she retorted.

The auditors' findings of private contractors' salaries were met with intense public scrutiny. Senator Diane Reynolds, a Legislative Oversight Committee member, said it was difficult "for average citizens to understand" why a "department does not have enough people to do their job, but" has "some $400,000 to have an outsider come in and tell us what we're doing wrong."

"There's hardly anybody worth that much money. The way these consultants were taken care of was ridiculous," said Woodward Mayor George Meyer, referring to Schilling's frequent stays at Embassy Heights, an exclusive hotel located close to the capitol building complex, and the costs associated with roundtrip first class airfare from Texas. In addition to Schilling's $380,000 salary over 22 months, he also "incurred $54,000 in travel expenses that were paid without proper authorization." The state auditor reported that the maximum allowable amount for food and lodging while on state business is $75 per day. Furthermore, first class air travel is not authorized for state business. The report concluded that Schilling should reimburse the state in the amount of $37,560.

Democrats suggested that Republicans were trying to stir up trouble for Governor Bartlett, a Democrat, as the two parties geared up for the fall legislative elections. Representative Phil Abbott, a Democrat, charged that committee cochairman Richard Stone, a Republican, was "playing 'gotcha politics' with the governor." Abbott also questioned the timing of the Schilling audit report by Davidson, a Republican, so close to an election.

DHS director Debra Foster was confronted by her critics at a hearing at the state capitol. She surprised lawmakers by accepting full responsibility for the contractual flaws identified by auditor Doug Davidson in Schilling and Kramer's lucrative consulting contracts. She stated that she might seek help from the attorney general in recovering the travel expenses from Schilling. Foster also stated that she intended to heed the advice of Davidson and other state officials for improving the department's handling of contracts. She defended the work, however, of both Schilling and Kramer, citing improved services. Lawmakers treated their meeting with Foster as a fact-finding session, not an interrogation.

When contacted by the media regarding his controversial recommendations, Schilling noted that the recommendations of consultants aren't always accepted and implemented by state agencies. When asked if the agency had become overly reliant on consultants for ideas on how to improve operations, he replied: "State agencies don't really listen to consultants."

Questions and Instructions

1. What political and management issues are you able to identify in the case? Please list them.

2. Is there a difference between patronage and cronyism? If yes, please make the distinction. What forms does patronage take in government at its various levels today?

3. Are patronage, cronyism, and favoritism found only in government operations, or are they also present in other areas of the economy—the private and nonprofit sectors? Explain.

4. If you were in Debra Foster's position, would you have made the political concessions that are presented in the case, and would you have defended the quality of the work provided by Kathy Kramer? Why or why not?

KEEP YOUR STICK ON THE ICE OR YOUR VIEWS TO YOURSELF*

John Snow was saddened about the way his childhood sport of hockey had changed since he was a young boy growing up in Duluth, Minnesota. Sure, the coaches demanded as much then as now, and there was the physical contact involved in checking other players, but the skills of skating fast and precisely always had to be finely honed. Some banter on the ice was permitted, but it was not mean-spirited and filled with obscenities, profanities, and statements about one's mother.

Today was different for John Snow. He became quite agitated as he read and reread the front-page story that appeared in his metropolitan newspaper, and he presumed that it had also received top billing in other newspapers across the country. For sure, it was the lead sensational story on all national and cable television news. The newspaper article featured two fathers who argued and then fought over the extent to which violence was being played out by adolescents in an ice arena in New England, and in the final analysis, one father ended up killing the other father, the game's umpire, while their children watched. "How can this be?" John wondered. "Why can't the senseless level of violence end in America? What is happening," he thought, "to our children who are fed a high caloric diet of violent encounters on a daily basis."

"Enough is enough," he said to himself. He opened a new document on his computer and wrote a letter to the editor of the local newspaper, *The Publics' Messenger*. His thoughts came quickly about a topic over which he had become outraged. It was during normal working hours, to be sure, and he knew that what he was writing was his own personal opinion, but he had to say something—if only to decry the magnitude and viciousness of violence in society. He wrote:

Dear Editor:

   Today, there is a low level of confidence and trust and a high level of cynicism and verbal abuse for those in positions of authority: police, government employees, teachers, social workers, librarians, members of Congress, and the judiciary. Indeed,

*Prepared by C. Kenneth Meyer and Lance Noe, Drake University

over the last 30 years, this trend is augmented by the declining confidence in the basic institutions of society, such as medicine, colleges and universities, journalism, and large companies. Correspondingly, is there any wonder why people don't trust or respect referees, umpires, coaches, and other players or fans? The legitimacy of coaches, umpires, referees, etc., as authority figures is challenged when they are spit upon, cursed, punched, shoved, and in a myriad of other ways, have pain, injury or suffering intentionally inflicted upon them by players and managers—and these acts take place in the noncombative sports. On the extreme side of the sports industry exist the totally obscene, decadent, and sought-after forms of behavior and "entertainment" displayed in boxing—"an ear or so for an alleged head butt"; in basketball—"a threat and choke for a reduction in pay and a short suspension"; in professional wrestling or "psycho-sexual sadism"—twisted around the themes of female objectification and the crudest forms of barbarism and human debasement; and the other combative "sports" of Ultimate fighting, kick boxing, and the totally cruel and vicious tough-man contests. These latter sports go well beyond the concerns of this letter.

Violence in sports should be categorized as a type of workplace violence (similar to violence that occurs in offices, factories, lumber mills, farms, taxicabs, warehouses, schools, and in "stop and robs"—convenience stores). If the safety and health of workers (players, umpires, coaches, and agents) and spectators is of concern, then the level of violence taking place on the court, field, floor, track, or in the arena might appropriately be addressed by the U.S. Center for Disease Control (CDC), the Occupational Safety and Health Administration (OSHA), and by professional labor unions, management, and team owners. The rationale underpinning a governmental policy that deals with sports violence is easily justified.

Seeing players fight one on one or as a gang on the field is common. Coaches routinely curse, rant and rave, and scream at players; they even throw clipboards, chairs, or other objects that are within immediate reach onto the playing floor and get "close and physical" with their charges. The players brawl and act viciously toward the umpires and other players, fight with, trip, hit, kick, and physically and verbally lash out at the spectators, and throw their bats, sticks, racquets, hats, etc., to the ground as if they are spoiled millionaire kids having a tantrum—which they largely are. Mothers of cheerleaders fight with one another, and one went so far as to put a contract for murder on another girl's mother; and, predictably, parents act violently toward their own kids who are involved in little league play. Most recently, the players' agents have entered into the fray and some even attempt to show that the spectators desire to see players snarl, scratch, claw, and be physically and mentally brutal and purposively violent in the arena. In fact, of the top twelve national sports stories recently voted for by members of the Associated Press, three dealt with violence: Tyson bites Holyfield (Rank 2), Marv Albert sex (biting) scandal (Rank 10), and Sprewell attack on Coach Carlesimo (Rank 12). Perhaps violence and winning, in a perverted way, have become the brass ring.

Violence does not end on the field or in the arena. Too often, violence continues after the game, and some players get involved in acts of abuse against wives, girlfriends, and paid or unpaid sexual partners and engage in other types of violent behavior (drug pushing, physical assault, and even rape). Even some of the all-stars on the U.S. Olympic Hockey Team trashed their hotel room in Nagano, Japan, when they found out that their crude, violent, and bullying behavior was not successful against their opponents. One might reasonably conclude that we spend more time reading the indictments by grand juries of those engaged in sports than we spend reading about the play of the day and the ultimate slam dunk.

Management, union officials, and players' agents all too frequently portray these attacks and outbursts as lapses in character. Or they claim that the player was driven over the edge by some unidentifiable cause, as if to justify a temporary aberration; they then do everything possible to keep them on the team so that a win can be marked-up, because winning is everything. The character and discipline formation of athletics gets lost in this win-at-any-cost mentality. And, to add to the problem, some club owners and sports announcers deride other owners, players, and associations and even engage in a unique type of violence—racism. The latest foray into the culture of spectator-approved violence was the simulated violent attacks by the San Diego Chicken against a purple dinosaur figure who resembles Barney, an icon of childrens' television. As the chicken attacks, pounces upon, and strikes the dinosaur, the cheers and applause are nearly palpable from the stands. These, of course, are all acts of violence.

Sports is not the sole proprietor of violent behavior in society. Generally, it is easy to uncover varying levels or intensities of violence in politics (injury by infringement, profanity, outrage, distortion, and need to control; electoral politics and the actions of special prosecutors come to mind); in musical lyrics (country to rap music); media; public policy (laws directed against women, minorities, children, elderly, lower income groups, and the underclass); video games; and in such areas as police-citizen interaction. More years of life are loss to violence each year than the total losses associated with cancer, strokes, and heart disease, according to the American Medical Association. Indeed, violence is of pandemic levels and is a major medical and public health problem. Each year, nearly one-half million visits to trauma and ER care centers involve violence. A recently conducted national survey of doctors, reported in the *Annals of Internal Medicine,* revealed that 87 percent and 94 percent of surgeons and internists, respectively, thought that gunshot wounds should be treated as a public health epidemic. The published report projected that death by gunshot will eclipse death by auto accidents by 2003. Further, some aspects of our society have become so violent that we can't seem to have the two sexes trained together, as is suggested by the recent allegations of rape, sexual abuse, and harassment in several of the military service branches.

Perhaps there is still some particle of hope among most of us that violence can be addressed in our systems of entertainment, economics, and politics. The public outrage concerning the slap on the wrist given to an NBA player who choked his coach provides some solace. If an employee in your workplace choked the CEO, CFO, or supervisor, would this result in employee suspension, termination, or the filing of a civil or criminal charge? Perhaps it is painfully evident for most to see how far we have permitted our society to depart from those idealized standards that ought to govern basic relationships among us—trust, caring, civility, compassion, and understanding.

John read and reread the letter. It included all the issues he wanted to put on the table at this time, and the tone had to be dramatic, he reasoned, if readers were to pay any attention to what he had to say. But no topic was more important to society than that of violence, he had spoken his mind, and now he would let the chips fall where they might.

Believing he had engaged in an act of citizenship, he proudly signed the letter: John Snow, Human Resources Counselor, City of Plainview. Now all he had to do was wait for the reactions of his friends and coworkers. He expected that other Letters to the Editor would follow, and he knew he would be ridiculed by some and praised by others. What he did not anticipate was his director's reaction. The e-mail was crisply written:

John, you have done it again! Your job is to counsel employees of the City of Plainview and their family members. It is not in your job description to take on every liberal, bleeding-heart cause that is presented on TV. To add insult to injury, your recent letter to the editor was signed using your official position title and that is forbidden, as you know, in the City of Plainview Employee Manual. I wish to discuss this irresponsible act with you and determine what steps need to be taken to ensure that you are appropriately disciplined. As you may already know, several members of the city council are fed up with your public tirades.

QUESTIONS AND INSTRUCTIONS

1. As the director of the Human Resources Department, what do you find objectionable, if anything, in what John Snow has penned to the Editor? Is the content of the letter relevant to your meeting with Snow? Be specific.

2. Does Public Employee John Snow give up any rights that he otherwise enjoys as Citizen Snow? If no, what is your reasoning or rationale? If yes, can you specifically identify any employee rights that are limited for public employees and why they are curtailed?

3. Should John Snow have signed his name and given his official organization affiliation? Was it acceptable, in your opinion, for John to write the letter he sent to the newspaper while at work and on the city time clock? Please elaborate. Would you see his expressed opinion as a concern for the HR director if he had signed it and given only his home address? Please explain.

NOTES AND RESOURCES

1. The term is borrowed from Joseph Califano, *A Presidential Nation* (New York: Norton, 1975).

2. Article II of the United States Constitution makes no mention of a bureaucracy beyond stating in Section 3 that "he [the president] shall take care that the laws be faithfully executed, and shall commission all the officers of the United States." Section 2 provides for the impeachment of all civil officers as well as of the president and vice president. From this we can infer an intention to create a bureaucracy.

3. The idea that the early leaders were trustees comes from the work of William E. Mosher and J. Donald Kingsley, *Public Personnel Administration* (New York: Harper & Row, 1930), p. 17.

4. On the history of American personnel policy, see N. Joseph Cayer, *Public Personnel Administration in the United States*, 2nd ed. (New York: St. Martin's Press, 1986); Paul P. Van Riper, *History of the United States Civil Service* (New York: Harper & Row, 1958); and Frederick C. Mosher, *Democracy and the Public Service*, 2nd ed. (New York: Oxford University Press, 1982).

5. Reproduced in James D. Richardson, ed., *Messages and Papers of the Presidents, 1789–1908* (New York: Bureau of National Literature and Art, 1909), pp. 213–24.

6. For a detailed discussion of the struggles and compromises that led to the framing of the Constitution, see Clinton Rossiter, *1787: The Grand Convention* (New York: Macmillan, 1966).

7. For a fuller discussion of the politics of this period, see Leonard D. White, *The Jeffersonians: A Study in Administrative History: 1801–1829* (New York: Macmillan, 1951).

8. *Marbury* v. *Madison*, 1 Cranch 137, 2 1. Ed. 60 (1803).

9. For a thorough discussion of the heyday of the federal patronage system, see Carl R. Fish, *The Civil Service and Patronage* (Cambridge: Harvard University Press, 1920), pp. 105–33; and Leonard D. White, *The Jacksonians: A Study in Administrative History: 1829–1861* (New York: Macmillan, 1984).

10. In more modern times, parties have seen to it that partisans are awarded automobile licensing franchises. Profits from these enterprises are shared with the party. The individual keeps a sizable share, and a percentage goes to the state. In some states, patronage appointees have been obliged to designate the party as the recipient of a share of their state salaries. Raymond E. Wolfinger, "Why Political Machines Have Not Withered Away and Other Revisionist Thoughts," in *Political Parties,* 2nd ed., David W. Abbot and Edward T. Rogowsky, eds. (Chicago: Rand McNally, 1971), pp. 51–74. For more complete treatments of the history of American political parties, see Frank Sorauf, *Politics in America* (Boston: Little, Brown, 1968); and Daniel Eldersfeld, *Political Parties in America* (Chicago: Rand McNally, 1964).

11. For a detailed discussion of Lincoln's travail with the spoils system, see Harry J. Carman and Reinhard H. Cuthin, *Lincoln and the Patronage* (New York: Columbia University Press, 1943).

12. For a sanitized version of the events surrounding the replacement of Simon Cameron as secretary of war, see John G. Nicolay and John Hay, *Abraham Lincoln: A History,* vol. 5 (New York: Century, 1886), pp. 111–23. Nicolay and Hay base their accounts on formal records and memos rather than the diaries and memoirs of participants in the discussion.

13. Harry J. Carmar and Reinhard H. Cuthin, *Lincoln and the Patronage,* pp. 278–84.

14. On the British origins of the merit system, see Paul P. Van Riper, *History of the United States Civil Service,* especially Chapter 5.

15. For a discussion of corruption at the federal level, see William D. Foulke, *Fighting the Spoilsmen: Reminiscences of the Civil Service Reform Movement* (New York: Putnam, 1919).

16. William L. Riordon, *Plunkett of Tammany Hall* (New York: McClure Phillips, 1905), p. 405.

17. An earlier piece of civil service legislation had been passed in 1871, giving the president broader powers than did the Civil Service Act that became law on January 16, 1883. The earlier legislation lacked adequate funding and widespread support in the Grant administration, however. Lewis Mayer, *The Federal Service: A Study of the System of Personnel Administration of the United States Government* (New York: Appleton-Century-Crofts, 1922), pp. 43–47.

18. For a fuller discussion, see Ari A. Hoogenboom, *Outlawing the Spoils: A History of the Civil Service Reform Movement, 1865–1883* (Urbana: University of Illinois Press, 1961).

19. *Angel G. Luevano et al.* v. *Alan Campbell, Director, Office of Personnel Management et al.,* Civ. A. No. 79–0271 93 F.R.D. 68, 1981 U.S. Dist. LEXIS 18023.

20. Perhaps the most prominent example of such behavior occurred in the Department of Housing and Urban Affairs during the Reagan presidency. See "Press: How Reporters Missed the HUD Story, A Multi-Billion Dollar Scandal during the Reagan Years Is Now Front-Page News. Where Was the Washington Press Back Then?" *Time,* July 4, 1989, p. 48.

21. The commission reports: "There are now more Schedule C appointees at GS 13–15 levels than there were total Schedule C appointees in 1976." National Commission on the Public Service Task Force, *Rebuilding the Public Service* (Washington, D.C.: National Commission on the Public Service, 1989), p. 163.

22. William Faulkner wrote of this phenomenon: "People seemed to hold that the one sole end of the entire establishment of public office was to elect one man like Sheriff Hampton big enough or at least with sense and character enough to run the country and then fill the rest of the jobs with cousins and in-laws who had failed to make a living at everything else they ever tried." *Intruder in the Dust* (New York: Random House, 1948), p. 31.

23. For a complete report, see William Reddig, *Tom's Town, K. C. and the Pendergast Legend* (Philadelphia: Lippincott, 1947).

24. For a detailed discussion of the corruption of county commissioners in Oklahoma and the movement of the FBI against them, see Frank S. Meyers, "Political Science and Political Corruption: The Case of the County Commissioner Scandal in Oklahoma," Ph.D. dissertation, University of Oklahoma, 1985, especially pp. 144–90. By the end of 1983, "nearly 250 incumbent commissioners, former county commissioners and suppliers had been convicted" (p. 6).

25. Harry Holloway, Frank S. Meyers, and Jeffrey L. Brudney, "Elite and Mass Attitudes toward Corruption," a paper presented at the annual meeting of the Southern Political Science Association, Birmingham, November 1983. These scholars found that, unlike state and federal elected officials, who are generally better educated than the electorate, county commissioners were slightly less educated than their constituents.

26. *Elrod Sheriff et al.* v. *Burns et al.*, 427 U.S. 347 (1976).

27. *Branti* v. *Finkel et al.*, 445 U.S. 507 (1980).

28. *Rutan* v. *Republican Party of Illinois et al.*, 497 U.S. 62 (1990) 1990 LEXIS 3298, 111 L Ed 2d 52 (1990).

29. Ibid., p. 66.

30. Ibid., p. 92. Scalia was joined in his dissent by the other Reagan appointees, Kennedy, O'Connor, and Rehnquist.

31. *O'Hare Truck Service et al.,* v. *City of Northlake et al.,* 518 U.S. 712 (1996).

32. *Vickery* v. *Jones et al.,* 100 F.3d 1334 (1996). Certiorari denied April 28, 1997.

33. Titled "The Hatch Reform Amendments," H.R. 20 was signed into law on October 6, 1993.

34. *Pickering* v. *Board of Education,* 88 S. Ct. 1731 (1968).

35. Ibid., pp. 1734–5.

36. *Waters et al.* v. *Churchill et al.,* 511 U.S. 661, LEXIS 4104 (1994).

37. *Fisher* v. *Walker,* 464 F2d. 1147 (1972).

38. *Jeffries* v. *Harleston,* 516 U.S. 862, LEXIS 6088 (1995).

39. Frederick W. Taylor, "The Principles of Scientific Management," in *Scientific Management* (New York: Norton, 1967), pp. 114–41.

40. Recommendation number two of the President's Task Force on Personnel Management Reforms called for an expansion of the rules "to allow selection from broader categories." *President's Reorganization Project Personnel Management Report*, vol. 1, Final Staff Report, December 1977, p. 27. For a discussion of the impact of veterans' preference points on the composition of the federal workforce, see *Hearings before the Committee on Post Office and Civil Service, House of Representatives Ninety-Fifth Congress, Second Session on H.R. 11280: A Bill to Reform the Civil Service Laws* (Washington, DC: U.S. Government Printing Office, 1978).

41. The actual number of candidates that may be considered as equals varies from the federal rule of three to as many as fifteen in states such as Oklahoma. The rule of fifteen can be used equally to reach qualified minority persons on the list or to practice nepotism or political cronyism, of course. A disabled veteran, however, may not be bypassed on an Oklahoma list of eligibles. The Supreme Court upheld the veterans' preference in *Massachusetts* v. *Feeney,* 442 U.S. 256 (1979).

42. *Angel G. Luevano et al.* v. *Alan Campbell, Director Office of Personnel Management et al.,* Civ. A. No. 79–0271 93 F.R.D. 68, 1981 U.S. Dist. LEXIS 18023.

43. Merit System Protection Board, *Restoring Merit to Federal Hiring: Why Two Special Hiring Programs Should Be Ended* (Washington, D.C., U.S. Merit System Protection Board, January 2000).

44. For an amplified discussion of the implications of decentralizing classification, see Bernard H. Baum, *Decentralization of Authority in a Bureaucracy* (Englewood Cliffs, NJ: Prentice-Hall, 1961), pp. 89–129.

45. The manual has been reprinted in Frank J. Thompson, ed., *Classics in Public Personnel Policy* (Oak Park, IL: Moore Publishing, 1979), pp. 159–88.

46. 5 U.S.C., Section 2301, <http://www.opm.gov/omsoe/merit/legal.htm> updated October 2, 1986.

47. Title II, Section 201 of the 1978 act defined the duties and responsibilities of the new Office of Personnel Management and its director as assisting the president in the making and administration of personnel policies, rules, and so forth. The presidential authority for personnel management may be delegated to the director of the OPM, who in turn may delegate authority to agency directors. The intent of the act, therefore, was the decentralization of routine personnel management functions.

48. The term *chief administrative officer* is borrowed from Richard Neustadt, *Presidential Power: The Politics of Leadership with Reflections on Johnson and Nixon* (New York: Wiley, 1976).

49. Presidential executive authority became complete with the advent of civil service reform in 1978. The president has had budgetary authority since 1921, with the passage of the Budget and Accounting Act. The Office of Management and Budget can also be directed to engage in performance audits of agency programs as a result of the 1969 changes in the Bureau of the Budget. For a review of the evaluation of presidential administrative authority, see Richard E. Neustadt, "Presidency and Legislation: The Growth of Central Clearance," *American Political Science Review* 48 (1954): 641–71. See also Ronald Randall, "Presidential Powers vs. Bureaucratic Intransigence: The Influence of the Nixon Administration on Welfare Policy," *American Political Science Review* 73 (1979): 795–810.

50. See, for example, Harold Seidman, *Politics, Position and Power: The Dynamics of Federal Organization,* 2nd ed. (New York: Oxford University Press, 1977).

51. Steven Hess, *Organizing the Presidency* (Washington, DC: Brookings Institution, 1976).

52. Lane, Larry M., "The Office of Personnel Management: Values, Policies and Consequences," in Patricia W. Ingraham and David H. Rosenbloom, eds., *The Promise and Paradox of Civil Service Reform,* (Pittsburgh: University of Pittsburgh Press, 1992), pp. 107–8.

53. For a thoughtful look at changes in the federal retirement system, see Robert W. Hartman, *Pay and Pensions for Federal Workers* (Washington, DC: The Brookings Institution, 1983).

54. See U.S. General Accounting Office, *Managing Human Resources: Greater OPM Leadership Needed to Address Critical Challenges* (Washington, DC: U.S. Government Printing Office, 1989), pp. 22–23. See also Patricia W. Ingraham and David H. Rosenbloom, *The State of Merit in the Federal Government,* an occasional paper prepared for the National Commission on the Public Service, June 1990.

55. Office of the Vice President, *Office of Personnel Management: Accompanying Report of the National Performance Review,* <http://www.pub.whitehouse.gov/uri-res/> posted July 16, 1994.

56. National Commission on the Public Service Task Force, *Rebuilding the Public Service* (Washington, DC: National Commission on the Public Service, 1989).

57. Office of the Vice President, *Office of Personnel Management: Accompanying Report of the National Performance Review,* <http://www.pub.whitehouse.gov/uri-res/> posted July 16, 1994, p. 4.

58. For in-depth reporting on the National Performance Review see Interagency Work Group on Performance Management, *Report to the President's Management Council on Managing Performance in the Government,* <http://www.opm.gov/perform/articles/2000/pmcrpt.htm> February, 2000.

59. Office of the Vice President, *Office of Personnel Management: Accompanying Report of the National Performance Review,* <http://www.pub.whitehouse.gov/uri-res/> posted July 16, 1994, pp. 15–25.

60. For an assessment of the difficulties facing those who attempt to make bureau chiefs accountable, see Harold Seidman, *Politics, Position and Power: The Dynamics of Federal Organization,* 2nd ed. (New York: Oxford University Press, 1977), pp. 304–12; also, Hugh A. Heclo, *A Government of Strangers* (Washington, DC: The Brookings Institution, 1977).

61. History is replete with examples of bureaucracies that take their time carrying out an executive order. See, for example, Max Weber, "Essay on Bureaucracy," in *Bureaucratic Power in National Politics,* 3rd ed., Francis E. Rourke, ed. (Boston: Little, Brown, 1978), pp. 85–96. For more modern documentation, see Graham T. Allison, "Conceptual Models and the Cuban Missile Crisis," *The American Political Science Review* 63 (1969): 689–718.

62. Reported in "Politics and Performance: Strengthening the Executive Leadership System," in National Commission on the Public Service Task Force, Rebuilding the Public Service (Washington, DC: National Commission on the Public Service, 1989), p.173.

63. *Reinventing Human Resource Management: Part 3* to accompany the National Performance Review of the vice president (September 1993) at <www.iiid/npronimprovingtheSES.htm>.

64. See, for example, James L. Perry, "Merit Pay in the Public Sector: The Case for a Failure of Theory," *Review of Public Personnel Administration* 7 (1986): 57–69. More recently, the same author found the bonuses to be linked to performance and program outcomes. James L. Perry and Theodore K. Miller, "The Senior Executive Service: Is It Improving Managerial Performance?" *Public Administration Review* 51 (1991): 554–63.

65. Merit System Protection Board, *Working for America: An Update* (Washington, DC: MSPB, July 1994).

66. Title 5 of the Code of Federal Regulations, Section 1201.115 (5C.F.R.) 1201.113.

67. U.S. General Accounting Office, *Report to the Ranking Minority Member, Committee on Government Affairs, U.S. Senate;* Merit System Protection Board, *Mission Performance, Employee Protections, and Working Environment* (Washington, DC: U.S. General Accounting Office, August 5, 1995).

68. For a discussion of the concept of whistleblowing, see Alan F. Westin, *Whistleblowing, Loyalty and Dissent in the Corporation* (New York: McGraw-Hill, 1981). The Merit System Protection Board and the Office of Special Counsel are not responsible for employees who take their complaints to the media rather than the MSPB.

69. For a report of who reports what to whom, see "Blowing the Whistle in the Federal Government: A Comparative Analysis of 1980 and 1983 Survey Findings," MSPB (Washington, DC: MSPB, October 1984).The strongest criticisms of the whistleblower protections came in a GAO report issued in 1984. Comptroller General of the United States, *Whistleblower Complainants Rarely Qualify for Office of Special Counsel Protection* (Washington, DC: U.S. Government Printing Office, 1985).

70. Section 1214(a)(3) of the Whistleblower Protection Act of 1989.

71. The Circuit Court of Appeals made its rulings in *Willis* v. *Department of Agriculture,* 141 F.3d 1139 (Fed. Cir. 1998) and *Horton* v. *Department of the Navy,* 66 F.3d 279 (Fed. Cir. 1995).

72. The broader protection view was offered by Beth S. Slavet, Vice Chair U.S. MSPB, in *Kenneth D. Huffman* v. *Office of Personnel Management,* Docket no. DC-1221-99-0178W-1, <http:www.mspb.gov/decisions/1999/dc178kho.html>.

73. The rules for test validity are included in the "Uniform Guidelines on Employee Selection Procedures," *Federal Register* 43 (August 25, 1978): 38290–38309. The PACE exam was discontinued under a 1981 consent decree. OPM, *OPM: The Year in Review* (Washington, DC:

OPM, 1984), p. 9. Subsequently, a federal court judge ordered OPM to begin using competitive exams to fill government positions. See Judith Havenmann, "The Government Has Been Sorely Tested and Been Found Wanting," *Washington Post*, March 23, 1987, National Weekly edition.

74. The FLRA was established by Title VII of the 1978 Civil Service Reform Act.

75. Office of the Vice President, *Reinventing Human Resource Management—Part 2*, <http:www.pub.whitehouse.gov/uri_res/12R?urn:pdi:oma.eop.gov.us/1994/7/16/5.text. 2.> July 14, 1994. The types of replacement incentives can be reviewed at Office of Personnel Management, Office of Merit Systems Oversight and Effectiveness, *Incentive Awards FY 1996–1997* (Washington, DC: U.S. OPM, August 1998).

76. General Accounting Office, *Civil Service Reform: Redress System Implications of the Omnibus Civil Service Reform Act of 1996* (Washington, DC: GAO, 1996).

TRENDS IN STATE AND LOCAL HUMAN RESOURCE SYSTEMS

State and local personnel systems have evolved along paths that were more or less parallel to that of the federal services. Such innovations as cadres of career executives responsible for implementing public policy were in play in some states before the 1978 creation of the federal Senior Executive Service. States also divided the personnel and merit protection functions before the federal government. State and local governments, moreover, also have adapted their policies to reflect the latest trends in managerial theory.[1]

STATE-LEVEL TRENDS

The ascendancy of the merit system of personnel management at the national level inevitably affected the structure of state personnel systems, partly because of a growing national consensus that merit was the appropriate basis on which to operate public personnel systems. Positive results at the federal level must have influenced forward-thinking state political leaders, although some states were in the vanguard of the reform movement and instituted merit systems before the federal government did.

The boom in state-level merit systems however, was a direct result of the rise of the positive state. The term *positive state* refers to such state-administered programs as health, welfare, education, and vocational rehabilitation.[2] All these programs are funded in part by the federal government; indeed, in some cases, the federal share may be as high as 90 percent of the total cost. One positive state requirement for federal funding prescribes that the agencies that administer these programs use merit-based personnel systems. To ensure compliance, the United States Civil Service Commission and its successor, the Office of Personnel Management, operated an assistance program between 1970 and 1980. The Reagan administration discontinued the practice of compliance monitoring in 1981 on the grounds that the office had substantially completed its mission to expand the applications of the merit principles, with the aim of upgrading the quality of government services. The notable exception was Illinois, whose leadership attempted a return to patronage in the absence of federal monitoring (see Chapter 1).

The absence of federal prodding to use merit systems—defined as civil service protections for government employees—has resulted in a number of innovations in state practices. The state of Texas never created a central personnel agency, preferring instead to invest its Railroad Commission with the merit protection function. In Illinois, the governor created his own central personnel office that was used to advance employees who shared the governor's partisan bent.

As noted in Chapter 1, the term *merit system* has come to imply the most up-to-date personnel techniques, including state-of-the-art classification systems and sophisticated performance review and financial reward systems, as well as protection from arbitrary, capricious, or otherwise unjustified disciplinary actions.

REORGANIZATION IN THE MERIT PROTECTION FUNCTION

Many states have reorganized their public personnel systems based on the federal reforms. The merit protection function has been assigned to a board or commission whose responsibilities include the definition and enforcement of merit principles in the state. These boards actually prescribe the merit rules, assigning enforcement responsibilities to a special counsel who investigates alleged misconduct and makes recommendations to the board. The counsel also schedules appeals hearings before examiners who are, in effect, administrative judges. These hearing officers rule on appeals by employees who maintain that they have been mistreated by their agencies.

The most radical departure from traditional models of civil service protection occurred in the state of Georgia, where state employees hired after July 1, 1996, no longer enjoyed civil service protections.[3] The goal of the legislature was to improve government service by making it easier to discharge an unsatisfactory employee. In 1999, however, the legislature attempted to reestablish a statewide grievance process available to all employees. The governor vetoed the legislation because he believed it might threaten the GeorgiaGain program which was a merit pay system to reward productive employees. Instead, the governor ordered all agencies to create internal grievance processes for all employees.[4] Thus, Georgia state employees are entitled to merit protection even without a centralized civil service system.

State employees covered by merit statutes have an automatic right to a hearing by an impartial examiner concerning the adverse actions of suspension, demotion, and discharge, but the aggrieved employee must, normally, file the appeal within ten working days. Other adverse actions, such as violations of state and federal civil rights laws or violations of merit rules of employment, may be appealed to the state merit protection commission or board for an investigation and possible scheduling before a hearing examiner. Decisions of the hearing examiners can be appealed to a merit protection commission, which is an oversight body of citizens. Going beyond the commission, an aggrieved employee or the agency may file suit in the state courts. When the issue involves a violation of the 1964 Civil Rights Act, employees have recourse to the Equal Employment Opportunity Commission.

Another innovation in the state merit protection commissions has been the certification of commission investigators as mediators. With this training, the commission staff can assist agencies and employees in finding a mutually satisfactory solution to their differences. Mediation can only be used if both parties agree. If the mediation process does not solve the problem, the employee is still entitled to a hearing before an examiner.

As dynamic as the innovations in merit protection have been, the unsung revolution in state personnel practices has principally occurred in the office of personnel director. Because they are now directly accountable to the governor, and because they now exercise hegemony over all state agencies, state personnel directors have the potential for becoming the instrument of reform in patronage as well as merit system agencies.

CHANGES IN STATE PERSONNEL MANAGEMENT

Reform laws usually make the state personnel director directly accountable to the governor by removing the nonpartisan oversight boards that previously shielded personnel operations from partisan politics. The director, as the policymaker, serves at the pleasure of the governor. Thus, reform-minded governors have direct access to personnel agencies staffed with highly trained specialists who can provide modern personnel services to all state agencies. How quickly these changes can be brought about depends on the governor's and the personnel director's commitment to reform and on the financial resources available.

Not all state agencies receive federal funds, and a state may choose to exempt the employees of entirely state-funded agencies from the merit system. The personnel routines practiced in such agencies are usually based on patronage. A widely believed myth in state government is that employees in patronage-system agencies serve at the pleasure of the governor. In reality, lower-level appointments are frequently made in consultation with members of the legislature whose districts the appointments affect. Thus, state-level patronage is as much a legislative phenomenon as it is an executive one.

As noted in Chapter 1, patronage employees can no longer be removed for partisan reasons unless they occupy policy-making positions.[5] Administrators of patronage-system agencies, therefore, are faced with the irony of being forced to accept persons with political connections who are less than qualified but who cannot be removed for partisan reasons.[6] The authority of political executives over lower-level patronage employees is further diminished because they are also protected by the general body of laws and court decisions that protect private- as well as public-sector employees from capricious personnel practices.[7] Particularly noteworthy in this regard are the equal opportunity provisions of the 1964 Civil Rights Act, which was amended in 1972 to extend coverage to state and local governments. Similarly, the 1991 Americans with Disabilities Act also applies to state and local governments.

The fact is that patronage agencies, no less than merit agencies, have need of skilled employees in such critical areas as budget and finance and computer programming.[8] These skilled positions require recruiting criteria beyond political partisanship, but patronage administrators formerly lacked access to the statewide recruitment and screening services provided to merit-system agencies. For all of these reasons, reform of state personnel systems can prove beneficial to agencies based on patronage as well as on merit.

Even those governors who would have been willing to upgrade the personnel practices of the patronage-system agencies lacked a staff sufficient to carry out reforms while simultaneously pursuing other administrative functions, legislative leadership, budgeting, and so forth. Prior to the creation of central personnel offices, the reform of personnel practices in even a single patronage-based agency would have required a major legislative fight to bring the agency under the merit system, with no guarantee of success to repay the expenditure of a great deal of political capital. Pragmatic reform-oriented governors, therefore, understandably focused their efforts elsewhere. With the advent of merit reform, however, great changes can be effected with an executive order implemented by state personnel office staff.

The types of changes possible are not limited to patronage-based agencies; they include the entire spectrum of human resource management. The advantages are illustrated below in the areas of recruitment, classification, and human resource planning. The section that follows goes on to suggest how governors can assert managerial leadership through the use of position control audits and sophisticated performance appraisal systems.

RECRUITMENT. Perhaps the most dramatic impact that separating personnel functions from merit protection tasks can have is on recruitment. The statewide recruitment mechanisms become available immediately to patronage agencies. Access to specialists such as computer programmers and fiscal and accounting experts as well as qualified pools of professional and clerical workers can be had through the lists of qualified candidates maintained by the state personnel office. To paraphrase an axiom, there is no Republican or Democratic way to type a memo!

UNIFORM CLASSIFICATION SYSTEMS. Uniform classification systems specify that persons performing substantially the same duties are to be paid the same, regardless of the agency in which they work. For example, no longer could a painter in a patronage-system agency be paid substantially more than his or her counterpart in nonpatronage agencies or in the private sector, on the basis of political connections. Other less obvious potential benefits of uniform classification systems are adjustments to the salaries of clerical workers under patronage systems, who normally are paid less than their counterparts under merit systems. Patronage-based agencies, therefore, would be in a better position to compete for the most qualified candidates for positions in state government.

Because of the cost, reforms such as uniform classification systems are normally undertaken on a statewide basis only in times of prosperity. In more austere times, these audits can be limited to ad hoc reviews of specific positions. Or, assuming that the classification systems of merit-based agencies are uniform and fair, those of patronage-based agencies can be audited, on a worst-first basis.

HUMAN RESOURCE PLANNING. In the past, human resource planning (HRP) involved best-guess projections of next year's human resource needs, based upon last year's needs. The HRP division of a statewide personnel office (if a separate division existed) also might have been called upon to project cost figures for proposed changes in the state retirement system, to calculate the costs of a salary increment for state employees, and so forth.

In the current era, HRP can involve the use of sophisticated computer programs that project staffing needs based upon precise definitions of the agencies' missions and the functional specialties necessary to accomplish those missions. These programs take into account turnover rates, retirements, and the addition or deletion of functional specialties that make up the workforce of an agency. For example, projecting the number of clerical workers that an agency will need for the foreseeable future would take note of turnover trends among clerical workers over the past several years and projected retirements based upon average length of employment figures in the various clerical classifications (clerk typist 1, clerk typist 2, executive assistant, and so forth). Any anticipated changes in the agency's word processing or data management system would also be factored into the figures. For instance, an agency in the process of automating its record-keeping system would need to adjust its clerical needs to reduce the number of typists while projecting increases in keypunch operators and computer programmers.

PERSONNEL REFORM AS A MANAGEMENT CONTROL FOR GOVERNORS

Like presidents, governors are chief executive officers. As such, they are responsible for the efficient and effective operations of state-level bureaucracies. Like presidents, they have legislative agendas that demand much of their time; unlike them, they cannot plead the demands of foreign relations and defense for inattention to administrative matters. Like presidents, many governors are responsible for formulating systemwide budgets; however, in many states much of the budget authority rests in the legislature. While both presidents and governors are responsible for administration, presidents have a considerable institutional bureaucracy at their disposal to assist in the task. No state provides its governor with the equivalent of the Executive Office of the President. State-level personnel offices, however, offer a considerable resource to governors for carrying out their policy agendas and can be instruments for making agencies accountable to the governor. As a tool of policy leadership, state personnel offices may be most helpful in such personnel-related policies as cost control, performance appraisal, equal employment opportunity, and labor relations.

CONTROLLING THE COST OF STATE GOVERNMENT. Once a state establishes a personnel office directly accountable to the governor and equips the agency with the sophisticated HRP technology previously described, the governor can begin to strengthen executive and legislative control of agencies through the device of position control audits.[9]

Position control audits review the number of positions an agency has requested during the previous fiscal year and require the agency to specify how many were unfilled. Unlike the federal government, some states allow agency directors to use funds allocated for unfilled positions for other purposes. Thus, an aggressive agency director can acquire considerable discretionary funding by asking for more positions than the agency really needs to carry out its mission or by leaving vacated positions unfilled for some time.

A more sophisticated method of control than position control audits is to have the classification section of the state personnel office review the stated work-force requirements of an agency and determine if, in fact, the number of positions requested (filled or not) is warranted. The technology involved in such audits overlaps significantly with sophisticated human resource planning models.

A number of governors have sought to reduce the cost of government through enhanced use of private contractors to perform state functions. They have also pushed for the use of more part-time and or temporary employees to perform various functions with time-certain end dates or to provide seasonal services such as snow removal in winter and road repair in summer.[10]

ACHIEVING POLICY OUTCOMES THROUGH PERFORMANCE APPRAISAL SYSTEMS. Goal-directed performance appraisal systems can also enhance a governor's power. Commonly known as management by objectives (MBO), these outcome-oriented systems allow top members of an administration (who serve at the pleasure of the governor) to negotiate the performance expectations they have for their immediate subordinates who are high-level career government employees. The system would operate in the same way regardless of whether the agency system were one of merit or patronage. Governors and other policymakers sometimes attempt to change the culture of state bureaucracies by introducing incentive systems designed to reward individuals for superior performance. Performance pay systems run counter to uniform classification systems that compensate employees on the basis of the qualifications and knowledge that are prerequisite to the position and the duties and responsibilities of the incumbent. It is rare that such systems are sufficiently funded to reward all deserving employees. This, in turn, can be destructive to employee morale and undermine agency loyalty and esprit de corps (see Chapter 9).

In MBO systems, policy-level executives receive their orders from the governor and, in turn, convey the desired outcomes to their subordinates. At this point, broad policy objectives are converted to specific outcomes and performance expectations in the course of the negotiations. Career employees, in turn, would negotiate with their subordinates realistic performance expectations for the various units within their purview. The system cascades down to the lowest levels of the agencies, so that everybody understands exactly what is to be accomplished and the specific goals for which he or she is responsible and will be rewarded.

Responsibility for developing the system and training the agencies in how to use it would belong to the state personnel director. Such a system would naturally take some time to implement because of the training involved. The energy and resources expended on developing the system, however, would be more than compensated by the long-term gains in executive control. Once such a system was up and operating, future governors would have no trouble achieving desired policy outcomes in agencies of either type.

EQUAL EMPLOYMENT POLICY. The simple fact is that all the executive orders in the world will not assure agency compliance with national and state equal employment policy. State personnel offices, with their direct accountability to the governor, are an ideal mechanism for asserting executive leadership and for ensuring that compliance. Particularly dramatic results could be achieved in states with significant minority populations. Organized into political coalitions capable of converting votes into political capital, such populations could achieve their desired policy outcomes.

A governor, for example, could issue an executive order specifying that agencies take steps to improve managers' and supervisors' awareness of the problems of minorities in the workplace and the problems of women working in areas formerly dominated by men. Such an order would have greater impact if it were accompanied by a schedule of mandatory training courses to be conducted by the personnel office. A governor also might direct the personnel agency to engage in a program of outreach recruitment in high schools and colleges with significant minority populations. Recruiters could dispense information directly to students and work closely with high school counselors and college placement specialists to make minorities aware of employment opportunities in state government.

Conversely, anti-affirmative-action groups have used the initiative process to amend state constitutions to strictly limit affirmative action in state and local governments. At this writing, the state of California has outlawed the use of affirmative action in state and local recruiting and contracting practices and university admission. State Proposition 209 was approved by California voters and upheld by the United States Supreme Court. Also at this writing, the state of Florida Supreme Court has delayed a scheduled 2002 vote on a similar proposition, because it was overly broad and violated that state's one proposition/one issue rule.[11]

LABOR RELATIONS POLICY.   A governor could also use the state personnel office to devise and implement viable policies regarding employee-management relations in state government. The labor movement has been more effective in gaining legislation enabling it to organize federal and municipal employees than it has been in achieving collective bargaining rights for state employees. Even without such legislation at the state level, a number of state legislatures and governors find themselves faced with well-organized and articulately led public employee associations. These associations lobby actively on behalf of state employees. They organize rallies, call press conferences, and generally direct public attention to their policy positions. They also offer legal representation to members who file grievances against state agencies.

These associations have secured legislation that specifies employees' bills of rights and have been instrumental in gaining immunity from persecution for employees who report irregularities in agency operations to members of the legislature. Finally, these associations have managed to persuade a number of legislatures to grant them dues checkoff privileges, requiring the state to collect dues from members just as if the associations had a collective bargaining agreement with the state. They have also developed full-blown grievance processes within existing frameworks and have established considerable legitimacy with members of the legislature, even though state statutes on public employee unionization make no mention of state-level employees. In some states, employees lack only the right to bargain directly with agencies over wages, salaries, and fringe benefits.

Some associations' ultimate goal is to gain full collective bargaining rights. Others are content to operate under the status quo. Like their federal counterparts, many state-level public employee associations have successfully achieved the right to participate in the political process by working in campaigns, donating to candidates and causes, and holding office in political parties. Also like federal employees, they may not seek partisan office while employed in state government.

There is also tension between collective bargaining statutes and civil service law. Issues arise over which statute should apply in such areas as classification, staffing, promotion policies, and employee discipline. This last can be particularly vexing because case law developing out of public employee relations boards' decisions may be in conflict with civil service law. What is needed is a system that integrates collective bargaining and civil service regulations into a single coherent package.

Whether treated as an instrument of modernization in state government or as an instrument of executive authority, the reform of state-level personnel management systems may be the most significant feature of the public management theories to come out of the 1970s, 1980s, and 1990s. Ironically, the states that did the least in moving from a patronage to a merit system of state-level personnel management stand to gain the most from these reforms.

EVOLUTION IN LOCAL GOVERNMENT

The unit of government closest to the people is city government, and it was here that the reform movement resulting in merit personnel systems began. Not all local governments operate merit personnel systems, however. Very small cities lack the resources to pay for separate personnel offices, much less to maintain external merit protection systems. Very large cities frequently rival state governments in the size and complexity of their services, number of employees, and so forth; they may operate full-blown merit systems and frequently do so. In some cases, however, patronage remains the operative principle of personnel management. The discussion here is confined to the city manager system of government that operates largely in medium-size cities. The city manager system epitomizes the notion of merit as the systematic application of management principles to the problems of government.

As shown in Table 2.1, full-time professional city managers are found most frequently in cities with populations of 2,500 to 50,000. Smaller cities simply cannot afford the services of full-time professional managers, but there is frequently too much to be done to rely on unpaid, elected council members. Often one or two secretaries perform the functions of city government, including budget preparation, utility billing, police and fire dispatching, and so forth. One promising alternative for small cities is the circuit rider system, in which professional managers establish record systems, organization structures, work priorities, and so forth for several small cities. The manager then visits each city on a routine basis and is available by phone for solving problems that require immediate attention. Mid-

■ TABLE 2-1

THE USE OF COUNCIL MANAGER FORM OF GOVERNMENT BY CITY SIZE

Cities with Populations of 2500 or More	Cities with Populations of 5000 or More	Cities with Populations of 10,000 or More	Cities with Populations of 25,000 or More
48.3%	53%	57%	63%

SOURCE: ICMA "Council-Manager Government . . . The Fastest Growing Form of U.S. Local Government Structure," at <http://www.icma.org/docs/105464.htm>, updated 3/23/00.

size cities possess sufficient resources to employ professional managers, yet their operations are not large enough to stimulate the political competition found in strong-mayor systems, where mayoral status can be a platform for grander political ambitions.

THE COUNCIL-MANAGER SYSTEM

City managers are accountable to elected city councils, which are responsible for program authorizations and resource allocations. Council members also select the manager and oversee his or her operations. Managers either serve at the pleasure of the council or work under contracts that are renewable by mutual consent. These contracts normally provide for discharge of the manager only for just cause. Managers are therefore somewhat insulated from the vagaries of politics that might result in their dismissal after a local election changed the composition of the council. Managers' contracts may also provide for removal of the manager for substantive policy disputes with the council. A typical contract might provide for early removal of a manager by a council vote of the same proportions that led to the appointment. For example, a city with a twelve-member council might appoint a manager by a vote of 8 to 4. Early removal would require another 8-to-4 vote. Managers who survive such challenges (e.g., a 6-to-6 or 7-to-5 vote) have been known to seek other employment.

The goal of the council-manager system is to bring the highest standards of professionalism to city government. Managers usually exercise virtually complete autonomy over day-to-day operations in the city. This autonomy is grounded in the theory that once the council makes a policy decision, its implementation is a matter of value-neutral management.

City managers are also supposed to advise the council on policy matters, based on their superior knowledge of what is needed in local government. The strength of this policy leadership role depends on the manager's personal style and on the political culture of the community. An assertive manager may be at risk if the city has a tradition of strong council leadership and hotly contested policy debates. On the other hand, the manager may play a strong role when the council has a tradition of laissez-faire attitudes toward the operation of its government and a substantial consensus favoring professionalism exists in the community. The appointment vote as well as his or her own policy proclivities temper the amount of policy leadership that a manager asserts. An appointment vote of 7 to 5 may indicate a council that is badly split over one or more policy issues. The wise manager will seek to identify areas of controversy, then tread lightly. At the very least, he or she will consult closely with all policy factions on the council during the policy development process.

The fact is that few managers spend an entire career in a single city, regardless of the stability of its political culture. The expected longevity of managers is sufficiently brief to cause professional managers to negotiate payments by the city to an independent retirement fund. Thus, if policy differences result in the nonrenewal of the manager's contract, he or she can move on without having to start over in a new retirement system.

This interchangeability of managers is actually the cornerstone of professionalism in city government. If managers were dependent on maintaining good relations with a single council for their entire careers, they would be much more susceptible to political pressure from the council. This pressure could take the form of suggestions or outright demands that this or that person be hired or that a contract for city services be granted to this or that contractor. In the final analysis, the city manager system is the antithesis of patronage in local government.

Managers are not the only policymakers in local government service. Police and fire chiefs and other department heads often exercise considerable policy discretion and may oversee the expenditures of millions of dollars. A recent trend is to remove high-level decision makers from under the protection of civil service. Department heads may receive fixed-term contracts, or they may be made to serve at the will and pleasure of the city manager.

The city of Los Angeles is a good case in point. The city's civil service system included the chief of police. The chief, therefore, could only be removed for just cause (misfeasance, malfeasance, or nonfeasance). In 1992, the leadership style of Police Chief Daryl Gates came under scrutiny in the wake of the Rodney King incident, the subsequent not-guilty verdict of the officers in state court, and the riots that followed. Council members challenged the chief's handling of the civil unrest and departmental policies that led to the beating incident.

Chief Gates's behavior was, at best, noncooperative and, at worst, defiant. The chief did nothing illegal nor could the problems be linked to personal mistakes by him. And, he could not be accused of not performing his job. A 1992 charter amendment limited the chief to two consecutive five-year terms. Another amendment ballot initiative that sought to remove the police chief and other top career officials from civil service protection failed to get voter approval in 1993.[12]

AT-WILL EMPLOYMENT

The movement to insulate public employees from partisan removal eventually came to protect high-level executives as well as rank-and-file civil service workers. In Chapter 1 we noted the creation of the Senior Executive Service, which allowed the transfer, demotion, or removal of federal executives who do not perform to administration standards. SES members have 180 days to demonstrate their cooperation with administration initiatives. Federal reforms were modeled on state-level initiatives most notable in California and Oregon. In California, agency executives well down into the bureaucracy serve at the pleasure of the governor who must give only 72 hours notice before removing them. Removed executives enjoy retreat rights back into the civil service bureaucracy. Executives in city and county governments, by contrast, are subject to removal for cause or policy differences.

H. G. Wood promulgated the at-will doctrine in 1870 in *Masters and Their Servants.*[13] An at-will employment contract can be terminated by either party at any time for any reason. Thus, a city manager could ask an at-will police chief for his or her resignation because the manager believed the chief was not effectively addressing unrest in the police union. Some cities provide retreat rights for executives who are promoted from the civil service protected jobs. So, a personnel director who had been promoted from the position of senior analyst would be able to retreat to that position. At-will executives appointed from outside the city enjoy no such rights.

Other innovations in local government personnel systems include contracting for some personnel services. The city of San Jose, California, for example, contracts with a private vendor to electronically screen applicants' resumes for required knowledge skills and experience. Many cities use private consultants to conduct comprehensive classification studies and so forth.

COUNTY GOVERNMENT

The least reformed level of government is the county. Most counties are concerned with road and highway construction. They also frequently administer state welfare and general assistance programs. Counties also provide law enforcement for unincorporated areas, and the county sheriff may provide incarceration services to local law enforcement agencies. In highly urbanized areas, there has been a trend toward making the county the principal unit of government. Honolulu, Hawaii, and San Francisco, California, have joint city-county governments. County governments also may provide public safety services on a contract basis to municipalities.[14]

Much like cities, counties too are reforming their personnel systems. These reforms are developing out of a pragmatic need for a competent and efficient civil service. Counties have also felt the pressure of federal and state merit requirements as preconditions for funding.

SUMMARY AND CONCLUSION

Personnel administration policies at the state and local levels reflect the values of the cultures in which they operate. Even states that have not fully embraced the concept of merit, however, find themselves faced with the necessity of upgrading their personnel policies in order to comply with federal laws such as equal employment opportunity and in response to elected state leaders' demands for the greatest possible return on their investments in government. The only way to achieve an adequate return on the investment in human resource management is through the adoption of modern personnel practices and techniques such as uniform classification systems and human resource planning. Public personnel managers are also faced with the necessity of dealing with organized employee groups, and some are already modernizing their personnel practices in order to effectively engage in collective bargaining with workers.

PROMISES REAL OR IMPLIED

After a grueling 14-month search and two interim chiefs, City Manager Margaret Egan was happy to announce the appointment of a permanent fire chief, Wilson Peebles. Peebles would be the city's second African-American fire chief. Herself an African American, Egan was pleased with the appointment.

The search process had taken so long due to considerable unrest among rank-and-file officers who wanted the position filled from within. The leadership of the firefighters union was particularly vocal. They openly expressed their resentment of the city's efforts to enhance diversity among the ranks of supervisors and managers in the department. The association of Black Firefighters, of course, saw the matter quite differently.

Egan's decision to go outside was backed by the mayor and city council, who believed with her that new leadership was needed to bridge the gap between the various factions within the department. The city charter provides that the fire chief serves at the will and the pleasure of the city manager. The chief is an at-will employee.

In their first meeting, Egan briefed Peebles on the recent turbulence within the department and urged him to move to bridge the gap while moving forward with city policies. Peebles assured Egan that he could handle the situation and that the best way to increase minority promotions was to improve performance on the promotion test.

Trouble started almost immediately when Peebles denied a request from the union to extend the time limit on the current list of eligible for promotion. The list was composed of everyone who had successfully passed the test in the last round. According to policy, the list must be refreshed after a year. The union urged the extension because a number of retirements were upcoming that would be filled from the current list of eligibles or by a new list. They argued that because no promotions had occurred and nobody on the list had retired, the list was as good as new. Peebles refused the request. The union appealed to Egan, who overruled the chief. The firefighters passed a no-confidence-in-the-chief resolution and sent it to Egan.

Peebles was understandably disappointed at Egan's decision. Nevertheless, he went ahead with his plan to improve the test-taking skills of minority firefighters. A test-taking class, open to anyone, was conducted. Only minority firefighters attended. Three months later, when the next list of eligibles was posted, minorities had not only passed but accounted for virtually everyone at the top of the list. The union cried foul, arguing that the only way that could have happened was if the chief had taught the minorities the actual test. They filed a lawsuit to have the test negated and demanded that Peebles be removed.

Egan decided that Peebles was not ready to manage a large urban fire department. She called him to her office and asked for his resignation. He refused to do so. A certified letter discharging him immediately was delivered to his office the next day. In it, Egan lamented Peebles's failure to bridge the gap with the union. She also noted that morale was awful, and training and safety issues were also not being adequately addressed. All pay and benefits were to end immediately and no severance package was offered.

Peebles hired an attorney and called a press conference. His attorney demanded that Peebles be given a hearing before the city council. He also demanded that Egan's letter be withdrawn and Peebles be reinstated as chief. He stated that his client, although an at-will employee, had been promised Egan's support. Further, the attorney alleged that Egan had promised to remove the chief only for just cause in order to strengthen his hand with the union.

The council refused to meet with Peebles, preferring instead to back Egan.

Peebles has filed a wrongful discharge suit asking for reinstatement and unspecified damages.

QUESTIONS AND INSTRUCTIONS

1. Did Egan make a mistake hiring a chief from a much smaller department?
2. Did Egan compound the problem by not monitoring Peebles's initiatives more closely?
3. What might Peebles have done to reach out to the union when he first came on the job?
4. Was Peebles at least entitled to some sort of severance package?
5. Is Peebles entitled to damages based on the way he was treated by the city?
6. If you were on the jury, how would you rule?

(Hint: even those who file successful wrongful discharge suits rarely get their jobs back. Instead, they negotiate a settlement that includes a lot of money.)

NOTES AND RESOURCES

1. For a discussion of the separation of policymaking and administration, see Woodrow Wilson, "The Study of Administration," *Political Science Quarterly* 2 (1887): 197–222; and Frank J. Goodnow, *Politics and Administration: A Study in Government* (New York: Macmillan, 1900).

2. For a discussion of the social and cultural variables that influence the policies of welfare, see Harold L. Wilensky, *The Welfare State and Equality: Structural and Ideological Roots of Public Expenditures* (Berkeley: University of California Press, 1975).

3. For a fuller discussion, see Stephen E. Condrey, "Reinventing State Civil Service Systems: The Georgia Experience" (presented at the 59th National Conference of the American Society for Public Administration, Seattle, WA, 1998).

4. See Ronald D. Sylvia, "Merit Reform as an Instrument of Executive Authority," *American Review of Public Administration* 17 (Summer/Fall 1983): 115–20.

5. The Supreme Court dealt what was thought to be a death blow to patronage as it was traditionally conceived in the cases of *Elrod* v. *Burns et al.,* 427 U.S. 347 (1976) and *Branti* v. *Finkel et al.,* 445 U.S. 507 (1980).

6. See Kenneth J. Meier, "An Ode to Patronage: A Critical Analysis of Two Recent Supreme Court Decisions," *Public Administration Review* 41 (1981): 558–64. Meier's views seem to have presaged the arguments of the minority in the subsequent case of *Cynthia Rutan et al.* v. *Republican Party of Illinois et al.,* 111 L Ed 2d 52 (1990).

7. See Chapter 11 for a detailed discussion of the discharge rights of public employees.

8. Francis Sorauf, "The Silent Revolution in Patronage," *Public Administration Review* 20 (1960): 32–33.

9. For a readable treatment of various human resource planning models and methods of forecasting organizational needs, see Gilbert B. Siegel and Robert C. Myrtle, *Public Personnel Administration: Concepts and Practices* (Boston: Houghton Mifflin, 1985), pp. 132–62; see also Chapter 8.

10. Keon S. Chi, "State Civil Service Systems," in Stephen E. Condrey, ed., *Handbook of Human Resource Management in Government* (San Francisco: Jossey-Bass, 1998) pp. 48–50.

11. *Coalition for Economic Equity* v. *Pete Wilson, Governor of State of California et al.,* No. 97, 15030, 9th Circuit (1997). "Fla. Court Rejects Measures Against Affirmative Action," *Los Angeles Times,* July 14, 2000.

12. "Civil Service Protections Are Upheld," *Los Angeles Times,* June 9, 1993, <http://latimes.qpass.com/html>.

13. Cited in Clyde W. Summer, "The Rights of Individual Workers: The Contract of Employment and the Rights of Individual Employees: Fair Representation and Employment At-Will," *Fordham Law Review,* 52 no. 6 (1984): pp. 1082–109.

14. Keon S. Chi, "State Civil Service Systems," in Stephen E. Condrey, ed., *Handbook of Human Resource Management in Government,* (San Francisco: Jossey-Bass, 1998) pp. 62–65.

EQUAL EMPLOYMENT OPPORTUNITY IN THE UNITED STATES

The 1964 Civil Rights Act was a turning point for the civil rights movement in the United States, beginning an era in which the rights of minorities and women to compete fairly for employment have been protected by federal statute. The legislation is important substantively as well as symbolically, because it established the Equal Employment Opportunity Commission to enforce the provisions of the law. Previous civil rights bills, such as a 1957 act, expressed the Congress's intent to provide for a color-blind society but provided no real enforcement mechanisms or statutory penalties for violators. According to Lyndon Johnson, Senate majority leader at the time, the 1957 act lacked teeth because there simply were not enough supportive votes in the Senate to cut off debate (stop a filibuster) and bring a stronger law to a vote.[1]

The current status of civil rights in the United States is a result of political movements, legislative enactments, agency enforcement policies, and court interpretations. Each of these is treated in turn. The focus here is on the struggle of minorities, especially African Americans. The struggle for gender equality is covered in Chapter 5.

THE CIVIL RIGHTS MOVEMENT

The 1964 act was the culmination of efforts that began nearly a century before with the abolition of slavery. The Thirteenth, Fourteenth, and Fifteenth Amendments to the Constitution outlawed slavery, guaranteed the rights of all citizens (civil rights), and guaranteed them the right to vote. Significantly, the end of each amendment states: "The Congress shall have power to enforce, by appropriate legislation, the provisions of this article." Insofar as the Constitution is a statement of intent, these amendments clearly express a desire for the equality of all citizens on the part of Congress and the states that ratified them. What seemed to be a national value statement in these three constitutional amendments was eroded by subsequent court interpretation. In 1896, the Supreme Court ruled in the case of *Plessy* v. *Ferguson* that separate but equal facilities were congruent with the Constitution. Legislation to make the Fourteenth and Fifteenth Amendments truly operational was not forthcoming until the Civil Rights Act of 1964 and the Voting Rights Act of 1965.

By the end of the nineteenth century, much of the fervor that had motivated the abolitionist majority had waned, and the former slave states began to pass "Jim Crow" laws that specified separate facilities for whites and blacks. These facilities came to include virtually all public accommodations, including transportation, restaurants, rest rooms, and schools.[2]

From its inception in 1909, the National Association for the Advancement of Colored People (NAACP) began working to overcome the Jim Crow laws that were sanctioned by the Supreme Court in the *Plessy* decision. In court challenges, NAACP representatives argued that separate facilities were by definition unequal and therefore denied black people their civil rights. The legal defense fund of the NAACP began its attack by challenging equal opportunity in higher education. The NAACP successfully challenged state programs that sent African Americans out of state rather than admit them to segregated state universities. They next challenged the equivalency of the Texas black law school and that of the University of Texas. Slowly and inexorably the NAACP worked its way down through the education system until 1954, when separate but equal per se was overturned in *Brown* v. *Board of Education*.[3] Other Jim Crow laws were subsequently overturned in a series of events involving sit-in demonstrations by civil rights activists and court rulings.[4]

Throughout its efforts in the first half of the twentieth century, the black civil rights movement pursued the goal of a color-blind society that would make no legal distinctions on the basis of race. In the 1950s and 1960s the movement gained momentum through sit-in demonstrations and mass rallies. It gradually gained the support of a large segment of white Americans and, perhaps more important, became a powerful issue in national Democratic party politics. Eventually, the emphasis progressed from the removal of arbitrary barriers to the opening of doors to all aspects of society. The movement was particularly interested in advancing equal opportunity in the workplace. For some, color-blind laws were insufficient; they believed that special programs were needed to speed the movement of blacks and other minorities into the mainstream of employment opportunities in both government and the private sector of the economy.

THE EVOLUTION OF AFFIRMATIVE ACTION

A HISTORICAL PERSPECTIVE

Scholars have divided the history of affirmative action (AA), particularly as it relates to federal government employment, into three distinct segments: the period of inaction, the period of reaction, and the period of proaction.[5] In the 1980s a fourth phase was entered into, one in which opponents successfully challenged some affirmative action programs as infringements on the rights of innocent members of the majority. Let us call this the reactionary period. In the current era, a substantial consensus exists that would protect the civil rights of all citizens. The debate over the amount of acceptable affirmative action continues. Hopefully, the debate will evolve into a period of accommodation.

THE PERIOD OF INACTION. The period of inaction, from 1883 to 1940, was so named because nothing whatsoever occurred. Prior to 1883, government employment was based upon partisan political appointment. During this era, the skin color or ethnic origin of a potential appointee was relevant only insofar as the individual was able to deliver votes to the victorious party.[6] In 1883, merit became the central criterion for government hiring decisions. The issue of equal employment opportunity became relevant then because, under a true merit system, women and minorities should occupy a proportion of government jobs equal to their representation in the pool of qualified candidates seeking government employment.[7]

THE PERIOD OF REACTION. Demonstrations on the part of civil rights activists did not begin in the late 1950s, as is commonly believed. Civil rights activists, under the leadership of Philip Randolph of the Brotherhood of Sleeping Car Porters, organized a series of local demonstrations in anticipation of a march on Washington, D.C., that was to take place in 1941. The purpose of the March on Washington movement was to demand that black people, as citizens of the republic, be given a fair opportunity to compete for jobs in organizations that consumed public monies. President Franklin D. Roosevelt reacted to the demand by issuing Executive Order 8587, prohibiting discrimination by government agencies and companies under contract to government agencies. By issuing the order, Roosevelt forestalled the planned march.[8] The timing of the planned march and Roosevelt's order were politically fortuitous. The president was otherwise occupied trying to mobilize the nation for World War II, which had begun in 1939.

The order also established the Fair Employment Practices Commission, whose task it was to use moral suasion to ensure compliance. The commission had no real power to compel compliance, nor any real administrative support system. In fact, the initial draft of Roosevelt's order applied only to government contractors; supporters of the order had to press hard to persuade the president to include government agencies. Presidents Truman and Eisenhower added executive orders of their own that expanded the prohibition against discrimination to include race, religion, color, and national origin. Perhaps the biggest leap forward in this period was the decision of President Harry S. Truman to racially desegregate the armed forces of the United States with Executive Order 9981, issued on July 26, 1948. The order was a courageous step for a president who succeeded into the presidency on the death of another and who had shortly to face a presidential election on his own.

Executive orders and court cases, however, must be viewed in the larger context of the civil rights movement, which was active on many fronts. The fact is that from 1941 onward there was evidence of a growing national consensus for a society in which race would not be a factor in matters of law and justice. Roosevelt's executive order, for example, was issued just ahead of congressional passage of the Ramspeck Act, which statutorily prohibited government discrimination on the basis of race.[9]

Civil rights issues appeared in the forefront of the national political scene when, in 1948, a group of dissidents calling themselves "Dixiecrats" walked out of the Democratic National Convention. Led by Strom Thurmond of South Carolina, the Dixiecrats walked out in protest of a keynote speech advocating civil rights by the young mayor of Minneapolis, Hubert Humphrey. The 1948 Democratic party platform included a call for a "square deal" for all Americans. Truman won the election despite a challenge by the Dixiecrats from the party's right and a separate fourth-party challenge from its left led by former Roosevelt vice president Henry Wallace. The walkout marked a major split in the coalition of big-city political machines, labor unions, farming interests, the South, and civil rights groups that had elected Democrat Franklin Roosevelt to the presidency four times.[10]

Brown v. *The Board of Education*, in 1954, was a unanimous expression of the Supreme Court's intent to change the criteria it would thereafter use to assess equality of treatment. Emphasis shifted from an endorsement of separate but equal facilities to the rationale that separate is inherently unequal. Additional evidence of a changing consensus is that the Eisenhower administration filed a brief in the *Brown* case supporting integration, thus pledging to enforce the ruling. Implementation of desegregation at the community level proved more challenging than the Court fight. In 1957, President Eisenhower sent elements of the vaunted 82nd and 101 airborne divisions to subdue unrest in the streets and to desegregate Little Rock Central High School. In 1962, President Kennedy dispatched thousands of federal troops to relieve 500 federal marshals, border patrol agents, and prison guards who were attempting to enforce a court order for the admission of James Meredith to the University of Mississippi.[11]

THE PERIOD OF PROACTION.   The term *proaction* is used here to mean that government began to define and enforce affirmative action standards for government agencies and federal contractors and to move vigorously to remove legal and institutional barriers to integration. Proactive involvement of federal authorities in the quest for equal opportunity for all citizens began with the administration of John F. Kennedy. The Justice Department of Kennedy's administration actively participated in the effort to integrate formerly segregated universities in the South and to bring an end to Jim Crow laws in general. The 1964 Civil Rights Act was also introduced to the Congress with the active support of the Kennedy administration. It was not until after the assassination of Kennedy, however, that President Johnson was able to make the proposed legislation law.[12]

President Kennedy in 1960 carried all the states that had comprised the Confederacy, while Johnson in 1964 lost all of them with the exception of his native Texas. These losses were directly due to the civil rights enforcement policies developed by the Kennedy administration. Johnson's presidency saw passage of the Voting Rights Act of 1965, which he considered his most significant achievement in an administration whose legislative successes numbered in the hundreds. Having guaranteed minorities the franchise, Johnson believed that their concerns could no longer be ignored.[13] Both Presidents Kennedy and Johnson also took administrative steps to advance the cause of civil rights in the area of government employment.

The term *affirmative action* can be traced to John F. Kennedy's Executive Order 10925, issued in 1961. This order instructed agencies to take "affirmative action" by reviewing their practices, engaging in recruitment on black college campuses, and developing plans and recommendations for needed changes. Upon entering office, Kennedy appointed an interagency taskforce to bring about change in the federal government. The taskforce noted that the government's own personnel office, the Civil Service Commission (CSC), employed only one African American above the rank of GS 12. Furthermore, in the entire period since Roosevelt's order, not a single contract had been terminated because the contractor had discriminated.[14]

Other nonstatutory actions in the 1960s included a 1962 attorney general's ruling that an 1870s law that permitted paying men more than women for doing substantially the same work was probably unconstitutional. Lyndon Johnson subsequently issued Executive Order 11375, which expanded the prohibition against pay discrimination based on sex.[15]

Richard M. Nixon defined more rigorously what was expected of federal agencies with regard to affirmative action with Executive Order 11478, issued in 1969.[16] This order directed agencies to provide sufficient resources to make affirmative action programs work; to engage in outreach recruitment; to make full use of current employees; to provide training and advice to managers; to engage in outreach activities beyond the agencies in the local communities; and, finally, to devise monitoring systems to determine how they were progressing. Perhaps the most significant feature of the Nixon order was the requirement that agencies allocate resources for the programs. If one is intent upon seeing a program fail, the surest way to proceed is to make its administration an additional duty for already overburdened officials. Failure can be further assured by not allocating adequate resources for the program.

The clear message to program administrators was the commitment of the various administrations to equal employment opportunity for minorities and women in the federal service. Exactly what was to be accomplished and how quickly, however, remained to be specified in a concrete way by public policymakers; hence, what and how fast became subject to administrative interpretation.

A COLOR-BLIND SOCIETY OR REMEDIAL AFFIRMATIVE ACTION?

The goals of the civil rights movement included a color-blind society, in which color would have no bearing on a person's opportunities for self-advancement. Civil rights activists were particularly concerned that the rights and privileges of citizenship in no way be curtailed on the basis of skin color. What were and are at issue, however, are the sorts of steps that should be taken to redress past injustices. For some, the objective is the establishment of a color-blind society; for them, laws that prohibit current and future discrimination are the goal. Others believe that prohibiting future discrimination is inadequate unless the effects of previous discrimination are compensated for by special remedies. The advocates of stronger measures suggest that discrimination is akin to a race between two runners, one of whose legs are shackled: removing the shackles halfway through the race would not compensate for the lead the unshackled runner had gained in the first half of the race.[17] Such advocates believe that minorities and women who now enjoy freedom from institutional barriers to equality of opportunity still face the experiential and educational advantages that white males gained while those barriers were in place. Thus, they favor preferential or "remedial" solutions such as establishing numerical quotas for minority employment and specific timetables for achieving them.[18]

There is a middle ground between the advocates of a color-blind society who would only remove institutional barriers and the remedial activists who would specify quotas. We shall call these moderates *proactive advocates.* Those who take the proactive middle path would establish goals rather than quotas and specify timetables for the attainment of those goals.[19]

Those opposed to affirmative action on any grounds see no real distinction between goals and quotas. The distinction, however, is valid and can be drawn most readily in terms of the consequences of failure to achieve the goals. If a goal is not achieved, an organization can examine itself for the reasons, asking whether the goal was realistic given the organization's turnover patterns and whether the various units responsible carried out their part of the task. The object in goal setting is to bring about change expeditiously without injury to individual members of the majority and without undermining the primary mission of the organization. Seeking to fill quotas, on the other hand, has met with little success. Unless they are court ordered to redress past blatantly discriminatory practices, attempts to enforce quotas may be struck down as violating the rights of individuals in the majority.

FEDERAL IMPLEMENTATION OF PROACTIVE AFFIRMATIVE ACTION

Federal, state, and local employees were not initially accountable to the Equal Employment Opportunity Commission under the 1964 act. Beginning in 1965, federal agencies answered to the Civil Service Commission. State and local governments came under the act with the 1972 amendments. Prior to 1972, federal agencies engaged in affirmative action only pursuant to various executive orders. In addition to forbidding discrimination, many of those orders prescribed structures for overseeing corrective actions by agencies and government contractors.

FREE-STANDING COMMISSIONS AND MORAL SUASION

In the absence of appropriate administrative structures, executive orders are merely broad statements of policy intent. When Franklin Roosevelt created the Fair Employment Practices Commission, whose purpose was to provide moral leadership and guidance to government agencies, its primary tool was moral suasion. The commission was underfunded and poorly staffed but did its best to provide leadership.

Under Presidents Eisenhower, Kennedy, and Johnson, leadership responsibility for equal employment activities was given to their vice presidents: Nixon, Johnson, and Humphrey, respectively. The name of the administrative unit responsible for equal employment opportunity in the federal government changed several times. Basically, however, membership consisted of representatives of various departments of the government. These EEO entities heard complaints and created policy largely on a case-by-case basis, often using informal persuasion to induce agency compliance. They lacked both the authority and the inclination to compel or even to pressure agencies to engage in stronger actions.

Despite the modest nature of their endeavors, the various committees and councils engendered political opposition. By 1965, opponents of the Equal Opportunity Coordinating Council managed to tie up appropriations for it on the grounds that funding for council activities and for programs in the line agencies that supported those activities constituted illegal duplication. This opposition no doubt played a part in the decision to transfer authority for equal employment opportunity enforcement to the Civil Service Commission.[20]

MOVEMENT TO THE CIVIL SERVICE COMMISSION

Oversight responsibilities for federal equal opportunity activities were assigned to the Civil Service Commission in 1965 by Executive Order 11246.[21] Even though the Equal Employment Opportunity Commission existed for private-sector enforcement, policymakers preferred to maintain CSC hegemony over all facets of personnel policy in federal agencies. This created a built-in contradiction in roles. An agency responsible for personnel management can hardly be expected to find serious fault with itself regarding equal employment opportunity. Assigning equal employment opportunity to the Civil Service Commission also caused a values clash within the agency.

The principle of merit in all personnel practices was the operant reference point for bureaucrats in the Civil Service Commission from its creation in 1883 until its functions were divided in 1978. Enforcement of equal employment opportunity in the federal service was consistent with the merit principle as long as the equal employment guarantee was defined as the assurance of color-blind laws. Merit came into conflict with equal employment opportunity, however, when the latter was defined as special recruitment and promotion programs for members of targeted groups. Steeped as it was in the merit tradition, the Civil Service Commission preferred to define equal employment opportunity as the removal of inappropriate barriers to entry and advancement in the federal service.[22]

Federal officials shortly came to realize that entry into the federal service was less of a problem than advancement into the middle and upper grades.

> For the most part, overt or conspicuous discrimination had become a lesser barrier to greater representation in the upper grades than the unavailability of minority group applicants who could meet the formal, and perhaps indirectly discriminatory, requirements for appointment and promotion to positions at these levels.[23]

Formal requirements of education and experience and, in some cases, performance on objective tests obstructed a timely conversion to adequate minority representation at the middle and upper levels of the federal bureaucracy. Therein lies the dilemma of the Civil Service Commission. On the one hand, it was responsible for encouraging the development of formal, objective standards for advancement; on the other hand, it was supposed to encourage and facilitate advancement opportunities for members of minorities.

PROACTION AS ADMINISTRATIVE POLICY. The commission's resistance to the use of goals and timetables ended in May 1971 with a memorandum to the agencies that stated, "The establishment of goals and timetables is a useful management concept and should be used when they will contribute to the resolution of equal employment opportunity problems."[24] The memorandum was in response to unilateral actions on the part of federal agencies that were taking more aggressive action than the commission had theretofore encouraged.

Most notable among those proactive agencies was the Department of the Army, to whom the memo was addressed. In 1971, the army announced its intention to move to a system of goals and timetables with regard to civilian employees. A participant in the May memo decision has pointed out that the memo did not mandate the use of goals and timetables, but rather expressed the commission's consent to their use when appropriate.[25] The memo must therefore be viewed as reactive rather than proactive. The commission apparently was fearful that the equal opportunity enforcement function might be transferred to the Equal Employment Opportunity Commission, resulting in more aggressive affirmative action policies that would threaten the merit system.

AFFIRMATIVE ACTION AND CONTRACT COMPLIANCE. The most vigorous federal proactive affirmative action initiative of the 1960s was undertaken by the Federal Office of Contract Compliance. The Office of Contract Compliance was created to implement the paragraph in Executive Order 11246 that required all contracts to have a nondiscrimination clause.[26] The office was part of the Department of Labor; its enforcement authority, however, could be delegated to other agencies until 1978, when Executive Order 12086 consolidated compliance enforcement activities in Labor.[27]

In 1969, the office issued an order known as the Philadelphia Plan, which required contractors on federal construction projects in that city to establish "specific goals and timetables for the prompt achievement of full and equal employment." The order required contractors to achieve annually increasing proportions of minorities in the skilled trades. (The term *skilled trades* normally refers to carpenters, plumbers, electricians, and pipe fitters.) The compliance order obviously had an impact on trade unions as well as on contractors dependent upon the unions for their supply of skilled craftsmen. In 1971, the Office of Contract Compliance generalized the use of goals and timetables by contractors by expanding its Order Number 4, which had originally required only the existence of an affirmative action plan.[28]

The government also sought to enhance opportunities for minorities by legislatively specifying that 10 percent of all contracts for services to the government be set aside for minority contractors. This policy withstood challenges to its legality in the 1980 Supreme Court case of *Fullilove* v. *Klutznick.*[29]

THE INSTITUTIONALIZATION OF EQUAL EMPLOYMENT OPPORTUNITY UNDER CARTER

By 1976, the task of equal employment opportunity enforcement had evolved into a complex set of programs that significantly overlapped one another in terms of responsibility and authority. At times contradictions in policy resulted, as exemplified by the differences in interpretation and initiative between the Civil Service Commission and the Department of the Army. By the mid-1970s, government commitment to active programs to achieve equal employment opportunity had come of age, but the various programs and administrative structures lacked clear-cut lines of authority. Program officials and government contractors had to cope with contradictory interpretations of what was possible or required under the law. A consolidation of the equal employment functions took place as a subcomponent of the Carter administration's 1978 civil service reorganization sooner than might otherwise have been the case, because it was part of a comprehensive overhaul of federal personnel programs.

EEO RESTRUCTURING. The dilemma of the Civil Service Commission was resolved in 1978 as part of the overall reform of the federal civil service system, when formal responsibility for equal employment opportunity in the federal government was transferred to the Equal Employment Opportunity Commission. The EEOC was also given responsibility for affirmative action leadership in the government. President Carter accomplished this move with Executive Order 12067, as part of Reorganization Plan Number 1 of that year. Carter's personal commitment to the goals of proactive affirmative action was evident in the arrangement for conflicts between agencies and the EEOC to be referred to the Executive Office of the President for resolution.[30]

Reorganization Plan Number 1 also transferred to the EEOC enforcement responsibilities regarding age and handicap discrimination. Responsibility for enforcing Title IX of the Civil Rights Act (dealing with educational opportunity) remained with the respective agencies. Finally, responsibility for initiating lawsuits against state and local governments was transferred to the attorney general's office.[31]

CONSOLIDATION OF CONTRACT COMPLIANCE. The 1978 reorganization consolidated contract compliance enforcement in the Department of Labor. Previously, actual enforcement had been delegated to a variety of agencies, making possible inconsistent policy and ragged enforcement. Executive Order 12086 effected the consolidation on October 5, 1978. Thus, the Labor Department assumed active responsibility for contract compliance, to realize the formal authority it had had since 1965. The consolidation should reduce the potential for inconsistent policy interpretations.

President Carter's final equal opportunity reorganization occurred on November 2, 1980, when he signed Executive Order 12250.[32] This order allocated leadership for and coordination of nondiscrimination laws to the attorney general's office. The goal of this coordination was to monitor agencies' enforcement of the nondiscrimination provisions of Section 504 of the 1972 Rehabilitation Act, which forbids discrimination for reasons of disability.

Federal commitment to equal employment opportunity evolved from presidential pronouncements to institutionalized components of the American bureaucracy in something less than forty years. This relatively swift transformation was possible because it was accomplished as part of a larger reform and reorganization of federal personnel programs.

EEO IN THE REAGAN ADMINISTRATION: THE REACTIONARY ERA

A review of both the presidential papers and the annual reports of the Office of Personnel Management and the EEOC indicates a commitment during Reagan's first term to improving employment opportunities for disabled persons in the federal service. Added weight was given those efforts by a 1981 ruling of the Fifth Circuit Court: in the case of *Prewitt* v. *The United States Postal Service*, the appeals court ruled that Congress, in its extension of coverage of Section 504 of the Rehabilitation Act, had intended to provide employment access to federally conducted programs.[33] Reports of the Office of Personnel Management indicate the Reagan administration was particularly concerned about the expansion of federal job opportunities for disabled veterans.[34]

Direct presidential involvement in equal opportunity programs in Reagan's first term was limited, with the notable exception of Executive Order 12320.[35] This order mandated federal assistance to improve the administrative structures of black colleges and increased the share of federal funding to those institutions.

REDUCTIONS IN GOVERNMENT AND MINORITY REPRESENTATION. A priority of Reagan's first term was the reduction, in both size and cost, of the federal government. This inevitably affected federal affirmative action policies. The reductions in force (RIFs) necessary to cut the costs of government hit minorities the hardest, because RIFs are based on seniority. Because minorities made up a disproportionate number of recent hirees, they were separated at a rate three times greater than their proportion of the federal workforce.[36] This prompted an OPM review of federal RIF policies and their heavy reliance upon seniority. Changes in the seniority policy to ease the adverse impact of future RIFs on minorities do not seem likely, however. It has been ruled that given satisfactory performance levels, innocent members of the majority may not be denied the benefits of seniority for such reasons.[37]

OTHER SIGNIFICANT ADMINISTRATIVE ACTIONS DURING THE REAGAN YEARS. The EEOC and the U.S. Commission on Civil Rights both rejected the use of comparable worth studies for determining pay equity between traditionally female-dominated and male-dominated occupations. These rulings and their endorsement by the courts were a significant setback to efforts of feminist groups to improve the lot of women in the workplace.[38]

The EEOC also changed its policy regarding the use of consent decrees to resolve EEO litigations. Consent decrees permit parties to a suit to negotiate a solution to their differences without the trouble and expense of a full-blown trial.

When an agreement is reached, "it is so ordered" by the presiding judge and is binding on both parties. Frequently these decrees involve remedial affirmative action, including establishing goals and timetables to correct past injustices. The EEOC had frequently been a party to such litigation. The addition of the Reagan appointees, however, resulted in a majority of commissioners who "quietly abandoned the use of hiring goals and timetables in settlements with private employers accused of race and sex discrimination."[39]

The Reagan administration was fundamentally opposed to the use of group remedies to correct past injustices. Group remedies are sometimes called remedial or compensatory affirmative action. When an employer (public or private) is found to have previously discriminated against one or another class of citizens, federal judges may order specific quotas to correct the injustice. These quotas are usually part of a consent decree, that is, the two parties agree to the quotas to settle the case without a full-blown trial. For example, a fire department might be ordered to hire a qualified black applicant for each white applicant hired until the proportion of blacks in the department matched their percentage in the relevant community. When the percentage is achieved, the court order is lifted. Courts have also ordered group remedies when minority plaintiffs are able to demonstrate discrimination in promotion policies.

White candidates for employment or promotion have challenged group remedies as discriminatory. They argue that they are being asked to bear the burden of societal sins for which they were not personally responsible. Furthermore, they argue that the injustice is compounded by the fact that the individual minority members who get the jobs or promotions were not themselves the victims of discrimination by the employer in question.

Reagan's Justice Department participated in challenges to current court interpretations of the 1964 Civil Rights Act. At issue was whether Section 706(g) of Title VII provided court-ordered remedies only for actual victims of discrimination or whether federal judges could impose goals and timetables or (in extreme cases) quotas for the hiring of members of a protected group as a whole. The Supreme Court rejected the Justice Department's interpretation of the act, which would have limited remedies strictly to individual victims of previous discrimination.[40]

All in all, little emphasis was placed on equal employment opportunity by the Reagan administration, which also opposed affirmative action—going so far as to file briefs opposing affirmative action in cases to which the government was not a party. Critics charged that Reagan's appointments to various commissions and administrative agencies dealing with equal employment opportunity represented an attempt to reverse previous policies. The Reagan administration was unable to deinstitutionalize structures already in place at the outset of his first term. Rather, changes were in the intensity of enforcement and in legal challenges to what can and should be done to correct past injustices.

THE REAGAN COURT.   The most significant actions of President Reagan were his appointments to the Supreme Court. His first appointment was Sandra Day O'Connor, the first female justice. Reagan then promoted William Rehnquist from associate justice to chief justice upon the retirement of Warren Burger, and he appointed

Antonin Scalia to the seat vacated by Rehnquist. Finally, Reagan appointed Anthony Kennedy.

The four Reagan appointees shifted the judicial philosophy of the Court significantly to the right regarding civil rights and employment. Most noteworthy were five narrowly decided cases in 1989 that began the erosion of precedent.

THE CIVIL RIGHTS ACT OF 1991

A series of amendments to the 1964 act, the Civil Rights Act of 1991 was signed into law by President George Bush on November 7, 1991, in the wake of the furor over his appointment of Clarence Thomas to the Supreme Court.[41] In fact, Bush had vetoed a nearly identical bill in 1990 on the grounds that it would encourage the use of quotas. The president expressed the belief that the damages provisions of the new act would place employers in such fear of lawsuits that they would hire proportional numbers of minorities, regardless of their qualifications, in order to avoid litigation.[42]

DAMAGES.   Quota bill or not, the damages provisions of the 1991 act allow for compensatory and punitive damages against employers (other than governments or government agencies) who engage in intentional discrimination. The 1964 Civil Rights Act allowed for compensatory damages for such things as lost wages and benefits. The 1991 act permits compensatory damages for "emotional pain, suffering, inconvenience, mental anguish, loss of enjoyment of life and other nonpecuniary losses." Punitive damages are available "if the complaining party demonstrates that the respondent engaged in a discriminatory practice or discriminatory practices with malice or with reckless indifference to the federally protected rights of an aggrieved individual."[43] The law limits these new compensatory and punitive damages by a formula tied to the number of employees. The bill further provides for a jury trial if either party so chooses when compensatory and punitive damages are sought.[44]

The damages provisions of the 1991 act specify that "Nothing in this section shall be construed to limit the scope of, or the relief available under, section 1977 of the Revised Statutes" (42 U.S.C. 1981).

Finally, Congress extended the damages provisions of the 1991 act to victims of intentional discrimination under the Americans with Disabilities Act of 1990 (discussed later in this chapter). Damages are not available, it should be noted, to persons who are the victims of unintentional discrimination. An unanticipated consequence of the act was the tremendous upsurge in complaints filed with the EEOC under the intentional discrimination provision. Many are bringing these suits against Type 1 sexual harassment (supervisors or managers seeking sexual favors as a condition of employment). By definition, such behavior is intentional.

GLASS CEILING PROVISIONS.   The intent of the various civil rights acts was to enhance employment opportunities for minorities (religious, ethnic, and the disabled) and women. These intentions have met with varying degrees of success, depending, in large part, on their good-faith implementation by employers. Although the law does provide judicial remedies, a lawsuit is a poor substitute for a paycheck. Congress, therefore, used the 1991 act to encourage employers to examine their top-level employment practices.

Congress noted that most of the successes to date had been at the entry and mid-levels of organizations. Many of the barriers to employment access have been toppled, and women and minorities have achieved a degree of success in gaining supervisory and managerial positions. The highest echelons of organizations, however, continue to be overwhelmingly populated with white males.

The 1991 act provides for the establishment of a Glass Ceiling Commission to study the problem by inquiring into the manner in which top positions are filled, how organizations develop employees for promotion, and how compensation decisions are made. The commission is also to present "an annual award for excellence in promoting a more diverse skilled work force at the management and decision-making levels in business."[45]

IMPLICATIONS OF THE ACT.   Clearly, Congress sought to reverse the Supreme Court decisions that it believed were inconsistent with the intent of the 1964 Civil Rights Act. In this regard, the 1991 act represents a watershed, with Congress rather than the courts becoming the most successful point of access for civil rights groups. The degree to which the Supreme Court will feel constrained by the new act, however, remains to be seen. The question loomed large with the two Bush appointees, David Souter and Clarence Thomas, who were expected to solidify the conservative majority. Justice Thomas has in fact sided with the conservative wing of the court. Justice Souter has proven to be moderate to liberal. The subsequent appointments by President Clinton of Ruth Bader Ginsberg and Steven Breyer have brought an uneasy balance on the court regarding permissible affirmative action. Justice O'Connor has emerged as the swing vote between the two factions.

THREE DEGREES OF AFFIRMATIVE ACTION

Of course, equal employment opportunity and affirmative action policies do not turn solely on the initiatives of the federal government. Various state and local entities have undertaken programs that extend affirmative action efforts beyond what is necessary to ensure equal opportunity. To put the matter in perspective: EEO/AA can be placed on a continuum with EEO compliance on one end and quotas on the other (see Figure 3.1). Since the passage of the 1964 Civil Rights Act, the American public has reached a substantial consensus that concurs with Dr. Martin Luther King's premise that we should each be judged on the content of our character rather than the color of our skin. In fact, opponents of group remedies have co-opted King's premise as the foundation of their opposition. On the other side are proponents of affirmative action who vary considerably as to what is acceptable and appropriate in the absence of demonstrable previous discrimination.

■ FIGURE 3-1

THREE DEGREES OF AFFIRMATIVE ACTION

Equal Opportunity		Proactive			Legally Suspect
Federal Compliance	Enhanced AA	List Expansion	Banding	List Certification	Quotas/ Set Asides
Self-examination Action Plan Outreach	Minority media Goals/Timetables Training to change organizational culture	Rule 3 to 7 to 15	Targeted recruitment	Test screens for minimum qualifications	Recruitment/ Promotions Contracting

PROACTION. The federal government requires state and local governments to annually submit a workforce analysis that looks at the composition of their workforce compared to the community from which it hires. At the next level, an agency may engage in enhanced outreach to targeted communities such as advertising on radio and television stations and in print media outlets that serve one or another ethnic group. Agencies might also work with institutions of higher education to develop internships and other work-study programs targeted at underrepresented groups.

Agencies can also further their efforts by expanding the list of eligible candidates. The federal government and many states use a *rule of three.* The top three scores on a test are considered equally qualified. The list of eligibles can be expanded to 7, 10, or even 15. In extreme instances, agencies use a technique called *banding* that allows the administrator to adjust the range of acceptable test scores to reach minority candidates.

When the applicant pool is very large and the number of positions to be filled is many, agencies sometimes use *list certification,* that is, a minimum passing score is established. Candidates for second stage screening are selected at random from the list of eligibles. Providing that the test is fair and widely advertised, list certification can achieve ethnically proportional numbers among eligible candidates.[46]

QUOTAS. Most controversial are quotas or set-aside programs wherein governments establish percentages of candidates or contracts to be awarded to members of targeted groups. The Supreme Court has been reluctant to approve quotas. They are only permissible under the strictest rules set out by the courts, as will be discussed. Unfortunately, opponents of affirmative action tend to paint all shades of affirmative action with the quota brush.

REACTION. Public opposition to affirmative action in government has boiled over in several states. In California, for example, voters amended the state constitution with Proposition 209 that reads in part:

> The state shall not discriminate against, or grant preferential treatment to, any
> individual or group on the basis of race, sex, color, ethnicity, or national origin in the

operation of public employment, public education, or public contracting. (Proposition 209,1996)

The U.S. Supreme Court has upheld the proposition's legality.[47] But, 209 does provide exceptions for affirmative action required by the federal government. Thus, outreach efforts to minority communities have continued on the part of state and local bureaucracies and the state's higher education system. The latter, however, may no longer use race (even as a partial factor) in admission decisions. On the other hand, in those areas of the state that favor the goals of affirmative action, considerable latitude remains. The city of San Jose's Office of Affirmative Action became the Office of Equality Assurance. It continues its efforts to recruit and retain minority employees and to increase the proportion of city contracts going to minorities. Proposition 209, moreover, provided no enforcement mechanism. It is therefore up to individuals who feel themselves aggrieved to expend their own resources in filing suits under the proposition. At this writing, the California Supreme Court is reviewing a challenge to the San Jose program.

AMERICANS WITH DISABILITIES ACT

The Americans with Disabilities Act (ADA) was signed into law on July 26, 1990. It is a landmark piece of legislation in the struggle of the disabled to gain equality of access to society. Along with the removal of physical barriers in public and private facilities, the act requires employers to provide reasonable accommodations for workers with disabilities. Most important for our purposes, it "prohibits discrimination against qualified individuals with disabilities in all aspects of employment."[48] Enforcement of the nondiscrimination-in-employment provisions of the act was assigned to the Equal Employment Opportunity Commission.

The ADA differs significantly from the 1964 Civil Rights Act, which prohibited any consideration of ethnicity, gender, and so forth. While the ADA prohibits discrimination against qualified persons with disabilities, it also draws the employer's attention to the disabilities of an applicant or employee and questions whether or not a reasonable accommodation could remove the barrier in question.

QUALIFIED PERSONS WITH DISABILITIES. The ADA is precise in its definition of a qualified individual with a disability:

> an individual with a disability who satisfies the requisite skill, experience, education and other job-related requirements of the employment position such individual holds or desires and who, with or without reasonable accommodation, can perform the essential functions of such position.[49]

In the selection process, employers can defend themselves against charges of disparate impacts by demonstrating that a selection criterion is job-related and constitutes a business necessity. For example, the use of a reading test for a job that requires substantial reading ability would not be discriminatory against a person with dyslexia.

An employer may also use qualification standards that limit access to the disabled if it can be shown that hiring a person with a particular disability might pose "a significant risk of substantial harm to the individual or others that cannot be eliminated or reduced by reasonable accommodation."[50] For example, an employer might reasonably screen out an applicant for a machinist job who had cerebral palsy that significantly affected his or her balance and motor skill, especially if the job entailed working around machinery with exposed moving parts.

On the other hand, the significant risk argument could not be used to preclude the hiring of a computer programmer to work in an office adjoining the plant whose duties required the incumbent to visit the plant occasionally to consult with operations personnel. In such a case, a reasonable accommodation would be for the plant personnel to come to the office for meetings.

Unlike the 1964 Civil Rights Act, which allowed no preemployment inquiries regarding such matters as child care for women, religious holidays, or ethnic background, the ADA permits inquiries regarding how an individual's disability would affect job performance:

> A covered entity may make pre-employment inquiries into the ability of an applicant to perform job-related functions, and/or may ask an applicant to describe or to demonstrate how, with or without reasonable accommodation, the applicant will be able to perform job-related functions.[51]

An employer can also require an after-offer medical examination and make passage of the exam a contingency before the employee begins her or his duties. But the examination must be required of all employees hired in the same job category.

REASONABLE ACCOMMODATION. This provision has several components that may include making existing facilities accessible and usable by persons with disabilities. It may mean reasonable adjustments of the application process to allow qualified applicants to apply. Reasonable accommodation can also mean restructuring a position so that its essential components can be performed by a person with a disability. Accommodation may also entail the acquisition or modification of equipment, the hiring of readers or interpreters, or the modification of examinations and training materials.[52]

UNDUE HARDSHIP. Employers need not make accommodations that result in undue hardship to them. The law is imprecise in defining what constitutes undue hardship, whether in difficulty or expense. Factors such as net cost of the accommodation, including tax benefits and external funding, may be considered. The overall size of the entity, its financial resources, the type of operation, and the number of persons employed may also be considered.

IMPLICATIONS OF THE ACT. The equal employment intent of the ADA is to knock down unreasonable barriers that have heretofore prevented persons with disabilities from entering into meaningful positions for which they are otherwise qualified. Placing enforcement of the act under the aegis of the Equal Employment Opportunity Commission is a significant expansion of what constitutes the civil rights of Americans, suggesting that the gains made by the disabled under this act may be the harbinger of future expansions of civil rights. The EEOC has vigorously enforced the ADA. Between 1992 when the act went into force and 1999, the EEOC reports that ADA suits have increased from 1.8 percent of its workload to 22 percent.[53] The types of cases that the commission has successfully pursued include the reinstatement of a gym teacher terminated because he had AIDS, the reinstatement of a phone company employee after being treated for depression, a case against a department store that illegally inquired regarding an applicant's amputated arm, and a case of a grocery store whose break room was inaccessible to employees with certain handicaps.[54] Furthermore, the federal courts have been receptive to the EEOC's ADA enforcement efforts. It reports a win rate of over 90 percent in the approximately twenty-four thousand cases it litigates each year. In time, discrimination based on sexual orientation or appearance may be included in federal, state, and local civil rights legislation. In fact, employment discrimination based on sexual orientation became a civil rights violation in California as of January 1, 1993.

EQUAL EMPLOYMENT OPPORTUNITY, AFFIRMATIVE ACTION, AND THE COURTS

The courts have played a central role in the equal employment–affirmative action controversy. Some of the decisions that will be presented involve EEO efforts in the public sector; others are private-sector cases that have ramifications for the public sector.

The discussion begins with cases involving preemployment or prepromotion barriers to equal employment opportunity. Employers, for example, sometimes use such candidate selection criteria as written examinations or intelligence tests that measure vocabulary skills. The developers of these exams frequently come from the middle-class, college-educated strata of society. Exam contents, therefore, may reflect the test makers' vocabulary skills rather than those necessary to perform the job. In some cases, vocabulary skills are less relevant to the position in question than other skills, such as the ability to work with hand tools or to operate heavy equipment. The Supreme Court has struck down inappropriate tests, stating that a test is valid only if it predicts the ability to perform the job in question. Tests that do not predict job performance constitute unwarranted barriers to equal employment opportunity.

The courts found it relatively easy to dispose of invalid selection procedures. More recent court decisions regarding civil rights have dealt with the stickier question of what employers must or may do to compensate for problems of the past. For example, the courts have addressed the fairness of voluntary programs that provide special hiring and promotional considerations for minorities underrepresented in the organization's workforce. The decisions in such cases have been both complex and mixed, dependent on the circumstances underlying the suit and the breadth of the solutions implemented.

The courts have also addressed the problem of preserving minority gains when layoffs are necessary. In such cases, they have adopted a more conservative standard, because their decisions affect innocent individual members of the majority as well as the overall composition of the organization's workforce. Furthermore, the Supreme Court has addressed the issue of how much power the federal courts may exercise in compensating for previous discriminatory practices. The Court has also extended the strict scrutiny standard it applies in employment cases to government contracting policies.

EEO and Barriers to Advancement

The Supreme Court set the parameters for determining whether or not a test was valid in the case of *Griggs* v. *Duke Power and Light Co.* in 1971.[55] Duke Power used a combination of criteria in its selection process. In order to be considered for employment, one had to perform satisfactorily on the Minnesota achievement test and possess a high school diploma. In the absence of either a satisfactory score or a diploma, one could still be employed at Duke Power, but only as a ditch digger.

The *Griggs* suit was filed on the grounds that black people as a group have disproportionately fewer high school diplomas and an average performance level significantly below that of whites on the Minnesota achievement test—statistics that reflect a pattern of educational and social discrimination in U.S. society as a whole. As a result, this combination of criteria restricted employment opportunities for blacks at Duke Power. The central issue of the suit, however, was whether the criteria used by Duke Power were valid predictors of the ability to perform the job in question. Presumably, in the Duke Power organization, a person without a high school diploma was not qualified to drive a truck or be a janitor. Duke Power officials believed they were within their rights to screen for the best possible applicants based on their own criteria.

In an amicus curiae (friend of the court) brief in the *Griggs* case, the American Psychological Association suggested three tests of validity that should prove useful to employers as they develop selection criteria.

CRITERION VALIDITY.   Selection criteria should bear a valid relation to job performance. For example, height and weight requirements can be challenged for validity in the selection of police officers and firefighters. There is no demonstrable relationship between being 5'9" tall and being able to perform successfully as a police officer. Similarly, a high school diploma does not guarantee the ability to perform any job. Employers traditionally required the high school diploma in the belief that it certifies basic math and language skills. If basic math and language skills are necessary to a job, however, valid tests exist for measuring them that may be more accurate guarantors than diplomas.

CONTENT VALIDITY.   A preemployment test can be demonstrated to be valid if it reflects the actual content of the job. Giving a prospective clerk typist a typing test would be valid if the preponderance of tasks in the job involved typing. But organizations can get into trouble by requiring a typing test for persons whose primary duties are answering the phone and dealing with the public.

CONSTRUCT VALIDITY.   Construct validity is probably the most difficult of the three standards to demonstrate. It means that the test predicts the ability to perform the job by measuring something other than the specific content of the job. For example, a reading comprehension test for potential paralegals would be justified on the grounds that they must read and interpret complex materials even though the job does not require formal legal training.

In the *Griggs* case, the company could not satisfactorily demonstrate the relationship between performance levels on the Minnesota test and the ability to do the job. Nor was the company able to demonstrate the relationship between possession of a high school diploma and the ability to perform successfully in the work environment. Griggs won the suit against Duke Power, and in the process the Supreme Court specified guidelines for employers on what is and is not a valid tool in the selection process. In brief, the message to personnel managers was, Does the selection device in question measure the potential to perform the job in question?

EEO SELECTION GUIDELINES

THE FOUR-FIFTHS RULE. The validity tests set out in the *Griggs* case were incorporated in the Uniform Federal Guidelines on Employee Selection Procedures issued jointly in 1978 by the Departments of Labor and Justice, the United States Civil Service Commission, and the Equal Employment Opportunity Commission.[56] These guidelines provide federal, state, and local governments and federal contractors with a standard by which they can determine whether their selection procedures discriminate. The standard, known as the four-fifths rule, establishes that any selection criterion, such as a written test, is presumed to be nondiscriminatory as long as the pass rate for minorities is at least four-fifths that of whites. If, for example, 90 percent of the white applicants who take a test pass, at least 72 percent of the minority applicants must also pass.

The four-fifths rule can also be used to test the appropriate representation of various groups in an organization's workforce as measured against the composition of the workforce in the surrounding community. For example, if 25 percent of the welders in the Metropolitan Statistical Area (MSA) surrounding the organization are black, then if the personnel policies of the organization are absolutely nondiscriminatory, 25 percent of the welders employed by the organization should also be black. Applying the four-fifths formula means that, at the least, the organization should have a 20-percent representation of black welders.

To use a real example, the federal government's professional entry-level exam was challenged on the grounds that it was discriminatory. The pass rate by white applicants was 42.1 percent as compared with the pass rate by black applicants of 5 percent and the pass rate by Hispanic applicants of 12.9 percent. Clearly the plaintiffs met the 80 percent standard. The suit resulted in a consent decree that is still in force at this writing some 19 years later.[57] The Merit System Protection Board has recommended that agencies expand their use of nondiscriminatory exams and that the scholar program and the Spanish language programs that were put in place as a result of the decree be ended, the former because it may discriminate against otherwise qualified applicants and the latter because the recruitment of Hispanics is no longer a problem.[58]

The four-fifths rule recognizes that individual employers cannot be held solely responsible for correcting injustices that have been wrought by the entire society. The standard therefore gives the employer an automatic 20 percent benefit of the doubt. More than a 20 percent discrepancy, however, may be interpreted by compliance agencies and the courts as prima facie (at first appearance) evidence that discrimination has occurred and justifies proceeding to a full-blown trial of the issues in the case. Failure by the plaintiff to establish a prima facie case results in a dismissal of the proceedings.

BURDEN OF PROOF.   Another significant feature of the *Griggs* ruling is the shifting of the burden of proof from the plaintiff to the defendant when a prima facie case of discrimination has been demonstrated. With *Griggs,* an employer must show a business necessity for selection criteria that violate the four-fifths rule. A nuclear power plant, for example, could justify the requirement of a college degree in nuclear engineering because such knowledge is essential to operating the plant. This would be a legitimate business necessity despite the relatively low numbers of women and minorities among engineers.

The *Griggs* rule was the law of the land until 1989, when the Supreme Court ruled that the burden of proof need not necessarily shift to the employer. In *Wards Cove Packing Co., Inc.* v. *Antonio* (1989),[59] the Supreme Court ruled that disparity must be demonstrated between minorities employed by the company and the relevant job pool. In this case, the ethnic composition of workers employed in the cannery was not the relevant yardstick for assessing noncannery employment practices. More important, the Court held that the plaintiff must identify the specific employment practice or practices causing the disparity. (At issue in *Wards Cove* were nepotism, separate hiring channels, and rehire preferences for noncannery workers.) The Court further ruled that the burden rests with the plaintiff to show that another method would meet the employer's need without discriminating.

The *Wards Cove* decision overturned what civil rights activists believed to be settled law. The 1991 Civil Rights Act was, in part, a congressional response to the *Wards Cove* decision. The 1991 act restored the *Griggs* rule. Once again, an employer must show a business necessity for selection criteria that have a disparate impact on minorities.[60]

EEO AND PROMOTIONS

The devices that an organization uses to determine who will be promoted were examined by the Supreme Court in 1975 in the case of *Albamarle Paper Co.* v. *Moody et al.*[61] The Albamarle Company was appealing its loss in the lower courts of a class action lawsuit filed by Moody on behalf of himself and other black employees of the company. Promotions in the company were based, in part, on an employee's performance on a standardized test and successful performance in the present job. In *Albamarle,* the Court extended to promotion decisions the rules validating initial employment tests established in *Griggs.* The decision is also important because the Court made its award to Moody and other parties to the suit retroactive. The Court did not find that the Albamarle Company had acted with malice in its selection of criteria for promotion. Thus, the decision put personnel managers on notice that despite their good intentions, their organizations could be severely penalized as a result of discriminatory personnel practices.

Public-Sector Promotion Testing. A case in point regarding the fairness of public-sector promotion procedures is *Connecticut* v. *Teal* (1982).[62] The Court ruled that the impact of a discriminatory process upon an individual member of a group was as important as the overall impact of the process upon the group.

Teal was one of four black employees of the State of Connecticut who were selected for promotion to supervisory positions on a probationary basis. Their promotions were to become permanent if they could demonstrate satisfactory performance as supervisors and pass the state's written examination for promotion to supervisor. Teal and the others did perform satisfactorily as supervisors but failed the written test and were therefore demoted. The four filed suit on the grounds that the test discriminated against black people.

Teal and the others based their claim on the fact that a disproportionate number of blacks failed the test. The pass rate for whites was 79.54 percent; blacks passed at a rate of 54.17 percent. According to the EEOC's four-fifths rule, the black pass rate should have been 63.63 percent.

The State of Connecticut used what is known as the "bottom-line defense": it pointed out that even though the pass rate for blacks was disproportionate to that of whites, black candidates were getting more than a fair share of the promotions to supervisor. The state noted that 11 out of 48, or 22.9 percent, of the black candidates who passed the test were promoted. Only 35 out of 259, or 13.5 percent, of the successful white test takers were promoted. Teal and the others won in the lower court, however, and the state appealed to the Supreme Court.

Disparate Impact versus Disparate Treatment. The Supreme Court was thus called upon to weigh the relative importance of the impact of one element of a selection process on an individual member of an affected group versus the impact of the total process on the entire group. The court ruled in favor of Teal (or the individual), stating that disparate treatment—that is, treatment that discriminates against individual members of a protected group—cannot be defended by proving no disparate impact on the group as a whole. In other words, an examination that discriminates against black people, and therefore adversely affects black individuals, cannot be defended on the grounds that the overall policies of the organization do not disadvantage black people as a subpopulation of society.

The *Teal* case is important from an administrative standpoint because the state's promotion policies were already consistent with EEOC compliance guidelines. From a public policy standpoint, government entities, like government contractors, face the necessity of complying with administrative policies set out by oversight agencies. At the same time, they must be ever mindful of the possibility of suits based on their actions brought by dissatisfied members of minority groups or by individual members of the majority who suffer from the organization's good-faith efforts at compliance.

Rulings such as those in the *Griggs, Albamarle,* and *Teal* cases are not unwarranted interferences in organizational processes but rather court attempts to remove personnel procedures that act as barriers to equal employment opportunity. When a preemployment, prepromotion written examination, or other selection criterion does not measure the ability to perform the job in question, and when the application of the criterion discriminates on any of the bases set out in Title VII of the 1964 Civil Rights Act, the courts can be expected to strike down the practice. Arbitrary barriers fly in the face of the American value of justice-as-fairness. On the other hand, special programs involving preferential treatment of groups who formerly suffered from discrimination may also be perceived by some as flying in the face of justice-as-fairness when they disadvantage individual members of the majority who had no hand in previous acts of discrimination.

REMEDIAL AFFIRMATIVE ACTION

Unlike the goals and timetables discussed under proactive affirmative action, court-sanctioned remedial affirmative action uses preferential recruitment or training programs available only to members of groups that have previously experienced injustices. Note that the impact of programs upon individuals is the one repeating theme running throughout the court opinions on remedial affirmative action programs.

ACCESS TO THE PROFESSIONS

Equal employment opportunity is one aspect of a controversy not limited to the workplace. Equality of educational opportunity is the underlying factor in determining whether equal employment opportunity exists in occupations that require specialized training as a prerequisite to entry. A case in point is the effort of Alan Bakke to gain entrance to the medical school of the University of California at Davis. Alan Bakke twice applied for admission to the Davis program and was twice denied admission, even though the university was admitting minority persons who ranked below Bakke in terms of the established criteria. Not being able to go to medical school, of course, effectively precluded Bakke from entry into the profession of medicine.

Alan Bakke sued the regents of the University of California under California's civil rights law.[63] Bakke's suit was based on the fact that sixteen seats in each entering class were set aside for members of disadvantaged groups. His grade point average was 3.65, while the average of those admitted under the disadvantaged program was 2.62. Bakke's performance on the medical aptitude exam placed him in the 97th percentile of all those taking the test; the average ranking of the persons admitted under the special program was in the 37th percentile. Bakke argued that he was objectively more qualified than those for whom the sixteen seats were reserved. He further argued that had the seats not been set aside for disadvantaged persons, he would have been admitted to medical school.

Most important, persons admitted under the disadvantaged program were members of racial minorities. The fact of their status as racial minorities, coupled with the different standards used to evaluate them, combined to discriminate against Bakke on the basis of his race. The California Supreme Court agreed with Bakke and ordered his admission; the regents appealed to the United States Supreme Court.

The Regents of the University of California v. *Bakke* (1978) has been interpreted as a victory by both sides in the equal employment versus affirmative action controversy, because the Court handed down what appeared to be two separate opinions supported by two separate 5-to-4 majorities. The Supreme Court upheld the lower court's decision, affirming Bakke's right to admission. The special admissions program at Davis had never really defined what constituted a disadvantaged person, nor had the faculty clearly established admissions criteria for the program. The Court concluded that the program used race as the sole criterion for admission and thus violated the 1964 Civil Rights Act prohibiting discrimination on the basis of race. Advocates for a color-blind set of laws interpreted this as a victory.

The decision, however, contained a second 5-to-4 majority that ruled that although race could not be the sole criterion for admission, it could be taken into account among other factors in the admissions decision. This majority ruled that the United States is a heterogeneous society of urban and rural dwellers from many backgrounds. All of these groups need medical services; therefore, admissions to professional programs such as medicine should not be so narrowly restricted as to deny representation of the heterogeneous groups that constitute the society. Race, then, could be a factor—among other factors—in admissions decisions.

In this complex ruling, the Court upheld the principle of equal opportunity defined as color-blind laws, but it also left the door open to programs that strive to redress former injustices but stop short of setting quotas. Had the University of California at Davis launched its new medical school by establishing goals for minority representation in its student body that were combined with outreach recruitment efforts, it might have accomplished two ends. First and most obviously, the university might have avoided lawsuits such as Bakke's. Second, through a true outreach effort it might have attracted highly qualified minority applicants who could have competed for admission without the establishment of a separate admissions program.

The use of race, even as a partial factor, in admissions to colleges and universities in California was made unconstitutional by the passage of Proposition 209. And while the Supreme Court has upheld the prohibition in California, public institutions in other states are free to consider race as an admission or hiring criterion among other criteria.

ACCESS TO THE SKILLED TRADES

The *Bakke* case established parameters to guide professional degree programs in their affirmative action efforts. Within a short time of the *Bakke* decision, the

Supreme Court ruled on the acceptability of a special training program for minorities in the workplace that ignored the principle of employee seniority.

In *Kaiser Aluminum and Chemical Corp.* v. *Weber* (1979),[64] a white employee filed suit on the grounds that a joint company-union training program favored blacks with less seniority than he had and therefore discriminated against him on the basis of race. The program had grown out of both the company's and the union's desire to increase the proportion of blacks employed by that company in the skilled trades. In reviewing the ethnic composition of the Louisiana community in which the plant operated (the MSA), Kaiser determined that the number of blacks employed by the plant by and large reflected black representation in the community: 39 percent. This representation was reflected in all job categories except the skilled trades, where blacks comprised only 2 percent of the Kaiser workforce. According to federal guidelines, Kaiser was required to have an ethnic employee distribution that reflected the *workforce* composition in the MSA, not the entire population distribution.[65] The only exception to this guideline was in filling jobs that required special training. Entry into the skilled trades further meant gaining membership in a union, and blacks had not been allowed equal access to union membership in Louisiana (as elsewhere). Kaiser chose to use the 39 percent figure even though, as these jobs required training, they were not obligated to do so. (The choice may not have been entirely voluntary, but rather the result of pressure from the Federal Office of Contract Compliance.)[66]

To achieve the goal of 39 percent black representation in the skilled trades, Kaiser and the United States Steelworkers decided to sponsor a training program in which 50 percent of the slots were reserved for blacks and the remaining 50 percent allocated on the basis of seniority. When the goal of 39 percent black skilled workers was achieved, all of the slots would be allocated on the basis of seniority. The training program was thus a case of a private-sector employer engaging in remedial affirmative action to correct problems in the social order for which the employer was not directly responsible.

Brian Weber filed suit on the grounds that two of the black people in the training program had less seniority than he. Subordinating seniority to race, Weber charged, was discriminatory. He won in the lower courts but lost in the Supreme Court on a 5-to-4 decision. The opinions produced in this case illustrate just how divided our society is on this issue.

The majority in the *Weber* case held that the Kaiser program was a private voluntary program of limited duration. The program therefore fell within the acceptable parameters of the 1964 Civil Rights Act. The majority interpreted the act and the debate leading to its passage as providing for corrective programs such as Kaiser's. The minority disagreed.

Dissenting, Chief Justice Burger wrote that if he were a member of the Senate being asked to vote for legislation that would provide for programs such as Kaiser's, he would support it. But, he reasoned, the role of the Court is to interpret the legislation as written, and the 1964 Civil Rights Act specifically states that such programs are not its intent.[67]

William Rehnquist went further in his dissent, pointing out that if Congress had intended to provide for exceptions to nondiscrimination on the basis of race, it knew how to do so. The 1964 law specifically exempts Indian preference laws from the provisions of the act, for example. (The Bureau of Indian Affairs is required to employ Indians in preference to other groups unless Indians are not available.) For Rehnquist, the goal is a color-blind law. Such an interpretation of the law, of course, would not allow for remedial affirmative action unless it were ordered by a court to correct overtly discriminatory actions on the part of an employer.

THE CONTROVERSY IN CONTEXT. The *Weber* case exemplifies a societal dilemma. On the one hand, black persons, through no fault of their own, lacked the skills necessary to qualify for skilled positions at the Kaiser plant. Neither Kaiser nor the Steelworkers' Union was directly responsible for the inequities of the workforce distribution. Unless something was done, however, the system would have perpetuated itself indefinitely.

On the other hand, Brian Weber was denied entrance to the training program, and thus to a better job, even though there was no evidence to suggest that he ever discriminated against anybody. Ironically, however, had there been no previous discrimination in the MSA and if black people had been proportionally represented in the skilled trades, there would have been no need for the training program, and the 50 percent of slots available for white employees at the Kaiser plant would not even have existed. Weber's "right" to gain access to a skilled trade through his employment as a steelworker would have been a moot issue. As a white man, however, he might have sought entry into one of the apprenticeship programs operated by one of the skilled trade unions at any time.

Another important issue that has been largely ignored by scholars is the role of the Federal Office of Contract Compliance in the case. The prescription of the Equal Employment Opportunity Commission to reflect the composition of the work force in the MSA and the pressure from the Office of Contract Compliance to reflect the actual population distribution were inherently contradictory and raise the fundamental question of how companies seeking federal contracts should proceed. A government based on laws should not have one set of administratively defined rules for those with government contracts and another for everybody else, when the rules in question interpret legislative intent. And employers who choose to question the interpretation of the Office of Contract Compliance run the risk of losing millions in federal contracts.

A nonlitigious channel is needed to allow contractors to challenge and clarify the rules made by the Office of Contract Compliance. One such channel would be a group of hearing examiners, housed in the Equal Employment Opportunity Commission, who could rule on the congruence of agency rules with the intent of the Civil Rights Act.

ACCESS TO SKILLED TRADES IN GOVERNMENT: PROACTIVE AFFIRMATIVE ACTION. The dilemma of how to equalize access to the skilled trades is even more perplexing for women than for minorities, because these are exactly the positions from which women have been excluded over the years. In the case of *Johnson v. Transportation Agency, Santa Clara County* (1987), the Court applied the *Weber* principle of reasonable voluntary programs to a case in which a woman was promoted over a male worker whose overall rating was higher than hers.[68] Both candidates were judged to be well qualified, and the county used a rule of seven; that is, the position could be given to any person ranked among the top seven candidates. A woman named Diane Joyce was ranked third, and Mr. Johnson was tied for second with another candidate. A review committee recommended that Johnson be given the job, but the agency director chose to promote Joyce as part of the county's efforts to move women into male-dominated job classes. The Supreme Court noted that the program had no goals or timetables, but that Joyce's promotion was instead part of a long-range effort to move women into skilled-trade positions in the county. The Court upheld Joyce's promotion, using the reasoning set forth in the *Weber* case.

COURT-SANCTIONED QUOTAS

The Supreme Court has also ruled on the appropriateness of remedial programs that seek to promote minorities into supervisory and managerial positions over more senior white employees. It has defined the parameters of lower court authority to use consent decrees to arrive at a mutually satisfactory solution without a full-blown lawsuit. Finally, it has rejected the notion that remedial programs should be limited to persons who were personally injured by previous discrimination.

CONSENT DECREES.   All of these issues were addressed in the case of *Local 93, International Association of Firefighters, AFL-CIO, C.L.C.* v. *City of Cleveland et al.*[69] In this 1986 case, a consent decree was used to settle a lawsuit brought by the Vanguards, an association representing the interests of black and Hispanic firefighters in Cleveland. Local 93, which represents the majority of Cleveland firefighters, filed a suit contesting the validity of the decree, to which it had not agreed. The union further contested the promotion plan on the grounds that it benefited persons who were not necessarily victims of past discrimination. The Reagan Justice Department joined Local 93 in this contention.

The Supreme Court upheld the plan by a vote of 6 to 3. Because Local 93 was not a party to the consent decree, it was not required to do anything under the terms of the decree and, therefore, could not protest its terms.

An even stronger challenge to the use of consent decrees was brought before the Court in the 1989 case of *Martin* v. *Wilks.*[70] White firefighters in Birmingham, Alabama, challenged the promotion decisions made based on a consent decree between the city and black plaintiffs. The claim put forward by Wilks on behalf of the white firefighters was that they could not be denied promotions based on a consent decree to which they had not been parties. The Supreme Court agreed (5 to 4). This decision opened the door to countless after-the-fact challenges to consent decrees.

The 1991 Civil Rights Act modified the *Martin* ruling by stating that after-the-fact challenges are not permissible if the challenger was given the opportunity to respond in a timely fashion to the original decree or if the challenger's claim raises an issue that was previously dealt with in the course of the suit.

In the case of *Local 93*, the judge had ordered the city and the Vanguards to consult with the white firefighters regarding the contents of the decree. Thus, even though they refused to accept the decree, they had been given the chance to challenge it.

WHO MAY BENEFIT.   Perhaps the most important aspect of the *Local 93* case, however, was the Court's rejection of the notion that the terms of the decree exceeded the remedies available under Title VII, Section 706(g) of the 1964 Civil Rights Act. The section reads, in part:

> *No order of the court shall require* the admission or reinstatement of an individual as a member of a union, or *the hiring, reinstatement, or promotion of an individual as an employee,* or the payment to him of any back pay, *if such individual* was refused admission, suspended, or expelled, or *was refused employment or advancement* or was suspended or discharged *for any reason other than discrimination on account of race,* color, religion, sex, or national origin or in violation of Section 2000e-3(a) of this title. (italics added by Justice Brennan)[71]

Local 93 and the Justice Department argued that the remedies available under the act were limited to actual victims of discrimination. The court majority reasoned, however, that consent decrees are voluntary agreements entered into to avoid litigation. As such, they are not subject to the same constraints that limit judicially imposed remedies. The incentive to reach an out-of-court settlement would be removed if the parties could not negotiate more than what would be possible by pursuing litigation. Writing for the court, Justice Brennan declared that "whatever the limitations Congress placed in Section 706(g) on the power of federal courts to impose obligations on employers or unions to remedy violations of Title VII, these simply do not apply when the obligations are created by a consent decree."[72]

THE AUTHORITY OF FEDERAL JUDGES.   On the same day, the Supreme Court laid down guidelines regarding the remedies available to federal judges in their attempts to seek compliance with Title VII. In the case of *Local 28, Sheet Metal Workers' International Association et al.* v. *Equal Employment Opportunity Commission et al.,*[73] the Court specifically addressed the authority of federal judges. In this case, the district court had found Local 28 guilty of egregious discrimination and, through the course of litigation, had imposed civil fines, ordered the establishment of a training fund for minority apprentices, set a goal for minority representation of 29.23 percent, and appointed an administrator to oversee compliance.

The union contested the terms of the order on the grounds that the fines levied were punitive and thus required a criminal contempt proceeding; that the order violated the Fifth and Fourteenth Amendment due process rights of nonminorities; and, most important, that the judge had exceeded his authority under Section 706(g) of Title VII. The union was joined in this last point by the solicitor general, representing the Reagan administration, in an amicus curiae brief.

The Supreme Court ruled 6 to 3 that the fines and fund establishment were meant to coerce compliance with the court order rather than to punish, that the order did not violate the due process rights of nonminorities, and that the judge had not exceeded his authority under Title VII. It held that the order was necessary to achieve the government's compelling interest in ending discrimination, including a racially classified remedy. The Court ruled that the judge did not exceed his authority under Section 706(g) by establishing compliance goals and that a lesser remedy might not have worked, given Local 28's history of egregious discrimination. Finally, the court interpreted the last sentence of Section 706(g) as *not* limiting relief to actual victims of past discrimination.

PROMOTION QUOTAS.   In the case of *United States* v. *Paradise et al.* (1987),[74] the Court ruled that a one-for-one promotion rate for black and white state troopers in Alabama was acceptable. Here again, the Justice Department objected to the extent of the remedies that had been agreed to by the other parties to a consent decree: the State of Alabama, Mr. Paradise, and the NAACP. A minority opinion, however, argued that a less extreme method, such as the appointment of an administrator to oversee the process or the imposition of fines, might have achieved the same result as the imposed promotion quotas.

The foregoing cases clearly illustrate the Supreme Court's willingness to go beyond providing remedies to actual victims of discrimination, thereby permitting remedial affirmative action. With the enactment of the 1991 Civil Rights Act, however, there may be less incentive to enter into consent decrees because of the possibility of collecting damages when plaintiffs can demonstrate intentional discrimination.

Court-sanctioned remedies that benefit persons who were not themselves the direct victims of discrimination are most likely in matters of recruitment and advancement when the harm to nonminorities is slight or widely diffused. The Court, however, has taken a narrower view when it can be shown that innocent individuals will suffer deprivation of employment to make way for minorities who are not direct victims of past discrimination.

AFFIRMATIVE ACTION AND PROTECTION FROM LAYOFFS

In the case of *Firefighters' Local 1784* v. *Stotts* (1984),[75] a black firefighter captain filed a class action suit against the city of Memphis, Tennessee, on the grounds that the city's hiring practices were discriminatory. In a consent decree, the city agreed to a remedial hiring program designed to increase the proportion of black firefighters to 35 percent. Some time into the program, the city found itself short of revenues and began cutting back across the board by laying off personnel in all its departments.

The city chose to lay off newly hired firefighters in alphabetical order, because they were all hired on the same day, but decided to skip over the names of three black firefighters in order to preserve some of the affirmative action progress it had made under the court-ordered consent decrees. The result was a layoff of twenty-one white and three black firefighters. Had the city adhered strictly to its alphabetical criterion, three more blacks would have been laid off, and three more whites would have kept their jobs.

THE RIGHTS OF INNOCENT INDIVIDUALS. The firefighters' union filed suit on behalf of the affected white firefighters, charging reverse discrimination. The Supreme Court ruled that it is inappropriate to deny an innocent employee the benefits of seniority in order to remedy the misdeeds of the organization. The minority reasoned, to the contrary, that this was a reversal of previous Court decisions, which had approved such actions to remedy classwide effects of discrimination or to prevent similar discrimination in the future.

Two factors in this case make the ruling particularly dramatic. First, the city's actions were based on a consent decree issued by a lower court, not the arbitrary or capricious actions of public officials acting on their own discretion. In Memphis, unlike at the University of California at Davis, previous discrimination had been documented. Second, the Court's ruling that the benefits of seniority cannot be denied used a strict definition of seniority, in light of the fact that all of the workers in question were hired on the same day. Here again, the test of discrimination is how individuals are affected.

THE COURTS AND UNION-SANCTIONED AFFIRMATIVE ACTION. In 1986 the Supreme Court reaffirmed the protections due innocent members of the majority in *Wygant* v. *The Jackson Board of Education.*[76] In this case, the Court issued a plurality opinion that struck down a layoff plan negotiated between the district and the local teachers' union. The plan called for proportional layoffs, so that the percentage of black teachers after a layoff would not fall below their proportion before the layoff. The purpose of the plan was to provide positive role models for black students in the district.

The Court stated the issue in these terms: "We must decide whether the layoff provision is supported by a compelling state purpose and whether the means chosen to accomplish this purpose are narrowly tailored."[77] It held that the Jackson plan did not meet this test and went on to rule that societal discrimination alone was not sufficient justification for race-conscious remedies. Rather, the Court insisted upon some showing of prior discrimination by the governmental unit involved before allowing limited use of racial classifications in order to remedy discrimination.[78] The Court specifically rejected the role-model justification offered by the district.

Writing for the plurality (himself and two other justices), Justice Powell specifically addressed the rights of innocent members of the majority:

> In cases involving valid *hiring* goals, the burden to be borne by innocent individuals is diffused to a considerable extent among society generally. Though hiring goals may burden some innocent individuals, they simply do not impose the same kind of injury that layoffs impose. Denial of a future employment opportunity is not as intrusive as loss of an existing job.[79]

What the Court did in the *Stotts* and *Jackson* cases was to apply a test of how the program affected individuals. In effect, the Court ruled that it was more important to protect the right of innocent members of the majority to maintain their employment status than it was to remedy the impact of past discrimination on an entire class of people.

STRICT SCRUTINY

The court began to lay out the parameters of strict scrutiny in the *Bakke* and *Wygant* cases. Two tests must be met to justify quotas: (1) a compelling government interest defined as demonstrable previous discrimination on the part of organization in question and (2) a narrow remedy. Previous discrimination is demonstrated using the eighty-percent rule. The narrow remedy provision is to protect innocent members of the majority from undue injury. Justice Powell eloquently expressed the sentiments behind the application of strict scrutiny in the *Wygant* case.

> No one doubts that there has been serious racial discrimination in this country. But as the basis for imposing discriminatory *legal* remedies that work against innocent people, societal discrimination is insufficient and overexpansive. In the absence of particularized findings, a court could uphold remedies that are ageless in their reach into the past, and timeless in their ability to affect the future.[80]

The two tests under strict scrutiny have also been extended to government contracting. In 1989 the Supreme Court struck down a 30 percent set-aside program in *City of Richmond* v. *J. A. Croson Co.* (1989) as overly broad for failing both prongs of strict scrutiny.[81] The Court further applied the standard to federal contracting procedures in the case of *Adarand* v. *Pena* (1995).[82] The Supreme Court found that a paving contractor named Adarand would very likely never get another highway subcontract because the federal highway program gave contractors bonuses for using minority subcontractors.

Richmond and *Adarand* are evidence of the Court's expanding the protection of innocent members of the majority. At the same time, the cases represent a continuity of Court reasoning between employment and contracting cases involving discrimination. Thirty-five years after the fact, the equality of opportunity promised by the 1964 Civil Rights Act is a matter of settled law, if not a fact of objective reality. The current Court probably will not be sympathetic to program administrators who initiate aggressive affirmative action programs without particularized findings of previous discrimination.

SUMMARY AND CONCLUSION

The Civil Rights Act of 1964 was the product of civil rights demonstrations and lawsuits and presidential leadership to bring about federal enforcement of basic civil rights. The primary beneficiaries of the act were expected to be African Americans, although the act covers a number of different illegal acts. Its enforcement was met with resistance and sometimes with violence. In the ensuing 35 years a substantial consensus has emerged supporting federal protection for a variety of rights. In 1999, only 37 percent of EEOC charges were filed for race discrimination. Another 32 percent were regarding sex discrimination, and the remainder involved discrimination on the basis of disability, age, religion, national origin, or violation of the equal pay act.[83] Clearly, equal employment opportunity enforcement has moved beyond race. But, if the anti–affirmative action initiatives begun in California spread to other states, it may become necessary for Congress to revisit the issue of appropriate group-based remedies.

A PROUD TRADITION OF AFFIRMATIVE ACTION*

Governor Maria Aura looked pleased and smiled broadly when she awarded the Department of Economic Development (DED) with the annual Governor's Affirmative Action Award. This award is given to those agencies or departments of state government that best demonstrated excellence in achieving the goals of promoting equal opportunity employment practices and increasing diversity in state employment. "Our state leads the way in challenging employment practices that hold people fast to the sticky floor of gender, racial, and disability stereotyping. Our state is committed to shattering the old hiring and promotion practices. We welcome the bright sunshine of affirmative action to improve opportunity for all qualified persons in our state. Tonight we recognize the Department of Economic Development as a leader in this mission," she said while presenting the large wall plaque to the department director.

Standing in the back of the dining hall, several midlevel managers of the Department of Economic Development were amused by what she had declared and snickered to each other, "Imagine the praise we would receive if our department actually reflected the diversity of the state!"

STATE AFFIRMATIVE ACTION REQUIREMENTS

1. Each department must submit a plan that addresses remedial hiring goals and the timetable for reaching their goal. Hiring goals are set utilizing the Equal Employment Opportunity Commission's (EEOC) "Guidelines on Affirmative Action Appropriate under Title VII of the Civil Rights Act of 1964," as amended 44 CFR 4422 (November 21, 1991), 29 CFR 1608. This standard holds that hiring goals should match the *proportional availability* of qualified women, minorities, and persons with disabilities in a given category of work. If a state agency employs a lower percentage of diverse individuals from the available qualified workforce pool, the agency is said to be in a condition of "underutilization," and additional affirmative action is needed.

2. Each department must submit an annual progress report to the Affirmative Action Compliance Board (AACB) which compiles the reports and creates the annual State Report on Equal Employment and Affirmative Action.

3. If the underutilization condition is found to exist, then a short-term and long-term plan must be developed to balance the workforce.

---

*Prepared by Lance Noe and C. Kenneth Meyer, Drake University

4. Additionally, a qualitative review of employment practices policy is to be completed to evaluate the potential for discrimination or underutilization of diversity that currently exists in the labor market pool.

Using these guidelines, the Department of Economic Development developed a program to address their underutilization levels. In assessing their hiring practices, they discovered that they had relied primarily on hiring from the private sector persons who recently retired or sold a business. This resulted in a workforce that reflected the workforce pool of the 1960s and 1970s, when white males dominated the private-sector management positions. By changing their hiring practices and through more extensive recruitment at public and private university campuses, they were able to improve the diversity of their department, moving them from underutilization status into short-term compliance. Last year, some employees who were reaching retirement age were offered attractive incentives to separate early which, in turn, opened added positions for new hires that were being recruited from the university ranks. However, some of the local university programs didn't seem to offer the level of diversity expected by the director of employment. In spite of this situation, talented persons were found and recruited to fill the open positions. Interestingly, the Department of Economic Development lacked compliance in all three categories (women, minorities, and persons with disabilities) prior to the current year.

Goals were set, and the results of their affirmative action program are as follows:

DEPT. OF ECONOMIC DEVELOPMENT

Benchmark Year

Total Workforce	Total Females Employed	Under-utilization	One-Year Goal	Total Minorities Employed	Under-utilization	One-Year Goal	Persons w/ Disabilities Employed	Under-utilization	One-Year Goal
250	75	25	10	20	4	2	20	5	2

Results: Year One

Total Workforce	Total Females Employed	Remaining Under-utilization	One-Year Goal	Total Minorities Employed	Remaining Under-utilization	One-Year Goal	Persons w/ Disabilities Employed	Remaining Under-utilization	One-Year Goal
250	85	15	Met	25	1	Exceeded	22	3	Met

QUESTIONS AND INSTRUCTIONS

1. In the case study, "underutilization" is determined by examining the diversity in the current qualified workforce pool in the state. The hiring goal is set so every agency maintains that level of diversity and no more. It does not assess underrepresentation within the qualified workforce

compared with the general population. Is such a program the best way to approach diversity? Does setting limits forestall the appointment of additionally qualified minorities?

2. Is there a danger that diversity attainment will be offset by poor morale and "quota resentment."

3. The Department of Economic Development did not reach full utilization but did reach or exceed its one-year goals. What approach is appropriate in both the short and long term to reach affirmative action goals in a given organization?

4. The Department of Economic Development reached its one-year hiring goals by meeting the exact number required in two categories and exceeding the goal by one in another. Does this result suggest that a "soft goal" is really just another term for "hard quota"? Do goals help or hurt in the quest for increased diversity?

5. What recommendations, if any, would you make to modify the affirmative action program for this state?

AIDS IN THE PUBLIC WORKPLACE*

The "Plague of the Millennium" is how Robert Hoyt referred to the pandemic known as acquired immunodeficiency syndrome (AIDS). Hoyt, as director of the state's Bureau of Personnel, was well versed on most of the statistics pertaining to the growth and pervasiveness of AIDS in the United States and around the world. In the U.S., for example, the Center for Disease Control reported a human immunodeficiency virus (HIV) infection rate decline of 9 percent between 1994 and 1998. The decline, however, was due to the drop among older women. The infection rate had nearly doubled for those in their early 20s. Further, the CDC estimated that nearly 40,000 new HIV cases were reported yearly in America and that these are disproportionately found among the age groups that make up the workaday world.

As personnel director, Hoyt was concerned that the treatment of AIDS patients might result in higher health insurance premiums for state government as well as for the society at large. Of less concern to Hoyt was its impact on the cost of life insurance, because life insurers could adjust premiums on a periodic basis. He wondered about the constitutionality of health insurance vendors testing for the AIDS virus based on their belief that soaring costs render them financially insolvent. AIDS-related medical costs were soaring into the tens of billions of dollars each year, and life insurance payments for AIDS victims were projected to soon exceed $100 billion. Hoyt realized that his organization must begin immediately to develop appropriate actuarial policies and AIDS-awareness programs for state employees. Hoyt also wanted to be sure that the rights of HIV-positive employees would be protected without unduly endangering their coworkers.

---

*Prepared by C. Kenneth Meyer and Lance Noe, Drake University

The civil rights issues were substantial and pertained to informed consent, privacy, and confidentiality as well as workers' Fourth Amendment protections against unreasonable searches. The situations was brought home dramatically to Hoyt when a valued employee named Joe Bauer reported that he was HIV positive during a work session to develop an AIDS-awareness program. Despite his knowledge of the subject, Hoyt's first thoughts were of what he should do to protect Bauer's associates and coworkers and to educate them and other state employees on the risk of contacting AIDS from sources other than contaminated needles, sexual behavior, and blood transfusions.

QUESTIONS AND INSTRUCTIONS

1. What programs, if any, should be developed by the Bureau of Personnel to deal with state employees who test positive for HIV? Please outline the details of the program.

2. Should HIV-positive employees be treated differently from those who may have other contagious diseases, such as hepatitis or tuberculosis? Please explain.

3. Does an employer illegally discriminate who refuses to hire an HIV-positive person? Please give the rationale for your decision.

4. Should Joe Bauer's coworkers be informed of his diagnosis, or should these matters be left confidential? Elaborate. How do you believe the Americans with Disabilities Act pertains to the protections of those with AIDS?

5. Did Hoyt overreact to Bauer's condition? What hope is there for HIV tolerance in the workforce if the director of personnel's first reaction is one of panic?

NOTES AND RESOURCES

1. Lyndon B. Johnson, *The Vantage Point: Perspectives on the Presidency, 1963–1969* (New York: Holt, Rinehart &Winston, 1971), p. 156.

2. The term *Jim Crow* referred to systematic discrimination against black people, especially with regard to public accommodations. For a detailed discussion of federal attempts to outlaw Jim Crow practices, see Leslie A. Carothers, *The Public Accommodations Law of 1964: Arguments, Issues and Attitudes in a Legal Debate* (Northampton, MA: Smith College, 1968). The Supreme Court upheld federal intervention in such practices under Title II of the 1964 Civil Rights Act in *Heart of Atlanta Motel* v. *United States*, 379 U.S. 241 (1964).

3. *Brown* v. *Board of Education of Topeka Kansas*, 347 U.S. 483 (1954).

4. For a detailed account of the transition to overt political action, see Aldon D. Morris, *The Origins of the Civil Rights Movement: Black Communities Organizing for Change* (New York: Free Press, 1984). Morris begins his analysis of modern confrontational civil rights tactics with an analysis of the 1953 boycott of the Baton Rouge, Louisiana, bus system.

5. The concept of a three-phase history of affirmative Action was taken from Nijole V. Benokraitis, *Affirmative Action and Equal Opportunity: Action, Inaction, Reaction* (Boulder, CO: Westview Press, 1978).

6. Ebeneezer Bassett was the first black person appointed to a high government post when in April 1869, he was appointed United States minister to Haiti. Samuel Krislov, *The Negro in*

Federal Employment: The Quest for Equal Opportunity (Minneapolis: University of Minnesota Press, 1967), p. 12.

7. The idea that the workforce composition of any given employer should reflect the work force in the surrounding community has been applied by the Equal Employment Opportunity Commission to both private employees and state and local governments. The federal government has attempted to reflect the population distribution of the entire U.S. society, a much more difficult standard to achieve. Women, for example, make up just over 50 percent of the population but comprise only 43 percent of the workforce; only 22 percent define themselves as managers. Thus, the whole-population standard is unrealistic. For complete statistics, see Office of the Secretary of Labor, Women's Bureau, *Time of Change: 1983 Handbook of Women Workers* (Washington, DC: U.S. Government Printing Office, 1983), bulletin 298.

8. See Aldon D. Morris, *The Origins of the Civil Rights Movement,* pp. x–xi; and Samuel Krislov, *The Negro in Federal Employment,* p. 29.

9. Samuel Krislov, *The Negro in Federal Employment,* p.29.

10. For a thorough discussion of electoral processes and coalition formation, see Gerald Pomper and Susan S. Linderman, *Elections in America: Control and Influence in Democratic Politics* (New York: Longman's, 1980).

11. For a fuller discussion of Eisenhower's decision, see Chester J. Pach Jr. and Elmo Richardson, *The Presidency of Dwight D. Eisenhower* (Lawrence, Kansas: The University Press of Kansas, 1991), pp. 137–59. For a discussion of the events at Oxford Mississippi, see Carl M. Brauer, *John Kennedy and the Second Reconstruction* (New York: Columbia University Press, 1977), pp. 181–204.

12. Passage of the 1964 Civil Rights Act was the highest priority in President Johnson's efforts to carry out the agenda of his slain predecessor. The matter came to a vote on July 2, 1964, through the efforts of a bipartisan coalition. This was the first time in the nation's history that the cloture rule (a Senate vote to stop debate and vote on the legislation) was successfully invoked for a civil rights bill. Lyndon B. Johnson, *The Vantage Point,* pp. 159–60.

13. Ibid., pp. 163–66.

14. See "Summary of Civil Rights Progress for the Nine Months: January 20 through October 1961," unsigned memo, POF of John F. Kennedy, Box 19, John F. Kennedy Library, Boston, MA. See also Harris Wofford, *Of Kennedys and Kings* (New York: Farrar, Straus and Giroux, 1980) pp. 168–69.

15. The order was issued on October 13, 1967. *Federal Register* 32, p. 14303.

16. The order was issued on August 12, 1969. *Federal Register* 34, p. 12985.

17. The shackled runner example is taken from Joseph Robison, "Giving Reality to the Promise of Job Equality," *Law in Transition Quarterly* 1 (1964): 104–17.

18. The term *remedial affirmative action* refers to using specific goals, quotas, and timetables to achieve results. The concept has also been called *preferential affirmative action* by David C. McGrice, *A New American Justice* (Garden City, NY: Doubleday, 1980), p. 7; and *compensatory affirmative action* by Samuel Krislov, *The Negro in Federal Employment,* pp. 76–85.

19. For an excellent discussion of these distinctions, see Elliott Zashin, "Affirmative Action, Preferential Selection in Federal Employment," *Public Personnel Management* 7 (1978): 378–93.

20. Samuel Krislov, *The Negro in Federal Employment,* pp. 30–45.

21. This order also specified that all federal contracts contain a clause requiring the contractor to promise not to discriminate. The Office of Contract Compliance was set up to administer enforcement, which it could delegate to other agencies. Richard A. Lester, *Reasoning About Discrimination: The Analysis of Professional and Executive Work in Federal Antibias Programs*

(Princeton, NJ: Princeton University Press, 1980), pp. 138–39 on contract compliance, pp. 209–38 on the role of the Civil Service Commission.

22. Elliot Zashin, "Affirmative Action, Preferential Selection in Federal Employment," p. 385.

23. David H. Rosenbloom, "The Civil Service Commission's Decision to Authorize the Use of Goals and Timetables in Federal Employment Opportunity Program," *Western Political Quarterly* 26 (1973): 236–51, p. 239.

24. Ibid., p. 236.

25. Ibid., pp. 246–48. Rosenbloom points out that the vagueness of the memo was a reflection of the commission's conflicting responsibilities for affirmative action leadership and merit protection.

26. Richard A. Lester, *Reasoning About Discrimination*, pp. 138–39.

27. *Public Papers of the Presidents: Jimmy Carter, 1978,* vol. 2, July 1 to December 31 (Washington, DC: U.S. Government Printing Office, 1979), pp. 1714–17.

28. Richard A. Lester, *Reasoning About Discrimination*, pp. 138–39.

29. *Fullilove* v. *Klutznick* 448 U.S. 448 (1980).The controversy involved the minority enterprise Provisions of the Public Works Employment Act of 1977.

30. *Public Papers of the Presidents: Jimmy Carter, 1978,* vol. 1, January 1 to June 30 (Washington, DC: U.S. Government Printing Office, 1979), pp. 1212–15.

31. *Public Papers of the Presidents: Jimmy Carter, 1980–1981,* vol. 3 (Washington, DC: U.S. Government Printing Office, 1982), pp. 2652–55.

32. Ibid.

33. *Prewitt* v. *The U.S. Postal Service,* 622 F2d (5th Cir.) (1981).

34. The OPM issued an order in 1982 instructing agencies to develop annual plans for the recruitment, placement, and advancement of disabled veterans. OPM, *OPM: The Year in Review, 1982* (Washington, DC: OPM, 1983), p. 11.

35. *Public Papers of the Presidents: Ronald Reagan, 1982,* vol. 2, July 1982 to December 1982 (Washington, DC: U.S. Government Printing Office, 1983), pp. 795–96.

36. OPM, *OPM: The Year in Review, 1982* (Washington, DC: OPM, 1983), p. 4.

37. The protection of the innocent members of the majority was set forth in the case of *Firefighters' Local 1784* v. *Stotts,* 427 U.S. 273 (1976).

38. For a detailed discussion of the comparable worth issue, see Chapter 9 and U.S. Commission on Civil Rights, *Comparable Worth, Issue of the 1980s: A Consultation of the USCCR,* vol. 2 (Washington, DC: USCCR, 1984).

39. "EEOC Abandons Hiring Goals, Timetables," *Public Administration Times* 1 (March 1986).

40. Two cases were decided by the Supreme Court on the same day, in which it upheld the affirmative action program in question and ruled against the position of the Reagan administration. See discussion of EEO and the courts later in this chapter.

41. Earlier, President Bush had appointed David Souter to the court, bringing to seven the number of consecutive conservative appointees.

42. In his veto message, the president explained: "Any measure that changes employment decisions to turn on factors of race, sex, ethnicity or religion—rather than on qualifications—is fundamentally unfair, and is at odds with our civil rights tradition." Message to the Congress Transmitting Proposed Civil Rights Legislation, October 20, 1990, *Public Papers of the President of the United States: George Bush* (Washington, DC: U.S. Government Printing Office, 1991), p. 1436.

43. Section 1977A of the 1991 Civil Rights Act.

44. Section 1977A sets the limitations as follows: for employers of more than 14 and fewer than 101 employees, the limit is $50,000; for 100 to 200, the limit is $100,000; for those employing 200 to 501, the per-victim limit is $200,000; for employers of 500 or more, the limit is $300,000 per victim.

45. Title II, Section 202 of the Civil Rights Act of 1991.

46. New York city uses list certification to good advantage in recruiting minorities. See "Higher Standards for Police Recruits," *New York Times*, November 28, 1995, p. 14.

47. *Coalition for Economic Equity et al.* v. *Pete Wilson, Governor of State of California et al.*, No. 97, 15030, 9th Circuit (1997). The Supreme Court refused to review the finds of the lower court.

48. Equal Employment Opportunity Commission, Final Rule, *Federal Register* 56 (July 26, 1991), p. 35726.

49. Part 1630.3 of the Equal Employment Provisions of the Americans with Disabilities Act.

50. Part 1630.2 of the Equal Employment Provisions of the Americans with Disabilities Act.

51. Part 1630.14 of the Equal Employment Provisions of the Americans with Disabilities Act.

52. Part 1630.9 of the Equal Employment Provisions of the Americans with Disabilities Act.

53. EEOC, "Charge Statistics from the Equal Employment Opportunity Commission FY 1992 Through FY 1999," at <http://www.eeoc.gov/stats/charges.html>, downloaded July 19, 2000.

54. EEOC, "Highlights of EEOC Enforcement of Americans with Disabilities Act: A Preliminary Status Report, July 26, 1992 through March 31, 2000," at <http://www.eeoc.gov/ada/status-prelim.html>, downloaded July 19, 2000.

55. *Griggs* v. *Duke Power and Light Co.*, 401 U.S. 424 (1971).

56. "Uniform Federal Guidelines on Employee Selection Procedures" (Washington, DC: U.S. Government Printing Office, 1978).

57. *Angel V. Luevano et al.* v. *Alan Campbell, Director Office of Personnel Management et al.*, Civ. A. No. 79–0271 93 F.R.D. 68, 1981 U.S. Dist. LEXIS 18023.

58. U.S. Merit System Protection Board, "Restoring Merit to Federal Hiring Practices: Why Two Special Hiring Programs Should Be Ended," (Washington, DC: Merit System Protection Board, 2000). The programs in question were the Outstanding Scholar Program and the Bilingual Bicultural Program.

59. *Wards Cove Packing* v. *Antonio*, 109 S.Ct. 2115 (1989).

60. Ironically, to secure passage of the 1991 Act in the U.S. Senate, Wards Cove Packing was exempted from the law.

61. *Albamarle Paper Co.* v. *Moody et al.*, 422 U.S. 455 (1975).

62. *Connecticut* v. *Teal*, 102 S. Ct. 2525 (1982).

63. *Regents of the University of California* v. *Bakke*, 98 U.S. 2733 (1978).

64. *Kaiser Aluminum and Chemical Corp. and United States Steelworkers* v. *Weber*, 443 U.S. 193 (1979).

65. *Hazelwood School District* v. *United States*, 433 U.S. 299 (1977).

66. In his dissent, Justice Rehnquist questioned the degree of voluntariness in the program, noting the pressure put on Kaiser by the Federal Office of Contract Compliance. *Kaiser Aluminum and Chemical Corp.* v. *Weber*, p. 2737.

67. Ibid., p. 2734.

68. *Johnson* v. *Transportation Agency, Santa Clara County*, 55 L.W. 4379 (1987).

69. *Local 93, International Association of Firefighters, AFL-CIO, C.L.C.* v. *City of Cleveland et al.,* 46 CCHS.Ct. Bull., p. B4521 (1986).

70. *Martin* v. *Wilks,* 109 S.Ct. 2180 (1989).

71. *Local 93* v. *City of Cleveland,* p. B4533.

72. Ibid., p. B4542.

73. *Local 28, Sheet Metal Workers' International Association et al.* v. *Equal Employment Opportunity Commission et al.,* 46 CCH S.Ct. Bull., p. B4437 (1986).

74. *United States* v. *Paradise et al.,* 55 L.W. 4211(1987).

75. *Firefighters' Local 1784* v. *Stotts,* 467 U.S. 561 (1984).

76. *Wygant* v. *The Jackson Board of Education,* 106S.Ct. 1842 (1986).

77. Ibid., pp. 1846–47.

78. Ibid., p. 1847.

79. Ibid., p. 1851.

80. Ibid., p. 1848.

81. *City of Richmond* v. *J. A. Croson Co.,* 488 U.S. 469 (1989).

82. *Adarand* v. *Pena,* 515 U.S. 200 (1995).

83. EEOC, "Charge Statistics from the Equal Employment Opportunity Commission FY 1992 Through FY 1999," at <http://www.eeoc.gov/stats/charges.html>, downloaded July 19, 2000.

WOMEN AT WORK

The organized struggle for gender equality, especially workplace equality, has gone on for more than one hundred and fifty years. The interests of women have often paralleled those of minorities; for example, the Seneca Falls Convention of 1848 that declared the rights of women included a number of abolitionists. Both were interested in achieving equality before the law, the voting franchise, and other rights and privileges pertaining to citizenship. At other times they diverged, as when African-American men gained the voting franchise 50 years before women. Of interest here is workplace equality with regard to employment access, pay, promotional opportunity, and the right to a work environment free from sexual harassment.

HISTORY OF WOMEN AT WORK

THE RIGHT TO WORK

The first challenges to state laws based on the Fourteenth Amendment's equal protection provisions were brought by women challenging state limitations on women's rights to vote and to enter men-only professions. In *Bradwell* v. *State of Illinois* (1873),[1] Ms. Bradwell challenged the state law prohibiting women from the practice of law in Illinois. She argued that as a law-school graduate she was entitled to sit for the bar. The Supreme Court disagreed, citing the delicate nature of women as making them unsuitable for the law. The women's movement continued to struggle, and state by state women began to gain the voting franchise, the right to own property, and the right to engage in gainful employment. All women, however, did not enjoy the right to vote until passage of the Nineteenth Amendment to the Constitution in 1920.

Participation in U.S. industry by white women was originally limited to premarital employment at low-skill, low-wage, sometimes backbreaking jobs in, for example, the garment and textile industries.[2] During slavery, African-American women, of course, were forced to toil at whatever task their masters set for them, from domestic chores and child rearing to agricultural field labor. Free women of all races also worked in low-paying service occupations, such as domestic and industrial cleaning and food preparation. Even in the nineteenth century, however, financial necessity often forced working-class women to work outside the home after marriage.

A few exceptions to the career limitations on women in the American social order were the teaching and nursing professions. Neither of these occupations could be characterized as leisurely, however, and both are lower paying than male-dominated occupations that require comparable skills and training. Finally, as the economy expanded and more paperwork became associated with the management of industry, clerical careers became available to women.

Early in the twentieth century, the National Consumer League pushed for special protections for women at work and won various protections, such as the ten-hour workday, based on the special needs of women. The goal was to improve working conditions for women who were frequently employed in sweatshop conditions doing sewing by the piece in substandard hygienic workplaces. Such protections were sought and won in *Muller* v. *Oregon* (1908).[3]

During World War II, women moved into the workforce in great numbers to replace men who were needed for military service. Rosie the Riveter became a familiar symbol of popular mobilization in defense of the nation. "Rosie the Riveter was depicted as a blue-eyed, rosy-cheeked woman with a kerchief on her head, a rivet gun across her lap, and a powder puff in her coverall pocket—the perfect combination of health, strength, and femininity."[4] Women performed virtually all categories of work and did them well.[5] The one exception was the limited access that women were afforded to managerial decision-making positions. The confinement of women to lower echelons was due in part to the fact that management positions are not at entry levels, where most women entered the workforce. Second, the men who were needed to fight the war were young, while management positions were usually the province of persons past the age of thirty. Finally, the dearth of women in positions of responsibility did not occur to the men in charge.

The extent of the work that women undertook during the war demonstrated that they were capable of performing virtually any task. Nevertheless, at the end of the war, returning veterans were given back their jobs, and the general demobilization of the war industry ended the widespread employment of women in male-dominated blue-collar occupations. Female participation in the economy returned to the traditional teaching, nursing, clerical, and service occupations until changes in the economy and the structure of families—and a growing women's movement—again began to alter the nature of the workforce beginning in the 1960s.

Economically, the male-headed nuclear family found it increasingly difficult to meet basic family needs on a single income. Most single incomes, moreover, were inadequate to satisfy the desires engendered by the proliferation of consumer goods. Consequently, married women began entering the work force in ever-increasing numbers. Meanwhile, divorce, once a stigma, became an acceptable solution to unsatisfactory relationships. The increase in the divorce rate brought with it a dramatic increase in the number of female-headed households. These women's paychecks were the family income rather than a mere supplement. By the mid-1980s, roughly 65 percent of women between the ages of eighteen and sixty-four were at work, and women constituted approximately 45 percent of the nation's workforce.[6] More significantly, by 1998 women held 46 percent of positions defined as executive, administrative, and managerial.[7]

Beginning in the mid-1960s feminist groups, most notably the National Organization for Women (NOW), sought to advance the cause of women by demanding full and equal legal status for women. These feminists argued that any divergence from a standard of absolute equality would only work to the detriment of women. Opponents of equality, it was argued, could point to the special statutes for women's protection as justification of unequal treatment. NOW managed to get two-thirds of the Congress to pass an equal rights amendment to the Constitution. The amendment narrowly failed, however, to gain ratification in three-fourths of the states. Had the amendment passed, it would have provided the legal vehicle for challenges to gender inequality throughout society.

The women's movement aggressively sought to break down artificial barriers to many career fields. Some of the strongest barriers were personnel policies based on the stereotypical belief that women should not be employed in hazardous or uncomfortable working conditions. In the public sector, these stereotypes virtually prevented women from becoming firefighters and severely limited their career opportunities in law enforcement. Other barriers resulted from civil service hiring criteria that limited female access to career fields for reasons that had little to do with the duties and responsibilities of the job in question. Chief among such barriers was the height requirement that typically prescribed a minimum height of at least 5'9" for public safety employees. When challenged, defenders of the standard were hard-pressed to justify it on the basis of job content. The requirement artificially discriminated against Hispanic and Asian males as well.

Congress continues to limit career opportunities for women in the armed services by denying them access to frontline combat positions. They have, however, won the right to fly combat aircraft and to serve on some combat ships. Furthermore, male and female members enjoy pay comparability. Thus, a female intelligence officer whose duties warrant the rank of major receives the same pay, benefits, and organizational privileges as her male counterpart.

EQUAL PAY

The women's movement secured the passage of the 1963 Equal Pay Act that prohibited paying women less than men for doing the same work. Then, in 1964, the interests of women and minorities in the workplace again conjoined in the 1964 Civil Rights Act. Title VII of the act prohibits employment discrimination based on "race, color, religion, sex or national origin . . . with respect to . . . compensation, terms, conditions, or privileges of employment."

During debates over the 1964 act, proponents found it necessary to demonstrate that the inclusion of gender and pay would not come into conflict with the 1963 act. They explained that the Equal Pay Act of 1963 prohibited discrimination for male and female employees performing the same work. The 1964 act would prohibit discrimination against women as a class.

The need for class protection for women is illustrated by the 1981 case of *Washington Co. Oregon* v. *Gunther*.[8] At issue was the disparity between the salaries received by female and male officers working in the county jail. The county argued that female officers also performed clerical duties, while male officers were engaged full-time in the oversight of prisoners. Thus, the two jobs were not the same as prescribed by the 1963 Equal Pay Act. The Supreme Court rejected this argument, noting that the female deputies as a class were entitled to protection under the 1964 Civil Rights Act. Otherwise, all any employer would have to do would be to change one or two duties, thereby making the jobs different. The case opened the door to broader challenges to government pay systems based on women as a class.

The state of Washington agreed to a union demand to conduct a wage and salary study of all state employees to identify any pay inequities. The consultant's report identified substantial disparity between the pay of men and women using a method of job analysis that determines the value of a job by using uniform criteria such as knowledge and ability, education, and communication skills. The methodology is sometimes called *comparable worth* but is better known as the *benchmark factor* classification system. The state legislature did not fund the report, and the union took its challenge to court in *AFSCME* v. *The State of Washington*.[9] The U.S. Court of Appeals rejected the trial court's decision in favor of the union on the grounds that a consultant's study could not bind the state legislature without its consent. While the matter was on appeal to the U.S. Supreme Court, the state funded the results of the study.

The methodology of comparable worth was subsequently rejected by U.S. Civil Rights Commission as a binding tool for achieving equity because it did not adequately consider market forces, and questions exist regarding its scientific objectivity. Nevertheless, the mechanics of comparable worth, or the benchmark factor classification system, is widely used in the public sector from the state and local to the national level. It has thus quietly brought about pay equity between male- and female-dominated job classes in many governments. In the city of San Jose, California, for example, the salaries of librarians were benchmarked against architects, which resulted in a substantial increase in librarian salaries. Despite such gains, pay disparity between the genders continues to be a problem in the private as well as the public sector.

In 1984 women on average earned 64 percent of the average salary paid to men.[10] In 1998 the gap had narrowed significantly to approximately 75 percent. Much of the disparity seems to be age related. Women under age 25 earn 89 percent and women 25 to 34 earn 83 percent of the wages paid to their male age cohorts. The gap then widens; women aged 35 to 44 earn 74 percent and older female workers, aged 55 to 64, earned only 68 percent of wages paid to men of a comparable age.

When controlled for education, the data reveal that earning growth for female college graduates has outpaced that of their male counterparts, having increased 21.7 percent since 1979 when controlled for inflation. The male increase for the same time span was only 8 percent, thus narrowing the pay gap between the groups to 75.3 percent.[11] In part, the human-capital factors of education, experience, and length of time in the workforce can explain the continuing gap. Women are more likely to leave and reenter the workforce or to move back and forth between full- and part-time employment because of childbearing. Some of the remainder must be attributed to continued disproportional concentrations of women in traditional female occupations (nursing, teaching, and clerical) and in managerial categories involving administrative support, such as human resource management. By contrast, men still dominate the higher paying categories of precision production, craft, and repair categories. The remainder of the disparity, however, must be laid at the door of residual sexism.

THE GLASS CEILING

In Chapter 3, we discussed the glass ceiling effect that seems to allow women and minorities to advance into higher management echelons but prevents them from achieving proportionality in top executive positions. Congress created a Glass Ceiling Commission as part of the 1991 Civil Rights Act. Private employers and government agencies are asked to examine their promotional practices to identify and remove barriers to advancement. The problem and progress towards its resolution can be illustrated by looking at the Senior Executive Service of the federal government. In 1990 women constituted 11.2 percent of the senior positions. By 1996 the percentage had increased to 20.4 percent; in 1998 women were 22.4 percent of the federal executives. By contrast, in the same period of time minorities had increased from 7.6 percent to 12.9 percent of the SES.[12] Clearly, gender parity in advancement has not yet been achieved.

SEXUAL HARASSMENT

The 1964 Civil Rights Act prohibited gender-based discrimination. Prior to the Supreme Court's ruling in the 1986 *Meritor Savings* case,[13] many believed that Congress could not have envisioned protecting women from unwanted sexual advances in the workplace. Critics argued that the courts would find it impossible to sort out harassment from normal courting behavior and what constituted welcome and unwelcome sexual advances. The critics were wrong.

Sexual harassment generally means any unwelcome sexual advance, or conduct or language that is sexually abusive or intimidating. When acceptance of unwanted advances or intimidating sexual behavior is made a condition of employment by a person in authority, or when the organization permits a hostile or intimidating working environment, it becomes discrimination under the act. Furthermore, every organization has a responsibility to provide for the protection of employees from hostile or intimidating behavior on the part of coworkers.

The *Meritor* decision defined two types of sexual harassment. The first involves making submission to sexual advances a condition of employment. The second involves creating or permitting a hostile or offensive work environment. Organizations should also provide mechanisms for registering harassment complaints and for the timely investigation and resolution of such complaints. These mechanisms, moreover, should be outside the chain of command. In the *Meritor* case the organization was found liable because the policy stated that an employee should report unwelcome advances to his or her supervisor. Such a reporting system is inadequate if the alleged harasser is the supervisor.

In the *Meritor* case there were questions as to whether the primary complainant had voluntarily engaged in sexual relations with the harasser initially, and when her participation became involuntary. Writing for the court, Chief Justice Rehnquist stated: "respondent's allegations in this case—which include not only pervasive harassment but also criminal conduct of the most serious nature—are plainly sufficient to state a claim for 'hostile environment' sexual harassment." The majority of the court stopped short of making employers automatically liable for the behavior of their supervisors (although the court did not preclude such liability in this case). A four-justice minority, however, wanted to provide automatic liability, because such a standard would be consistent with other Title VII cases where employers are automatically liable for the discriminatory practices by supervisors in matters of race and religion.

The unanimous *Meritor* decision cemented protection for workers from sexual harassment in the workplace. Then the 1991 Civil Rights Act provided for the award of punitive damages for civil rights violations when it can be demonstrated that the harassing behavior was intentional on the part of the employer. Type one harassment is almost always intentional. The amount of the potential award is a function of the size of the organization and the number of victims. Civil rights laws in some states do not contain such limitations. In 1989, for example, a California jury awarded three female sheriff's deputies nearly $2.2 million because their employer failed to protect them from retaliation by other deputies for having reported being harassed by a supervisor.[14]

The decision in the *Meritor* case was further refined by a series of cases in the 1990s. In *Harris* v. *Forklift Systems, Inc.* (1993),[15] the court took up the issue of the amount of damage that a victim must suffer to be entitled to compensation, and it refined the standard for determining harassment. Harris had been the victim of comments and conduct from her supervisor that were severe, lewd, and pervasive. Overturning a lower court ruling, the high Court ruled that a victim need not have suffered severe psychological damage as the result of the harassment nor must the harassment have interfered with the ability to perform work duties. The Court also established the *reasonable person* standard for determining what is offensive. Lower courts had stated that the standard should be what a reasonable woman would find objectionable. Such a standard would be beyond the capacity of male members of a jury to apply, and it would have been inappropriate for judging the claims of male victims.

Sexual harassment is sometimes so intolerable to the victim that he or she believes it necessary to quit rather than endure the treatment. Suits that are filed after the victim quits are filed under the standard of the *constructive discharge*. That is, the environment was so offensive that the victim's having quit was tantamount to being fired. In the case of *Burlington Industries, Inc.* v. *Ellerth* (1998),[16] the victim alleged that her supervisor repeatedly threatened adverse actions if she did not submit to his overtures. The court ruled that Ellerth had been the victim of a constructive discharge even though her supervisor never carried out the threats and she had received rewards for her performance.

In the case of *Faragher* v. *City of Boca Raton* (1998),[17] the Court revisited the issue of the amount of protection an employer must provide. Faragher alleged that her lifeguard coworkers had harassed her and the city had not protected her. The Court ruled that the city had not provided reasonable protection, including notification of the employee's rights and routes of appeal. Employers must make the effort to post their policies and make every employee aware of how to file a complaint.

Finally, in *Oncale* v. *Sundowner* (1998)[18] the Supreme Court took up the issue of same-sex harassment and, in the process, greatly expanded the protections. Oncale was employed on an oil rig in the Gulf of Mexico. There, he alleged, he was repeatedly harassed by his coworkers, who belittled him and threatened him with sexual assault. When he could no longer endure the treatment, Oncale resigned and sued the company for constructive discharge. Oncale's position was that he was harassed and that the harassment was of a sexual nature based on his gender. He did not allege that his harassers, who were male, were homosexual. The court refused to excuse the behavior as rough horseplay.

SUMMARY AND CONCLUSION

The problems of gender stereotyping and wage comparability are uniquely female. Even if the last vestiges of racial, religious, and ethnic discrimination were miraculously to disappear, female members of minority groups would be faced with gender-related discrimination. Sexual harassment may be directed at either sex but remains the special concern of women in the workplace. None of these problems, moreover, can be resolved by general-level prohibitions against discrimination. Concerned managers, especially human resource managers, must therefore develop solutions and programs specifically tailored to the resolution of these gender-based problems. These include diversity training for all employees and establishing clear and accessible complaint mechanisms for reporting discrimination that are outside the chain of command. Employers should also ensure timely investigations of discrimination allegations. And, investigations should be conducted in a manner that protects the dignity of the person making the complaint and the alleged perpetrator. When allegations of discrimination or harassment prove true, the organization must take immediate corrective action. Finally, the employer must take pains to protect victims from retaliation for having come forward.

TRUST AND COMMITMENT

Sarah Ryder, a single parent of two school-age children, was delighted when she landed a job as an English as a second language instructor for Central Coast College in California. Her contract was semester by semester and the pay was not great, but as a .50 employee she was entitled to participate in the school's health care and retirement plans. In each case, she was entitled to one half the benefits of a full-time faculty member, and her rates were adjusted accordingly. The job had the advantage of holidays and summers off, which allowed Sarah to be home when her two children were. Her income, combined with the support payments from her former husband, allowed her to barely make ends meet.

Two years into her employment, her department chair retired and was succeeded by Elmer Smith, a handsome intellectual who was just Sarah's age. The two hit it off immediately and began to see each other socially. When the dean authorized the department to offer an additional section of English as a second language, Elmer offered the class to Sarah who accepted without hesitation. The .75 appointment meant reduced costs for insurance as well as extra income.

Midway through the semester, Sarah's social relationship with Elmer turned sour. Sarah was seeking a commitment that Elmer was unwilling to give. He cut quite a figure in the small coastal community with his rugged good looks and advanced degrees. He explained that he had recently gone through a difficult end to a ten-year marriage. He said that he had feelings for Sarah but was not ready to stop seeing other people.

Part way through the spring semester, the couple stopped dating at Sarah's behest. She told Elmer that she hoped they could still be friends and colleagues. Elmer said he understood completely, and things seemed to work out. Sarah immersed herself in her classes and her children. Elmer was elected president of the local yacht club and zipped around town in his sports car with three or more different women per week.

During the summer, Sarah began to date her ex-husband, Bob. They spent the summer on family outings to the beaches and nearby mountains. One Saturday, Elmer and his date ran into Sarah and her ex-husband and children as they were buying supplies at the marina. Sarah introduced the two men, and they exchanged pleasantries before separating. "What's his problem?" Bob asked as they walked away. "Did you see the look he gave me?" Sarah had noticed a certain discomfort in Elmer's eyes but chalked it up to embarrassment at his being with a twenty-year-old.

A few days later, Sarah received a certified letter informing her that she was being cut from one of her classes. The letter indicated that an over-extension of department resources made the cut necessary. It was signed, "Affectionately yours, Elmer." Sarah could only wonder what this meant. She called the department to schedule a meeting with Elmer but was told he would be out of town until school started.

Sarah and her ex-husband decided to travel to Las Vegas and remarry over the Labor Day weekend. The fall semester started the Wednesday before the holiday. In the past this had meant just starting a semester then taking a three-day hiatus from school. Unfortunately, this time it posed a problem. Try as she might, Sarah could not get a return flight from Las Vegas on the holiday. The earliest arrangement that could be made was for Tuesday evening. This would require her to miss her two Tuesday classes.

Sarah arranged for a colleague to cover her classes and thought nothing more about it. After all, department members routinely covered for each other for illnesses or to attend conferences or training sessions. The Ryders took their children with them and had a wonderful four days in Las Vegas.

When Sarah came into the office on Wednesday, she found two messages from Elmer on her phone and a note on her door instructing her to come to his office after her last class. The tone of Elmer's voice on the phone messages was friendly, and she inferred that perhaps a last-minute opportunity for a third class had opened.

Sarah found Elmer with his feet on the desk chatting on the phone. It was obviously a social call, so Sarah waited in the hall for Elmer to finish his conversation. Upon seeing Sarah, Elmer smiled and motioned for her to come in and take a seat, which she did. Sarah sat quietly, trying her best not to eavesdrop for nearly five minutes while Elmer went on and on about what a great weekend he had apparently passed with the person on the other end of the phone line.

When he finally put the phone down, his mood shifted perceptibly. Without any preliminaries, Elmer launched into the purpose of the meeting. He demanded to know why Sarah was not in class the day before. Sarah was taken aback by the aggressiveness of Elmer's manner. She stammered as she explained that she had gone to Las Vegas to get married and could not get an earlier flight back.

"Absolutely unacceptable," Elmer's voice trembled with rage as he tossed the faculty handbook across the desk. "You have to get my permission to miss class. Even when you are sick, you must clear the absence with me. We just can't allow everybody to come and go as they please, trading classes to go off partying and such," he concluded. "I am going to have to dock you a day's pay, and I am putting a letter of reprimand in your file. If this happens again, you will be fired. Do you understand?"

Sarah was so shocked that she was unable to speak. She rushed from the office choking back the tears of anger and humiliation. That evening with her husband, Sarah discussed her options. Once she convinced Bob that there was nothing to be gained by breaking Elmer's jaw, she decided to quit her job after the current semester. She also filed a sexual harassment claim with the school's personnel officer. To her mind, the reprimand had more to do with her marriage than with missing class.

QUESTIONS AND INSTRUCTIONS

1. Was Sarah in violation of school policy by missing work without permission?

2. Is Sarah correct in her inference as to Elmer's motives for the reprimand?

3. Does she have a valid claim for sexual harassment?

4. Would her claim be substantiated in a court of law?

5. Is there sufficient merit to her claim for the school to take administrative action?

6. Do you believe Elmer overreacted to the infraction based on his feelings for Sarah?

7. What would the reaction be in your agency if this sort of thing had occurred?

8. Given the events described here, are agencies justified in policies that forbid dating between supervisors and subordinates? Does the same hold true for faculty dating university students?

NOTES AND RESOURCES

1. *Bradwell* v. *State of Illinois*, 83 U.S. 130 (1873). The opinion cited women's destiny as fulfilling "the noble and benign offices of wife and mother. This is the law of the Creator."

2. See, for example, Mabel H. Willet, *The Employment of Women in the Clothing Trade* (New York: Columbia University Press, 1902).

3. *Muller* v. *Oregon*, 208 U.S. 412 (1908). Future Supreme Court Justice Lois Brandies represented the plaintiffs in this landmark case.

4. Doris Kearns Goodwin, *No Ordinary Time* (New York: Simon and Schuster, 1994), p. 365.

5. See Susan M. Hartman, *The Home Front and Beyond: American Women in the 1940s* (Boston: Twayne, 1982).

6. Office of the Secretary of Labor, Women's Bureau, *Time of Change: 1983 Handbook of Women Workers* (Washington, DC: U.S. Government Printing Office), bulletin 298.

7. "U.S. Department of Labor, Bureau of Labor Statistics Summary 99—5 May 1999," *Issues in Labor Statistics: What Women Earned in 1998* (Washington, DC: U.S. Government Printing Office, 1999).

8. *Washington Co. Oregon* v. *Gunther*, 452 U.S. 161 (1981).

9. *AFSCME* v. *The State of Washington*, 770 F2nd 1401 (1985).

10. U.S. Department of Commerce, *Women in the American Economy*, Series P-23, no. 146 (November 1986).

11. "U.S. Department of Labor, Bureau of Labor Statistics Summary 99—5 May 1999," *Issues in Labor Statistics: What Women Earned in 1998* (Washington, DC: U.S. Government Printing Office, 1999).

12. United States Office of Personnel Management, *The Fact Book* (Washington, DC: OPM, 2000), p. 56.

13. *Meritor Savings Bank, FSB, Petitioner,* v. *Mechelle Vinson et al.*, 54 LW 4703 (1986).

14. *Bates* v. *Co. of Santa Clara*, C892328 Cal (1989). In a retrial of the case involving the largest judgment, the amount of the award was reduced from $1.6 million to $700,000.

15. *Harris* v. *Forklift Systems, Inc.*, 510 U.S. 17 (1993).

16. *Burlington Industries, Inc.* v. *Ellerth*, 524 U.S. 742 (1998).

17. *Faragher* v. *City of Boca Raton*, 524 U.S. 775 (1998).

18. *Oncale* v. *Sundowner Offshore Services, Inc.*, 523 U.S. 75 (1998).

WORKFORCE CHANGES AND FAMILY ISSUES

The United States workforce was revolutionized in the latter half of the twentieth century by the entry of women into the workplace. The changing gender composition of the work force (45 percent female in 1999) will keep family issues at the center of discussions regarding human resource management well into the new millennium.[1] Because women also continue to bear principal responsibility for child rearing, family issues are primarily women's issues.

The traditional two-parent American household in which only the father works outside the home now describes a small minority of families. Recent Labor Department statistics reflect the dramatic changes that have taken place. In 1940, 68 percent of households were traditional families; in 2000, the figure is 20 percent. Another 17 percent of households are headed by single women.[2]

Traditionally, employers did little to break down the firewall between work and family—no longer. Households have continued to evolve, and employment markets have tightened. Employers who wish to recruit and retain competent workers are altering the benefits, work schedules, and services that they provide to employees. Workers who once had to worry about themselves and their children, now are faced with caring for aging parents as well. Some of the more innovative approaches have come from government.

The Family and Medical Leave Act of 1993 was the first legislation signed by incoming president Bill Clinton. The act provides up to twelve workweeks of uncompensated leave in any twelve months for family or medical problems. Also in 1993, the Federal Employees Leave Sharing Amendments Act was passed, which allows workers to share accrued leave benefits with fellow workers who have family or personal medical emergencies. Many state and local governments and private employers have also adopted this policy. In 1994 federal employees became eligible for applying up to 104 hours of sick leave to care for a sick family member or to deal with the death of a family member.[3]

DOMESTIC PARTNERS

A growing minority of households consists of unmarried partners committed to long-term relationships in which they accept mutual responsibility for each other's welfare, debts, and in many cases, children. These households are often same-sex relationships, but many are heterosexual partners who choose not to marry.

Whether to extend employee benefits such as health care and sick leave to domestic partners caused considerable controversy in the early 1990s. Opposition came from religious groups opposed to same-sex unions. Some employers feared that without the proof-of-marriage requirement, benefit costs could skyrocket as the definition of what constitutes a family was left up to individual employees. Today, the Campaign for Human Rights lists 108 Fortune 500 companies, 118 colleges and universities, and 94 state and local government employers who provide domestic partner benefits.[4] The city of Berkeley, California, was one of the first cities to extend the benefit. Berkeley found that only 16 percent of those seeking the benefit were same-sex couples.[5]

Nationally, the trend is towards accepting alternative definitions of family households. The state of Vermont, for example, has established a domestic partners registry that allows gay and lesbian couples to identify themselves as families for legal purposes such as inheritance. A number of cities have begun providing domestic partner registries. The formal step of registering relationships can be a benefit to employers as well as the partners in question. If registration becomes a trend, it will prevent employees from designating roommates and friends as domestic partners merely to secure them benefits under the company's health care plans. Finally, as more and more organizations extend the benefit, those organizations that do not provide them will find themselves at a competitive disadvantage in tight labor markets.

DAY CARE

A central problem for working parents of preschool-age children is day care. It is also a problem for parents of school-age children, because children often must be dropped off before school officially begins in order for parents to arrive at their places of employment on time. Similarly, school days normally end before the workday. Summers, holidays, and teacher conference days also pose day-care problems for working parents.

Recognizing the necessity of day care, the U.S. tax code provides a child-care deduction. Some school districts also assist parents by providing before- and after-school programs for working parents. Workers with preschool children must rely on private day-care facilities that vary greatly in cost and program quality.[6]

Even when parents are able to make suitable child-care arrangements, most facilities will not accept sick children, which leaves parents with few options. They can either leave the child with family or friends or miss work. However, women find it necessary to call in sick to care for children more frequently than men. Family-friendly employers allow employees to use sick leave to care for family members.

A recent survey of private organizations with more than 100 employees reported that 9 percent provided day care on or near the work site.[7] Growing numbers of employers are providing on-site day-care facilities for their employees. On-site day care allows parents to spend time with their children on a drop-in basis. Having children nearby, moreover, solves a number of logistical problems for working parents with preschool children. On-site day care is less of a boon for parents of school-age children, who need before- and after-school care. The problem is particularly acute for employees who live some distance from the work site. These parents cannot leave work to collect their children and bring them back to the on-site facility.

The response of government employers, too, has varied. The federal government operates a modest on-site program for children of federal civilian employees. Under the federal system, the facilities are located in government buildings, but the cost of the centers is borne by the employees on a per-child basis.

By contrast, the uniformed services operate day-care centers at locations in the United States and abroad. These centers serve some thousands of children, and the military pays two-thirds of the cost.[8] The military supports day care because uniformed personnel are on call twenty-four hours a day and are subject to abrupt shifts in duty assignments or deployment. (Uniformed personnel are expected to have prearranged child care should deployment become necessary.) Providing day care, therefore, is a mission-relevant and necessary expenditure.

Other innovations include programs that allow employees to open pretax accounts to pay for day care. Fifty percent of employers surveyed by the Families and Work Institute report such programs. Another 5 percent report providing vouchers for day care. Another 6 percent report reimbursing for child-care costs when employees travel or have to work late.[9] The federal government now subsidizes day-care costs for its low income employees.[10]

ELDERCARE

The U.S. population is aging as well as growing. The fastest-growing segment of the population consists of those over the age of 85. Stereotypes to the contrary notwithstanding, less than 5 percent of these people live in nursing homes. Those who maintain their own homes often rely on their children and other relatives to assist them with transportation, shopping, housework, and so forth. Others live with their adult children by choice or economic necessity.

The amount of assistance needed varies from family to family. Surveys reveal that responsibility for assisting aging parents falls mostly to adult children between the ages of 40 and 60 and primarily to daughters.[11] These adult children are coming to be known as the "sandwich generation" because they are pressured by the needs of their children as well as their parents. Many 40-year-olds are no longer faced with the need to find day care for children, but their parenting responsibilities are far from over. Overall, studies estimate that between 23 and 30 percent of the workforce have some form of eldercare responsibilities, and 40 percent of these have child-care as well as eldercare responsibilities.[12]

Employers recognize that, like child-care demands, eldercare problems can detract from productivity, as workers seek to meet such needs of their parents as scheduling medical appointments, filing Medicare forms, and finding an eldercare facility to watch parents while the adult child works. Caring for the elderly sometimes causes employees to miss work. This can result in use of leave time in an erratic pattern that disrupts workflow or, in some cases, an abuse of sick leave.

Government and concerned groups began recognizing the need for eldercare a decade ago, which resulted in a number of private and public partnerships. The New York City Department of Aging, for example, received grants from the American Express, Philip Morris, and J. P. Morgan companies to develop counseling services for caregivers.[13] These services include group sessions at the work site as well as individual counseling regarding service availability. In addition to counseling services, employers respond by offering their employees the options of flextime, flexiplace, and job sharing, which also help employees with child-care problems. The 1998 Business Work-Life Study (BWLS) reports that companies have responded to the eldercare problem as follows. Twenty-three percent of companies provide eldercare referral services, and 9 percent provide a long-term-care insurance option for family members.[14]

FLEXIBLE SCHEDULING

FLEXTIME

The human tradition of working during daylight hours and sleeping at night is probably the first cause of nine-to-five business schedules. The necessity to interact with customers and suppliers also contributed to the concept of "regular business hours." Manufacturing using sequential production methods further contributed to the notion that everybody must be at the work site at the same time.

In the current era, much of what is done is paperwork, computer analysis, accounting, and the like, tasks that are accomplished by individual workers. Furthermore, such public services as law enforcement, health services, and fire protection are provided around the clock. Thus, it becomes possible for many workers to set their own hours within a framework that protects the organization's interests and needs. Some workers opt to put in a forty-hour week in four days of ten hours each. Others choose to alter their starting and stopping times to accommodate school schedules, parents' transportation needs, and so forth. Still others may alter their schedules to avoid the crush of rush hour traffic. The BWLS survey reports that 68 percent of the companies responding allow periodic changes in starting and stopping times and 24 percent permit this on a daily basis.[15]

Flextime schedules can prove quite useful for government agencies that wish to extend their operating hours to facilitate citizen access to services. A secretary at an urban university, for example, wanted to work a schedule of four 10-hour days. Arriving at work a full hour before the faculty enabled her to set up the office before the rush began, and the fact that she worked until six o'clock meant that evening students could get service from the department before the start of night classes. Because her schedule ran Monday through Thursday, she was absent on the lightest day of the week. In compensation for her extended hours, she had three free days a week. Similarly, public service shift workers whose facilities are open seven days a week may choose to work more than a standard five days in a row in order to achieve greater blocks of time off. The federal government too permits schedule flexibility. Employees may opt for a standard 8-hour day 40 hours per week or they may choose eight 9-hour days and one 8-hour day in a two-week period. Employees needing a more compressed schedule may opt for ten hours a day for four days a week or 13 hours and twenty minutes three days a week.[16]

JOB SHARING

Flextime can be an even more powerful management tool when combined with job sharing and part-time employment. Traditionally, job sharing allows two workers to occupy the same position. Each works four hours and receives benefits on a prorated basis. That is, they earn 50 percent of the sick leave and vacation time of a full-time worker. They may also be required to bear a greater portion of the cost of health insurance than would be expected of a full-time employee.

Job sharing requires a high degree of communication between the two workers if they work on the same projects. Jobs can be shared on a less segmental basis in caregiving facilities such as hospitals or custodial facilities such as prisons. In both instances, staffing is required on a 24-hour basis and involves group and individual interactions between agency staff and clientele.

The federal government has generally lagged behind other employers in recognizing the need for part-time employment. In 1978, however, Congress passed the Federal Employees Part-Time Career Employment Act, and in OPM's 1990 appropriation it mandated that a system of job sharing be established. Participation in part-time employment in the federal service has remained low overall, 3 percent in 1998. This constant overall proportion, however, masks an increase in participation at the higher grades accompanied by a decrease at the lower grades.[17]

FLEXIBLE STAFFING

Flextime allows management to increase or cut back staffing according to program needs. In place of the standard three 8-hour shifts, some workers can be assigned to bridging shifts that maximize staffing during peak need periods. The staffing possibilities become particularly dramatic when full-time positions can be divided up, enabling part-time employees to share their positions without sequentially tying their work assignments to a single other worker.

A residential mental health facility for children, for example, needs to maximize nursing staffing during the evening period when children are in the dorm but not engaged in organized activities. Extra help is also needed when children are being transported on recreational outings, to medical appointments, and so forth. Maximum staffing is also necessary to get the children bathed and into bed at night and up and dressed in the morning. By contrast, much lighter dormitory staffing is desirable on the overnight shift when the children are normally asleep or during school hours when children are in classrooms staffed by teachers and their aides.

Such variations in staffing can be accomplished by converting a set number of positions from full-to part-time. Suppose, for example, that the agency in question has been allocated 80 full-time employees. By converting 10 positions to half-time slots, the agency would acquire 20 employees available for 20 hours each of flexible assignments ranging from 2 to 6 hours in length. Employees with family responsibilities might welcome such flexibility in their schedules as would persons attending school.

Government workers who are employed half-time or more must retain the protections of the civil service system, and they should be entitled to a prorated share of benefits. Otherwise, government service agencies will run the risk of being operated like fast-food franchises that are unable to attract and retain high-quality workers.

FLEXIBLE LEAVE

Some employers are rethinking the entire concept of leave. Rather than segmenting sick leave from vacation and holiday time, some employers grant a finite amount of annual leave that can be used for whatever purpose the employee chooses. Employees who do not use the leave may accumulate same or accept a cash payment for the unused portion.

The 1978 Pregnancy Discrimination Act required that pregnancy be included under employers' short-term disability programs. As of 1984, 95 percent of the Fortune 1500 companies provided for short-term disability leave for pregnancy. The time allowed was from 1 to 12 weeks. The same report indicates, however, that few companies allow paid maternity leave after delivery.[18] The 1993 Family and Medical Leave Act require companies with over 50 employees at a work site to provide up to 12 weeks of uncompensated medical, maternity, or adoption leave. The BWLS survey reports that some companies provide leaves well beyond the basic requirement, and 53 percent of the companies reported some replacement pay for maternity leave. Thirteen percent reported paid paternity leave, and 12.5 percent reported paid leave for adoptions.[19]

FLEXIBLE LOCATION

Flexiplace is perhaps the most innovative of the changes in the employment landscape. Under flexiplace, employees whose schedules permit are allowed to perform their duties at places other than the work site. The arguments for flexiplace suggest that fax machines, computer links, and conference calling have rendered the notion of assembled workers passé. This is especially true of professional employees who largely work independently, such as technical writers and computer programmers.

Flexiplace does not require that an employee work exclusively at home. For the concept to work, the employee must have sufficient flexibility in his or her job assignment to allow at least one day per week of activities away from the work site. For example, employees who do a good deal of writing could plan blocks of time away from the bustle and interruptions at the agency.

University professors are an example of how informal flexiplace systems have been working for years. When not in the classroom, it really matters little where the professor prepares lectures, conducts research, and writes manuscripts. The research output of the individual over time and student assessments of relative levels of professorial preparation for class are two measures of how effectively the individual professor has employed his or her time.

Unfortunately, critics of flexiplace can also use the professor example to illustrate their concerns: there is no way to check on how much of a professor's time is actually spent on these legitimate pursuits of the university. Flexiplace does not allow for efficiency checks on how time is being used from moment to moment or hour to hour. Organizations whose managers possess a high need for control will not benefit from the flexiplace approach.

Nor has flexiplace caught on well with workers, a great many of whom enjoy the act of going to work each day. For some, the need to go to work is a cultural imperative; that is, they do not feel right about accepting the paycheck without regularly appearing at their employer's place of business. For others, going to work fulfills the social need of interacting with other adults. Finally, some workers choose to segment their working environments from their home situations, which may prove too distracting to get the work done. Whatever the reasons, the federal government reports that employee participation in its pilot flexiplace programs has been low.[20] In the private sector, 33 percent of the BWLS companies report allowing employees to work at home on a regular basis and another 55 percent allow it occasionally.[21]

SUMMARY AND CONCLUSION

Changes in the conventions that govern the way we think about work (such as scheduling and employee benefits) portend a new world of work in the twenty-first century. The majority of workers will be either single or joint heads of families, with some combination of child- or parent-care responsibilities. Insofar as these family responsibilities affect workers, so too are their employers affected. If the current economic expansion continues, moreover, government employers will be forced to accommodate work schedules and benefit packages to the new reality or risk being unable to fill positions.

BETTING ON FAMILY LIFE*

The message from the local American Federation of State, County, and Municipal Employees (AFSCME) union was clear, "Benton City Casino is UNFAIR to working families who wish to maintain a good family life." These signs were placed on the windshields of all patrons who parked in the Benton County Casino parking lot. What sparked the controversy was a change in the shift rotation for the all-night gambling center. Employees were told that they were now required to work staggered shifts. Previously, workers were assigned one of three regular shifts. As

*Prepared by Lance Noe and C. Kenneth Meyer, Drake University

employees moved up the seniority ladder, they could apply for the shift of their choice. The director of human resources was facing a recruiting crisis and was struggling to find enough employees to fill the overnight shift. Thus, he proposed to management that a staggered shift would give everyone a chance to enjoy a "good" shift while eliminating the hiring problems that were crippling the operation. With the new plan, everyone was rotated through all shifts four times each year, like it or not.

Marcus Grimly was a long-time casino employee with an above-average employment record. Upon being notified that he would be rotated through the all-night shift, he immediately contacted his union steward and then filed a grievance citing his illness and how he was protected under the Americans with Disabilities Act (ADA). He claimed that fluctuating blood sugar levels affected his ability to perform his assignment in the overnight shift. An employee who claimed she couldn't drive at night and needed to be accommodated by remaining on the day shift filed another grievance. Others complained that family life was now going to be in a constant state of flux, with parents now unable to find permanent child care. Of even more concern was the expected impact that a constantly changing work schedule would have on family life.

QUESTIONS AND INSTRUCTIONS

1. Because Benton City Casino is owned and operated by the city, is there a special obligation to family and community life that impacts this issue? Does the city have a moral obligation to ensure that family life is protected and children are raised in the most stable environment possible?
2. What issues, ADA and otherwise, are impacted by the move from a fixed to staggered shift schedule?
3. What is the most equitable way to deal with operations that require employees to be on duty 24 hours per day? Please elaborate.

LEAVE IT TO THE BEREAVEMENT POLICY*

As the final draft of a letter was submitted to Barb Rosen, director of human resources, for her approval and signature, she sighed with relief that this issue was finally laid to rest! What should have been an easy interpretation of a blue-collar union contract rule turned into a fierce internal battle with cultural overtones. "I hope we did the right thing here," she remarked while signing the letter.

One month earlier, Max Buckman, director of parks and recreation for Scottsville, was completely frustrated by Denish Mawisa, a parks and recreation maintenance employee, who had left the country and missed eight consecutive days of work. In an angry tone of voice he stated to Barb and others within hearing distance in the human resources office: "I am sick and tired of these guys from other countries going home for long visits whenever they feel like it and believing they should be paid for it at the same time." Although Barb didn't appreciate the tone of the comment, she had to agree that some foreign-born nationals did not

*Prepared by Lance Noe and C. Kenneth Meyer, Drake University

seem to appreciate the notification requirements and limits on leave for family issues, such as illness and death. Barb expressed her frustration to Kevin Clark, the labor relations manager, "Why do we spend days arguing over these contracts when most of our employees just do what they want to do anyway?"

Denish Mawisa, a recent immigrant to the U.S., was by all accounts doing a great job. However, six months into the job, he called the office from overseas to explain that his "sister died and that he would be back in a week." This was allowed by the union contract, which allows 40 hours of bereavement leave for an immediate family member, defined as: a parent, sister, brother, spouse, son, daughter, employee's grandparent(s), mother-in-law, father-in-law, grandchildren, stepchildren domiciled in employee's household.

In Mawisa's case, however, a week turned into eight days, and the subsequent information called in to the office by his spouse didn't match the final information he provided upon his return to work. Mrs. Mawisa called the office on the sixth day of her husband's absence and stated that he couldn't return due to illness. Then, on the seventh day she called stating that he couldn't return due to passport problems. When Mr. Mawisa returned to work on the ninth day, he claimed that while home for the funeral of his sister, a second sister died, resulting in the need for an additional 40 hours of bereavement leave.

Upon hearing this request, Parks and Recreation Director Buckman sought approval to terminate Mr. Mawisa. "Two sisters dying within three days of each other—give me a break!" Max complained to anyone in human resources who would listen. The second death claim, especially in light of the last-minute calls claiming sickness and passport troubles, did seem incredible. However, Barb Rosen convinced Buckman that he should "play it straight" and request the documentation allowed for by the contract. "We fought hard for the language allowing management to request documentation in certain cases. Let's use the contract to deal with this issue, not our emotions," she reasoned with him.

Both Buckman and Rosen were surprised to receive official documentation in the form of two government death certificates a few days later. Apparently, Mr. Mawisa had thought to request official documentation while on his trip. When they sat down to look at the materials, they quickly found the documentation was not in English. Rosen, now determined more than ever to follow the "rules of the game," had to find someone who could translate the documents into English. Fortunately, Paulette, a secretary who primarily dealt with pension and retirement, was also a native of Mr. Mawisa's home country, so a meeting was arranged.

Although it looked like one of the documents supported his claim, the second death certificate seemed to show that a cousin, not a sister, had died. Cousins are not in the contract, so his documentation appeared not to support his claim. However, in a follow-up meeting with Mr. Mawisa, he repeatedly claimed that in his home country, a cousin is often considered to be a "sister" in the family. "You don't understand our culture, we are as close to our cousins as to our brothers and sisters," Mr. Mawisa told a bewildered Barb Rosen and a skeptical Max Buckman. This claim was supported by the translator, although she repeatedly said that she did not want to take sides.

Max wanted to hold firm. Barb, however, wanted to learn more about the cultural values of Mawisa's home country, and she spent added time talking with

Paulette about family values in her homeland. She also went on-line and accessed the U.S. Department of State's Web pages for foreign countries. There she found a great deal of information on Mawisa's country's spoken languages, its history, culture, and economic and political system; she also found the information on cultural and religious practices to be useful.

The results of the meeting and subsequent final action are recorded in the letter to Mr. Mawisa from Barb Rosen, Director of Human Resources, Scottsville.

Dear Mr. Mawisa:

On October 1, you sent me a letter in which you stated that the Parks and Recreation Division did not allow bereavement leave for the full time period that you were in your home country to attend funeral services for two sisters who died a few days apart. According to your letter, the Division did not approve your leave because of the difference in the last names of your sisters, raising questions regarding the claim that both were, in fact, your sisters.

I contacted Parks and Recreation, who provided me with the following information related to the events that led to their decision. On September 27, the day you were due back from an initial five-day bereavement leave due to the death of your sister, the Division reported that they received a call at 6:30 A.M. from Mrs. Mawisa, who said that you were home sick and would not be reporting for work. She was advised that per Division policy, the employee must personally call the Division unless unable to do so due to extenuating circumstances. The Division reports that they did not receive a call from you on that day.

The following day (September 28), Mrs. Mawisa came into the office and reported that you were experiencing passport troubles and could not leave your home county to return to the U.S. Mrs. Mawisa was then told of the dock-in-pay policy that would be implemented per the blue-collar contract agreement. On Thursday, September 30, you reported for work and explained that while in your home country for the funeral of your sister, a second sister passed away delaying your stay and that you were requesting a second week of bereavement leave. The Division explained that in order to be granted bereavement leave, documentation establishing the relationship with the employee can, per the contract, be required. At this time they asked for such documentation, which you subsequently provided. As you know, the documentation was not in English, but it was initially determined by an employee of Scott County, who served as a translator, that the documentation *did not* establish the sister relationship between yourself and both persons represented on the death certificates.

Due to the unique nature of the certificates, we arranged a meeting with you to clarify the issue. In that meeting, we agreed that the first certificate showed that the parents of the deceased were Mr. A. Mawisa and Mrs. M. Suruses, also both deceased. The death certificate for the second person showed her parents to be Mr. R. Mawisa and Mrs. J. Lormara. You then stated that Mr. A. Mawisa was your father and Mr. R. Mawisa is his brother—meaning the second person was your cousin, not your sister. Based on this information and the fact that no single parent appears on both documents, you have only established that one of the persons was your sister.

Therefore, we recommended to the Division that you be granted 40 hours of bereavement leave in accordance with the Blue Collar Bargaining Agreement (Article 11 Bereavement Leave, Section 1) and not 80 hours as you requested. However, I am also recommending that the Division allow you to use emergency annual leave for September 27, 28, and 29, which will be deducted from your annual-leave total, even though the proper procedure was not followed in requesting such leave. In the future, if you do not accurately follow the procedural requirements of the contract, you will be subject to appropriate disciplinary action.

As you can see, much effort has been expended in response to your claim. We regret the losses you and your family have suffered.

Sincerely,

Barb Rosen, Director
Human Resources

Cc   Parks and Recreation—Division Director
     Human Resources—Labor Relations Manager

QUESTIONS AND INSTRUCTIONS

1. Assess the actions recommended by Barb Rosen. Did her recommendations result in an action that was fair to all parties? If not, who was ill served by her recommendation? Please elaborate.

2. Should leave policy take into account differences in cultural values and traditions? If so, how would you incorporate these values and traditions into policy?

3. As you read the case study, what was your reaction to the events leading to Mr. Mawisa being asked to provide documentation? What did you think motivated the initial claims of sickness and passport troubles? Please discuss.

4. What do you believe is important to know about the international and multicultural dimensions of human resources management? Does culture really make a difference? Explain.

5. Did the human resources director undermine the authority of the line manager by trying to fix the problem rather than disciplining the employee?

TIME AND TIME AGAIN*

The Springfield Cancer Research Center (SCRC) is a small public health–research clinic located in the Northeast. It is a satellite site to the main clinic located 100 miles away in Greenfield. The clinics represent 2 of 50 sites located across the country that are conducting a study on the prevention and treatment of breast cancer in women. The goal of each clinic is to contact as many women as possible who have been diagnosed with breast cancer and to follow them throughout their treatment. Kay Smith, R.N., was hired as the clinic manager for the new clinic in Springfield, and she recently hired a nurse practitioner, a data coordinator, and a project manager. The new project manager, Tammy Wells, previously worked at the central clinic in Greenfield before she was transferred to SCRC.

---

*Prepared by Mary Beth Mellick and C. Kenneth Meyer, Drake University

The working hours for both Greenfield and Springfield cancer centers were identical: 8:00 A.M. to 4:30 P.M., with a half-hour for lunch. Tammy, the project manager, said that the Greenfield "supervisors were *very* strict about hours," and if anyone came to work late—even just a few minutes late—they were required to take vacation time for the minutes lost. Tammy also said that the project manager in Greenfield would stand at the copy machine every morning and monitor the time of arrival for all employees. Flexibility was not an option; she noted, for example, that "no one was allowed to take an extra half-hour lunch and stay at work an extra half-hour at the end of the day,"—the flexibility that some wanted.

When Kay heard about the attendance rules in Greenfield, she proclaimed that "there was no way her clinic would operate in such an autocratic manner." She further explained that on certain high-patient-load days, her coworkers may not get a half-hour for lunch, but when the patient load was low they could take long lunches, as long as no one took advantage of the flexible time. Kay told her staff, "I refuse to be as rigid as the Greenfield clinic with hours. The way they treat their employees is so unprofessional; they might as well work in a factory. After all, we are not a colony of ants." By this time, everyone had come to like and trust Kay, and the four staff members became almost like family.

The one exception to Kay's flexible style was her insistence that all members of her staff be at work by 8:00 A.M. every morning—no excuses, no exceptions. It was easy for Kay to be at work by 8:00 A.M.—she woke up every morning at 4:30 without an alarm, made her family breakfast and also dinner for that evening, did laundry, and left for work sometimes as early as 6:30. She loved to get things done in the morning. Her employees, however, did not have Kay's energy in the morning. Tammy lived one hour away and was a single mother with two kids. She had to get them to school and day care before leaving for the one-hour drive to work. Sarah Parker, the data coordinator, had trouble being on time—especially in the morning. Sarah and Tammy were usually late, but usually not more than 5 minutes. Since they did not see patients, their work was not affected. Kathy Jones, the nurse practitioner, on the other hand, was usually at least 15 minutes late and had patients waiting for her when she reached the office. Kay reminded everyone that 8:00 A.M. was the time to be at work.

Staff members at the Springfield clinic were told that the patient load would be high, and the rumor mill communicated that additional staff would be hired. During the next few months the clinic staff did an exceptional job of getting the work done. Although there were only four of them, the SCRC staff maintained a 98 percent subject-retention rate, the highest of all the clinics nationally, and much higher than those clinics that had 15 or 20 employees. However, Kathy, the nurse practitioner, only did average and sometimes below-average work. She had many personal problems that interfered with her job, including separating from her husband, taking care of her mentally ill daughter, and occasionally providing assistance to her elderly mother. The staff sympathized with Kathy and didn't think twice about picking up the slack for her.

The employees at the Springfield CRC were busy, but not busy enough. They only had one research study, whereas the other clinics had between 5 and 10 going on at one time. But new studies were pending, and it wouldn't be long, they were told, before they would be swamped. Until then, Kay told her staff it was okay to take long lunches.

In the beginning, everyone started with a one-hour lunch break, but over time, the norm became two hours. With business slow, Kay seemed unconcerned. However, Kathy sometimes stretched the lunch hour to three hours and kept patients waiting until she returned. Kay told her that three-hour lunches were too long and that she could not keep her patients waiting like she did.

As months passed, work remained extremely slow. The new research studies that were pending had fallen through. And as the Springfield staff became more familiar with their jobs, they were able to get their work done well before 4:30. Not only did Kay allow her staff to continue to take long lunches, she also told them that once their work was done, they could do whatever they wanted—as long as they stayed at work. So the staff brought magazines, books, and crossword puzzles to work to make the days go by faster. On exceptionally slow days, Kay would let her staff go home a half-hour or more early. No one argued with Kay about the 8:00 A.M. rule, because they didn't want to cause friction. They really liked and respected her as a clinic manager.

Kay continued coming to work by 7:00 every morning, even if there were no appointments until later in the day. She read the newspaper or worked on crossword puzzles until the first appointment. But Kathy, Sarah, and Tammy did not change their late arrival habits. They did not understand the rationale of "breaking their necks to get to work by 8:00," only to read magazines and do crossword puzzles as Kay did. Tammy wanted to use the extra time to spend with her kids, while Sarah wanted to sleep in longer in the morning. But Kay was adamant about being to work by 8:00 A.M. and became increasingly angry as the staff continued its late arrival. As Sarah and Tammy strolled in at 8:05 and 8:10, and Kathy between 8:15 and 8:30, Kay would be sitting at the front desk working on a crossword puzzle. She would not even say "hello," but would instead look up at the clock to see what time it was. She also would not talk to anyone for about the first half-hour of work, until she cooled off.

As tensions grew about the issue of time and hours, Kay decided to put her foot down. She said that if anyone on her staff were 10 minutes late or more, they would have to take vacation time for the lost time. Sarah and Tammy usually made it to work by 8:05, but sometimes it was 8:10. Kathy continued to be 15 minutes or more late. Kay had everyone filling out vacation slips for being late. Lunches remained flexible, although Kathy continued to take three-hour lunches, and Kay continued to confront her about it.

The vacation records that were filled out for lost time were sent to the main office in Greenfield, where all staff benefits were handled. Of course, the Greenfield clinic was not happy with the numerous vacation records they had to process. All the 5- and 10-minute vacation slips going to Greenfield every week embarrassed Kay, so she decided to stop having Sarah and Tammy use vacation time when they were late, but she continued having Kathy use it. Although tensions continued to be high, the staff—for the most part—remained a tight-knit group, and the clinic held onto its Number 1 national ranking!

Sarah and Tammy knew Kay was at her wits' end and made a stronger effort to get to work by 8:00 A.M. They had hoped Kathy would do the same, but she did not. In fact, she only got worse. Kathy's work, although never more than satisfactory, started going further downhill. Her personal problems worsened, and she began to take between two and three weeks off each month for sick time, vacation time, or family leave. She continued to come to work late and take long lunches. Kay eventually started making Kathy fill out vacation slips for long lunches. Kathy then began making up excuses to get out of work by saying she was going to the lab in another building, when really she was running errands or taking her mother to the doctor.

The staff's sympathy for Kathy grew to frustration. The more Kathy came to work late and took time off, the more Kay became angry, and the more work everyone had to do to pick up the slack. Even when Kathy was at work, her mind seemed to be somewhere else. The clinic was becoming an unbearable place to work. But no matter how many rules Kathy broke, and no matter how angry Kay got with her, Kay would not reprimand her because she knew if she did, Kathy would retaliate. Kay felt that if she tried to fire her, Kathy would say that Kay allowed the staff to do crossword puzzles and read magazines at work. Kay—and everyone else at the clinic—could lose their jobs as a result. Kay felt the only thing left to do was to make Kathy's life hell so she would eventually quit. But it didn't work. Months went by, and Kathy showed no signs of leaving. Meanwhile, Sarah and Tammy started back in their routine of being 5 or 10 minutes late for work.

Finally, Kay told her staff that there would be no more long lunches, even if there was no work to do and no patients to see: "Half-hour lunches only. . . . If you choose to run an errand for a half-hour and still want to eat lunch, you'll have to eat at your desk while you work." She continued to confront people when they were late, although no vacation time had to be used. Kay later pulled Sarah and Tammy aside and told them: "Since Kathy can't follow the rules, then everyone will have to be punished."

Over the next few months, morale and productivity at the clinic quickly dropped. The group of employees that was once like a family slowly began distancing itself from one another. The tension between Kay and Kathy grew into shouting matches. Meanwhile, Tammy and Sarah began looking for new jobs.

QUESTIONS AND INSTRUCTIONS

1. Was Kay's flexible approach appropriate in a publicly funded agency? Why or why not? What does flextime really mean? Explain.

2. Was Kay's punish-everyone strategy an appropriate response to Kathy's work and family problems? Should Kay have fired Kathy?

3. Should Kay have reprimanded Tammy and Sarah for not getting to work on time? Why or why not?

4. If this case had transpired 20 years ago, do you think it would have been more acceptable to reprimand someone for being late? Are time clocks passé in the new public administration?

NOTES AND RESOURCES

1. U.S. Department of Labor, *Facts of Working Women*, Publication No. 90–2, September 1990, p. 1.

2. For a fuller discussion of these figures, especially with regard to child care, see Edward L. Suntrup, "Child-Care Delivery Systems in the Government Sector," *Review of Public Personnel Administration* 10 (1989): 48–59. For a discussion of female-headed households, see Linda L. Swanson, "Household Structure and Resources in Female-Headed Family Households," presented at the annual meeting of the Population Association of America, San Francisco, April 1995; at <http://www.cpc.unc.edu/pubs/paa_papers/1995/swanson.html>.

3. *Muller* v. *Oregon*, 208 U.S. 412 (1908).

4. See Human Rights Campaign "Domestic Partners" at <http://www.hrc.org/worknet/dp/index.asp/>

5. "Domestic Partner Coverage Found Not to Increase Costs," *BNA Employee Relations Weekly Report*, April 27, 1992, pp. 24, 29.

6. See General Accounting Office, *Child Care: State Efforts to Enforce Safety and Health Requirements* (Washington, DC: GAO, January 2000).

7. Families and Work Institute's 1998 Business Work-Life Study at <http://www.familiesandwork.org/summary/worklife/pdf>.

8. United States Merit System Protection Board, *Balancing Work Responsibilities and Family Needs: The Federal Civil Service Response* (Washington, DC: MSPB, 1991), pp. 18–21.

9. Ibid., p. 5.

10. The rules regarding the federal government program can be found in the Office of Personnel Management, 5 CFR Part 792 RIN 3206-A193, *Federal Register*, vol. 65, no. 50 (March 14, 2000) or at <http://www.opm.gov/fedregis/2000/65–13659-a.htm>.

11. See Subcommittee on Human Resources, "Exploding the Myths: Caregiving in America," Select Committee on Aging, U.S. House of Representatives, Comm. Pub. No. 100–665, August 1988.

12. Margaret Magnus, "Eldercare: Corporate Awareness, But Little Action," *Personnel Journal* 67, no. 6 (June 1988): 19, 23.

13. "Partnerships Formed for Eldercare Needs: Agencies Pilot Eldercare Information Referral Service," *Employee Benefit Plan Review* 46, no. 2 (August 1991): 26–29.

14. Families and Work Institute's 1998 Business Work-Life Study at <http://www.familiesandwork.org/summary/worklife/pdf>, p. 6.

15. Ibid., p. 3.

16. Office of Personnel Management, "Handbook on Alternative Work Schedules," at <http://www.opm.gov/oca/aws/html/appende.htm>.

17. Despite OPM's efforts, part-time employment in the federal service has remained low during the 1990s. It reached a high of 4 percent in 1993 but fell back to 3 percent by 1996. OPM, *The Fact Book: Federal Civilian Workforce Statistics* (Washington, DC: OPM, 1999): 15.

18. The data are summarized from the *Labor Relations Yearbook* (Washington, DC: Bureau of National Affairs, 1985).

19. Families and Work Institute's 1998 Business Work-Life Study at <http://www.familiesandwork.org/summary/worklife/pdf>, p. 4.

20. Merit System Protection Board, *Balancing Work Responsibilities and Family Needs: The Federal Civil Service Response* (Washington, DC: MSBP, 1991), pp. 47–54.

21. Families and Work Institute's 1998 Business Work-Life Study at <http://www.familiesandwork.org/summary/worklife/pdf>, p. 4.

HUMAN RESOURCE PLANNING

Human resource planning is a critical subset of an organization's strategic planning efforts.[1] Without a thoughtful plan, each line manager must decide how to allocate resources and prioritize unit activities with guidance only from the next higher echelon. Agencies that take the time to plan are better able to coordinate the efforts of various units toward agreed-upon objectives.

Planning is a fact of agency life whether agency managers wish it or not. Few organizations can afford to remain static because of changes in the agency's environment. Shortfalls in projected revenues, for example, frequently spur public executives to rethink the resources that are allocated to various components of the mission. The election of a new public executive whose view of government radically differs from that of the previous administration also may stimulate a spate of planning activities in agencies.[2]

THE PLANNING CONTEXT

Whether generated from the executive's own sense of direction for the organization or demanded by outside actors, agencies sooner or later engage in systematic planning efforts. The textbook way of doing this is as follows:[3]

1. Agency executives define the mission as precisely as possible.
2. They then decide where they wish the agency to be in three to five years.
3. Various strategies and program options are explored as possible means of getting the agency from where it is to where it should be.
   a. In the course of these deliberations, alternatives are assessed in terms of their primary or intended outcomes.
   b. The potential secondary outcomes of alternatives, which may be either positive or negative, are also assessed.
   c. Care must be taken to gather information from a variety of sources rather than relying solely on the best guesses of those engaged in the discussions.
   d. The alternatives are assessed and reassessed in the context of the factors that come to light during the course of the discussions.

4. Next, an alternative is selected and implemented.

   a. Implementation requires apprising rank-and-file workers of the new direction the agency is taking.[4]

   b. Key players are carefully assigned responsibilities for implementation to assure that the plan is carried out as specified.[5]

   c. A program monitoring system is put in place to make management aware of problems as they emerge and to report on the progress of the plan.[6]

5. Finally, the new program is evaluated to see if the outcomes that occur were those that were intended and whether new alternatives should be explored.[7]

Steps 1 and 2 of this model may vary according to the preferences of those planning the project. Persons with strong views about what their organization should be doing may first wish to arrive at a consensus about where the organization should be headed before precisely examining what is in fact being done. The order of steps 1 and 2 is less important than making absolutely certain that both are achieved before designing the change strategy.

THE HUMAN COMPONENT IN AGENCY PLANNING

Assessing human resource needs is a vital part of steps 3 and 4 of the planning process.[8] The existence of an overall agency plan enables the human resources division to plan for the recruitment and training of new workers and the retraining of current workers to achieve the mission. Projecting human resource needs is thus a vital and ongoing part of the personnel mission.

The personnel division may, in fact, contribute critical human resources information to those engaged in the planning process. More important, it is impossible to assess accurately the funding required to implement a plan without input from the human resources division, because 70 percent or more of operating costs can go toward salaries and benefits for workers.

PLANNING FOR CHANGE

Suppose that a city manager and his or her key staff decide to automate the billing system for the city's water and refuse collection services.[9] Such a change may require equipment acquisition, the hiring of workers with new skills, and the retraining of current staff. The system's conversion will require a transition period containing both manual and automated billing procedures. Finally, because the new system will require a different skills mix, a decision will have to be made on what to do with the employees who operate the current manual system. Obviously, such a transition will require close cooperation between the utilities division and the human resource planning staff.

Suppose further that the manual system employs a division head and nine billing clerks and that the conversion to the computer system and its subsequent operation will require the employment of a division head, a computer programmer, and three data entry clerks. At the most basic level, the needs are for five employees rather than ten. Planners may conclude that the conversion will require the hiring of one new employee (the programmer), the retraining of three clerks, and the layoff of six others.

A more refined assessment, however, may indicate a less dramatic impact on the lives of the current employees. An analysis of turnover patterns, for example, might reveal that the clerks in the division have a 50 percent annual turnover. In the past, that is, half the clerks quit each year. The needed reductions might therefore be accomplished by attrition rather than layoffs. The computer programmer, moreover, would only be needed to get the system up and running. Therefore, the programming might be contracted out to a private firm. The contract could include retraining the current clerks on the new computer system.

Other relevant considerations include providing time for conversion from the current to the new system and meeting customer needs in the interim. Finally, bringing the new system on-line and completing the conversion could take as long as two years. Thus, the issue becomes one of training and adaptation rather than hiring and layoffs. Providing the planning group with this information and scheduling the training are among the responsibilities of the human resources division. Finally, human resource planners can be most helpful when brought into the process early.

SUCCESSION PLANNING

Nationwide, state and local governments are at a crossroads. In 1999 42 percent of their employees were between the ages of 45 and 64.[10] Most government retirement systems provide for maximum benefits at age 55 with 30 years of service. The problem is even more acute for high-level management positions. While many public agencies are aware of the impending turnover, few have put in place plans to replace managers who retire.[11] Because the problem is uniform across the country, agencies cannot realistically plan to recruit outside replacements in a recruiting environment that adds all other government entities to the competition pool.

Forward-thinking agencies are dealing with the impending crisis through succession planning programs that combine the techniques of human resource planning and employee development. Succession planning involves a five-step process:

1. Identifying positions that are likely to experience retirements in the near term.

2. Organizing management teams to identify critical skills necessary to the positions. These might include decision making, financial analysis, leadership skills, and so forth.

3. Identifying mid-level personnel who either possess the requisite skills or who have demonstrated the potential for acquiring them. This may include historical analysis to identify the lower-level positions from which successful senior managers were promoted.

4. Design in-house training programs to provide the needed skills.
5. Develop a mentoring program in which high-level managers work with specific subordinates to help them hone their managerial skills.

The foregoing steps are more easily achieved if the agency has a database of employee skills that includes education, experience, and current performance-appraisal information. Of course, succession planning may have a phase two in which the agency identifies successful first-line supervisors and professionals to succeed the middle managers who are moved up. Finally, agencies may wish to use the impending turnover as an opportunity to reconfigure the organization to deal with changing demands for service, more efficient patterns of workflow, and strategies for worker empowerment through delegation and the formation of work teams to replace hierarchies where appropriate.

PLANNING FOR CUTBACKS

The interdependence of human resource planning and overall program planning is as important in times of austerity as in times of growth and change.[12] When program managers are ordered to slash their budgets, up-to-date human resources information becomes vital to preserve the mission and minimize the negative effects on employees. When ordered to cut their budgets, public executives must often seek more creative solutions than those considered in the private sector. In private companies, cutbacks usually result from a slowdown in demand for the company's products. The private manager then decides which plants to close and how many employees to lay off in order to balance the books.

Public programs, by contrast, are often entitlements, which means that services cannot be interrupted regardless of budget shortfalls. A county welfare agency, for example, must provide welfare benefits to families with dependent children when the parents can demonstrate eligibility. Benefits are mandated by federal and state law and cannot be denied. During an economic downturn, tax revenues may decline at the same time as the demand for services go up. And while the formula for federal payments of the benefits triggers an automatic increase in payments to the county, the increased cost of personnel to provide the services is not automatic. Thus, the director of the welfare agency may be faced with an increased demand for services and a simultaneous need to cut the cost of service delivery.

The role of the human resources division is critical in times of austerity because public programs are labor-intensive activities. Thus, the preponderance of the cuts must come from the staffing budgets.

Program managers may choose initially to make their cuts across the board. This approach usually means that the manager considers all elements of the mission to be substantially equal in importance. It also normally means that the manager hopes that the cutbacks will be temporary and that harder choices among program components can be postponed or avoided altogether.

The across-the-board strategy involves first making projections on turnover in the agency. That is, the human resource division provides data on the number of retirements that are anticipated for the coming year and the number of vacancies that currently exist. Retirements and hiring freezes can sometimes cover short-falls. In some instances, senior employees are encouraged to take early retirement by offering them "golden handshakes," allowing them additional years of age or service credit to make retirement more attractive.[13]

When attrition is not enough, it may become necessary to begin laying off employees. Union contracts and civil service law maintain that layoffs must be made on the basis of seniority: the last hired is the first fired. A public university that is in retrenchment may find it necessary to lay off large numbers of junior faculty. Curricular impacts are greater in across-the-board layoffs because junior faculty salaries are low, and more faculty must be laid off to achieve the desired effect than would be the case if programmatic cuts involving senior faculty were made.

Programmatic cuts call for tough decisions regarding mission that most public executives are reluctant to make. Nevertheless, agencies can choose to preserve priority programs at the expense of less-valued ones. Many colleges and universities, for example, find the greatest student demand for their engineering and business management programs. Research universities may also derive significant funding from research grants to their science divisions. In such cases, layoffs would first come in the arts, humanities, and social sciences.

To minimize the impacts of the cuts, deans of schools and department chairs who are forced to cut may find it beneficial to appoint some faculty in more than one department, such as history and political science or philosophy and humanities. By this means, programs can continue to offer needed courses even with reduced faculty resources. Some junior faculty can also be retained by such creative efforts.

Organizations must also use caution to be sure that their headquarters staff is not preserved at the expense of service delivery. This is a natural outcome of cutbacks designed and implemented from the center. The military refers to this problem as maintaining an appropriate ratio of "teeth to tail." As bases are closed, units reassigned, and whole divisions eliminated, care must be taken to assure that headquarters staff are proportionally reduced.

BUMPING BACK

Public agencies may find it necessary to abolish some service delivery units, transferring more senior employees to other offices and laying off less senior employees on a bump-back basis. Suppose, for example, that a state vocational rehabilitation agency operates assessment centers in every large city in the state and several mid-size cities as well. These centers provide diagnostic services to clients to determine the extent of their disabilities and the services that are available to them.

Rehabilitation services (like welfare payments) must be provided; however, the convenience of service access is not specified. When faced with the necessity of cutting the budget, therefore, a rehab director might choose to close several diagnostic centers and relocate more senior employees to the centers that remain open.

Thus, a supervisor at a center that is closing would have the right to bump back (take the position) of a less senior supervisor at a diagnostic facility that is not closing. The supervisor being bumped would then have the option of bumping back into the position of a senior rehab counselor who, in turn, would bump a less senior employee.

THE DARK SIDE OF LAYOFFS

Bumping back can lead to a good deal of antipathy among employees and a loss of worker morale. Other potential casualties of strict adherence to the seniority rule are the merit principle and affirmative action gains. The merit principle may suffer if energetic, promising workers lose their positions to more senior, mediocre performers. This is not to imply that senior workers are automatically less competent than more junior employees; the opposite is often the case. But sweeping layoffs must surely sacrifice some promising workers who constitute the future of the agency.

Some government units faced with layoffs have sought to ameliorate the impact of seniority by developing layoff formulas that also give points for exceptional performance. Of course, giving partial recognition for exceptional performance cannot offset months or years of seniority. An exceptional employee with a few weeks' less seniority than a mediocre peer, however, might be retained.[14]

Last hired, first fired can also have a devastating impact on agency affirmative action programs. Years of effort to diversify the workforce by recruiting minority and female applicants can be wiped out by a seniority-based layoff. Agencies that have sought to preserve their affirmative action gains by building a race factor into the layoff procedures have had their efforts rebuffed by the courts. On at least two occasions, the Supreme Court has ruled that innocent members of the majority may not be denied the benefits of seniority in order to achieve larger social goals. The cases of *Firefighters Local 1784* v. *Stotts* (1984)[15] and *Wygant* v. *The Jackson Board of Education* (1986)[16] are detailed in Chapter 3. Suffice it to say here that minority persons cannot retain their positions over more senior employees unless the minority person in question was personally the victim of previous discrimination by the agency and gained his or her position by means of a court order.

Human resource analysis is also important in routine year-to-year planning for maintenance of current programs and services, normal employee attrition, and growth in the demand for services. Having the human resources planning capacity in place, moreover, facilitates decision making when more dramatic human resource planning decisions become necessary.

THE TECHNOLOGY OF HUMAN RESOURCE PLANNING

HUMAN RESOURCE PLANNING AS FORECASTING

Forecasting human resource needs involves projecting demand for organization services, appropriate reallocations of resources, and the development of new resources, as necessary.[17] The best predictor of the future currently available to planners is the past. Trends in demand for services over the past several years are a fairly reliable predictor of future demand. Welfare professionals know, for example, that an excellent predictor of the demand for agency services is the percentage of the population who are women of childbearing age. This information can then be combined with data on the health of the local economy to predict service demand.

Historical analysis is the term used to describe human resource forecasting that predicts the future based on the past. Public administrators look at previous demands for services and then estimate the resources that will be necessary to cope with the demand. Public hospitals, for example, are required by regulation to maintain certain ratios of licensed to unlicensed nursing personnel. Total staffing, in turn, is tied to the patient census. Human resource planners must provide decision makers with probable service demands and staffing needs based on past patterns. Projecting demand and assuring adequate staffing ratios is also essential to be eligible for public and private insurance payments.

Variables such as mandatory staffing ratios are known in human resource planning language as *sovereign factors*. A sovereign factor is used as a constant to allocate resources. Thus, once the patient census factor is known, the sovereign factor is used to arrive at the staffing needs. Further refinements in the needs analysis are achieved by adding in predicted staff retirements, replacements necessitated by employee leaves, and so forth.

Turnover analysis involves more than simple addition and subtraction. The human resources division must analyze turnover with an eye to skills specialization among employees. Our hospital planner may find that while the projected turnover is high, prospects for replacement of especially skilled persons such as nurses may be particularly grim.[18]

COMPLEXITY OF DEMAND.   The task of forecasting can become complicated as the demand for services becomes complex. Nowhere is this more evident than in the melting pot that is California. Large metropolitan school districts should carefully monitor population trends to predict service demands. In cases such as Los Angeles, keeping up with the demand is virtually impossible given the rate of immigration. Each month thousands of new students apply for admission to the schools. Some of these have migrated from other states; the vast majority, however, are new immigrants from Asia and Latin America, which further compounds the planning process.

School administrators must make hiring bilingual educators a priority to ensure service to the new immigrants. The district must therefore recruit large numbers of bilingual teachers and teachers trained to offer courses for non-English-speakers. Student diversity, therefore, is a recruitment and development problem as well as a program planning and project development challenge.

The district goes to extraordinary lengths to recruit new teachers with bilingual teaching credentials. At the same time, pay incentives and district payment for language training encourage current teachers to update their skills to meet the challenge.

Until recently, bilingual education meant English/Spanish programs.[19] While challenging, the task of preparing for such bilingual programs could be accomplished because of the large Hispanic population, a number of whom become teachers. Now, however, the situation is much more complex because of the influx of immigrants from various Asian countries speaking languages such as Vietnamese, Cambodian, various Chinese dialects, and the languages of the Indian subcontinent. This multilingual demand has forced a rethinking of education programs simply because the pool of persons who speak these languages who can immediately be trained as teachers is small. In a few years, Cambodian-speaking teachers, for example, will be more available as the population becomes assimilated. In the interim, however, alternative education programs must be developed to bridge the language gap and accelerate the learning of English. Such a program requires extensive training and development of teachers, in turn requiring careful planning and allocation of resources.

Bilingual education is only one example of the types of challenges human resource planning can present to existing organizations seeking to adapt to changing demands from the environment. Human resource planning is also a vital part of start-up planning for new programs or facilities.

FORECASTING FOR NEW OPERATIONS. Forecasting may or may not be computer assisted. Unassisted forecasts involve *expert estimates* of needs and costs based on the experience of the experts in setting up and operating similar programs. Normally, expert estimates rely extensively on the experience of line managers. These manager-experts can be quite adroit at defining most phases of a project. Line input is useful in planning program goals and objectives. Line managers are also invaluable for estimating construction costs and space allocations. And although line managers rarely place a premium on projecting human resource needs, they can greatly assist human resources planners.

Computer-assisted forecasting often involves the introduction of sovereign factors into the program planning process using computer models.[20] Suppose, for example, that the Department of Defense (DOD) wishes to convert a military base in northern Japan from a small naval air station that also serves as an electronic intelligence-gathering facility into an Air Force base with a primary tactical air mission.[21] That is, the DOD wishes to station a wing of F-16 fighters at the base to deter potential threats to Japanese airspace and to protect commercial flights over the northwest Pacific.

Planning for the conversion would use sovereign factors in both the construction and human resource planning processes. On the construction side, knowledge of how many F-16s were to be deployed would introduce such sovereign factors as hangar space, runway requirements, underground fuel-storage facilities, and housing facilities.

On the human resource side, the sovereign factors might again include the number of aircraft involved. By knowing the number of aircraft, the human resource planners also know the number of pilots (which might be three per aircraft) and ground crews needed to maintain the planes. The number of planes and level of training activities would also dictate the air traffic control facilities and the number of personnel needed to operate the tower. The size of the force directly involved in the tactical mission would also trigger the sovereign factor of medical support facilities and staffing requirements.

Other human resource sovereign factors might include whether the uniformed personnel stationed at the base are to be deployed on twelve-month unaccompanied or two-year accompanied rotations. An accompanied assignment means that the families of the troops are to come with them. When families are present, planners must also utilize the sovereign factors of housing, schools, shopping facilities, and other support activities.

Each new factor that is introduced into the process complicates the task of the planners. By using sovereign factors, however, at least the preliminary model can be developed relatively quickly. Using the factors as a starting point, the agency can seek congressional authorization. Once funding has been secured, the agency can begin facilities planning and logistical support planning, begin negotiating construction contracts, and undertake the recruitment, training, and deployment of military and civilian personnel.

Few organizations strictly adhere to either manual or computerized approaches; most use some mixture of the two. Prudent planners use experts to review the outcomes of even the most sophisticated computer planning models. Whether manual, automated, or mixed, human resource planning models must take into account assets that are currently available within the organization before they can adequately determine what must be procured. The best way to assess current human resources is by means of an inventory of current employees' skills.

SKILLS INVENTORIES

All organizations maintain a file on each employee. By computerizing the process, organizations can maintain current housekeeping records, such as date of appointment, salary, and benefits coverage, so that they are accessible by a computer keystroke. In addition, the computer can be programmed to survey current records on a variety of parameters of interest to organizations as they plan projects and make work assignments. For example, if the systems division of a NASA facility has a project that requires an engineer with specialized training in mathematical modeling, the position can be filled in one of several ways. The personnel division can be asked to conduct a nationwide search; various project chiefs can be contacted to see if they know any qualified candidates; or, if NASA maintains an electronic database on employees (known as a skills inventory), a list can be quickly generated of engineers who possess the needed skill.[22]

A dramatic example of the importance of such a skills inventory occurred during the Vietnam War on the occasion of the incursion into Cambodia by U.S. ground troops. During the operations, it became necessary for the English-speaking crews of U.S. gunships to communicate with Cambodian forces on the ground who were combating the mutual enemy. English among the Cambodians was as limited as Cambodian among the Americans. The problem was addressed by the manpower planning division of the United States Air Force in Saigon. A search of the Air Force skills inventory generated a list of U.S. Air Force personnel in Vietnam who spoke French, a language that was common among the Cambodians.

CONTENTS OF THE INVENTORY. Besides the obvious employee identification information, such as name and social security number, skills inventories contain a variety of information useful to the organization. Each inventory is specially tailored, in that the data contained in individual employee records are organized into categories of interest to the organization. For example, an inventory might contain information on the employee's history with the organization, documenting training and experience such as financial management, line supervision of employees, client relations, or legislative liaison. Other special skills might include computer training, facility with mathematics, engineering skills, or other specialized training of interest to the organization. Additional variables might include advanced degrees, foreign language skills, or any special licenses the employee might hold.[23]

BENEFITS OF THE INVENTORY. The principal benefit of a skills inventory is internal recruitment. By seeking inside first, organizations are able to draw on a previously screened pool of candidates for a given position. These candidates, moreover, have already exhibited their loyalty to the organization, and access to information on their work habits and reliable references are assured.

The obvious benefit to employees is the boost in morale that comes from knowing that their previous service to the agency places them first in line for positions that represent career advancement. The inventory also facilitates the creation of an employee development program.

Employee development may involve a mentoring program, in which lower-ranking employees work with more senior colleagues to map out career advancement strategies. Such a strategy would include identification of needed skills that the subordinate lacks and assistance from the organization to facilitate the employee's training. This support might include in-house training sessions, centralized training provided by the personnel office, and tuition reimbursement for classes that the employee attends on his or her own time.

Updates of the inventory's contents are essential so that each employee can gain its full benefits. The organization, too, benefits from updates through increased morale, employee loyalty, and self-improvement efforts that employees anticipate will lead to promotion. Employees who are pursuing advanced degrees, for example, can optimize their potential for advancement by notifying personnel each time they complete another job-relevant class.

Implicit in the use of skills inventories (especially those that are augmented by an employee development program) is a commitment to promote from within whenever possible. The civilian branch of the United States Air Force has such a system. Whenever an upper-level opening occurs, the Air Force seeks to fill the position from within. This loyalty to existing personnel is laudable and builds esprit de corps, although the practice poses a threat to the federal merit system as envisioned by its founders.[24]

A hallmark of the American merit system is the opportunity for lateral entry into the career service at the middle and upper levels. The British merit system, by contrast, normally allows for entry only at the bottom and the appointment of policymakers at the upper levels of the organization. The American logic is that lateral entry invigorates the bureaucracy from the infusion of new ideas. Lateral entry is also an artifact of patronage systems, which trades off career opportunities in the interest of citizen accountability. Proponents of entry-level-only recruitment systems argue that lateral entry is a disincentive for employees to develop themselves or to remain loyal to their agency.

In the current era, most public organizations find that mid- and upper-level positions in their organizations require strong familiarity with the agency's own policies and procedures. Public and private executives prefer to maintain the option of rewarding their subordinates with promotions for demonstrated loyalty, creativity, initiative, and plain hard work. This approach is facilitated by the existence of skills inventories that support systematic human resource planning.

The human resource planning services performed by the personnel division can prove invaluable to managers and executives who wish to implement planned changes in an orderly fashion. Both growth plans and cutback efforts must depend on reliable human resources information to avoid disruption and chaos. Cutbacks are especially disruptive to agency operations when they are undertaken without due consideration for employee seniority and bump-back rights. Hastily taken cutback decisions can result in a plethora of grievance hearings and wrongful discharge appeals.

The positive aspects of a well-thought-out human resource planning function are hard to overstate. The returns to organizations of computerized employee databases are potentially manifold, whether the organization is planning for growth or seeking to minimize the impact of cutbacks.

SUMMARY AND CONCLUSION

Human resource planning is central to organization survival and well being. Whether an organization is expanding, contracting, or merely maintaining the status quo, it must identify human resource needs. The organization can then develop recruitment, promotion, and training strategies. The technology of electronic databases has greatly enhanced the ability to adapt to changes in mission as well as personnel turnover. The indispensable component to good human resource planning, however, will remain a commitment to the process by high-level management outside the personnel department. Only when mainline executives engage in systematic organization planning, can human resource professionals effectively plan for change.

NOTES AND RESOURCES

1. On strategic planning, see Ernest C. Miller, *Advanced Techniques for Strategic Planning* (New York: American Management Association, 1971); see also Stephanie K. Marrus, *Building the Strategic Plan: Find, Analyze and Present the Right Information* (New York: Wiley, 1984).

2. See William H. Lucy, *Close to Power: Setting Priorities with Elected Officials* (Washington, DC: Planners Press, American Planning Association, 1988).

3. For a detailed discussion of the process, see Patrick M. Wright, Lee Dyer, and Michael G. Takla, *Execution: The Critical "What's Next?" in Strategic Human Resource Management*, (New York: Human Resource Planning Society, 1999); see also Patrick J. Below, *The Executive Guide to Strategic Planning* (San Francisco: Jossey-Bass, 1987). For a public-sector treatment, see Barry Bozeman and Jeffrey D. Straussman, *Public Management Strategies: Guidelines for Managerial Effectiveness* (San Francisco: Jossey-Bass, 1990).

4. Without employee cooperation, implementation is difficult. The latest thought is that rank-and-file workers should be involved in all phases of the production and planning processes. W. Edwards Deming, *Quality, Productivity and Competitive Position* (Cambridge, MA: MIT Center for Advanced Engineering Study, 1982). For Deming's prescriptions for handling the current imbalances between the United States and other industrial nations, see *Out of the Crisis* (Cambridge, MA: MIT Center for Advanced Engineering Study, 1986).

5. See Joseph W. Weiss, *The Management of Change: Administrative Logics and Actions* (New York: Praeger Special Studies, 1986).

6. See F. Beckhart and R. T. Harris, *Organization Transition: Managing Complex Change* (Reading, MA: Addison-Wesley, 1977).

7. See Ronald D. Sylvia, Kathleen M. Sylvia, and Elizabeth M. Gunn, *Program Planning and Evaluation for the Public Manager*, 2nd ed. (Prospect Heights, IL: Waveland Press, 1997).

8. For an up-to-date set of readings on human resource planning, see Richard J. Niehaus and Karl F. Price, *Bottom Line Results from Strategic Human Resource Planning* (New York: Plenum Press, 1991).

9. When referring to local government planning, most scholars mean planning the physical environment of the city; see John K. Friend, *Local Government and Strategic Choice: An Operational Research Approach to the Processes of Public Planning* (New York: Pergamon Press, 1977).

10. See Jonathan Walters, "Employee Exodus," *Governing.com*, (March 2000) at <http://www.governing.com>. For a complete discussion of succession planning, see Robert A. Levitt and Christine Gikakis, eds., *Shared Wisdom, Best Practices: Development and Succession Planning* (New York: Human Resource Planning Society, 1994).

11. See Katy Saldarini, "Agencies Neglect Workforce Planning, Officials Say," *Government Executive Magazine*, (March 2000) at <http://www.govexec.com/>.

12. For a comprehensive collection of readings on cutback management, see Charles H. Levine, Irene S. Rubin, and George G. Wolohojian, *The Politics of Retrenchment: How Local Governments Manage Fiscal Stress* (Beverly Hills, CA: Sage, 1980). For a discussion of how cutback principles can be misused, see Ronald J. Stupak, "Perversions of Cutback Management: Executive and Managerial Leadership Is 'the' Critical Element in the 90s," *The Bureaucrat* 18, no. 4 (Winter 1989): 9–12. For a discussion of local government issues, see Jonathan P. West and Charles Davis, "Administrative Values and Cutback Politics in American Local Government," *Public Personnel Management* 17 (1988): 207–23.

13. The 1991–1993 fiscal crisis in California prompted the state to offer public employees a golden handshake. Professors in the state college system who were at least 50 with five years of service were given four years' extra service credit; other state employees were given two years' credit. The aim was to encourage higher paid, more senior employees to retire, thus preserving the positions of newer employees. See California Assembly Bill 1522 (1992).

14. For a discussion of seniority and layoffs, see Leif Danzinger, "Implicit Contracts, Seniority Rights, and Layoffs Under Symmetric Information," *Journal of Comparative Economics* 14 (1990): 372–84. For a discussion of the impact on morale and productivity, see Joel Brockner, "Managing the Effects of Layoffs on Survivors," *California Management Review* 34, no. 2 (Winter 1992): 9–29.

15. *Firefighters Local 1784* v. *Stotts*, 467 U.S. 561 (1984).

16. *Wygant* v. *The Jackson Board of Education,* 106 S.Ct. 1842 (1986).

17. The standard reference for human resource planning is by the staff of the Human Resource Planning Society, *Human Resource Planning: A Case Study Reference Manual* (New York: McGraw-Hill, 1986). For a shorter treatment, see Elmer H. Burack and Nicholas J. Mathys, eds., *Human Resource Planning: A Pragmatic Approach to Manpower Staffing* (Lake Forest, IL: Brace-Park Press, 1983).

18. For a discussion of the problems faced by nurse administrators, see National Conference on Nursing, *Patterns in Nursing: Strategic Planning for Nursing Education* (New York: National League for Nursing, 1987).

19. Bilingual education has occasioned much debate. See Dick Kirschten, "Speaking English," *National Journal,* June 17, 1989, pp. 1556–62. In 1998 California voters outlawed bilingual education in the state with the passage of Proposition 227. Proponents of the proposition maintained that teaching students science and math in their native tongues forestalled the learning of English. Nevertheless, many districts have chosen to continue their bilingual program. And, whether or not subjects continue to be taught in foreign languages, the need for bilingual teachers will continue.

20. See, for example, Emily S. Bassman and John P. Fernandez, eds., *Human Resource Forecasting and Strategy Development: Guidelines for Analyzing and Fulfilling Organizational Needs* (New York: Quorum Books, 1990); see also Robert E. Sibson, *Strategic Planning for Human Resources Management* (New York: American Management Association, 1992).

21. The U.S. Air Force has three major subdivisions: the nuclear response component, known as the Strategic Air Command; the Tactical Air Command, which provides nonnuclear responses (such as in the 1992 U.N. war with Iraq; and the Military Airlift Command, which moves people and materials in support of the other two missions. For a fuller discussion of forecasting, see Dan Ward, Thomas P. Bechet, and Robert Tripp, *Human Resource Forecasting and Modeling* (New York: Human Resource Planning Society, 1994).

22. See, for example, Roscoe H. Adams, "Management, Analysis and Planning for Skill Development in the 1990s," *S.A.M. Advanced Management Journal* 54, no. 4 (Fall 1989): 34–40.

23. See John T. Payne, "Distributed Control Systems—Personnel," *ISA Transactions* 31, no. 3 (September 1992): 9–23. Payne argues for developing employee training programs based on the contents of the inventory.

24. See Paul P. Van Riper, *History of the United States Civil Service* (New York: Harper & Row, 1958).

RECRUITMENT SYSTEMS

If asked what the personnel office does, the layperson is likely to respond: recruitment. This response is understandable because the most common personnel encounter occurs when people apply for work in an organization. The personnel-as-recruitment illusion may be particularly strong in the public sector because of the elaborate and time-consuming nature of the process.[1]

Recruitment processes in the public sector have evolved from patronage mechanisms for rewarding the party faithful into systems to ensure merit selection. Most recently, public-sector recruitment systems have been instruments for achieving social equity. The discussion that follows describes the recruitment process under patronage and merit systems. The latter includes a discussion of the impact of affirmative action programs on merit recruitment systems.

The discussion is laced throughout with examples of improvements that administrators have made to streamline public recruitment systems in order to compete for the best employees in the workforce. The chapter concludes with a discussion of the importance of staffing in organization performance and the potential for merit recruitment systems to obstruct optimal performance in government.

RECRUITMENT UNDER PATRONAGE

Chapter 1 discussed the history of patronage systems. Suffice it to say here that these systems are manifestations of the principle "to the victors go the spoils."[2] The spoils system, at times, has involved the diversion of public funds to private benefit. It may also involve the direct taking of bribes by career and elected officials to achieve program outcomes favorable to the bribe-giver. The system condones using knowledge gained while performing one's duties to line one's pockets. It is not unusual, for example, for officials (or their families and friends) to buy land surrounding the planned site of a new public facility in anticipation of increased property values.

By far the most common characteristic of traditional spoils systems was the use of government positions to reward loyal party members for their work in elections. The demands of modern government, however, require that policymakers have as their direct assistants the most competent staffs possible.[3] Rank-and-file positions in the bureaucracy also often require specialized skills that preclude appointments based purely on party affiliation. Positions requiring specific skills, such as computer programmer or bulldozer operator, or special training and licensing, such as doctor or nurse, all limit the usefulness of patronage to parties.

The patronage positions that remain include upper-level appointees in merit agencies where critical policy choices are made. The remainder are in arcane bureaucracies, often in rural areas. Many of these positions are at the lower end, where the low-skill and semiskilled jobs go to the party faithful or their friends and families.

Upper-echelon patronage positions are filled based on skills and abilities as well as a willingness to carry out the policies of a given administration. Persons who occupy such positions may or may not have participated actively in the political campaign or made large contributions to the party or incumbent officials.

Those who are not politically active are normally sponsored by some member of the inner circle of the administration. When, for example, a midwestern governor wished to appoint a new head of the state personnel office, he sought the counsel of his political advisers, especially those who headed state agencies. The person finally appointed was a management consultant of extraordinary energy and creativity but limited political involvement. He was recommended to the governor by the head of the state welfare agency, who was also an old family friend of the consultant. Of course, the prospective candidate still had to convince the governor of his personal willingness to carry out the governor's agenda.

Rank-and-file patronage jobs are most common in the current era in city and county government. Selection for one of these positions can be through direct involvement in politics or through sponsorship.[4] In Ohio, an applicant became the first black deputy sheriff in a particular county by means of sponsorship. His appointment came about because when he was the right guard on his high school football team, the future sheriff's son was the left guard.

A more detailed example of a patronage appointment can usefully demonstrate the patronage selection process for lower-level jobs. The person in question (whom we shall call Tom) was having difficulty finding employment, so his father-in-law (the former district attorney) called the county Democratic party chairperson. The chairperson indicated that Tom might be a candidate for several vacant positions and should stop by the office the next day.

A brief interview determined that Tom had little work experience and even fewer job skills. Nevertheless, the chairperson was able to offer Tom a position on the county bridge-painting crew. Before Tom could be hired, however, he had to provide the chairperson with certification from the county board of election that he had never registered to vote in a Republican primary. As a candidate for a Democratic-controlled patronage position, Tom could not have been appointed if he were a Republican. This step did not present much of a hurdle for Tom because he had never voted at all. The chairperson found this fact amusing but hardly an obstacle to Tom's employment. Tom was instructed to be at the county yard at 7:00 A.M. the following Monday. Tom asked if he should call first and let the supervisor of the bridge crew know he was coming. The chairperson indicated that Tom could call to be polite, but the hiring decision rested with the chairperson alone.

The point to be gained from Tom's tale is that, under the patronage system, the chair of the majority party controls government hiring and must consult only with the members of the central committee.[5] Neither the chair nor the committee members hold public office, nor are they accountable to the people.

Tom's appointment is also a commentary on the outdated patronage system in the current era of media-based election campaigns. Legions of party workers are no longer necessary to get out the vote. Nor is it necessary to reward the faithful with government positions, because many of them are employed in the private sector. Their political involvement is motivated by a sense of citizen responsibility or ideological identification with the goals of the party.[6]

By far the greatest reason for the demise of patronage, however, was the grass-roots reform movement that sought to eliminate corruption in government by instituting merit systems of selection.

RECRUITMENT UNDER MERIT SYSTEMS

The growth of merit systems in government came about as a reaction to the excesses of patronage. The reasons for the widespread acceptance of merit systems are presented in Chapters 1 and 2. In the modern age, even states resistant to merit systems have succumbed to the pressures of reformers and federal merit requirements as a precondition for receiving federal funds.

What follows is a generic discussion of the process, from consultation to advertising the position to testing, list construction, interviews, and other screening activities, to the actual offer of employment. Variations on the generic approach are also presented to illustrate the potential for a more dynamic recruitment approach whereby public employers can more effectively compete for good candidates in the job market. The discussion concludes with some observations on the impact of affirmative action programs on merit-based recruitment systems.

As noted in the previous chapter, governments will undergo significant turnover over the next 15 years. Experts note that 44 percent of government workers are over 45 years of age; in the private sector they make up 30 percent.[7] Public agencies may view this as one more challenge to be dealt with as it comes up or they may undertake systematic planning efforts that include succession planning and employee development. In either case, recruitment will remain a center-stage feature of human resources management for the foreseeable future.

POSITION ANALYSIS

The process involved in a merit-based selection system ideally begins with a close consultation between the personnel office and the officials wishing to fill a vacancy. These discussions include a careful review of the position description to determine whether the current specifications are consistent with the skills the agency needs.[8]

Not infrequently the incumbent of a position dramatically alters its content from the description that is on file in the personnel office. Suppose, for example, that the secretary of an executive decides to retire after twenty years of service with the city—five years of that service in the current position with a classification of secretary 2. During this five-year tenure, the secretary may (through personal initiative) have significantly expanded the responsibilities of the position. Thus, a secretary 2 may actually be performing the duties of an administrative assistant, which would entitle the secretary to a promotion and raise.

Ideally, the supervisor would have monitored this development and sought a reclassification action to get the secretary the pay grade and title appropriate to the position. Oftentimes this is not the case, however, and the employee is reluctant to initiate the action on his or her own behalf. The result is a loyal employee of considerable initiative who is underpaid.

What the supervisor might have done is moot considering the employee's imminent retirement. At this point, the supervisor can only seek to prevent compounding the problem by appointing a successor at a similarly low rate. What is more important, from the perspective of the manager, is the impact of the oversight on the recruitment process. Neglecting to upgrade the position to administrative assistant most likely would result in the appointment of an entry-level secretary 2 who is not capable of performing the current duties of the position.

Unfortunately, managers who neglect to get appropriate classification upgrades for their subordinates frequently do not review the duties of the position before submitting a recruitment request to personnel. The result is a successor of lower talent, knowledge, and abilities than the retiring incumbent. Such problems can be avoided if public managers will take the time to understand the dynamics of both the classification and recruitment processes.

Upon learning of a prospective vacancy, a manager should consult with others in the work group to determine the exact nature of the skills they hope the new employee will bring to the position. The next step is to confer with the personnel office to draft a position description to match those needs.[9] Only then should the recruitment process commence.

THE RECRUITMENT PROCESS

FEDERAL AGENCIES.   Since the passage of the 1978 Civil Service Reform Act, federal agencies have been responsible for most of their own recruitment efforts. Agencies must comply with the procedures set forth by the Office of Personnel Management, the Merit System Protection Board, and the Equal Employment Opportunity Commission. Procedural constraints notwithstanding, agencies enjoy much more autonomy than they did when the Civil Service Commission handled the recruitment process.[10]

STATE AND LOCAL GOVERNMENTS.   In small cities, the city manager may be entirely responsible for all phases of the process, from advertisement to hiring. The situation is much the same for rural county governments. Medium-size cities have personnel officers who handle the task for the manager. Cities over 100,000, urban counties, and state government agencies normally operate central personnel offices.

In some jurisdictions, freestanding personnel agencies are responsible for all phases of the recruitment process; these agencies can be grouped under the rubric

Office of Personnel Management. In other localities, the same agency also houses the merit protection function and is referred to as the Civil Service Commission. Regardless of whether the agency also protects merit, the recruitment process must comply with the merit protection statute of the jurisdiction.

ADVERTISING.   A merit system, by definition, is the selection of the most qualified candidates from a broad-based pool of applicants drawn from society without regard to race, gender, ethnicity, or creed.[11] Thus, the first step in the merit process is to advertise the position broadly enough to ensure that all qualified candidates are aware of the position and given the opportunity to compete for it. Traditionally, this principle was more evident as a matter of intent rather than a characteristic of operation.

Public agencies normally post their job announcements on bulletin boards throughout the agency and at the central personnel office. Very ambitious recruiters might also send announcements to neighboring government personnel offices as well as the state department of employment services. Traditionally, money was not available to advertise in the local or statewide media. Recognizing the shortcomings of narrow advertising, however, governments have taken the first steps toward broad-based advertisement of vacancies.[12]

The candidate pool from a passive effort is usually composed of friends and relatives of current employees who pass the word that the agency is hiring. Others in the candidate pool are those with a sufficient knowledge of public personnel systems to know where to check for potential openings. Candidates in the latter group are normally current or former civil service employees and persons whose vocational preparation focused on a class of positions that exist primarily in the public sector.

Schoolteachers and police officers are two employment categories in which limited advertising can generate an adequate pool of qualified candidates to fill the open positions in all but the tightest labor markets. Persons interested enough in teaching as a career to obtain academic certification will probably figure out how to negotiate the labyrinth of public employment systems. They also enjoy the assistance of faculty mentors who help them find suitable employment.

Similarly, police science majors at the local junior college or criminal justice majors at the university also learn about the public employment process. But police departments must provide law enforcement and police protection services to an entire community whose ethnic composition may be quite diverse. To adequately serve such a community, the police department needs to recruit persons from various subcommunities, and that diversity cannot be achieved passively.[13]

Passive advertising efforts presume that persons interested in public employment know when, where, and how to apply. This approach is less useful for occupational categories requiring more general skills, such as clerical workers and general management professional categories. Workers seeking employment in these categories are much more likely to check the newspaper or visit an employment agency than they are to visit a government office.

Insofar as the object of the merit system is to attract to public service the best-qualified workers, passive advertising is inadequate at best. At worst, it can be used by malintentioned public managers as a way to circumvent the merit system. For example, some jurisdictions have variable standards on how long a position must be posted (advertised) before applicant screening can begin. At a minimum, jobs must be posted for seventy-two hours. A manager wishing to appoint a personal friend might plead with the central personnel office for a seventy-two-hour posting. The plea might be based on the critical nature of the position and the limited number of qualified candidates, largely within the agency. If approved, the short period would allow the agency to post the job on Friday afternoon in its own offices and begin screening candidates on Tuesday morning. The result is predictable: the manager notifies the preferred candidate, who may be the only applicant. In fairness, the person recruited in this fashion may be qualified for the position and do a fine job; the method of appointment, however, has only a limited resemblance to commonly accepted definitions of merit.

OUTREACH RECRUITMENT.   Public employers cannot hope to attract the best possible candidates by passive methods. Positions should be advertised in newspapers and in the electronic media. Where the community to be served is diverse, advertisements on foreign language stations may be particularly appropriate. Minority recruitment can be improved by sending recruitment teams to campus career days at high schools and colleges with significant minority populations. These efforts can be further enhanced by sending recruiters who are members of minorities. For example, President John F. Kennedy instructed the U.S. Civil Service Commission to administer the entry-level examination (the PACE) on black college campuses as part of his affirmative action order, Executive Order 10925, in 1961.

Government entities interested in selecting from the broadest possible pool of candidates have undertaken a number of innovations. One such innovation is to give examinations in the evening and on weekends, thereby increasing the chances of attracting currently employed candidates.

Another innovation is to recruit prospective employees on campuses much as aggressive private companies do. Like their private counterparts, public agencies dispatch teams to recruit promising seniors for public-service careers. Unlike their private-sector counterparts, however, government recruiting teams are unable to offer employment on the spot to outstanding candidates. The most government recruiters can do is offer candidates information packages on public-service careers and advice on how to navigate the government's application process.

Government outreach efforts are not confined to college campuses. The need for large numbers of clerical workers has encouraged some state agencies to send circuit riders to high schools to advertise the benefits of government employment. Truly innovative personnel officers have taken to waiving the requirement that all clerical applicants pass a typing speed and accuracy test administered by the personnel office. Instead, current typing-speed certifications by high school typing teachers are accepted, thus expediting the screening process. This innovation can be particularly useful for state personnel offices in rural states. The combination of circuit rider recruiters and teacher typing certifications allows state government to recruit talented young people from small towns who might not otherwise have considered state employment.

Government agencies (particularly at the state level) have also entered into cooperative agreements with state offices of employment services. When a person seeking employment visits the employment office, he or she is invited to review the current postings of state government jobs. The process is expedited by employment counselors who are knowledgeable regarding current positions and what constitutes qualifying experience. By assessing the person's education and experience, the employment counselor need only suggest those positions for which the applicant is qualified.

INTERNSHIPS. Agencies at all levels of government operate internship programs to attract promising candidates.[14] Some internships, such as the presidential management internships of the federal government, are available only to persons who have completed a master's degree. Normally, internship candidates are nominated by their education institutions and then undergo a rigorous screening process. Those selected spend two years in a mixture of revolving job assignments and training seminars at the rank of GS 9. Successful completion of the first year of an internship results in promotion to GS 11. After two years, an intern is eligible for a GS 12.

A number of state and local government entities also offer postdegree internship programs. Cities such as San Jose and Los Angeles in California; Phoenix, Arizona; Miami, Florida; and Washington, DC have used internship programs to recruit some of their most promising managers. State governments from New York to California also offer internship programs.

A number of government agencies offer pregraduation internships to undergraduate and graduate students. The interns, who are usually paid, also receive college credit for work experience. Faculty supervisors meet regularly with interns to assess their progress and counsel those experiencing difficulties. Most important from the academic point of view is for the intern adviser to relate interns' work experiences to their academic training.

Cooperation between universities and agencies has made internships meaningful learning experiences for students considering public-service careers. Such cooperation, moreover, can result in the additional benefit of faculty efforts to recruit women and minorities for government service careers. Internships are thus one of the least threatening ways for public employers to enhance the percentage of minorities and women employed in government without obstructing the rights of members of the majority.

ELECTRONIC RECRUITMENT. The Internet has revolutionized the job search in the public as well as the private sector. Those seeking a position with the federal government can visit <http://www.fedworld.gov/jobs/jobsearch.html>. There they will find a list of all current vacancies in the federal government that can be searched by job type, state, or region. Many states and their subsidiary agencies also maintain electronic databases of the open positions and, in many cases, candidates can submit their resumes on-line.

At a more advanced level, government agencies can use scanning technologies to review resumes for relevant job skills and experience in less than a second. This technology will change the way personnel agencies work and the way applicants construct their resumes. For example, computer scanning of resumes potentially can reduce the number of personnel assigned to reviewing resumes. The city of San Jose, California, contracts for the scanning services, thereby avoiding the start-up costs of purchasing equipment and training personnel. Of course, pains must be taken to ensure that city personnel determine the relevant skills and knowledge that will be programmed into the computer. Although the computer can scan resumes to find qualified candidates, real humans must conduct the interviews and make the selection decision. For their part, job candidates no longer need abbreviate their resumes. A twelve-page resume, like a one-page resume, can be scanned in the blink of an eye.

THE SCREENING PROCESS

Once the recruitment process has yielded a pool of candidates, the screening process may involve a number of elements in addition to resume assessment, such as written examinations, medical exams, reference checking, list construction, and candidate interviews.

TESTING. The use of written examinations in the public sector is a time-honored tradition that is rooted in the philosophy of scientific management.[15] This philosophy holds that there is one best way of doing every job. Proponents of scientific management believe that by carefully observing the tasks involved in a given job, the analyst can discover a more efficient way of organizing them.[16] If there is one best way to do every job, then there must also be one best person for the job. All the personnel analyst needs to do is study the position in question and devise screening criteria that will produce the best candidate. The most popular screening method in civil service is the written examination. A given exam can be specifically tailored to determine which candidates possess the requisite knowledge and reasoning skills to succeed in the position.

Examinations normally are not tailored to specific positions. Instead, personnel experts seek to develop examinations suitable for assessing abilities applicable to a range of positions. For example, arithmetic and language skills testing, along with items that test a candidate's ability to do simple reasoning tasks, are popular components of civil service exams for entry-level positions. The positions for which such an exam might screen candidates include clerical worker, file clerk, medical technician, and security guard. More complex tests aimed at abstract reasoning, sophisticated math skills, and the ability to read and interpret complex written materials might be used to screen for broad ranges of professional positions.

Broad-spectrum examinations can be questioned regarding whether they provide data sufficiently relevant to the position in question to allow meaningful comparisons among candidates. This is especially true when large numbers of candidates score within a few points of one another.

A more serious charge against such tests, however, is that the test makers are largely representative of upper-middle-class white society. The terms used in the test, therefore, reflect the middle-class experience. The resulting performance disparity between middle-class white applicants and black and Latino test takers has led to successful legal challenges to the testing system (see Chapter 3). These challenges have resulted in test revisions to eliminate items that appear to be consistent stumbling blocks only for minority candidates.[17]

Even with the elimination of biased items, the advantage remains for those who are good at taking standardized tests. Persons educated in school systems that rely heavily on standardized multiple-choice examinations will score better on standardized civil service examinations than those who lack such training.[18] Middle-aged and older candidates may find themselves at a particular testing disadvantage when competing against younger candidates with more recent test-taking experience.

For many government positions, standardized testing is of little use. For professional-level positions, the ability to write clearly and succinctly is a far more important skill that standardized exams are ill-equipped to measure. At lower echelons of government, such as custodial positions, the skills measured by the written exam may have no relevance whatsoever to the actual duties of the position.[19] The mere knowledge that a written exam is required, however, may be an impediment to otherwise qualified candidates who lack test-taking skills.

Recently, the Merit System Protection Board revisited the issue of testing. The board noted with concern that the abandonment of written exams for assessments of skills, knowledge, and experience limits an agency's ability to predict performance. Grade point average, for example, has less than 4 percent correlation with job performance for recent college graduates and even less for those who have been out of school for some time. Written tests of cognitive skills, by contrast, can have a performance predictability rate of upwards of 40 percent. The board urges agencies to invest the time and resources to develop nonbiased job-related examinations and to expand their use of such programs as the Cooperative Education Program, in which prospective employees are observed in advance of permanent employment.[20] Thus, the federal government may have come full circle to written examinations of cognitive abilities.

RANKING CANDIDATES. Before interviews begin, candidates are ranked according to their scores on the written examination or the central personnel office's assessment of their qualifying experience and education. In some jurisdictions, the central personnel office gives the examination to all qualified applicants, then conducts screening interviews to assess their fitness for the job in question. The test and interview scores are combined into a composite score that is used to construct the list.

For example, let us suppose that a recently retired army sergeant has applied for a job as a security guard for a local transit district. Suppose that the candidate achieves a score of 78 out of a possible 100 on the written test, with 70 as the minimum qualifying score. In the interview, however, the applicant reveals that 18 of his 25 years in the military were spent as a military police officer. This information might move the interviewer to assign a score of 98 to the interview portion. If the relative weights assigned to the two components are 70 percent for the written exam and 30 percent for the interview, then the former sergeant would receive a combined score of $(78 \times .70) + (98 \times .30)$, or 84.

Suppose now that the transit authority has openings for 10 guards. Suppose further that 150 persons taking the exam achieved scores of at least 70 and that 25 of those achieved scores of 90 or better. Under these circumstances, our former sergeant would be high in the ranking but still not among the realistic contenders for the position, despite his obvious qualifications that so impressed the interviewer. Not even the addition of 5 points for being an honorably discharged veteran would greatly improve his chances. (Veterans' preference is discussed later in this chapter.)

Personnel managers defend the use of written exam scores to rank candidates on the grounds that the exams do measure basic reasoning and analytic skills of value in government service. Furthermore, without some device for ranking candidates, agencies would be left with the prospect of interviewing everybody with qualifying experience, which could lead to hundreds of interviews. In circumstances such as the one described here, however, the weight of the test should be reevaluated.

INTERVIEWS. Perhaps the greatest impact a manager can have on the final selection of job candidates is in the interview process.[21] By personally interviewing all finalists (whether there are three, seven, or more), the manager can assess both the potential candidates and the effectiveness of the selection process. The latter can be judged against the overall quality of the applicant pool and the special skills of the finalists. The weight given to the interview is another matter.

For interviews to be effective screening criteria, they must elicit information that is not readily accessible in the application file, and they must be given appropriate weight.[22] Interviews are excellent for assessing worker compatibility, communication skills, and the speed with which the candidate can formulate and deliver an answer. If the position in question does not require high-level social skills, other criteria such as knowledge and experience should be weighed more heavily. Candidates' capacities for analytic thinking in a job-related situation can be assessed in a structured interview process in which they are presented with situations they are likely to encounter on the job.[23]

CLOSED VERSUS OPEN LISTS. Although still widely used, closed candidate lists are declining in popularity. In the closed system process, the position is posted, and prospective employees take the examination. Very often closed systems use assembled examinations, which means that all candidates must come together on a previously announced date to take the written portion of the examination. Candidates are then ranked, and the list is sent to the agency. The distinguishing feature of closed lists is that no new applications for the position are taken until the number of qualified candidates on the list is sufficiently depleted to warrant construction of a new list.

The advantage of closed lists is that they free the personnel office from continually screening job candidates. The disadvantage of the closed system is that the usefulness of the list decays rapidly as those on it find other employment, move out of the area, or otherwise lose interest in government employment. Few if any of these dropouts notify the personnel office that they are no longer interested. Closed lists, moreover, defeat the purpose of merit selection. A list of 200 might have no more than 25 highly qualified applicants. Thus, after a few months, declining the applications of recent applicants in all probability will lead to the hiring of mediocre employees.

A second disadvantage of the closed list is that excellent candidates must wait, sometimes for months, before they become eligible for government employment. Persons seeking work, of course, will not wait. Denying excellent candidates the opportunity to compete for government jobs while persons of lesser ability await placement from the list undermines the basic concept of merit.

This problem can be solved by making lists open and continuous for positions that experience frequent turnover (such as clerical or entry-level professional jobs). That is, qualified applicants can take the test anytime during regular business hours and be placed on the list ahead of all those with lower scores. This has the effect of enhancing the merit process and continually updating the list with interested persons. Computerized testing, moreover, provides instant scoring and list placement of the new candidate.

CANDIDATE SELECTION

The list of qualified candidates is referred to the agency, which then schedules interviews with top candidates and makes the final selection. The number of scheduled interviews depends on the agency's merit rules and the number of positions to be filled.

RULE OF THREE. Merit standards have long recognized that tests have their limits for discerning the most qualified applicant for a position. The rule of three is used by the federal government and many state and local authorities. However, many appointing authorities have expanded the rule to seven, for two reasons. First, there is often little difference in test performance among a number of candidates. Second, by expanding the rule, the probability increases that traditionally underrepresented groups will become finalists.

Under the rule, the top three candidates are considered equal on all previous factors. Thus, if candidate number one had a written test score of 99, number two had a score of 95, and number three scored 89, all are equal coming into the interview. So, the top scoring candidate cannot challenge the outcome of the interview process. The rule is most important in large organizations. In small municipalities who advertise in the local newspaper, managers may count themselves fortunate if they get an application from a single qualified candidate.

VETERANS' PREFERENCE. The federal government and most state and local governments give veterans' preference points to honorably discharged persons who served in the armed forces prior to the creation of the all-volunteer military. Veteran status is extended to persons who had 180 days of active duty before May 7, 1975. More recently, Congress has extended veterans' preference to Gulf War veterans and to those who served in the Bosnia expedition.[24] The impact of veterans' preference on women, however, is lessened, because they have the opportunity to serve in the all-volunteer military.

Additional points are awarded to disabled veterans. In some localities, a disabled veteran receives ten points; in others, disabled veterans receive absolute preference. This means that once a disabled veteran passes the examination, he or she moves ahead of all nondisabled candidates. Massachusetts operates one of the most generous veterans' preference programs, in which all veterans move ahead of nonveterans. The result is a disproportionate representation of veterans among Massachusetts state employees. The program was challenged unsuccessfully in the case of *Personnel Administrator* v. *Feeney* (1979).[25] The Supreme Court upheld the right of public employers to give hiring preference to persons who had honorably served the nation.

One problem with veterans' preference points is that there are no time or frequency limitations on their use. This places women at a disadvantage in the competition for government employment. The disadvantage is ameliorated somewhat in jurisdictions that have expanded the rule of three to a rule of seven or fifteen. Even then, however, a disabled veteran who achieves a place on the final list cannot be bypassed.

Less than scrupulous managers who wish to hire a particular candidate can sometimes circumvent the absolute veterans' preference rules. The preferred applicant is hired on an "emergency appointment" basis pending the outcome of the selection process. The anointed one is encouraged to take the test and get on the list for the position in question. The agency then requests a copy of the list from the central personnel office. If the preferred candidate is among the upper ranks of those taking the test, the candidate can be reached in the interview process. Agency personnel need only find one reason or another for not hiring those ranked ahead of the preferred candidate. If an absolute veteran is on the list, the agency simply continues the emergency appointment until some other agency hires the veteran.

MERIT RECRUITMENT AND SOCIAL EQUITY

The Congress of the United States and federal enforcement agencies have produced a plethora of statutes and regulations requiring governments and their contractors to remove barriers to the employment of women and minorities. For the most part, the courts have upheld the legality of these programs (see Chapters 3 and 4).

When it comes to implementation, however, a debate rages between affirmative action advocates and opponents over what the law and the courts will permit. Without delving into the nuances of court opinions, recruitment seems to be the phase of human resource management about which the courts are most tolerant of direct positive actions to correct past injustices.

In Chapter 3, a distinction was drawn between court-ordered set-aside programs and proactive affirmative action. The latter was defined as an extra effort to recruit and retain underrepresented groups without the use of set-aside programs. Even proactive affirmative action, however, has been criticized as antithetical to efficient operation of a merit-based employee recruitment program. Merit advocates argue that there is a fine line between encouraging line managers to recruit proactively and bringing pressure to bear on them to give hiring preference to underrepresented groups.

A precise application of merit would meticulously define selection criteria—for example, experience, education, and performance on a written test—and the weight to be given to each. Merit advocates would then rate the applicants on the criteria and select from only the top performers. Of course, there is nothing in the foregoing that would preclude agencies from making extra efforts to ensure that the minority community is fully aware of the job opening. Conflicts emerge, however, over the criteria and their weights and whether gender or ethnicity should be a consideration in the actual selection process.

CRITERIA AND THEIR WEIGHTS

Experience is the criterion most often challenged. When an agency is recruiting for middle- or entry-level jobs, strongly weighting experience may give undo advantage to white males. When a well-paid, secure government position comes open, there is a high probability that white males will constitute a disproportionate percentage of the applicants who possess the qualifying experience. This is because white males hold a disproportionate share of managerial and professional positions in the workforce. If most of the eligibles are experienced white males, the probability is low that a female or minority candidate will emerge near the top of the list.

The real issue is the amount of weight experience warrants in the recruitment process, especially for mid- and entry-level positions. The problem is that experience may not be additive. At lower echelons, two years of comparable experience may be the maximum amount that actually represents growth in knowledge and skills; any additional years may simply involve repetition of the same experience. Ten years of experience, in reality, may be two years repeated five times.

The same criticism applies to the education criterion. Again, white males have a disproportionate level of educational achievement. Education beyond that needed to perform the job may give unwarranted selection advantage to those with higher, but not necessarily relevant, educational achievement. As noted earlier, the MSPB has questioned the use of educational attainment, especially grades, in ranking candidates.

WEIGHTING GENDER AND ETHNICITY

Strict adherence to merit principles would preclude giving any weight to gender or ethnicity. Affirmative action advocates believe that, at a minimum, such considerations should be used to break ties among substantially equal candidates. Merit proponents would break such ties with a coin toss.

A more proactive stance would give weight to affirmative action considerations in assessing the qualifications of individuals. This stance is consistent with the guidance provided by the Supreme Court in the *Bakke* case,[26] in which the Court ruled that race could be used as one factor among several in determining admission to medical school. Relying on race alone, however, would result in unlawful discrimination against white applicants. The justices went on to state that all communities have need of professional services (in *Bakke,* the profession was medicine), and the best way to ensure the provision of those services is by giving weight to the applications of persons from groups underrepresented in the profession.

The same justification applies to the public service. All groups receive services and contribute taxes to pay for them. Meeting the needs of the various communities served by government may require recruitment of employees from those communities. This argument is most cogent when applied to police and fire services in immigrant communities whose residents lack English language skills, and who may distrust authorities and members of the majority. The same holds true, to a lesser degree, for such services as tax collection, social services, and public utilities.

A partial solution to the language issue is to make foreign language skills a bonus in ranking candidates. Some agencies pay a bonus to employees with the requisite language skill regardless of an employee's background. When language is essential, it can be included in the position description, thus excluding monolingual candidates.

Language is a start, but language alone cannot overcome cultural barriers. Spanish-speaking white people may be able to communicate with members of the Latino community, but most whites cannot expect to identify automatically with Latino people, and they certainly cannot serve as undercover or plainclothes police officers in that community. For that matter, undercover police services to most physically identifiable ethnic groups make ethnicity an essential consideration in the selection process for police officers.

AFFIRMATIVE ACTION AS SOCIAL POLICY

Government employers and contractors are responsible for doing everything possible to ensure equality of employment opportunity in American government and in those companies that do business with the government. Affirmative action zealots would go so far as to mandate that gender and ethnicity be given weight in much the same way as veterans' preference points. Such a system would give extra points to members of protected groups.

To date, neither Congress nor the courts have given their consent to such a system because it is viewed as potentially unfair to innocent members of the majority. As noted in Chapter 3, the courts have begun to question more ambitious efforts to achieve social equity through government hiring and contracting. In California, for example, the 1998 passage of Proposition 209 prohibited using race, gender, and so forth as criteria in government hiring, contracting, and university admissions. Such prohibitions, however, do not absolve agencies from the requirements of federal law for outreach recruitment and incorporation of affirmative action considerations into their strategic planning efforts.

PERSONNEL MANAGEMENT UNDER THE MERIT SYSTEM

Personnel management is one of the few areas of program implementation that enable career managers (especially at the middle and lower echelons) to lastingly affect their organizations. Top executives, of course, are active participants in policymaking and budget formulations. By contrast, mid-level and front-line managers, by and large, are confined to implementing policies.

Unfortunately, this potential is lost on many managers, who throw up their hands at the complexities of the merit hiring process. Managers are frustrated by the time it takes to fill a vacancy and the myriad forms required to complete an appointment. For some, the merit process is at best an obstacle to overcome and at worst a frustration to be avoided whenever possible. The traditional, cumbersome civil service system was exhibit A for those who advocated the reinvention of government in the mid-1990s.[27] Their argument that patronage and corruption the system was designed to prevent may have been overstated; nevertheless, the system was slow and in need of streamlining. Government employers simply cannot be competitive in a full employment market if they take weeks or months to make a hiring decision.

Cumbersome or not, managers who seek advancement in their careers would do well to master the process. Only by staffing one's agency or division with the most competent, hardworking, and loyal subordinates possible can one hope to shine as a manager. This is because the success of even the most inspired administrative decision is directly dependent on the enthusiasm with which rank-and-file employees implement it. Managers can best ensure employee enthusiasm by personal involvement in the recruitment and selection process.

A manager's involvement in recruitment might include identifying promising candidates through networking in professional organizations. Establishing internships with local universities is another useful tool, as is maintaining contacts with one's own university. For example, the manager of one small California city recruits interns from local institutions and from as far away as Utah. Similarly, diversity in the workforce as well as quality of hirees can be enhanced by establishing ties with universities that serve ethnically diverse student bodies.

Protectors of the passive status quo in merit recruitment might balk at such management initiatives as having the potential for nepotism or opening the door to political patronage. Such concerns are largely unfounded, because the goal of the merit system is to locate and recruit the best possible candidates. Proactive efforts by managers should enhance rather than dilute the quality of the applicant pool.

Proactive recruitment becomes a merit problem only if the manager substitutes his or her efforts for the regular merit process. If, on the other hand, the outreach effort attracts high-quality applicants, they should eventually emerge among the finalists referred to the agency from the central personnel office.

Implicit throughout the discussion of the merit system was the need for hands-on managerial involvement in every phase of the process. From drafting the position description to determining the selection criteria to conducting interviews with finalists, managers cannot simply assume that things will be done according to the merit system or in the best interest of the agency.

The importance of line-manager involvement can be illustrated with an historical example. The personnel division of a NASA research center discovered that a majority of its aerospace technicians would be eligible to retire within five years. The manager of the recruitment division consulted with the heads of the various operating divisions to get their sense of what skills were needed.

The various division chiefs concluded that the quality of research conducted at the center would benefit greatly if the recruits had a strong background in math, science, and engineering. Experience, the chiefs reasoned, was less important than education because the recruits would have to learn to do things the NASA way regardless of previous experience. The personnel office, therefore, sent recruiters on a circuit of two-year technical colleges, some of which were at a considerable distance from the facility.

The result of this effort was a raft of job inquiries from persons with exactly the skills the agency hoped to attract. The position was advertised by the Civil Service Commission, which administered the test, evaluated applicants, and sent a list of eligibles to the agency to begin the final screening process.

As it turned out, those at the top of the list were persons with several years' experience in related technical fields. Many were veterans whose qualifying experiences were in positions such as radio operator, electrical crew, or aircraft or heavy equipment repair. Almost none of the candidates with the desired educational background were high enough on the list of eligibles to have a chance of being selected.

Understandably perplexed, the personnel officer began an immediate review of the process. The reason that educationally superior candidates were not on the short list of eligibles was that nobody at NASA had bothered to inform the Civil Service Commission that the agency wanted technical education weighted most heavily. Without a clear instruction from the agency, the commission evaluated candidates primarily on the amount of qualifying experience they had.

This episode occurred before the 1978 Civil Service Reform Act, which delegated most of the recruitment function to the agencies. The shift came about, in part, because of incidents such as this. Nevertheless, the same sorts of problems can occur in large federal agencies with a centralized personnel function, and they remain common in state and local governments that have not decentralized the personnel function.

The response of some line managers is to give up in despair and leave recruitment to personnel. Taking this path means that agencies must simply accept whomever personnel sends them. The proactive approach means actively working the system—no matter how frustrating—to recruit the best possible workers.

Proactive managers, moreover, will not passively accept cumbersome policies and procedures. Even though such policies are created to preserve merit, they cannot be permitted to impede effective recruitment. In defense of central personnel agencies, it must be stated that their sometimes exclusive hegemony over the recruitment process is often the result of agencies' shunning their personnel responsibilities. If public employers hope to recruit and retain the best possible employees, a middle ground must be found. When line managers are willing and eager to involve themselves in the recruitment process, the personnel office should assist rather than resist them. Conversely, when managers are unable or unwilling to get involved, the personnel office must act on their behalf. At a practical level, this flexible approach is the most viable because most state and local government agencies are too small to operate their own full-blown personnel offices, and extreme decentralization compounds the problems of merit protection.

SUMMARY AND CONCLUSION

Public personnel recruitment in many organizations has undergone changes that border on a revolution. Innovations in technology have provided the wherewithal for recruiters to reach a wide range of candidates who may apply electronically or on paper. Computers also allow personnelists to screen the applications for qualifications and to operate open continuous lists of eligibles. Reinvention efforts, moreover, have empowered line managers to control the hiring process without sacrificing the requirements of merit.

The transition, however, is not yet complete. Many small agencies simply lack the resources to take advantage of the new technologies. Nevertheless, the growing availability of private-sector contractors who specialize in electronic recruitment services to governments can potentially expedite the hiring process at all levels of government. Moreover, insofar as merit is defined as advertising widely, government agencies who post their job announcements with electronic recruiting services can recruit on a national and international level. Doing less will make it difficult to compete with private employers for the best recruits.

RECRUITMENT EXERCISE

THE RECRUITMENT PROCESS

1. The first step in the recruitment process is to review the current position description to determine whether it matches the current configuration of duties performed by the incumbent in the position. The hiring manager may also wish to discuss with his or her colleagues any changes in organization goals or functions that may require new skills. For purposes of this exercise, we will assume that the skills listed for the position of a police officer are appropriate.

2. Second, the agency should review the position description to determine the appropriate selection criteria. In the case of a police officer, these would be divided into minimum qualifications and qualifications upon which candidates would be ranked. Minimum qualifications might include

passing a physical, having a clean driving record, and minimum education attainment. Additional credit could be given for additional education, especially education relevant to police work. Other criteria may include emotional stability and decision making under stress.

3. The selection criteria should then be weighted. Minimum qualifications, for example, might be weighted 50 percent. Other criteria would be weighted between 5 percent and 50 percent. The weights of all the criteria should sum to 100 percent.

4. Next, the selection team decides which criteria should be tapped in the interview process and which can be tested or require written submissions from the candidates.

5. Having determined the criteria to be rated in the interview process, the next step is to generate a set of questions to tap each of the interview criteria. For the selection process to be fair, each applicant should be asked questions designed to tap each of the interview criteria. For example, if a team decided that decision making under stress was an appropriate selection criterion, they might design several open-ended scenarios that an officer might face. That way, every candidate need not be asked the same question.

This classroom exercise should take between an hour and an hour and one half. Students should be divided into groups of 3 to 5 students. The groups should read and discuss the position description provided and develop selection criteria from it. Criteria should then be weighted. Students should then develop interview questions to tap the relevant criteria (about 30 minutes).

The professor should then choose candidates to undergo an interview by members of groups other than their own. Designated candidates should be asked to leave the room so that they cannot hear the questions posed to other candidates. A selection panel made up of three students from a particular group should then conduct an interview with two or more candidates and rank them on the criteria that they have selected. Each interview should be no more than 10 to 15 minutes in length.

When each group has had the opportunity to interview and rank at least two candidates, the scores given to each candidate should be posted on the board. The instructor may then conduct a discussion of the civil service system and note any scoring disparities between interview panels. The professor might also solicit from the candidates whether any of them are veterans entitled to 10 extra points.

As time allows, the professor may wish to discuss particular strengths and weaknesses displayed by particular candidates. The discussion should also include the effectiveness of interviewers in drawing out candidates, getting them to express themselves, and the ability to build on another panelist's questions.

POLICE OFFICER

JOB SUMMARY

This position is located in the Police Department. The patrol officer's major function is the enforcement of city, state, and federal laws and to protect lives and property of the citizens of Pleasantville.

Patrol Duties

1. Patrols assigned area, being alert to possible criminal activity and citizens in need of assistance. Patrol may involve vehicle operation or foot patrol.

   a. Vehicle operation is performed in accordance with department regulations for safe vehicle operation.

   b. Foot patrol includes security checks of businesses and residences for indications of criminal activity. This involves the checking of doors to be certain they are secured and alertness to other signs of criminal activity such as broken windows.

2. Enforcement of traffic laws by means of issuing citations, written warnings, and oral warnings to motorists in violation of traffic laws. Directs traffic as necessary in case of signal malfunctions, heavy traffic flow, and emergency situations such as traffic accidents, fires, etc.

3. Responds to traffic accident dispatches via two-way radio. Extricates victims from vehicles, administers first aid, directs traffic, calls ambulance, etc., as necessary.

   a. Collects evidence such as measuring skid marks, interviewing witnesses, etc.

   b. Issues citations as necessary.

4. Responds to nontraffic dispatches for disturbances, assaults in progress, prowlers, burglaries in progress, armed robberies in progress, family disputes, etc.

5. Upon arrival at the scene of events listed in 4, the officer's duties include:

   a. Intervention and suppression of mutual combat between antagonists or victims and assailants.

   b. Engages in foot searches of the vicinity for perpetrators.

   c. Apprehends felony and misdemeanor suspects in accordance with departmental regulations and state and federal laws—taking care to protect the safety of citizens.

   d. Arrests, secures, and transports suspects to the station for disposition or incarceration.

   e. Interviews witnesses, takes crime report.

   f. Secures crime scenes and summons investigators and supervisors as necessary.

   g. Advises citizens of the availability of such things as counseling services and grievance remedies available under civil law.

6. Serves warrants and subpoenas.

7. Gives testimony in court and by deposition.

Support Duties

1. Files reports.

2. Reads logs from previous shift to determine activity in the assigned patrol area.

3. Checks assigned vehicle for minor damages or mechanical malfunctions and reports same to superior officer.

4. Attends in-service training sessions as required.

JOB REQUIREMENTS

1. Knowledge of the English language in order to effectively communicate both orally and in writing.

2. Ability to make decisions based on concrete and abstract factors in stress and nonstress situations.

3. Ability to meet and deal effectively with others.

4. Knowledge of city, state, and federal laws.

5. Knowledge of all departmental regulations and procedures, such as procedures for:

   a. Responding to traffic emergencies.

   b. Responding to any type of natural or human-made emergency.

   c. Arrest, apprehension, and incarceration.

6. Proficiency in the use of firearms.

7. Knowledge of civil law and available counseling services.

8. Knowledge of procedures for testifying in court.

9. Ability to operate a vehicle safely under normal and high speeds.

10. Ability to work steadily and quickly.

11. Ability to work in all weather conditions.

12. Successful completion of 220-hour training course.

13. Successful completion of two-week orientation.

14. Successful completion of background check.

15. Successful completion of psychological testing.

OTHER SIGNIFICANT FACTS

Difficulty of Work

This position consists of work tasks that are both repetitive and variable. The incumbent makes complex decisions based on concrete and abstract factors requiring a high degree of accuracy. Decisions are frequently made under stress, and the officer is held accountable for end results. Life-and-death situations occur that may involve the risking of lives to save lives or the taking of a life.

Working Conditions

The incumbent works a 40-hour week on a rotating schedule. The incumbent is subject to constant stress while on duty due to the anticipation of emergency calls and episodic encounters with emergency and dangerous situations while on routine patrol, requiring immediate, independent action on the part of the officer.

Officers routinely encounter health and safety hazards and may occasionally be subjected to bodily harm or life-threatening situations. The incumbent is subject to emergency call out and occasionally works extended tours.

Interpersonal Relations

The patrol officer interacts with persons from all economic and social backgrounds, frequently under stressful circumstances. The officer is expected to enforce the law fairly, tactfully, and without personal rancor. The officer works closely with other governmental and nongovernmental agencies.

Physical Effort

The officer must remain in good physical condition in order to run various distances, climb, and jump or otherwise surmount various obstacles in the performance of duties. The officer may be called upon to lift and move people and heavy objects. The officer may be called upon to engage in physical combat in order to defend self and others or to effect an arrest.

Supervision Received

The officer receives work assignments from the shift supervisor who provides guidance, direction, and assistance.

NOTES AND RESOURCES

1. For an up-to-date treatment of the process, see John P. Wanous, *Organizational Entry: Recruitment, Selection, Orientation and Socialization of Newcomers* (Reading, MA: Addison-Wesley, 1992). See also Christine White, *Managing the Recruitment Process* (New York: Law and Business, 1982).

2. On corruption, see George Amick, *The American Way of Graft: A Study of Corruption in State and Local Government, How It Happens and What Can Be Done about It* (Princeton, NJ: Center for Analysis of Public Issues, 1976). See also John D. Haeger and Michael P. Weber, eds., *The Bosses* (Saint Louis: Forum Press, 1979). The classic treatment in the field is Carl R. Fish, *The Civil Service and the Patronage* (Cambridge, MA: Harvard University Press, 1920). For more recent treatments, see Bruce M. Stave and Sondra Astor Stave, eds., *Urban Bosses, Machines, and Progressive Reformers* (Malabar, FL: R. E. Krieger, 1984).

3. See Francis Sorauf, "The Silent Revolution in Patronage," *Public Administration Review* 20 (1960): 32–33. Much of the change in patronage has been motivated by court cases. See Cynthia Granta Bowman, "We Don't Want Anybody Sent: The Death of Patronage Hiring in Chicago," *Northwestern University Law Review* 86 (1991): 57–111. See also David Herman, "*Rutan v. Republican Party of Illinois* and Patronage Employment Practices: Clarification or Confusion?" *Northern Illinois University Law Review* 11 (1991): 375–409. For a treatment of the special problems faced by local elected officials in selecting municipal executives, see David N. Ammons, *Recruiting Local Government Executives: Practical Insights for Hiring Authorities and Candidates* (San Francisco: Jossey-Bass, 1989).

4. See Wilbur C. Rich, *The Politics of Urban Personnel Policy: Reformers, Politicians and Bureaucrats* (Port Washington, NY: Kennikat Press, 1982).

5. This was substantially the case in *Elrod et al.* v. *Burns et al.,* 427 U.S. 347 (1976), where sheriff's office employees could keep their jobs by producing a sponsor on the Cook County Democratic Central Committee. The Supreme Court ruled the practice unconstitutional.

6. See Frank M. Bryan, *Political Parties in Rural States: People, Parties and Process* (Boulder, CO: Westview Press, 1981). See also William Crotty, ed., *Political Parties in Local Areas* (Knoxville: University of Tennessee Press, 1986).

7. Maureen Smith, "Innovative Personnel Recruitment/Changing Workforce Demographics," *IPMA News* (March 2000): 12–14.

8. See Lyle Yorks and David A. Whitsett, *Scenarios of Change: Advocacy and the Diffusion of Job Redesign in Organizations* (New York: Praeger, 1989).

9. For a detailed discussion, see Sidney Gael, ed., *The Job Analysis Handbook for Business, Industry and Government* (New York: Wiley, 1988); and Kurt Landau and Walter Rohmert, eds., *Recent Developments in Job Analysis: Proceedings of the International Symposium on Job Analysis* (New York: Taylor and Frances, 1989).

10. The decentralization of the function is particularly dramatic when combined with noncareer appointments by political executives. See Patricia W. Ingraham, "Building Bridges or Burning Them? The President, the Appointees and the Bureaucracy," *Public Administration Review* 47 (1987): 425–35.

11. The 1978 Civil Service Reform Act altered the definition of merit to include equal employment opportunity as the second of its nine principles of merit. The first was to recruit from a broad pool of candidates. For a discussion of what agencies are undertaking, see: Ronald D. Sylvia and Peter J. Haas, "Affirmative Action in Municipal Government, Political, Structural and Demographic Determinants of Alternative Strategies," *Social Science Journal* 35, no. 4 (October 1998): 615–25.

12. See Paul Schofield, "Local Government Job Ads: The Good, the Bad and the Ugly," *Personnel Management* 24, no. 4 (April 1992): 41–45.

13. Diversity notwithstanding, employers must treat minorities first and foremost as qualified candidates. See Jennifer J. Laabs, "Affirmative Outreach," *Personnel Journal* 70, no. 5 (May 1991): 86–92.

14. For a complete report, see U.S. Office of Personnel Management, *Report on the Presidential Management Intern Program* (Washington, DC: U.S. Government Printing Office, 1989).

15. Frederick W. Taylor, "The Principles of Scientific Management," in Jay Shafritz and J. Steven Ott, eds., *Classics of Organization Theory*, 2nd ed. (Monterey, CA: Brooks/Cole, 1987).

16. The job analysis process is part and parcel of classification and can be combined with organization planning and design in the process known as job design. See Jai Ghorpade, *Job Analysis: A Handbook for the Human Resource Director* (Englewood Cliffs, NJ: Prentice-Hall, 1988).

17. See Bernard R. Gifford, ed., *Test Policy and Test Performance: Education, Language and Culture* (Boston: Kluwer, 1989). See also Don Rubin, "Cultural Bias Undermines Assessment," *Personnel Journal* 71, no. 5 (May 1992): 47–53.

18. On the impact of test items, see Michael G. Aamodt and Teige McShane, "A Meta-Analytic Investigation of the Effect of Various Test Item Characteristics on Test Scores and Test Completion Time," *Public Personnel Management* 21 (1992): 151–60.

19. The Supreme Court set forth its rules on job relevance and screening criteria in *Griggs* v. *Duke Power and Light Co.*, 401 U.S. 424 (1971).

20. Merit System Protection Board, "Employee Selection Methods Need to be Better," *Issues of Merit* (Washington, DC: MSPB, 1999): 1–4.

21. For a detailed discussion, see Robert L. Dipboye, Gerald R. Ferris, and Kendrith M. Rowland, eds., *Selection Interviews: Process and Perspectives* (Cincinnati: South-Western, 1992).

22. Gerald T. Gabris and Steven M. Rock, "Situational Interviews and Job Performance: The Results in One Public Agency," *Public Personnel Policy* 20 (1991): 469–80.

23. Daniel Christopher and Sergio Valencia, "Structured Interviewing Simplified," *Public Personnel Management* 20 (1991): 127–36.

24. Section 2108 of U.S. Code Title 5 provides for veterans preferences as part of the Military Authorization Act. The act also extends preference to widows of veterans and to mothers of those killed in combat provided they are widows themselves or no longer married to the soldier's father and have not remarried. The full text of the act can be accessed at <http://www.4.law.cornell.edu/uscode/5/2108.text.html>.

25. *Personnel Administrator* v. *Feeney*, 422 U.S. 256 (1979).

26. *The Regents of the University of California* v. *Bakke*, 98 U.S. 2733 (1978). In *Bakke*, race could be a factor in admission decisions, but it could not be the only factor.

27. David Osborne and Ted Gaebler, *Reinventing Government: How the Entrepreneurial Spirit is Transforming the Public Sector* (Reading, MA: Addison-Wesley, 1992).

CLASSIFICATION SYSTEMS

"Position classification is a term of art whose meaning and purpose are not immediately obvious to most people, even though its underlying concepts are quite prosaic."[1]

Classification systems grew out of a desire to impose order on the morass of positions that make up government agencies. As noted in the human resource planning chapter, the number and types of positions in organizations ideally should be tied to the agency's mission. For example, a branch welfare office serving an estimated 3,200 clients might require a supervisor, four social workers, eight eligibility workers, and four general clerical employees. Appropriate staffing levels are determined by the nature of the work to be performed. Fortunately, the planners of this hypothetical office need only define the service levels necessary and make staffing plans based on agency experience with client–staff workload ratios. The relationship of the various positions, one to another and to other positions in the organization, is determined by the agency's classification system.

Classification also involves attaching appropriate pay to positions in government. In an enterprise as vast as government, chaos would ensue if the pay of employees were determined in direct negotiations with their supervisors. Such a system could result in substantial inequities in the salaries of persons doing identical work for different supervisors. A uniform classification system is therefore necessary to assure like rewards for like positions.[2]

TYPES OF CLASSIFICATION SYSTEMS

The types of available classification systems fall into three broad categories: rank in person, rank in the corps, and rank in position. Each of these will be discussed in turn.

RANK IN PERSON

Private-sector organizations, and a growing number of public agencies, operate two-tier systems of classification that assess the value of managers on a case-by-case basis. Nonmanagerial workers are grouped into job classes in which persons with similar duties receive the same pay rate with some recognition of seniority and previous performance. Often, the wages of these employees are prescribed by union contracts. Rank-in-person systems used to determine the relative worth of professional and managerial employees are much more complex.

Rank in person designates a system that determines the pay of individuals on a case-by-case basis. The pay one receives may be a recognition of actual contributions to the organization, or it may reflect a judgment by management that the person in question has demonstrated intellectual or leadership qualities that will benefit the organization in the future. For example, recent engineering graduates who come highly recommended by their professors may receive initial salaries designed to ensure that the recruits will remain with the organization until they realize their full potential. Similarly, a seasoned engineer possessing a successful track record on previous projects for another company may be recruited by offering a substantial salary increase, stock options, and so forth.[3]

Rank-in-person systems allow for market forces by paying more to valued employees or promising recruits, in part to keep them happy and out of the hands of competitors. The executive/managerial recruitment industry is substantial. Many placement specialists make their living locating quality employees and luring them away from their employers on behalf of competing companies.

Rank-in-person systems also allow organizations to differentially reward managers at the same hierarchical level to compensate for demonstrated leadership qualities and initiative or to ensure the retention of gifted employees for future leadership roles.

These systems place employees in the position of negotiating individual services contracts. Employees also expend considerable time and energy worrying about whether their pay is equitable, given their perceptions of their individual contributions to the organization. Some employees engage in elaborate schemes to learn the salaries of those they believe to be their peers. Management theorists warn that the amount of one's salary is less important than its relationship to that of one's perceived peers in forming judgments about salary fairness. Thus, a salary differential of a few hundred dollars between peers can be devastating to morale. Worse still is the disruption that can occur if an individual learns that he or she is paid less than another whose performance is considered to be less contributory to the organization's success than his or her own.[4] Ironically, the perceived inequality can cause lower-paid but valuable employees to leave an organization even when their actual salaries are relatively high for the industry.

Although generally associated with private companies, these systems are growing in popularity in the nonprofit and public sectors. Rank-in-person systems exist, for example, in many private and public universities.[5] Individual faculty members negotiate their initial salaries, and yearly raises are awarded based on the university's assessment of individual performances and potential contributions.

As in industry, these universities would prefer that individual salaries be kept private, because what is important to universities is that members believe that their salaries are just. For example, a professor who receives an 8 percent raise and a letter of praise could be satisfied unless he or she learns that a peer received the same letter and a 10 percent raise. Public universities rarely achieve the privacy end because salary records are open to anyone who cares to look. Thus, the specter of disgruntlement often looms large in the not-so-nonmaterialistic halls of ivy.

Rank-in-person salary systems are also coming into wider use in state and local government. Such top-level public executives as city managers, their assistants, the heads of special districts, and state-level program chiefs and their top assistants all negotiate their salaries. Here again, the compensation packages are open to scrutiny by the media, interested citizens, or disgruntled peers. Therefore, even though their salaries are negotiable, public administrators must take care to ensure that the amount is not out of line with standards acceptable to the public and its elected representatives.

A recent case in point was the resignation of the head of the United Way of America. When the amount of his salary and perks became public knowledge, many local chapters refused to forward their agreed-upon payments to the national office. The outcry occurred even though the organization had grown and prospered under his leadership.[6]

Few public administrators are given to excess. Most lack the budgetary autonomy to negotiate salaries that are out of line with comparable state agencies or nearby municipalities. Nevertheless, public-sector rank-in-person systems have made it possible to negotiate executive compensation packages that can attract highly skilled managers who otherwise might not consider careers in government. The flexibility of these systems, moreover, extends beyond salaries to include such items as retirement contributions, expense accounts, housing, and car allowances.

An incoming city manager might receive an ample base salary, a contribution to an individual retirement account, individual and family health-care coverage, moving expenses, and car and telephone allowances. Obviously, considerable flexibility exists in the amount of pay and the form taken by that payment. A more rigid system governs the compensation received by persons employed under rank-in-the-corps and rank-in-position systems.

RANK IN THE CORPS

The rank-in-the-corps system is generally associated with commissioned officers in the military services.[7] The idea behind the system is to inspire a sense of esprit de corps by grouping individuals with like amounts of seniority and competency into a single pay grade. Each year, a fresh crop of second lieutenants is commissioned. Those who demonstrate appropriate leadership skills and potential for advancement become first lieutenants, much like a graduating class; those without the appropriate military potential are encouraged to seek careers in the civilian sector.

When the time is right, the group advances to the rank of captain. However, differentiations are made among candidates based on their performance as lieutenants, and some are promoted sooner than others. Of course, a certain attrition occurs as some leave the service for other careers and the military again finds it necessary to separate those who do not show the requisite potential for continuation. This is often accomplished by denying promotion to captain on two separate occasions. The military hopes that individuals who are passed over twice get the message. Being passed over for promotion a third time results in automatic separation.

The process is repeated, with some achieving the rank of major and others being passed over. The military uses the selecting out process to accommodate the narrowing organizational pyramid that occurs naturally at the upper echelons of the hierarchy. There are not enough major slots to accommodate every captain who desires to become a major. With the end of the Cold War, the military underwent serious downsizing that required a pruning at all levels within each branch of the service. Regular officers were given preference over reserve officers, and additional credit was given to officers who had graduated from the military academies. Those who were separated were given generous allowances to compensate them for ending their military careers before being eligible for retirement.

The aspect of the rank-in-the-corps system that is of importance to classification is that all officers at a given rank receive the same base pay regardless of their duties. A captain employed in intelligence gathering is paid at the same basic grade as one who commands troops or pilots jets. Those whose duties involve personal risk, such as pilots and paratroopers, receive a bonus for the hazardous component of their assignment. If reassigned to a nonhazardous position, however, they lose the bonus.

Other exceptions to the rank-in-the-corps pay system are hard-to-fill critical-need positions such as nuclear engineers, who are vital to the navy's mission, and medical doctors, who earn so much in the private sector that the military finds it necessary to pay a doctor's bonus. By and large, however, the exceptions are few, and pay is determined by rank, not by duties and responsibilities.

In the resulting system, pay is a matter of indifference, and neither time nor energy is lost seeking to learn the salaries of others.

RANK IN POSITION

By far the most common classification system at all levels of government is rank in position. Under this system, the duties and responsibilities of the position and the qualification necessary to perform them are evaluated to determine the pay of the incumbent. Thus, no matter what educational degrees one possesses, no matter what special training and skills, no matter how glib or reticent the incumbent, the pay received is determined by the needs of the position. Thus, a person with a college degree who took a position as a clerk typist in a government agency would be compensated only as a typist, regardless of his or her educational achievements.

Persons with similar duties and responsibilities are grouped into such job titles as police officer, personnel specialist, program analyst, and eligibility worker. Persons with similar but not identical duties are collectively referred to as a job class. Thus, police officers and firefighters might be classed as public safety officers. Persons from a variety of job titles and classes may be grouped together into the same rank in an organizationwide or governmentwide salary scheme. Normally, however, uniformed personnel are compensated using ranking systems that recognize the uniqueness of their special training and the physical risk associated with their positions.

Other employees of the same unit of government are often grouped into a common salary scale. Thus, billing clerks in the office of the county tax assessor, the secretary to the county administrator, and ward clerks at the county medical center might all be grouped together in a clerical job class. The salaries paid to clericals could put them in the same pay grade as maintenance workers, ambulance dispatchers, and so forth.

How often employees are evaluated varies considerably with the size of the agency and the resources available for the classification function. Small counties and municipalities, for example, rarely examine their classification systems simply because their personnel offices are small, overworked units that must prioritize between reviewing classification systems and the demands of recruitment and testing, labor relations, administering the retirement and benefits systems, and complying with federal and state equal employment and employee safety requirements. The situation has improved somewhat with the introduction of computers. Small entities can also receive salary survey data from their professional associations that permit overall comparisons of their salary schedules. Such aggregate data are less useful for determining the value of individual positions because workers can increase their duties and responsibilities via individual initiatives.

Full-blown reviews of all positions are rare and are usually contracted out to consulting firms that specialize in classification. These evaluations are often the result of pressure from women's groups or labor unions who perceive the interests of their particular clientele as being ill-served by the current system.

On the other hand, large municipalities, urban counties, and state governments often maintain elaborate personnel offices that employ highly competent classification specialists.[8] These specialists routinely undertake classification reviews of individual positions, and classification units engage in systematic reviews of entire agencies upon request or during periodic review cycles.

How individual positions are evaluated and assigned to a given pay scale will be discussed in later sections of this chapter. Regardless of the specific technique employed, however, most echelons of American state and local government have accepted rank in position as the fairest and most equitable means for determining the salaries of their employees; so, too, has the federal government.

CLASSIFICATION IN THE FEDERAL CIVILIAN SERVICE

Uniformity in the federal service came about with the Classification Act of 1923. A Classification Board, then housed in the Civil Service Commission, was given the responsibility for administering the classification system.[9] The commission added classification to its other duties, such as recruitment and protection of the merit system. The complexity of the classification task grew along with government. The 1949 Classification Act, therefore, assigned overall classification authority to the Civil Service Commission but delegated the actual classification task to the agencies.[10] Much the same arrangement continues under the Office of Personnel Management.

Not all federal employees are under the uniform classification system. Exempt employees include those in the Department of State and various intelligence agencies as well as employees of the Congress, the federal judiciary, and the president's personal staff. The military services, of course, are not covered, and the postal service operates its own personnel system. In addition, separate wage systems are operated for federal blue- and white-collar employees. The total civilian federal workforce in 1998 was 2.7 million. Of these, 871,500 were employed by the U.S. Postal Service. Of the remainder, the Department of Defense employed 718,000. The remaining roughly 1.1 million are spread among the rest of federal agencies. These figures represent a ten-year decline of roughly 43,000 people or approximately 1.5 percent.[11]

OPM administers the broad classification grades (GS 1 through 18) and the criteria whereby a position would fall into a given grade. The agencies analyze their positions and assign the appropriate grade.

The terminology in the federal system of classification is the same as in other echelons of government, largely because the latter have emulated the federal system to be eligible for federal funding of programs.[12] A large number of positions entailing substantially the same duties and responsibilities constitute a job class. A pay grade in the federal service may contain a number of job classes of similar complexity and requiring similar levels of skills and qualifications. Thus, a groundskeeper for the General Services Administration might be a GS 3 along with a clerk typist at Defense and a roustabout in a crew for the Bureau of Land Management.

CLASSIFICATION AS A DYNAMIC SYSTEM

Individuals under rank-in-position systems can affect the classification of their positions. Talented people may seek additional responsibilities and can then seek a reclassification from the personnel office of the agency. Getting reclassified to a higher grade is facilitated by having the support of a supervisor willing to corroborate the change of duties and responsibilities. Even supervisory support may not result in a reclassification if the classification specialist deems the change in duties and responsibilities insufficient. When this happens, the employee can appeal to the head of the classification unit or to the centralized classification agency for the federal government, the Office of Personnel Management.

Support from one's supervisor is also important in the appeals process, especially within the agency. With or without supervisory support, however, employees have the right to challenge their current job class. Frequently, this is done with the help of a public employee labor union.

A successful appeal of a classification decision may not always result in a position reclassification. Because of budgetary limitations, monies frequently are unavailable in a given year to pay for a reclassification. A successful appeal can thus result in a reassignment to less interesting duties rather than a raise.

In one actual case, a GS 12 federal employee believed that over the years his responsibilities had become sufficiently challenging to warrant an upgrade to the rank of GS 13. He approached his supervisor who, while agreeing that the increase was warranted, noted that funding for the increase was not available in the current budget. The would-be GS 13 rejected the supervisor's suggestion that he delay his request until the next budget cycle, when the supervisor promised to be supportive.

The employee petitioned for an immediate reclassification. The agency's classification division determined that the duties indeed were those of a GS 13. The agency's budget officer, however, informed the employee he would have to wait until funding was available.

Determined to have immediate justice, the employee appealed the matter to the then Civil Service Commission. The commission ordered that the agency either grant an immediate increase in grade to GS 13 or restructure the employee's position to reflect duties appropriate to his current pay grade of GS 12. Unfortunately for the employee, his superiors chose to restructure his duties by removing those responsibilities that the employee found challenging and interesting—the same duties that warranted the promotion. The employee was thus left with a rather pedestrian set of GS 12 duties that were not likely to change during his tenure in the position.

JUSTIFYING A RECLASSIFICATION. Classifiers are most sympathetic to a reclassification when the duties and responsibilities become more complex and require greater skills and abilities. They are less sympathetic to classification petitions based on volumes of work. That is, one cannot succeed in getting a reclassification to a higher grade simply by producing more of the same. Superior performance should be rewarded by a within-grade pay increase. When an employee's impact on his or her position is to such a degree that a reclassification is appropriate, the reclassification normally lasts until the incumbent leaves. At that point the position reverts to its old grade level unless managers can convince personnel that the reclassification should be continued.

PAY RAISES WITHIN THE SAME RANK. Under most rank-in-position classification systems, superior performers are rewarded by step increases within their current grades. This is made possible by the fact that each grade of the classification scheme is divided into steps. The federal GS system is divided into ten steps, each of which represents a pay increase. Satisfactory performers advance one step each year.

STEP INCREASES AND MERIT. The step system was originally intended to recognize and reward merit. Marginally satisfactory and deficient performers were not to receive the raise.

In many systems, increases are thought of as the legitimate right of all employees who remain in their positions. As the systems were envisioned, supervisors would have to identify an employee as a superior performer to warrant the increase. As the systems have evolved, however, a supervisor must justify the withholding of a step increase to a nonperformer.

REWARDING LONGEVITY. In fairness to those who work in the system, one must acknowledge that there is something to be said for longevity awards. Employees who work away in the trenches of the bureaucracy understand how things are done and why. Employees come to know whom to call to resolve this or that problem. They also remember what has been tried in the past with success and what has failed. Thus, senior workers become valuable assets to the organization simply by continuing in their current positions. Presumably they become more efficient and require less supervision.

A number of organizations recognize and reward the loyalty represented by longevity by providing their employees with an annual longevity bonus based on their years of service. Using bonuses has the further advantage of not building longevity into the base pay of employees.[13]

THE TECHNIQUES OF CLASSIFICATION

WHOLE-JOB EVALUATION SYSTEMS

Whole-job evaluation is a relatively unsophisticated system of job evaluation. It involves ranking positions from the most to the least valuable based on the evaluator's subjective perceptions. Its simplicity of application is limited to relatively small organizations; it is impractical for large organizations with complex divisions of labor and multiple job categories.

POSITION CLASSIFICATION SYSTEMS

Position classification systems, found most often in government, elevate classification to an art form. This approach utilizes a uniform set of job evaluation criteria to evaluate a position: the *qualifications* necessary to assume the position, the *duties* of the position, and the *responsibilities* of the incumbent. The job class into which a position is placed and the salary the incumbent receives are functions of the configuration of qualifications, duties, and responsibilities. These are weighed by the evaluator against uniform standards that dictate the rank and pay to which the incumbent is entitled.

QUALIFICATIONS. Qualifications include formal education, specialized training, and official certifications. Some qualifications are general, such as requiring a college degree in any of several subjects. For example, an eligibility worker announcement may call for a bachelor's degree in social work, sociology, psychology, or a closely related discipline. Other positions require highly specialized training in medicine, engineering, or law, or a graduate degree in public administration or social work. Some positions may require the added qualification of state licenses.

DUTIES. The complexity of the duties associated with a position is the second factor that affects its value. The duties of a police officer, for example, might include enforcing state and local laws, directing traffic, responding to nontraffic dispatches, serving warrants and subpoenas, and giving testimony in court. The duties of the manager of a county mental health unit might include policy administration, conducting therapy with patients, supervising a staff of five professionals and fifteen paraprofessionals, and the routine preparation of reports.

RESPONSIBILITIES. Responsibilities, which may overlap somewhat with the duties category, are the program activities and components for which the incumbent is held accountable. Our mental health unit manager might be responsible for the effective administration of all program activities within the unit as well as for preparing the budget document and making specific policy recommendations to his or her superiors in the organization.

Classifiers at various levels of government undergo dozens of hours of in-depth classification training along with carefully supervised on-the-job training before being allowed to autonomously evaluate a given position. For years, this training involved reading the classification manual of the agency, examining a specific position, and attempting to arrive at an appropriate classification determination. The principles of classification were specific in theory but vague in application. The actual classification of a given position allows considerable discretion on the part of the classifier, who makes a good-faith effort to be fair to the incumbent of the position while preserving the integrity of the position classification system.

BENCHMARK FACTOR SYSTEMS

To the layperson, the traditional classification process is largely a mystery. To understand the system one simply had to work in it. Many private- and public-sector employers have now adopted quantitatively based classification systems, known variously as benchmark factor and point factor systems. Their use began early in this century as part of the scientific management movement.[14]

These systems apply standardized benchmark descriptions of qualifications, duties, and responsibilities. For each criterion, a set of standardized benchmark descriptions are applied to jobs from the lowest worker to the chief executive officer. The number of factors used may range from 5 to 15.[15] Under "complexity of decision-making responsibilities," for example, the lowest benchmark might state: "The incumbent makes simple choices requiring little or no interpretation of standardized policies and procedures." At the upper end, the benchmark might state: "The incumbent makes complex decisions which have long-term impact on program success, using abstract concepts and reasoning where information is limited."

Benchmark factor systems are used to assess individual positions, as in the case of an employee seeking a classification upgrade. Frequently, however, point factor systems are used to assess whole organizations to equalize the pay of workers in various job classes whose organizational contributions are judged comparable.

What follows is a step-by-step description of how such a study might be conducted. The federal government currently uses nine factors in its point factor evaluation system:

Factor 1, Knowledge Required by the Position

Factor 2, Supervisory Controls

Factor 3, Guidelines

Factor 4, Complexity

Factor 5, Scope and Effect

Factor 6, Personal Contacts

Factor 7, Purpose of Contacts

Factor 8, Physical Demands

Factor 9, Work Environment

Most of the foregoing are self-evident, however, Factor 3, Guidelines, refers to the parameters that the organization places around the individual's ability to make decisions using desk manuals and policies and procedures. The more freedom allowed, the more points received. Factor 5, Scope and Effect, refers to the depth and breadth of the work assignment and its impact in and outside the organization. Factors 6 and 7 are highly interrelated, and a classifier is normally expected to assign the same weight to each. Factor 6, Personal Contacts, looks at with whom the employee has contact on a regular basis and the type of information that is exchanged. Thus a secretary who calls agency managers and union officials to schedule a meeting with a hearing examiner receives fewer points than the examiner who meets with the same people to discuss contract interpretation, work rules, administrative procedures, and so forth.[16] The complete list of the factors and benchmark definitions used by the federal service are included in the classification exercise at the end of the chapter.

CHOOSING A SYSTEM.   The first step in the process is to choose a job evaluation system that meets the needs of the organization. Several variables should guide the organization's decision. Some point factor systems are proprietary and require the consent of the developers.[17] Other systems, notably those developed by the federal government for its own use or for use by state and local governments, may be used without charge.[18]

Two other considerations in the choice of a job evaluation system are organization time and resources. If the study must be done quickly, the organization may wish to use a consultant to conduct the job evaluations. If, on the other hand, the organization intends to adopt a quantifiable job evaluation system for ongoing use, it may want to spend the necessary time to train its own human resource management staff in a particular methodology.

POSITION ASSESSMENT SURVEYS.   Each employee receives a questionnaire that asks for a listing of the duties and responsibilities of his or her position and the qualifications that the incumbent must possess. Specific information is requested on the primary duties, responsibilities, and qualifications necessary to the position. Specific topics in the survey include requests for information on the financial responsibilities of the position, the number and types of persons supervised, and so forth. Job analysts evaluate these questionnaires and assign points to various responses.

Other sections of the questionnaire ask with whom the employee communicates regularly and what these communications involve. More points are assigned for policy-making communications than for communications that seek guidance and instruction or that comply with routine reporting requirements. For example, a senior-level social worker who routinely consults with the agency director regarding policy receives more communication points than a social worker whose primary contact is with clients.

Finally, the questionnaire seeks to identify the types of decisions that the incumbent makes. The decisions of a truck driver might include the selection of routes to take and decisions about the safety of the vehicle and needed maintenance. The head of the transportation department would make more complicated decisions regarding the purchase of equipment, duty assignments of employees, and the order in which work is to be accomplished, as well as personnel and budgetary decisions.

When the survey method is used, individual employees have an impact on the evaluation of their contributions that ultimately will determine their pay grades. The survey team also consults with supervisors to determine if the duties and responsibilities reported in the employee questionnaires are accurate.

The questionnaires of persons whose positions have the same title are compared so that multiple position descriptions need not be written. There are cases, however, in which an individual employee performs duties and has responsibilities that are significantly different from those of his or her peers. A clerk typist 3 who works for a department head, for example, might take responsibility for tasks that exceed those of other employees with the same job title. When this occurs, a reclassification to, say, executive assistant is in order. Such reclassifications normally result in pay increases.

Persuading employees to respond to the job survey is more critical in position surveys than in other survey research projects. If public opinion pollsters do not get a high response rate, they must question the reliability of their findings and interpret the findings with caution. A job survey team, however, cannot afford to miss a single person. Employees who refuse to participate or do not return their questionnaires in a timely fashion may read the results of a comprehensive job survey only to learn that their positions have been eliminated. Supervisors must be careful to fill out the survey for vacant positions. Normally, a follow-up survey is necessary to ensure that everybody participates—including those who ignored the first-round questionnaire. Desk audits by subject matter experts and consultations with supervisors are needed to ensure the accuracy of survey responses.

POSITION ANALYSIS. The next step in the process is to assess individual positions and assign points for the various components. This step varies with the methodology used. In some methodologies, points are assigned to positions based on the reviewer's assessment of the questionnaire. That is, evaluators have a range of points that they can assign for a particular criterion, such as decision complexity or financial responsibility.

The more common approach is to assess the position using benchmark definitions of the type described earlier. The evaluator reviews the questionnaire (or position description, in some approaches), then compares this information to the established benchmarks. Thus, the process has two steps. First, the evaluator determines the appropriate benchmark for each criterion. The points associated with each benchmark are predetermined. After all benchmarks have been applied to a given position, the total points are calculated.

POSITION DESCRIPTIONS. The analyst need not rewrite a position description when the purpose of the analysis is to determine whether a specific employee is entitled to a raise in salary. Frequently, all that is necessary is to change the title. For example, a secretary 1 might petition for a reclassification to a secretary 2 position based upon his or her evolving duties. If the reclassification is warranted, all that may be necessary is to designate the position a secretary 2.

If, on the other hand, the analysis is part of a revamping of the entire classification system, new position descriptions are required for every job class. Normally, the classification team need not draft a new description for each position. Police officers, for example, constitute a large job class, and only one police officer description is needed. The class would include officers engaged in patrol activities or who work in the jail as well as those assigned to the canine unit or plainclothes duty. Separate descriptions would be written for seasoned officers with broader duties such as training and supervising new officers. Separate descriptions would also be needed for detectives, whose duties are substantially different from patrol officers, and police managers and supervisors of advanced rank.

Once position descriptions have been developed and appropriate point values assigned, the classification team can undertake the critical and sometimes controversial business of constructing a pay scale.

CONSTRUCTING A PAY SCALE

There are basically two approaches to constructing a pay scale: the bottom-up approach and the benchmark-position approach. The simpler bottom-up approach will be described first.

BOTTOM-UP SCALES

The classifiers, in consultation with management, first tentatively decide the number of pay grades that are appropriate for the organization. This number can be changed later if the estimate proves unrealistic. The number of positions included in each grade is determined by multiplying the base position by a predetermined spreader factor. An example of how the spreader factor is used will illustrate not only how the system works but why it is so important to choose a spreader factor based on organization needs and a concern for equity.

HOW THE SPREADER FACTOR WORKS.   Suppose that an organization chooses a 10 percent spreader factor. The first pay grade is constructed by calculating 10 percent of the adjusted score assigned to the lowest position in the organization. If the lowest job score is 160 points, the analyst will determine the adjusted value of the position by subtracting the minimum possible score from 160. This step is necessary because the minimum score would be assigned if a worker did nothing more than show up for work each day. Let us suppose that the minimum score in the system we are using is 35. The true value of the lowest position, then, is 160 minus 35, or 125.

The range of points that fall within pay grade 1 is determined by multiplying the adjusted score by the spreader factor: $125 \times .10 = 12.5$. The result is rounded up to the nearest whole number, and 13 points are added to the lowest score of 160. Grade 1, therefore, will include all positions whose point value falls between 160 and 173.

Grade 2 is arrived at using the same procedure: subtracting the minimum value from the bottom of the grade, multiplying by the spreader factor, and adding the result to the base number. In this example, $174 - 35 = 139$, and $139 \times .10 = 13.9$. Rounding the result to 14 means that grade 2 will range from 174 to 188. Notice that the range of point values included in a grade increases with each calculation because the base number is larger. The result is that at the upper end of the scale many more positions are accounted for in each succeeding grade.

CHOOSING A SPREADER FACTOR.   The appropriate spreader factor is neither cast in stone nor scientifically derived. The smaller the spreader factor is, the fewer positions will fall into a particular pay grade. The more pay grades there are in a system, the more opportunities there will be for justifying pay distinctions between classes of workers. Conversely, increasing the spreader factor collapses larger numbers of positions into the same grade. When job studies occur in union environments, the size of the spreader factor can occasion considerable debate because of its impact on raise opportunities.

The choice of a spreader factor is based on many factors—the number of echelons in the organization, the degree of job specialization, and so forth—and is normally decided by the classifiers in consultation with agency managers. These deliberations may also include union officials, representatives of women's groups, and such political decision makers as members of the city council, representatives of the mayor's office, or state legislators. Broadening participation in the formulation of decision criteria enhances acceptance of the findings. Regardless of who participates in the spreader factor decision, it should be made before the pay scale is constructed to avoid even the appearance that those in authority might be manipulating the outcome. Anytime an agency undertakes a comprehensive review of its classification system, it is well advised to bring labor unions into the process as early as possible. Labor unions have a tendency to distrust complex classification schemes that they may not fully understand. Normally, unions favor smaller spreader factors that result in multiple grades containing multiple steps that allow for maximum worker advancement. On the other hand, unions tend to resist classification schemes that attempt to eliminate steps or grades in the interest of broadening the flexibility of management in assigning work. Management's flattened hierarchy that collapses job classes and pay grades in the name of worker empowerment and team approaches to problem solving may mean a flatter paycheck and an inability to advance to a rank-and-file union member.

PAY AND GRADE.   Under a bottom-up system, appropriate pay for each grade can be determined by applying a flat percentage increase from one grade to the next. Thus, positions in pay grade 2 might receive 6 percent more than positions in pay grade 1. Positions in grade 3, in turn, would receive 6 percent more than grade 2, and so forth.

Of course, the percentage differential may be an appropriate topic for union bargaining just as the actual base pay attached to a grade is negotiable. Another factor that may affect the construction of a pay scale is any previous use of pay steps within grades.

The bottom-up method is most appropriate for small organizations with a limited number of positions. The method may also be useful in ad hoc situations such as when the object is to equitably realign the pay between firefighters and police officers. These simple multiplier approaches lose some of their value for more complex organizations. If, for example, a state wishes to equalize the pay of traditionally male- and female-dominated positions, the analysis should include a salary survey of other employers to consider market forces. Determining the fair market value of every position in a state government would be time-consuming and prohibitively expensive. The alternative is to use benchmark positions.

BENCHMARK POSITIONS

The difference between the benchmark-positions and bottom-up approach lies in how the pay for the various grades is determined. The benchmark-position alternative selects a number of positions from all strata of the organization, taking care to ensure that they are representative of the diversity of skills and responsibilities in the hierarchy. Next, classifiers determine the economic value of benchmark positions by surveying similar employers. Once the survey has been completed, the salaries of the benchmark positions can be adjusted in light of their market value.[19] The salaries of other positions within the same grade are also adjusted accordingly.

THE SALARY SURVEY.   The survey assesses the market by contacting other employers in the city, state, or region regarding the appropriate value for each of the benchmark positions. It must be constructed with care because the resulting salary scale will have a major economic impact on the organization and may meet with stiff resistance from employee groups.

The extensiveness of the survey depends on the size and resources of the organization and the availability of comparable pay information. A metropolitan bank, for example, might confine its inquiry to other banks in the same city. A city might survey other cities with comparable populations, economic conditions, and so forth. Finding a comparable city nearby, however, can be difficult in regions of the country with few population centers.

A city government might seek information on county, state, and federal wages, or it might survey local private-sector employers or use Department of Labor data to determine the competitiveness of city wages in the local marketplace.[20] Public/private-sector matches can be difficult because many public positions—not only uniformed services, but urban planners, housing inspectors, recreation specialists, and others—lack private-sector counterparts.

Similarly, state governments may wish to compare their salaries with those of other states in the region, local governments, and federal employees, as well as comparable private-sector positions. Such breadth ensures an accurate reflection of the total job market rather than relying solely on either public or private comparisons.[21] For example, state accountants may seem grossly underpaid if compared only with those in private firms. Many private accountants, however, are entrepreneurial developers of customers, and many are partners with profit-sharing benefits and loss risks not found in the public sector. State salaries may be much more in line with the pay of local and federal accountants. The same is also true of physicians employed by government hospitals that could not hope to match the earnings of specialists in private practice.

The contents of the survey must seek information on the total compensation of the positions surveyed. A municipality, for example, might pay its truck drivers two to three dollars less per hour than the unionized employees of large trucking firms in the region. Part of the pay of privately employed union truck drivers, however, goes directly to the union, which in turn provides the workers with insurance and retirement benefits. When government fringe benefits are included in the comparisons, the compensation of government truck drivers is more favorable.[22] The same sorts of pay and benefit considerations apply to unionized members of such skilled trades as carpenter, electrician, and pipe fitter. Public employees in the skilled trades, moreover, are not subject to seasonal layoffs.

The federal government sets the wages of its skilled trades by comparisons to local labor markets. Salary comparability of other federal employees to the private sector is determined by the president based on the recommendations of the Federal Salary Council. These decisions are supported by data gathered by the Office of Personnel Management. And, as noted above, national and local salary information is routinely collected by the Department of Labor.

POINT FACTOR SYSTEMS. These systems operate much like the benchmark factor systems.[23] The principal difference is that each point assigned to a position represents an increment in salary. Thus, when the analysts finish their review of a position, its salary is determined. Such a system does not lend itself to the construction of position classes nor to the collective negotiation of salaries.

There exists the possibility that, during the analysis, the classifier will adjust the point values assigned to a job in order to keep the final salary in line with the evaluator's preconceived idea of the position's value. Tampering with point values is also possible in the benchmark factor system, but the two steps in the benchmark system lend it greater objectivity.

ONGOING APPLICATIONS AND ISSUES

Comprehensive evaluations of employee salaries are much too expensive to conduct on a regular basis. The salaries of some professionals, such as nurses, however, are subject to more frequent changes than those of other public employees. Thus, government nursing salaries might be comparable to those paid by private medical facilities at the time of the survey but fall dramatically behind the market in subsequent years.

Such pitfalls can be avoided by ongoing monitoring of Department of Labor data on regional trends. When salaries for a given specialty fall behind the trend, they must be adjusted; otherwise, governments may experience difficulty in recruiting and retaining workers in high-demand specialties.

Quantifiable systems, with their benchmark definitions and salary surveys, are rapidly gaining acceptance at all levels of government. The ability to factor in market forces can be especially useful in achieving appropriate compensation systems.

These quantified systems of job evaluation, however, are sources of controversy for two reasons. First, the reliance on quantification is criticized as further dehumanizing an already bureaucratic working environment.[24] Second, the systems are at the center of the comparable worth debate.

HUMANISTIC CONSIDERATIONS

Despite its appeal to the women's movement and labor unions based on comparable worth considerations, benchmark methodology can be criticized on humanistic grounds. Critics of bureaucracy point out that the reduction of government services to predetermined work routines limits the amount of discretion and creativity that government workers can exercise in their positions. Government workers, moreover, are thought by some to be unappreciated for their individual contributions. Instead, they are treated as interchangeable parts of a great bureaucratic machine that cares as little for the individual worker as it does for the agency's clients, who are reduced from the status of persons to case numbers.[25]

Nowhere is this more evident than in point factor classification systems. The analysis in such systems is of the content of the position rather than the contribution of its incumbent. The position is broken down into its component parts, and points are assigned to each part. The whole value of the occupant is the sum of the various subcomponents of the position.

Under this system, a position can be broken down by duties and responsibilities and reformulated to achieve a grade outcome without consideration for the impact on the incumbent. An example of this was described previously in the restructuring of the position of a GS 12 in response to his request for a reclassification. In that example, the restructuring was done purposefully in response to the classification appeal. Such restructuring can also occur on a larger scale in the design or redesign of an organization.

When a point factor system is used, no consideration is given to loyalty, dedication, or willingness to contribute more than the minimum requirements to the mission. (These sorts of extra efforts by career bureaucrats are much more frequent than is acknowledged by the popular press.) Long hours or a willingness to come in on the weekend or holidays to complete a project count for nothing. Because the point factor system cannot systematically account for these individual contributions, it leaves them out of the classification decision.

Another criticism of point factor systems is the relative value placed on the various criteria. Decision complexity and supervisory and financial responsibilities are valued more highly than physical effort and job hazards. In fact, danger and discomfort often account for less than 5 percent of the classification decision.

One might argue, with some justification, that managerial decision making is more highly valued in point factor systems than other work factors precisely because it is so valued in our business-oriented culture. Be that as it may, one would be hard pressed to convince firefighters (the most dangerous occupation in the U.S.) or garbage collectors (one of the dirtiest) that their contribution is so small in comparison to managers who work in climate-controlled offices. Equally plausible is the argument that job evaluation systems overvalue the contribution of managers because those who design and conduct the job evaluation study are themselves members of the managerial professional class and because managers authorize payment for the study. Ironically, factors such as contacts and communication skills that give the advantage to managers, also benefit the clerical workers with whom they work.

SUMMARY AND CONCLUSION

Traditionally, the distinctions between rank in person, rank in the corps and rank in position were clear, but no longer. Rank in person is no longer a private-sector phenomenon, as more and more public executive positions lose their civil service status. The down side for these employees is that they are now at-will employees serving at the pleasure of their supervisors. On the upside, they can negotiate individual compensation packages far beyond what is traditional in the public sector.

The distinctions between rank in the corps and rank in position are being diluted by the necessity for extra pay for specialized skills in the military. On the civilian side, programs such as the Presidential Management Internship recruit entry-level professionals who are advanced through their first two grades as a cohort. In effect, these interns operate under rank in the corp.

Classification systems have become more quantified. Previously, classification was an art form in which the classifier attended training to obtain the requisite sensitivity to the relationship between a given job skill or cluster of skills and the appropriate pay grade in the organization. Benchmark factor systems have substantially altered the task of the classifier. Ironically, the combination of talent, experience, and analytic skills that constituted classification has been broken down into its component parts so that the techniques can easily be taught and learned.

A second-order benefit of using benchmark factor systems is their applicability across positions whose contents are very different. This has resulted in an equalizing of pay between traditionally female- and male-dominated positions. In effect, benchmark factor systems have brought about de facto comparable worth as a classification standard in agencies that use them.

A CLASSIFICATION EXERCISE

In this exercise students will go through the actual process of evaluating positions using the U.S. Government's point factor system. The exercise will take about an hour. Students should be divided into groups of 3–5 students. They should then individually read the two position descriptions provided. Groups will then apply the factor criteria provided and collectively decide on the benchmark and points warranted by a given position. For example, if the group believes that the appropriate knowledge benchmark for the secretary is Level 1–2: *Knowledge of basic or commonly-used rules, procedures, or operations that typically require some previous training or experience,* then a point value of 200 would be applied. When all nine factors have been applied, the points for each can be totaled, which will determine the appropriate GS grade for the position.

The instructor will then provide students with the grade that the federal classifiers actually assigned to the position, and the class can discuss any variance between their rating and the federal answer. Normally, first-time classifiers tend to over-value the knowledge, skills, and responsibilities contained in the position description.

The instructor may also wish to have a discussion of the fairness of the various point values that are possible and the relative weights given to executive decision complexity and the value given those who work under extreme conditions or whose jobs are quite dangerous.

POSITION 1

Standard Position Description

Classification Title: Secretary (OA)
Organizational Title: Division Secretary (OA)
Organizational Location: Servicewide
Position Information:

Standard Position Description

(This position is one grade level below the full-working-level Secretary, and requires closer supervision than that described in the full-working-level position description.)

Introduction:

Provides principal administrative and clerical support to a division chief or supervisor of an equivalent organization and is the recognized authority on division administrative policies and procedures.

Major Duties:

Receives telephone calls and personal visitors. Refers those not requiring the manager's personal attention to appropriate office. Provides information on office functions to those from other organizations and advises manager of contacts which are of a sensitive nature.

Establishes overall policies and procedures for correspondence control and routing, requests for personnel actions, travel arrangements, files administration, and internal memoranda throughout all levels of the office.

Provides advice, assistance, and training to secretaries and clerical support positions in the subordinate organizational segments; and reviews, coordinates, and assembles the work products of subordinate counterparts as required.

Screens incoming correspondence and routes to the appropriate organization, establishing specific response dates and maintaining and monitoring suspense dates.

Maintains a calendar of appointments and commitments for the manager and provides pertinent informational items for conferences and meetings. Makes all necessary travel arrangements for the manager and/or his/her designees.

Performs other duties as assigned.

Knowledge:

Knowledge of the organization's programs, responsibilities, policies, priorities, commitments, and structure to provide effective administrative and clerical assistance.

Functional knowledge of other organizational segments to provide advice and direction to subordinate counterparts on administrative support functions such as preparation of correspondence and mail routing.

Knowledge of agency regulations, directives, and procedures pertinent to establishment, maintenance, and retention of office files, requisition of supplies and equipment, travel, and preparation of correspondence.

Knowledge and ability to effectively operate a variety of office automation equipment such as personal computers and printers. A fully qualified typist is required.

Effective communication skills to advise and train subordinate secretaries, interact with peers, and respond and provide information to officials within and outside the organization.

Standard Position Description

Knowledge of Security, Disclosure and Privacy Act procedures to provide guidance to subordinate clerical staff and other personnel within the office.

Knowledge of spelling, grammar, punctuation, formatting, and capitalization to prepare and review correspondence.

Work Situation: B The staff is organized into subordinate segments and is directed through intermediate supervisors. The subordinate groups differ from each other in various aspects, and formal internal procedures and administrative controls require extensive coordination between the office and subordinate levels.

Level of Difficulty:

The employee receives closer supervision than what is normally incurred at the full working level. The supervisor makes assignments, sets priorities, deadlines, and objectives and assists on assignments, as needed. Additional, detailed instructions are provided for new, difficult, or unusual assignments. Incumbent independently organizes and carries out recurring work, referring only problems and unfamiliar situations not covered by instructions to the supervisor for help. The supervisor assures that completed work is accurate and in compliance with instructions. Guidelines for most administrative aspects of the work include agency manuals, policy statements, and local office procedures. The guidelines do not cover many of the work situations encountered and thus require the incumbent to exercise considerable judgment. The incumbent is expected to recognize the need for and develop internal procedures and directives for use by secretaries in subordinate segments of the organization. The incumbent establishes complex internal administrative policies and procedures for subordinate secretarial and clerical positions and is required to consolidate reports and correspondence that require input from more than one branch. Work is normally sedentary and takes place in an office setting.

Assignment:

Guidance and advice provided to counterparts in subordinate organizational segments impact on the administrative efficiency of the division as well as the effective operation of the entire office.

Communications:

Contacts are with managers and employees in the division and counterparts in other organizations. Occasional contacts occur with officials at all levels of the organization as well as with representatives from other agencies, private concerns, taxpayers, media representatives, and elected officials. Contacts are to coordinate the administrative and clerical functions of the office and its subordinate organizations.

POSITION 2

Internal Revenue Service
Standard Position Description

Title: Tax Technician
Organizational Title: Tax Auditor (Tax Shelter)
Location: District Examination Division, Examination Support Staff

Exempt Merit Pay: No Bargaining Unit Status
Duties and Responsibilities Approved: 11/23/81

Duties

The incumbent serves as a Tax Auditor in the Examination Support Staff in the Office of the Chief, Examination Division. In this capacity, the incumbent serves as a member of a team of Revenue Agents, Tax Technicians, and support personnel engaged in monitoring and controlling 918-A and tax shelter returns. The program is designed to prevent fraudulent or sham transactions resulting in tax abuse, and to assure uniformity and consistency in the examination and disposition of shelter cases. The incumbent participates in the coordination, control, and identification of abusive tax shelter schemes and devices.

More specifically, the incumbent performs the following duties:

Assists in the identification, control, and coordination primarily of individual returns associated with the Tax Shelter Program, and 918-A cases aimed at minor areas of noncompliance with tax laws.

Classifies individual returns before placing them in suspense for issues other than the tax shelter issue.

Prepares Statutory Notices of Deficiency for cases in which either the taxpayer has refused to extend the statute or the taxpayer cannot be located or does not respond to IRS correspondence, for those cases in the Staff.

Analyzes returns and supporting data to determine whether adjustments other than those directly related to the program will be required. May prepare examination report on appropriate key case explaining the justification for technical determinations and adjustments.

When the key case is closed, determines adjustments to be made to income, credits, expenses, deductions, etc. claimed on returns, and prepares written technical reports of examination explaining justification for determinations and adjustments. Cases examined involve legal, financial, investigative, or valuation issues of a minor nature.

Upon closing of the key case, determines the appropriate disposition of the case through the administrative process based on the technical issues involved and the facts and circumstances in each case.

Communicates with taxpayers and their representatives to discuss case issues, resolve problems, and attempt to reach agreement on adjustments.

1. Knowledge Required by the Position

Knowledge of basic accounting principles, practices and terminology. Problems encountered are characteristically minor or average, and may involve controversial points of law mingled with related factual and accounting issues.

Knowledge of Internal Revenue Code, Internal Revenue Manual, and other applicable statutes and guidelines, as well as precedent setting cases.

General knowledge of business conditions and trade practices to permit analysis and evaluation of reasonableness and validity of items of income, expense, and deduction.

Skill in dealing and negotiating with taxpayers and their representatives, who are specialists in their fields, and persons of considerable professional attainment. Mature tact, diplomacy, and technical competence are essential.

2. Supervisory Controls

The incumbent works under the general supervision of the Chief, Examination Support Staff. Assignments are performed without direct technical supervision although the Chief, Examination Support Staff is available for discussions on policy interpretations, selection of alternatives on key issues, and application of precedents. Completed cases are reviewed for adequacy, sound judgment, and consistency with law, regulations, and IRS procedures.

3. Guidelines

Specific guidelines are few in number, consisting primarily of portions of the Internal Revenue Code, Internal Revenue Manual, court decisions and precedents, and written communications from the National Office regarding various projects. The incumbent is, of course, guided by statutes, manuals, etc., but some situations may require the incumbent to interpret these broadly stated, nonspecific guides to cover specific cases and issues at hand. For major issues, precedents are normally directly applicable.

4. Complexity

The work is technical in nature, involving the administrative aspect of the District's tax shelter program. Because of magnitude and diversity, specific tax shelters frequently cross district and regional lines, creating many administrative problems. Cases are typified by average interrelationships of legal, factual, and accounting issues, and the extent of business activities of particular taxpayers can largely be determined on the basis of logic and the application of general business and accounting knowledge.

5. Scope and Effect

Work involves the administration and control of tax shelter returns that are designed to assure the examination of abusive tax shelters. Programs are designed to assure uniformity and consistency in the agency's approach to abusive tax shelters. Determinations made affect the internal operations of the district, current and future tax liabilities of significant numbers of taxpayers nationwide who have engaged in abusive tax practices, and may have significant deterrent effects on other taxpayers in the community.

6. Personal Contacts

Personal contacts include agency personnel both within the district and in other districts and regions, and taxpayers and their professional representatives. Taxpayer contacts are frequently persons of considerable professional attainment, position, personal wealth, and political or business connections.

7. Purpose of Contact

The purpose of contacts is to assist in planning and coordinating the District's tax shelter program, to advise various individuals associated with the program of progress or operating problems, to disseminate information, and to motivate individuals working toward the objective of controlling abusive tax shelters. Contacts with taxpayers and their representatives are to explain and justify actions taken by the agency on taxpayer accounts.

8. Physical Demands

There are no unusual physical requirements.

9. Work Environment

Work is performed in an office setting.

Primary Standard

The Primary Standard serves as a standard-for-standards for the Factor Evaluation System (FES). Factor-level descriptions for position classification standards are point-rated against the Primary Standard. Thus, it serves as a basic tool for maintaining alignment across occupations.

The Primary Standard has descriptions of each of the nine FES factors and the levels within each factor as well as the point values appropriate for each level. The nine factors are:

Factor 1, Knowledge Required by the Position
Factor 2, Supervisory Controls
Factor 3, Guidelines
Factor 4, Complexity
Factor 5, Scope and Effect
Factor 6, Personal Contacts
Factor 7, Purpose of Contacts
Factor 8, Physical Demands
Factor 9, Work Environment

Factor 1, Knowledge Required by the Position

Factor 1 measures the nature and extent of information or facts that a worker must understand to do acceptable work, e.g., steps, procedures, practices, rules, policies, theories, principles, and concepts, and the nature and extent of the skills needed to apply this knowledge. To be used as a basis for selecting a level under this factor, a knowledge must be required *and* applied.

Level 1-1—50 points Knowledge of simple, routine, or repetitive tasks or operations that typically include following step-by-step instructions and require little or no previous training or experience;

OR

Skill to operate simple equipment or equipment that operates repetitively, requiring little or no previous training or experience;

OR

Equivalent knowledge and skill.

Level 1-2—200 points   Knowledge of basic or commonly-used rules, procedures, or operations that typically require some previous training or experience;

OR

Basic skill to operate equipment requiring some previous training or experience, such as keyboard equipment;

OR

Equivalent knowledge and skill.

Level 1-3—350 points   Knowledge of a body of standardized rules, procedures, or operations that require considerable training and experience to perform the full range of standard clerical assignments and resolve recurring problems;

OR

Skill, acquired through considerable training and experience, to operate and adjust varied equipment for purposes such as performing numerous standardized tests or operations;

OR

Equivalent knowledge and skill.

Level 1-4—550 points   Knowledge of an extensive body of rules, procedures, or operations that require extended training and experience to perform a wide variety of interrelated or nonstandard procedural assignments and resolve a wide range of problems;

OR

Practical knowledge of standard procedures in a technical field, requiring extended training or experience, to perform such work as adapting equipment when this requires consideration of the functioning characteristics of equipment; interpreting results of tests based on previous experience and observations (rather than directly reading instruments or other measures); or extracting information from various sources when this requires considering the applicability of information and the characteristics and quality of the sources;

OR

Equivalent knowledge and skill.

Level 1-5—750 points   Knowledge (such as would be acquired through a pertinent baccalaureate educational program or its equivalent in experience, training, or independent study) of basic principles, concepts, and methodology of a professional or administrative occupation, and skill in applying this knowledge in carrying out elementary assignments, operations, or procedures;

OR

In addition to the practical knowledge of standard procedures in Level 1-4, practical knowledge of technical methods to perform assignments such as carrying out limited projects that involve use of specialized complicated techniques;

OR

Equivalent knowledge and skill.

Level 1-6—950 points
Knowledge of the principles, concepts, and methodology of a professional or administrative occupation as described at Level 1-5 that has been either: (a) supplemented by skill gained through job experience to permit independent performance of recurring assignments, or (b) supplemented by expanded professional or administrative knowledge gained through relevant graduate study or experience, that has provided skill in carrying out assignments, operations, and procedures in the occupation that are significantly more difficult and complex than those covered by Level 1-5;

OR

Practical knowledge of a wide range of technical methods, principles, and practices similar to a narrow area of a professional field, and skill in applying this knowledge to such assignments as the design and planning of difficult, but well-precedented projects;

OR

Equivalent knowledge and skill.

Level 1-7—1250 points   Knowledge of a wide range of concepts, principles, and practices of a professional or administrative occupation, such as would be gained through extended graduate study or experience, and skill in applying this knowledge to difficult and complex work assignments;

OR

A comprehensive, intensive, practical knowledge of a technical field, and skill in applying this knowledge to the development of new methods, approaches, or procedures;

OR

Equivalent knowledge and skill.

Level 1-8—1550 points   Mastery of a professional or administrative field to:
- Apply experimental theories and new developments to problems not susceptible to treatment by accepted methods;

OR

- Make decisions or recommendations significantly changing, interpreting, or developing important public policies or programs;

OR

Equivalent knowledge and skill.

Level 1-9—1850 points   Mastery of a professional field to generate and develop new hypotheses and theories;

OR

Equivalent knowledge and skill.

Factor 2, Supervisory Controls

Supervisory Controls covers the nature and extent of direct or indirect controls exercised by the supervisor, the employee's responsibility, and the review of completed work. Controls are exercised by the supervisor in the way assignments are made, instructions are given to the employee, priorities and deadlines are set, and objectives and boundaries are defined. Responsibility of the employee depends upon the extent to which the employee is expected to develop the sequence and timing of various aspects of the work, to modify or recommend modification of instructions, and to participate in establishing priorities and defining objectives. The degree of review of completed work depends upon the nature and extent of the review, e.g., close and detailed review of each phase of the assignment; detailed review of the finished assignment; spot-check of finished work for accuracy; or review only for adherence to policy.

Level 2-1—25 points For both one-of-a-kind and repetitive tasks the supervisor makes specific assignments that are accompanied by clear, detailed, and specific instructions.

The employee works as instructed and consults with the supervisor as needed on all matters not specifically covered in the original instructions or guidelines.

For all positions the work is closely controlled. For some positions, the control is through the structured nature of the work itself; for others, it may be controlled by the circumstances in which it is performed. In some situations, the supervisor maintains control through review of the work. This may include checking progress or reviewing completed work for accuracy, adequacy, and adherence to instructions and established procedures.

Level 2-2—125 points The supervisor provides continuing or individual assignments by indicating generally what is to be done, limitations, quality and quantity expected, deadlines, and priority of assignments. The supervisor provides additional, specific instructions for new, difficult, or unusual assignments, including suggested work methods or advice on source material available.

The employee uses initiative in carrying out recurring assignments independently without specific instruction, but refers deviations, problems, and unfamiliar situations not covered by instructions to the supervisor for decision or help.

The supervisor assures that finished work and methods used are technically accurate and in compliance with instructions or established procedures. Review of the work increases with more difficult assignments if the employee has not previously performed similar assignments.

Level 2-3—275 points The supervisor makes assignments by defining objectives, priorities, and deadlines; and assists the employee with unusual situations that do not have clear precedents.

The employee plans and carries out the successive steps and handles problems and deviations in the work assignment in accordance with instructions, policies, previous training, or accepted practices in the occupation.

Completed work is usually evaluated for technical soundness, appropriateness, and conformity to policy and requirements. The methods used in arriving at the end results are not usually reviewed in detail.

Level 2-4—450 points The supervisor sets the overall objectives and resources available. The employee and supervisor, in consultation, develop the deadlines, projects, and work to be done.

The employee, having developed expertise in the line of work, is responsible for planning and carrying out the assignment, resolving most of the conflicts that arise, coordinating the work with others as necessary, and interpreting policy on own initiative in terms of established objectives. In some assignments, the employee also determines the approach to be taken and the methodology to be used. The employee keeps the supervisor informed of progress and potentially controversial matters.

Completed work is reviewed only from an overall standpoint in terms of feasibility, compatibility with other work, or effectiveness in meeting requirements or expected results.

Level 2-5—650 points The supervisor provides administrative direction with assignments in terms of broadly defined missions or functions.

The employee has responsibility for independently planning, designing, and carrying out programs, projects, studies, or other work.

Results of the work are considered technically authoritative and are normally accepted without significant change. If the work should be reviewed, the review concerns such matters as fulfillment of program objectives, effect of advice and influence on the overall program, or the contribution to the advancement of technology. Recommendations for new projects and alteration of objectives usually are evaluated for such considerations as availability of funds and other resources, broad program goals, or national priorities.

Factor 3, Guidelines

This factor covers the nature of guidelines and the judgment needed to apply them. Guides used in General Schedule occupations include, for example, desk manuals, established procedures and policies, traditional practices, and reference materials such as dictionaries, style manuals, engineering handbooks, and the pharmacopoeia.

Individual jobs in different occupations vary in the specificity, applicability, and availability of the guidelines for performance of assignments. Consequently, the constraints and judgmental demands placed upon employees also vary. For example, the existence of specific instructions, procedures, and policies may limit the employee's opportunity to make or recommend decisions or actions. However, in the absence of procedures or under broadly stated objectives, employees in some occupations may use considerable judgment in researching literature and developing new methods.

Guidelines should not be confused with the knowledge described under Factor 1, Knowledge Required by the Position. Guidelines either provide reference data or impose certain constraints on the use of knowledge. For example, in the field of medical technology, for a particular diagnosis there may be three or four standardized tests set forth in a technical manual. A medical technologist is expected to know these diagnostic tests. However, in a given laboratory the policy may be to use only one of the tests; or the policy may state specifically under what conditions one or the other of these tests may be used.

Level 3-1—25 points   Specific, detailed guidelines covering all important aspects of the assignment are provided to the employee.

The employee works in strict adherence to the guidelines; deviations must be authorized by the supervisor.

Level 3-2—125 points   Procedures for doing the work have been established and a number of specific guidelines are available.

The number and similarity of guidelines and work situations require the employee to use judgment in locating and selecting the most appropriate guidelines, references, and procedures for application and in making minor deviations to adapt the guidelines to specific cases. The employee may also determine which of several established alternatives to use. Situations to which the existing guidelines cannot be applied or significant proposed deviations from the guidelines are referred to the supervisor.

Level 3-3—275 points   Guidelines are available, but are not completely applicable to the work or have gaps in specificity.

The employee uses judgment in interpreting and adapting guidelines such as agency policies, regulations, precedents, and work directions for application to specific cases or problems. The employee analyzes results and recommends changes.

Level 3-4—450 points   Administrative policies and precedents are applicable but are stated in general terms. Guidelines for performing the work are scarce or of limited use.

The employee uses initiative and resourcefulness in deviating from traditional methods or researching trends and patterns to develop new methods, criteria, or proposed new policies.

Level 3-5—650 points   Guidelines are broadly stated and nonspecific, e.g., broad policy statements and basic legislation that require extensive interpretation.

The employee must use judgment and ingenuity in interpreting the intent of the guides that do exist and in developing applications to specific areas of work. Frequently, the employee is recognized as a technical authority in the development and interpretation of guidelines.

Factor 4, Complexity

This factor covers the nature, number, variety, and intricacy of tasks, steps, processes, or methods in the work performed; the difficulty in identifying what needs to be done; and the difficulty and originality involved in performing the work.

Level 4-1—25 points   The work consists of tasks that are clear-cut and directly related.

There is little or no choice to be made in deciding what needs to be done.

Actions to be taken or responses to be made are readily discernible. The work is quickly mastered.

Level 4-2—75 points   The work consists of duties that involve related steps, processes, or methods.

The decision regarding what needs to be done involves various choices that require the employee to recognize the existence of and differences among a few easily recognizable situations.

Actions to be taken or responses to be made differ in such things as the source of information, the kind of transactions or entries, or other differences of a factual nature.

Level 4-3—150 points   The work includes various duties involving different and unrelated processes and methods.

The decision regarding what needs to be done depends upon the analysis of the subject, phase, or issues involved in each assignment, and the chosen course of action may have to be selected from many alternatives.

The work involves conditions and elements that must be identified and analyzed to discern interrelationships.

Level 4-4—225 points   The work typically includes varied duties that require many different and unrelated processes and methods such as those relating to well-established aspects of an administrative or professional field.

Decisions regarding what needs to be done include the assessment of unusual circumstances, variations in approach, and incomplete or conflicting data.

The work requires making many decisions concerning such things as interpretation of considerable data, planning of the work, or refinement of the methods and techniques to be used.

Level 4-5—325 points   The work includes varied duties requiring many different and unrelated processes and methods that are applied to a broad range of activities or substantial depth of analysis, typically for an administrative or professional field.

Decisions regarding what needs to be done include major areas of uncertainty in approach, methodology, or interpretation and evaluation processes that result from such elements as continuing changes in program, technological developments, unknown phenomena, or conflicting requirements.

The work requires originating new techniques, establishing criteria, or developing new information.

Level 4-6—450 points   The work consists of broad functions and processes of an administrative or professional field. Assignments are characterized by breadth and intensity of effort and involve several phases pursued concurrently or sequentially with the support of others within or outside of the organization.

Decisions regarding what needs to be done include largely undefined issues and elements and require extensive probing and analysis to determine the nature and scope of the problems.

The work requires continuing efforts to establish concepts, theories, or programs, or to resolve unyielding problems.

Factor 5, Scope and Effect

Scope and Effect covers the relationship between the nature of the work, i.e., the purpose, breadth, and depth of the assignment, and the effect of work products or services both within and outside the organization.

In General Schedule occupations, effect measures such things as whether the work output facilitates the work of others, provides timely services of a personal nature, or impacts on the adequacy of research conclusions. The concept of effect alone does not provide sufficient information to properly understand and evaluate the impact of the position. The scope of the work completes the picture and allows consistent evaluations. Only the effect of properly performed work is to be considered.

Level 5-1—25 points The work involves the performance of specific, routine operations that include a few separate tasks or procedures.

The work product or service is required to facilitate the work of others; however, it has little impact beyond the immediate organizational unit or beyond the timely provision of limited services to others.

Level 5-2—75 points The work involves the execution of specific rules, regulations, or procedures and typically comprises a complete segment of an assignment or project of broader scope.

The work product or service affects the accuracy, reliability, or acceptability of further processes or services.

Level 5-3—150 points The work involves treating a variety of conventional problems, questions, or situations in conformance with established criteria.

The work product or service affects the design or operation of systems, programs, or equipment; the adequacy of such activities as field investigations, testing operations, or research conclusions; or the social, physical, and economic well-being of people.

Level 5-4—225 points The work involves establishing criteria; formulating projects; assessing program effectiveness; or investigating or analyzing a variety of unusual conditions, problems, or questions.

The work product or service affects a wide range of agency activities, major activities or industrial concerns, or the operation of other agencies.

Level 5-5—325 points The work involves isolating and defining unknown conditions, resolving critical problems, or developing new theories.

The work product or service affects the work of other experts, the development of major aspects of administrative or scientific programs or missions, or the well-being of substantial numbers of people.

Level 5-6—450 points The work involves planning, developing, and carrying out vital administrative or scientific programs.

The programs are essential to the missions of the agency or affect large numbers of people on a long-term or continuing basis.

Factor 6, Personal Contacts

This factor includes face-to-face contacts and telephone and radio dialogue with persons not in the supervisory chain. (NOTE: Personal contacts with supervisors are covered under Factor 2, Supervisory Controls.) Levels described under this factor are based on what is required to make the initial contact, the difficulty of communicating with those contacted, and the setting in which the contacts take place (e.g., the degree to which the employee and those contacted recognize their relative roles and authorities).

Above the lowest level, points should be credited under this factor only for contacts that are essential for successful performance of the work and that have a demonstrable impact on the difficulty and responsibility of the work performed.

The relationship of Factors 6 and 7 presumes that the same contacts will be evaluated for both factors. Therefore, use the personal contacts that serve as the basis for the level selected for Factor 7 as the basis for selecting a level for Factor 6.

Level 6-1—10 points   The personal contacts are with employees within the immediate organization, office, project, or work unit, and in related or support units;

AND/OR

The contacts are with members of the general public in very highly structured situations, e.g., the purpose of the contact and the question of with whom to deal are relatively clear. Typical of contacts at this level are purchases of admission tickets at a ticket window.

Level 6-2—25 points   The personal contacts are with employees in the same agency, but outside the immediate organization. People contacted generally are engaged in different functions, missions, and kinds of work, e.g., representatives from various levels within the agency, such as headquarters, regional, district, or field offices, or other operating offices at the immediate installation;

AND/OR

The contacts are with members of the general public, as individuals or groups, in a moderately structured setting. For example, the contacts generally are established on a routine basis, usually at the employee's workplace; the exact purpose of the contact may be unclear at first to one or more of the parties; and one or more of the parties may be uninformed concerning the role and authority of other participants. Typical of contacts at this level are those with persons seeking airline reservations or with job applicants at a job information center.

Level 6-3—60 points   The personal contacts are with individuals or groups from outside the employing agency in a moderately unstructured setting. For example, the contacts are not established on a routine basis; the purpose and extent of each contact is different; and the role and authority of each party is identified and developed during the course of the contact. Typical of contacts at this level are those with people in their capacities as attorneys; contractors; or representatives of professional organizations, the news media, or public action groups.

Level 6-4—110 points The personal contacts are with high-ranking officials from outside the employing agency at national or international levels in highly unstructured settings, e.g., contacts are characterized by problems such as that the officials may be relatively inaccessible; arrangements may have to be made for accompanying staff members; appointments may have to be made well in advance; each party may be very unclear as to the role and authority of the other; and each contact may be conducted under different ground rules. Typical of contacts at this level are those with members of Congress, leading representatives of foreign governments, presidents of large national or international firms, nationally recognized representatives of the news media, presidents of national unions, state governors, or mayors of large cities.

Factor 7, Purpose of Contacts

In General Schedule occupations, the purpose of personal contacts ranges from factual exchanges of information to situations involving significant or controversial issues and differing viewpoints, goals, or objectives. The personal contacts that serve as the basis for the level selected for this factor must be the same as the contacts that are the basis for the level selected for Factor 6.

Level 7-1—20 points The purpose is to obtain, clarify, or give facts or information regardless of the nature of those facts; i.e., the facts or information may range from easily understood to highly technical.

Level 7-2—50 points The purpose is to plan, coordinate, or advise on work efforts or to resolve operating problems by influencing or motivating individuals or groups who are working toward mutual goals and who have basically cooperative attitudes.

Level 7-3—120 points The purpose is to influence, motivate, interrogate, or control people or groups. The people contacted may be fearful, skeptical, uncooperative, or dangerous. Therefore, the employee must be skillful in approaching the individual or group in order to obtain the desired effect, such as gaining compliance with established policies and regulations by persuasion or negotiation, or gaining information by establishing rapport with a suspicious informant.

Level 7-4—220 points The purpose is to justify, defend, negotiate, or settle matters involving significant or controversial issues. The work usually involves active participation in conferences, meetings, hearings, or presentations involving problems or issues of considerable consequence or importance. The people contacted typically have diverse viewpoints, goals, or objectives requiring the employee to achieve a common understanding of the problem and a satisfactory solution by convincing them, arriving at a compromise, or developing suitable alternatives.

Factor 8, Physical Demands

The Physical Demands factor covers the requirements and physical demands placed on the employee by the work assignment. This includes physical characteristics and abilities, e.g., specific agility and dexterity requirements, and the physical exertion involved in the work, e.g., climbing, lifting, pushing, balancing, stooping, kneeling, crouching, crawling, or reaching. To some extent the frequency or intensity of physical exertion must also be considered, e.g., a job requiring prolonged standing involves more physical exertion than a job requiring intermittent standing.

Level 8-1—5 points The work is sedentary. Typically, the employee may sit comfortably to do the work. However, there may be some walking; standing; bending; carrying of light items such as papers, books, or small parts; or driving an automobile. No special physical demands are required to perform the work.

Level 8-2—20 points The work requires some physical exertion such as long periods of standing; walking over rough, uneven, or rocky surfaces; recurring bending, crouching, stooping, stretching, reaching, or similar activities; or recurring lifting of moderately heavy items such as typewriters and record boxes. The work may require specific, but common, physical characteristics and abilities such as above-average agility and dexterity.

Level 8-3—50 points The work requires considerable and strenuous physical exertion such as frequent climbing of tall ladders, lifting heavy objects over 50 pounds, crouching or crawling in restricted areas, and defending oneself or others against physical attack.

Factor 9, Work Environment

The Work Environment factor considers the risks and discomforts in the employee's physical surroundings, or the nature of the work assigned and the safety regulations required. Although the use of safety precautions can practically eliminate a certain danger or discomfort, such situations typically place additional demands upon the employee in carrying out safety regulations and techniques.

Level 9-1—5 points The environment involves everyday risks or discomforts that require normal safety precautions typical of such places as offices, meeting and training rooms, libraries, residences, or commercial vehicles, e.g., use of safe work practices with office equipment, avoidance of trips and falls, observance of fire regulations and traffic signals. The work area is adequately lighted, heated, and ventilated.

Level 9-2—20 points The work involves moderate risks or discomforts that require special safety precautions, e.g., working around moving parts, carts, or machines; exposure to contagious diseases or irritant chemicals. Employees may be required to use protective clothing or gear, such as masks, gowns, coats, boots, goggles, gloves, or shields.

Level 9-3—50 points The work environment involves high risks with exposure to potentially dangerous situations or unusual environmental stress that require a range of safety and other precautions, e.g., working at great heights under extreme outdoor weather conditions, subject to possible physical attack or mob conditions, or similar situations where conditions cannot be controlled.

GRADE CONVERSION TABLE

Total points on all evaluation factors are converted to GS grade as follows:

GS GRADE	POINT RANGE
1.	190–250
2.	255–450
3.	455–650
4.	655–850
5.	855–1,100
6.	1,105–1,350
7.	1,355–1,600
8.	1,605–1,850
9.	1,855–2,100
10.	2,105–2,350
11.	2,355–2,750
12.	2,755–3,150
13.	3,155–3,600
14.	3,605–4,050
15.	4,055–up

NOTES AND RESOURCES

1. Merit System Protection Board, *OPM's Classification and Qualification Systems: A Renewed Emphasis, A Changing Perspective* (Washington, DC: MSPB, 1989), p. 5.

2. For a history, see Civil Service Assembly, *Position Classification in the Public Service* (Chicago: Public Personnel Association, 1965).

3. For a fuller discussion, see "Executive Compensation," *Employee Benefit Plan Review* 45, no. 10 (October 1991): 56–79.

4. The most obvious current examples of equity theory are found in the salary structures of professional sports. See for example, Joseph W. Harder, "Equity Theory v. Expectancy Theory: The Case of Major League Baseball Free Agents," *Journal of Applied Psychology* 76 (1991): 458–64. For a comprehensive discussion of equity theory, see J. Stacy Adams, "Inequity in Social Change," in Richard M. Steers and Lyman W. Porter, eds., *Motivation and Work Behavior* (New York: McGraw-Hill, 1975), pp. 138–54.

5. The most vexing problem for those trying to apply equity theory to faculty salaries is the issue of market forces. Professors of business and engineering traditionally are paid more than social scientists and humanities professors. See "Market Inequity: Incorporating This Critical Element," *CUPA Journal* 40, no. 1 (Spring 1989): 37–47.

6. See Felicity Barringer, "Charity Board Learns to Be Skeptical: United Way of America Scandal Has Embarrassed Board Members," *New York Times,* April 19, 1992, p. 10. Similarly, the chancellor of the California State University system resigned under pressure over inordinate pay and benefit packages for herself and her top administrators. See "Head of Cal State Quits in Dispute on Raises," *New York Times,* April 21, 1990, p. 7.

7. The distinction between rank in person and rank in the corps is unique to this text. Others use two divisions, with rank in person and rank in the corps treated as one category and rank in position as the other. See, for example, O. Glenn Stahl, *Public Personnel Administration,* 8th ed. (New York: Harper & Row, 1983).

8. See Robert J. Green, "Which Pay Delivery System Is Best for Your Organization?" *Personnel* 58, no. 5 (May–June 1981): 51–58.

9. For an early history, see Darrell H. Smith, *The United States Civil Service Commission: Its History, Activities, and Organization* (Baltimore: Johns Hopkins Press, 1928).

10. Steven W. Hays and T. Zane Reeves, *Personnel Management in the Public Sector* (Boston: Allyn & Bacon, 1984), p. 103.

11. U.S. Office of Personnel Management, *The Fact Book 1999 Edition: Federal Civilian Workforce Statistics* (Washington D.C.: U.S. OPM, 1999).

12. Merit was one of the requirements for state agencies that administer federal funds. Part of merit (as it is conventionally thought of) is a rational classification system. Many states modeled their systems on that of the federal government. The aid formulas and the conditions for receiving aid change with each administration. See Edwin J. Benton, "The Effects of Changes in Federal Aid on State and Local Government Spending," *Publius* 22, no. 1 (Winter 1992): 71–83.

13. See Richard C. Kearney and Kathy S. Morgan, "Longevity Pay in the States: Echo from the Past or Sound of the Future?" *Public Personnel Management* 19 (1990): 191–201.

14. The early pioneers of these systems, known collectively as the universal compensable factors approach, included Merril R. Lott, *Wage Scales and Job Evaluation: Scientific Determination of Wage Rates on the Basis of Services Rendered* (New York: Ronald Press, 1926); Eugene J. Berge, *Job Evaluation and Merit Rating* (New York: National Foremen's Institute, 1946); and Edward N. Hay, "Characteristics of Factor Comparison Job Evaluation," *Personnel* 23 (1946): 370–75.

15. The most widely used system is American Association of Industrial Management, *Job Rating Manual (Shop)* (Melrose Park, PA: AAIM, 1969), which uses eleven factors.

16. U.S. Office of Personnel Management, *Introduction to the Position Classification Standards* (Washington, DC: U.S. OPM, 1999): 44.

17. The most widely known of these government-applicable systems is owned by Hay and Associates. See W. G. Van Horn, "The Hay Guide Chart-Profile Method" in Milton Rock, ed., *Handbook of Wage and Salary Administration* (New York: McGraw-Hill, 1972): 2–86.

18. Developed in the 1970s, the federal system is known as the Factor Evaluation System (FES). For a discussion of the implementation of the FES, see Lawrence L. Epperson, "The Dynamics of Factor Comparison/Point Evaluation, *Public Personnel Management* 4 (1975): 38–48.

19. The original approach to benchmark positions was developed by Merril R. Lott, *Wage Scales and Job Evaluation: Scientific Determination of Wage Rates on the Basis of Services Rendered* (New York: Ronald Press, 1926).

20. See Charles Fay, Howard Risher, and Paul Hempel, "Locality Pay: Balancing Theory and Practice," *Public Personnel Management* 20 (1991): 397–408. Determining an appropriate market wage can be difficult. See Sara L. Rynes and George T. Milkovich, "Wage Surveys: Dispelling Some Myths about the 'Market Wage,'" *Personnel Psychology* 39, no. 1 (Spring 1986): 71–90.

21. For a review of state practices in controlling wages, see Wendell C. Lawther, Earle C. Traynham, and Kenneth M. Jennings, "Compensation Control Mechanisms in the American States," *Public Personnel Management* 18 (1989): 325–38.

22. For a detailed discussion of benefits, see Jerry S. Rosenbloom, ed., *Handbook of Employee Benefits: Design, Funding and Administration* (Homewood, IL: Dow-Jones Irwin, 1984).

23. Developed as a modification to the benchmark factor approach, the system is sometimes called the "weighted in money method." It was developed by Eugene J. Berge, *Job Evaluation and Merit Rating* (New York: National Foremen's Institute, 1946).

24. The same criticism regarding loss of the individual as a whole person was leveled at the production improvement techniques of Frederick Taylor, *Principles of Scientific Management* (New York: Harper & Row, 1911).

25. For a critique of government bureaucracy as a dehumanizing experience for both workers and clients, see Ralph P. Hummel, *The Bureaucratic Experience*, 3rd ed. (New York: St. Martin's Press, 1987).

9

COMPENSATION

Nothing is more central to the human resources functions of government than compensation. Indeed, Max Weber in his famous essay on bureaucracy wrote that adequate salaries were essential for recruiting and retaining top flight professionals. Adequate pay was also necessary as a barrier to employees feeling the need to take bribes in order to feed their families.[1] In the modern era, governments compete among themselves and with private employers. Compensation has come to mean more than just salary paid for hours worked. Compensation also includes health and life insurance, retirement, leave packages, vacation, and medical necessity. Compensation also means incentives for performing well and includes individual and group bonuses and permanent pay increases that set superior performers apart from their peers. These merit pay systems have become the topic of considerable controversy among management and labor unions as well as management theorists. Other incentives include extra days off with pay, plaques, and other nonpecuniary rewards.

COMPARABILITY

Government must pay substantially comparable wages to the private sector to compete for the best employees. For the bulk of their employees, state and local governments have met the challenge. The Bureau of Labor Statistics (BLS) reports that, taken in the aggregate, state and local government employees earn more than comparable private employees (see Table 9.1).[2] On average, state and local employees earn more in base wages and in benefits. In the past, government benefit packages and the relative security of civil service employment were the features of government service that made them competitive, but no longer.

Roughly 32 percent of the compensation difference between private-sector and government positions is found in the benefits packages received by government employees. Some of the differences disappear when individual job categories are compared. State and local clerical workers earn only $.12 an hour more than their private-sector peers. Public-sector executives, administrators, and managers earn on average $1.53 per hour less than their private-sector peers but make $.87 more in retirement benefits.

Government employers have altered their static compensation practices to compete. The federal government, for example, provides for bonuses under a program that the Office of Personnel Management has labeled "the 3Rs."[3] This stands

■ TABLE 9-1

BLS Per-Hour Salary Comparisons of State and Local Government and Private-Sector Employees, March 2000

	Wages	Benefits	Total Compensation
State and Local Employees	$20.57	$8.48	$29.05
Private Sector Workers	15.36	5.80	21.16

for Recruitment, Relocation, and Retention. Under the program, OPM authorizes agencies to pay individuals up to 25 percent of their base salary as a bonus. The agency must demonstrate, however, that the position in question is critical to the agency and particularly difficult to fill. NASA and other science-based agencies find the program useful in recruiting and retaining specialists.

Government salaries are least competitive among top executives. Compensation packages for top executives in the private sector run into the millions of dollars and include outright grants of company shares as well as the option to buy shares in the future at the current value. Executives also receive bonuses when the performance of their division or throughout the company hit specified targets. When companies are successful, the value of each share of stock also increases providing executives an additional increase in their personal wealth.[4]

The top step of the federal Senior Executive Service, by contrast, pays $122,400 with no stock options or built-in performance incentives.[5] The government does provide incentive awards for superior performance, as will be discussed, but these are in no way comparable to private-sector incentive systems. Government must therefore rely on the public-service orientation of their top employees as a source of satisfaction and reward.

Sometimes, however, the desire to serve is not enough. State and local governments in high cost-of-living areas have found it necessary to provide unique incentives to compete for qualified professionals. The state of California recently signed into law a bill to exempt public school teachers from state income taxes in amounts that range from $150 to $300 depending on the teachers' years of service.[6] The state is able to offer this incentive because its booming economy has provided record surpluses. The economy has also driven up the cost of living, making teachers' salaries noncompetitive. School districts in high-cost areas are building apartment complexes on district land and will offer rents at approximately half the market rate. One district has also entered into an arrangement with the Intel Corporation to pay $500 per month toward the mortgages of teachers.[7]

MOTIVATION

HUMAN RELATIONS THEORY

Organizational psychologists have long argued over the relative importance of pay as a motivating factor in worker productivity. The human relations school, especially Frederick Herzberg,[8] groups pay with security and a sense of belonging as lower-order needs. Certainly, they argue, organizations must compensate their employees fairly. But, they argue, real job satisfaction stems from the gratification of higher-order needs such as esteem, autonomy, and the ability to find personal fulfillment, known as self-actualization, in one's work. To motivate workers, therefore, the organization must provide for opportunities to gratify these higher-order needs.

Herzberg in particular emphasizes the elusory nature of motivation systems predicated on pay. He notes that systems that rely solely on monetary rewards have little to offer employees once their monetary needs have been gratified.[9]

Critics of this line of thinking point to the complex nature of pay, noting that pay is not only a salary to provide basic needs. They note that properly constructed incentive systems can be used for recognizing superior performance and are therefore a manifestation of the esteem in which the organization holds the employee.

EXPECTANCY THEORY

Motivating workers through monetary rewards requires several factors. First, the incentive offered must be sufficient in the workers' eyes to warrant an effort beyond current levels. Second, the workers must believe they are capable of obtaining the productivity levels that trigger the reward. Third, there must be no negative secondary outcomes attached to pursuing the goal. Frederick Taylor introduced piecework in factory settings to motivate workers.[10] Piecework compensates individuals for the product they produce rather than how many hours they work. Thus, following the logic of expectancy theory,[11] the per-piece reward must be set so that workers will produce more in a given hour within the limits of human output and safety considerations. Suppose that a factory paid its production workers $8.00 per hour or $64.00 per day. Suppose that the average units of production per worker were 50 per hour. Management would thus offer $.16 per unit.

A worker who maintained the current production levels would continue to earn $8.00 per hour; however, a worker who increased his or her productivity to 60 units per hour would receive $9.60 per hour. Although the system is attractive at face value, the new incentive system might not lead to increased productivity if the workers perceive it as a threat. For example, the workers might suspect that management's real agenda is to determine how many units per hour they could really produce. Then when the new rate was established, management would go back to paying $8.00 per hour with a quota of 60 units per hour. Another negative might be the suspicion that management had no real need of the extra per hour production but that it wanted to reduce its workforce. By increasing the per worker output to 60 per hour, management could reduce its workforce by 20 percent with no loss of output ($60 - 50 = 10$, $10 \div 50 = 20\%$). The result would be just over a 5 percent reduction in labor costs.[12]

If the proposed incentive system were viewed under the latter two scenarios, it is unlikely that workers would increase the productivity even if it meant a temporary loss of pay. A much higher probability is that the shift of payment would lead to unionization of the factory, thus forestalling future changes in compensation without consultation. On the other hand, if management consults closely with workers, explaining why the new system is being put in place and assuring them that there are no hidden agendas aimed at injuring the workers, piece work can work to the benefit of both parties.

An organization need not adopt piecework to use money as an incentive for productivity. Stock packages have been used with great success in the private sector. A new manager, for example, is given 10,000 shares in the company that will vest over five years. At the end of the first year he or she owns 2,000 shares outright; at the end of two years the worker has 4,000 shares, and so forth. The worker has a great incentive to remain with the company and to do everything in his or her power to increase the per-share value of the stock. Stock options are often given to workers as a further incentive. Suppose that our new manager was given an option to purchase an additional 5,000 shares of stock at the current market value after five years of service. Suppose that the stock was trading at $15.00 per share on the date the worker was hired. Suppose that in the interim five years, the value increased to $75.00 per share. The worker could exercise all or any part of his or her option, buying and selling shares on the same day at a profit of $60 per share. Of course, the worker has the option of holding the shares for a longer time.

The entrepreneurial boom in the Silicon Valley has been fueled by the willingness of venture capitalists to fund start-up companies and the companies' use of stock incentives to attract and retain managers and engineers willing to work 100 hours a week or more to make the company succeed. If the company succeeds, the manager is well rewarded; if it fails, he or she is out of work with a portfolio full of worthless stock.

There is nothing to prevent the workers from jumping ship. In our example, the manager has just over a million dollars in stock and options. He or she may choose to remain with the company or go on the market and sell his or her services to the highest bidder, thus undermining the loyalty the company sought to purchase. In a particularly competitive market, workers leave with only a partial vestment of their shares for bigger packages at other companies.

INCENTIVE PAY

Governments have no capacity for rewarding workers with stock. Governments have, however, sought to establish incentive systems that reward high performers at the expense of their less productive peers or by extra compensation for superior performers. The success rate of such programs has been mixed.[13]

The 1978 Civil Service Reform Act contained an incentive system designed to reward superior performers at the expense of their less productive peers. Prior to 1978 there were 18 grades in the federal compensation system. Within each grade there were 10 steps. An employee who performed to the satisfaction of his or her superiors could anticipate a step increase without a change of grade. Originally, superior performance was to be the criterion for a step increase. A supervisor would recommend a good employee for a step increase on the basis of his or her having grown in the position. Over the years, however, it had become necessary to justify withholding the step. In effect, a minimally satisfactory employee could anticipate a step for each year of service within a grade.

The 1978 Civil Service Reform Act sought to change the automatic step dynamic to one in which superior performance was rewarded and substandard performance was penalized. Initially, the system provided merit pay for managers above the rank of GS 12. If, for example, the Congress provided for a 3 percent cost-of-living increase, the managers would receive only half, or 1.5 percent. The other 1.5 percent, plus any steps that would normally have been given, were to go into a pool to be distributed on the basis of merit. The assumption of the system was that there were enough substandard performers in government to penalize in order to reward superior performers. In addition, the system left very little for rewarding satisfactory workers. Problems with the system led to a 1985 reform known as the Performance Management and Recognition System (PMRS).[14]

The PMRS used a five-step system to tie rewards more closely to the performance appraisal system. Persons receiving a rating of 1 or 2 received no increase. Persons at levels 3, 4, and 5 varied in the awards they received. The 1985 reforms also required agencies to set aside a small percentage of their budgets for performance awards. These monies were to be bonuses on top of employees' salaries.

The PMRS system was an improvement over the original zero-sum game, but problems persisted. Limited funds forced managers to rotate rewards among deserving employees. Supervisors and managers were frequently in the same salary pool as those rated, causing a built-in conflict of interest. Charges were leveled that most of the rewards went to headquarters managers to the great disadvantage of those working in the field. Finally, Congress did not reauthorize the PMRS program in 1993.[15]

One overarching criticism of differential reward systems is that the reward for superior performance in a given year is folded into the employee's salary base. Thus, through cost-of-living allowances, he or she is repeatedly rewarded in subsequent years based on the earlier performance. One-time bonuses are viewed as a much fairer way to reward superior performance.

The federal government, for example, has a two-level system for rewarding superior performance by executives known as the Presidential Rank Award.[16] Award winners undergo a rigorous selection process involving recommendations from their agency's head and a review by a panel of private citizens. An SES member who is designated a Distinguished Executive receives a lump-sum payment equivalent to 35 percent of his or her base salary. No more than 1 percent of the SES can receive this award in a given year. An additional 5 percent of the SES are eligible for the Meritorious Executive award, which is a lump-sum payment equivalent to 20 percent of the executive's base salary.

Merit award programs such as those described that can benefit no more than 6 percent of the Senior Executive Service are more an award for substantial service to the nation rather than a tool for motivating workers to greater efforts. SES members receive the Meritorious Executive award for years of superior performance.

GROUP REWARDS

Group incentives can provide motivation to workers to achieve outcomes desired by the organization. For them to work, the organization's workflow must have been stable over time, and there should not have been any substantial change in technology that affects the efficiency of the group. The first step is to calculate the productivity or cost in a given area of work over the last several years. Management then proposes to pay the members of the group for productivity improvements or cost savings. Skeptics might question if such a system could work in a government agency where there is no profit motive. But they can and have worked.

The federal government ran an experimental group reward program known as Pacer Share at McClelland Air Force Base until it was closed as part of defense cutbacks.[17] Whole ranges of employees across several grades were lumped together into a single pay pool. Step increases and individual performance appraisals were eliminated. Cost-of-living raises were paid as usual. In addition, workers as groups were rewarded one half of any cost saving over the average of the last three years. Thus, if the cost of overtime paid to repeat work that was not performed correctly the first time was reduced by 5 percent, the group would divide one half of the savings. Projects such as Pacer Share are best undertaken in the context of a total quality management approach to an agency's mission. Goals are clearly set and rewards are geared to desired outcomes. Such systems have worked well in modern Japanese industry and rewards based on outcomes have been adopted at the Saturn division of General Motors Corporation.

Group incentives can be used in systems much less far-reaching than the Pacer Share program. A city, for example, might use group rewards to reduce its workers' compensation costs. Analysts might first determine workers' compensation claims paid by the city in each of the last five years. An average of the per-year costs would then be the benchmark for the incentive system. If the city was unionized, the matter would first have to be negotiated with the appropriate bargaining units. Once the unions were in agreement, the program could begin. The city might agree to lump-sum payments to be distributed evenly among all members of the bargaining unit and managerial employees. The amount might be 50 percent of the saving or a different percentage could be negotiated. The point is that substantial savings can be obtained at no cost to the city.

LONGEVITY PAY

As noted above, the step increases in many civil service systems have at times degenerated into automatic raises based on the employee having completed another year of service. True longevity pay is not folded into an employee's base. Instead, it is given annually as a lump-sum payment based on years of service. Normally, the amount of the payment is not more than a few hundred dollars, but longevity pay can be an expression of gratitude for loyalty to the organization.

SKILL PAY

Skill pay is supposed to encourage workers to acquire specific skills that the organization values. A fire department, for example, might provide a 5 percent pay increase for firefighters who complete training as Emergency Medical Technicians. An abundance of EMTs in the department allows for flexibility of work assignments to ambulance duty and can pay great dividends in citywide emergencies like floods or tornadoes, as well as more limited problems like large fires or chlorine gas leaks at refineries.

The state of California projects that it will need 300,000 new teachers over the next decade to accommodate projected retirements and population growth. The shortage is so acute that many districts must hire teachers on temporary credentials. Interdistrict competition for fully qualified teachers causes the impact to fall most heavily on the weakest schools. The state appropriated funds to increase the minimum starting salary for teachers in the state from $32,000 to $34,000. Further, in an effort to enhance the credentials of teachers, the state is offering a one-time skill bonus of $10,000 for public school teachers who attain certification from the National Board for Professional Teaching Standards. The amount can increase to $20,000 if a nationally certified teacher agrees to teach for four years in a low-performing school.[18]

BENEFIT PACKAGES

RETIREMENT. In the past, noncompetitive government salaries were offset somewhat by attractive retirement packages. Under the Reagan OPM, federal retirement benefits were adjusted to bring them in line with those paid to private employees with comparable salaries. The analysis on which the decision was based looked only at salary and benefits. It would have been more appropriate to assess the duties and responsibilities of the position as well. The retirement benefits of persons employed before 1987 are substantially better than those who joined after the new program took effect in 1987.

Persons joining the federal civil workforce since 1987 are under the Federal Employees Retirement System. FERS has a three-tiered system based on employee participation in the social security system plus an annuity program into which employees pay less than 1 percent of their income that vests in five years. Federal employees were not included in the Social Security system prior to 1987. Federal employees are also eligible to participate in a voluntary "Thrift Savings Plan," in which they may place up to 10 percent of their salary in a tax-sheltered savings plan (up to a current limit of $10,500). The government contributes a matching amount up to 4 percent of the employee's wages.[19]

City managers serve at the will and pleasure of the city council. Normally, they are hired with set contracts, often five years, that specify that the manager can be removed for cause or for substantive policy differences with the council. City managers, therefore, do not have an expectation of long tenure in a given city. Their association, therefore, operates a retirement system that the individual takes with him or her from city to city. The contribution amount is a subject of negotiation in formulating the contract.[20]

HEALTH CARE. Traditionally, employers would provide a health-care benefit for employees with a narrow range of choices as to the mix: one size fits all. In the current competitive market, employers find it advantageous to provide cafeteria benefits. A married employee whose spouse also works might need no coverage from the employer. In such circumstances, the employer might offer cash payment in lieu of the insurance. Similarly, employers might give employees a choice of various combinations of eye and dental care and so forth. The packages might vary the co-payment for doctor's office visits or prescription drugs. The federal government boasts more than 350 different packages.

The amount of coverage and the relative contribution of the employee and the employer is variable. Labor unions often seek additional insurance coverage in lieu of wage increases because such benefits are pretax. An employer who provides free coverage to the employee but charges the employee for family, will find union negotiators willing to trade a percentage of their wage demands for family coverage.

LIFE INSURANCE. This benefit also is highly variable. The federal government, for example, offers a death benefit equal to the employee's annual salary. The state of California pays an amount equal to 150 percent of the employee's annual salary. Some employers offer coverage to family members at the employee's expense. Many employers also offer low-cost supplemental death and dismemberment plans.

ANNUAL LEAVE. Employers take a variety of approaches to the issue of time off. Normally, leave includes a set number of vacation days that is determined by the length of service and a set number of holidays off. Beginning federal employees currently accrue annual leave at a rate of 13 days per year, and they get 10 holidays per year.

Employers normally will cap the number of vacation days that an employee can accumulate. Ninety days is not an unusual number. Two reasons underlay this policy. First, employees need to take time off to refresh and regroup. Second, employers resist having a large liability on the books in the form of unused leave.

SICK LEAVE. The rate at which sick leave accumulates can vary, but a frequent rate of accumulation is eight hours of sick leave per month. Normally, employers will not limit the number of days of sick leave that an employee can accumulate. In some cases, unused days can be counted towards the retirement accumulation. So, a 30-year employee who only lost 20 days of work to illness would have an additional 72 weeks of service credit at the time of retirement.

Some employers allow employees to assign a portion of their sick leave to another employee who, through an extended illness, has exhausted his or her benefit. In addition, some employers allow employees to charge time off to care for dependent children to their sick leave rather than vacation time.

Some employees view their sick leave as a benefit to be utilized to its fullest each year. From time to time, they feel the necessity to take a "mental-health day." They do this rather than tap into their annual leave. This can be a sore subject between these employees and their supervisors. Some organizations therefore make no distinction between sick days and annual leave, thereby avoiding the problem. Employees consume credits from the same pool regardless of the purpose.

NONMONETARY REWARDS AND PERQUISITES.   Many organizations utilize such nonmonetary award systems as plaques and certificates for employee of the month, quarter, or year. Often the employee will be given extra days off as a form of reward, or he or she might get a designated parking spot for the ensuing month. Announcing the award at a ceremony can be as important as the award itself. Having one's peers applaud one's accomplishments builds esprit de corps and employee loyalty.

Other perquisites that executives and managers have come to expect include being assigned a preferred office space, a designated parking spot, and the use of an organization vehicle with a cell phone paid by the organization. Managers sometimes negotiate car allowances for the use of their own vehicle in lieu of mileage reimbursements. These allowances can be an income supplement provided that the manager does not drive the vehicle many miles per month. Finally, the organization may pay the manager's cost of membership in professional organizations and pay for the manager's personal liability insurance policy.

SUMMARY AND CONCLUSION

Government organizations offer a variety of incentives and benefits to attract and retain employees. In general rank-and-file government employees are paid wages and benefits that favorably compare to private-sector employees. Certain professional employees, notably public school teachers, are rewarded more than their private counterparts, but neither group is paid enough to attract the best and the brightest to the profession. Given the educational requirements for entry into the profession, teachers' salaries are substantially below comparably trained persons in other professions. Recognizing this inequity, many states are making extra efforts to enhance the rewards paid to teachers.

Government executives are underpaid in comparison to the responsibilities they assume. Top government executives earn between $100,000 and $150,000 per year. Although such salaries are enviable to many rank-and-file workers, they are in no way comparable to the compensation packages of private-sector executives with comparable responsibilities.

Over the past twenty years, governments at various levels have utilized reward systems that seek to reward superior performers. Extra compensation for extra effort and achievement is laudable. Unfortunately, these systems often require that the reward pay come from a pool that takes from lesser performers to reward the superior. The underlying assumption is that the number of substandard performers in the pool is at least as large as the number of superior performers. This is often not the case, and superior performers can only be meaningfully rewarded by depriving the fully satisfactory as well as the underachievers.

Such systems pit employee against employee, break down esprit de corps, and remove the incentive to cooperate even when cooperation is critical to the mission. Individual merit pay, some insist, is a viable system of motivating workers, based on private-sector experience. They should recognize that the rewards that are possible in the private sector make the system worthwhile. Unless or until government merit pay systems are fully and meaningfully funded, they should be left aside.

Most government work is the product of group rather than individual performance. A number of private- and public-sector organizations, therefore, find gainsharing or group rewards a better way of achieving increased productivity and/or cost reductions.

Most important, rewards for superior productivity, whether group or individual should be distributed as one-time lump-sum payments rather than pay increases that are folded into the employee's base salary. Base salaries in government are supposed to be based on the knowledge, skills, and responsibilities undertaken by the incumbent.

NOTES AND RESOURCES

1. Max Weber, *Essays in Sociology* (Oxford: Oxford University Press, 1946). Weber's points are summarized in "Bureaucracy," Jay Shafritz and Albert C. Hyde, eds., *Classics of Public Administration*, 4th ed. (Fort Worth: Harcourt, 1997): 37–43.

2. U.S. Department of Labor, Bureau of Labor Statistics, "Employment Cost Trends" at <http://stats.bls.gov/news.release/ecec.t02.htm>, and <http://stats.bls.gov/news.release/ecec.t04.htm>, revised 6/10/2000.

3. For an explanation of the Recruitment Bonus Program, see U.S. Office of Personnel Management, "Recruitment Bonuses" at <http://www.opm.gov/oca/Pay/html/recbonfs.htm>. For more information on the retention and relocation bonus program see Office of Personnel Management, "Recruitment Bonuses" at <http://www.opm.gov/oca/pay/html/Q&ARRR.htm>.

4. See C. Cuny and P. Jorion, "Valuing Executive Stock Options with a Departure Decision," *Journal of Accounting and Economics* 20 (1995): 193–205; and S. Huddart "Employee Stock Options," *Journal of Accounting and Economics* 18 (1994): 207–31.

5. U.S. Office of Personnel Management, "Senior Executive Service: Compensation" at <http://www.opm.gov.ses.compensation.html> updated 7/10/00.

6. "$2.4 Billion OK'd to Aid Education" *San Jose Mercury News*, July 6, 2000, p. 4B.

7. "Housing for Santa Clara Teachers: A Creative Idea," *San Jose Mercury News*, June 26, 2000, p. 10B.

8. Frederick Herzberg, *Work and the Nature of Man* (Cleveland, OH: World Press, 1966).

9. Frederick Herzberg, "One More Time: How Do You Motivate Employees?" *Harvard Business Review* 46 (January–February 1968): 53–62.

10. Frederick Taylor applied his "one best way" philosophy by modifying the size of the shovel used in the steel factory where he worked. By finding the perfect size (nine pounds), he increased per-worker per-day output from 16 to 59 tons. His payment system increased wages from $1.15 to $1.88 per day. Worker skepticism about the methodology is understandable given that Taylor reduced the workforce from 600 workers to 140. Those interested can read his philosophy of scientific management in Frederick W. Taylor, "Scientific Management," in Jay Shafritz and Albert C. Hyde, eds., *Classics of Public Administration*, 4th ed. (Fort Worth: Harcourt, 1997): 30–32.

11. For a detailed explanation of expectancy theory, see Victor Vroom, *Work and Motivation* (New York: Wiley, 1964) and Edward E. Lawler III, *Aligning Organizational Strategies and Pay Systems* (San Francisco: Jossey-Bass, 1990).

12. If a factory employed 100 workers at $8.00 per hour, its cost per hour would be $800.00. If it reduced its workforce by 20 percent to 80 workers who were paid $9.60 per hour, the total cost would be reduced to $768.00 per hour, for a savings of 4 percent. But when we add in an average benefits cost of an additional 27 percent of wages, the savings rises to just over 5 percent.

13. Gerald T. Gabris, "Merit Pay Mania: Transforming Polarized Support and Opposition Into a Working Consensus," in Stephen E. Condrey, ed., *Handbook of Human Resource Management in Government* (San Francisco: Jossey-Bass, 1998): 627–58.

14. The rules regarding PMRS are taken from *Federal Register* 50, no. 69 (August 31, 1985).

15. For an assessment of the Federal merit pay experiment, see U.S. General Accounting Office, *Analysis of OPM's Report on Pay for Performance in the Federal Government 1980–1992* (Washington, DC: U.S. Government Printing Office, 1993). Criticism of the proposed system began almost immediately; see Frederick Thayer, "The President's Management 'Reforms': Theory X Triumphant," *Public Administration Review* 38 (1978): 309–15.

16. U.S. Office of Personnel Management, "Presidential Rank Awards," at <http://www.opm.gov/ses/presrankaward.html> updated 5/10/2000.

17. See B. W. Schay, "In Search of the Holy Grail: Lessons in Performance Management," *Public Personnel Management* 22 (1993): 649–68. See also Gilbert B. Seigel, "Three Federal Demonstration Projects: Using Monetary Performance Rewards," *Public Personnel Management* 23 (1994): 153–64. For a general discussion of gainsharing, see B. Graham-Moore and T. L. Ross, *Gainsharing* (Washington, DC: Bureau of National Affairs, 1990).

18. California State Senate Bill 1666 at <http://info.sen.ca.gov/pub/bill/sen/sb.html> August 10, 2000.

19. U.S. Office of Personnel Management, *Benefits,* at <http://www.opm.gov/ses/benefits.html>. Please note that the benefits for top executives in the federal service are the same as for rank-and-file employees.

20. The International City/County Management Association (ICMA) created a retirement corporation as a separate nonprofit organization in 1972 to management the retirement assets of city managers. Currently, more than 5,500 employers participate along with some 450,000 individual participants. See "About ICMA-RC," at <http://www.icmarc.org/about/restory.html>.

10

PERFORMANCE APPRAISAL SYSTEMS

The literature of human resource management offers a myriad of reasons for organizations to operate performance appraisal systems. Among these are organizational planning, managing for results, employee development, and employee counseling and discipline. Each of these uses is treated in this chapter. New approaches to government, such as flattened hierarchies and team projects as well as an emphasis on achieving specified outcomes, have raised the issues of who should evaluate whom and when. The chapter concludes with a discussion of several widely used appraisal instruments and their relative merits for achieving these purposes.

APPRAISAL SYSTEMS AND ORGANIZATION OUTCOMES

The single greatest potential of performance appraisal systems lies in their usefulness for conveying organization plans and strategies to professional-level employees.[1] In the same vein, appraisal systems offer a mechanism for assuring that desirable outcomes are achieved.

Management theorists have long recognized the need for organizations to engage in planning.[2] In the public sector, planning can usefully be divided into three categories: compliance, strategic, and operational planning.

Compliance planning is used here to describe planning efforts that are imposed by external agencies, such as when federal funding agencies require states to submit one- to five-year planning documents as a condition of funding. Inexperienced state administrators may expend an inordinate amount of time and resources to assure that all mid- to upper-level managers take part in the process and approve of the plan, in the belief that federal audit officials will somehow hold the agency accountable (and withhold funding) if the plan does not reflect what is actually taking place in the agency. The reality is that federal agencies lack the resources to check up on planning compliance. They are much more likely to review how an agency allocates funding to clients and whether benefits are going to appropriate recipients. As a result, the best-written plans by state agencies will probably be relegated to the same obscure filing cabinet as the worst planning documents.

Strategic planning is another matter entirely. Public executives are well advised to assess the mission and goals of their programs in the manner set out in Chapter 6. And they should involve a broad spectrum of professional employees in the planning process, for two reasons. First, broad involvement enables the agency to draw on the experience, expertise, and creativity of line employees, who bring a practical program perspective to the planning effort. Second, if rank-and-file professionals develop the plan, they both understand it and are willing to implement it when the time comes. Even if top management could devise a better strategic plan without consultation, they would still be faced with the necessity of persuading the rank and file to implement the plan.

Program planning has to do with the distribution of organization resources and the assignment of people to various tasks. The distribution of resources is normally prescribed by senior executives and implemented by middle and first-line managers. The allocation and monitoring of work assignments generally follow the same channels. Herein lies the principal benefit of a well-designed and implemented performance appraisal system: assuring the good-faith implementation of program plans.

The best-laid plans for organizational change can fall short of the intended goals. Normally, the shortfall occurs during the implementation phase because management fails to build the changes into the managerial agenda. As a result, the hoped-for changes slip from sight in the press of day-to-day office routines.[3]

These failures are ironic in light of the fact that most organizations have elaborate chains of command to ensure that agreed-upon outcomes occur. Unfortunately for organization innovators, these systems exist largely to implement what is already in place. Most line managers, as well as rank-and-file employees, understand and are committed to current program priorities. Accountability systems are designed to ensure that current outcomes continue. Thus, it is not enough to conduct a planning retreat and decide where top managers want the organization to go. Managerial systems must be put in place to coordinate change, or it may well not occur.

Coordination of change should take place at two levels. First, the planning group must devise a specific timetable for implementing the desired change. This should include specific milestone meetings in which progress toward goals is reviewed and strategies for adaptation are devised. In this connection, individuals should be given specific responsibilities for implementing various aspects of the change strategy.[4]

Second, achieving the proposed changes must be incorporated into the evaluation and reward systems of the organization. This process can be facilitated through the use of open-ended evaluation systems such as management by objective (MBO).[5] Responsibility for various aspects of the proposed plan are incorporated into the short- and long-range expectations placed upon professional employees. Professionals should be made aware that accomplishment of the goals will be a significant component of their performance ratings during the life of the project.

MANAGING FOR RESULTS

Appraisal systems that do not link performance to mission will function in a mediocre fashion, at best. And organizations that have reward systems linked to factors other than the desired outcomes can hardly expect good-faith implementation of the plan. For example, a private company that wishes to expand its market base by recruiting new customers for a product line must convey this message to its sales professionals; otherwise, they will pursue their proven methods of trying to sell products to existing customers because it is easier to sell to a current client than a new one. The best way to assure new customer contacts is by making it a priority in the performance appraisal system.

A PUBLIC-SECTOR EXAMPLE. Governments, too, have focused on intended outcomes as the standard for measuring individual and program performance. For example, if a county government stated a goal of providing affordable health care to all children, the goals would then be manifested in the goals of the health-care and social service agencies. The welfare agency could begin with a review of its files. Programs could also be set up to outreach through schools and primary care physicians to identify potential recipients. Public health clinics and area hospitals could also be involved. The county board could use the performance appraisal system to hold administrators of the various agencies responsible for achieving the stated goal with the understanding, no progress, no raise. Then, through a system of top-down appraisal known as management by objective, lower-level supervisors and professionals would be judged on the program's success, that is, program outcomes. Of course, care would have to be taken to ensure that delivery in this program did not push out other equally desirable outcomes.[6] There are many such situations in the public sector. Suppose, for example, that a state director of vocational rehabilitation services wanted agency counselors to place greater emphasis on services to the severely disabled. Federal government statistics indicate that of all rehab clients served nationwide, 35 percent are severely disabled; in the director's state, the average is only about 20 percent.

In this hypothetical case, the director instructed the manager of field services to order counselors to increase services to severely disabled clients. One year later, in reviewing the annual report, the director noted a disappointing 3-percent increase in successful rehabs of severely disabled clients. A review of month-to-month performance reports indicated that a respectable upswing occurred shortly after the director's memo was issued, followed by a return to previous levels. Puzzled, the director met with the central office professional staff to analyze the situation.

In that meeting, the politically appointed director learned that the problem was not a lack of willingness to serve the severely disabled; instead, the problem lay with the agency's appraisal system, which distributed merit pay and promoted counselors on the basis of the total number of successful rehabs achieved.

The vocational rehabilitation process consists of twenty-six steps, from an initial screening interview to the placement of a client in a meaningful work role. Intermittent steps include diagnosis and treatment by medical doctors and provision of vocational training. Under the agency's appraisal system, a counselor's performance was measured by the number of twenty-sixes achieved.

Severely disabled clients require extra services and higher expenditure, with no guarantee that they will ever reach the point of holding a job; by contrast, persons with relatively minor disabilities (say, the loss of a limb) can be treated, trained, and placed relatively quickly at substantially lower cost. Thus, counselors were understandably reluctant to take the extra time and risk involved in serving severely handicapped clients.

The director formed a task force to restructure the appraisal system, giving greater weight for serving the severely disabled. A regular twenty-six was given a value of 1; a severely disabled twenty-six was weighted as 1.4. The change was carefully explained to counselors, who were told that their appraisal would depend a great deal on their service to the severely disabled. Within three years, this hypothetical agency should be well above the national average in service to the severely disabled.

When Ends Are Less Obvious. Because rehab counselors are given substantial autonomy over their caseloads, it is possible to measure the outcomes of individual performances. The work of most public employees, however, is contributory to collective end results.

When employee productivity is contributory, it becomes necessary to develop evaluation criteria that assess performance against standards of desired conduct. Such criteria as quality of services to clients, quantity of work performed, and timeliness of report filing are generalizable to most positions. Such criteria facilitate comparisons between employees for purposes of recommending workers for merit pay increases and aid in the assessment of employees for promotion.

The intent of these systems is to ensure overall quality of service to the public. Without tying these general criteria directly to the responsibilities of individuals, however, it becomes difficult to utilize the appraisal system as a tool for employee development and counseling.

Two Faces of Evaluation. Dennis M. Daley makes a useful distinction between appraisal systems that develop and those that judge.[7] Very often, however, the same system is asked to determine whether specific program outcomes are achieved, and it asks the supervisor to act as a mentor to subordinate employees. Systems that seek to develop employees use different criteria from outcome systems. Developmental systems often identify organizationally critical skills and abilities. Supervisors then consult with employees to help them develop through on-the-job experience gained through creative work assignments. Very often, the employee is counseled to acquire advanced academic training or to participate in training and development activities provided by the organization. Judgmental systems hold employees accountable for achieving organization ends. To be meaningful, judgmental systems must be fair and objective and tied directly to the organization's reward system.

EMPLOYEE DEVELOPMENT

A central responsibility for every manager is the development of subordinate employees.[8] This development has two aspects. First, each supervisor should explain to employees why things are done in certain ways, in order to teach them organization norms and procedures. Second, supervisors should assess the strengths and weaknesses of subordinates as a means of fostering their personal development.

ESTABLISHING PRIORITIES. The most important component of an effective judgmental system is a clear understanding between supervisors and subordinates regarding the organization's work expectations. This should be done in a formal, one-to-one discussion in which the supervisor states clearly the goals and objectives of the organization and the expectations that the organization has of the work unit. These expectations can then be translated into the duties and responsibilities of the individual worker.

With professional employees, who exercise substantial autonomy over their schedules and priorities, it is appropriate to work out goals and objectives for specific time frames. For managers and supervisors, these goals and objectives can be tied to the productivity of the units they supervise.

The appropriate time frame for reviewing progress toward fulfilling individual roles varies according to the agency and its mission. Service agencies engage in ongoing programs that, to a large extent, react to demands from citizens. Biannual and sometimes annual performance reviews are sufficient for professionals in these agencies. When the assignments of individual professionals involve special projects, however, quarterly and even monthly reviews are appropriate to ensure that the project is not lost in the crush of routine service delivery.

Agencies that engage in project management can establish program goals to be accomplished by specific dates, with progress assessed on a routine basis. Examples at the national level would include NASA and the Army Corp of Engineers. State transportation agencies that construct highways and rail systems can also make good use of time-certain systems. Local examples might include water districts and redevelopment agencies.

PROVIDING FEEDBACK. Systematic and specific communication regarding worker performance is critical to employee development and the achievement of organization outcomes. More to the point, ongoing routine feedback regarding workers' performance is an integral part of basic supervision. Nothing is more demoralizing to employees than to work an entire year at a performance level they believe to be at or above the agency standard only to find out at appraisal time that their work is considered inferior.

SETTING STANDARDS. All agencies have standards of performance for their employees. These may be based on systematic analysis or evolve as informal norms based on custom and precedent. Either way, new employees should not be forced to ferret out standards on their own, then wait a year to find out if their information is correct.

In an ideal world, workers (especially professionals) would come to the agency with a sense of what is a minimal performance level. Clerical workers, for example, should have learned reasonable standards of speed and accuracy in typing class. Unfortunately, the subject of government caseload expectations is absent from the curricula of most schools of social work. Likewise, public administration programs are more prone to teach their students how to prioritize budget cuts in times of austerity than they are to teach their students how to do more with less after the budget axe falls. The fact is that entry-level professionals are often ill prepared for the workload expectations of government service.

Frequently, neither the policy and procedure manual nor the employee handbook makes reference to performance standards. This may be because management wishes to maintain flexibility in dealing with individual employees, or it may be a matter of sloth. Nevertheless, standards are a very real part of agency culture and are used to assess employees.

Returning to rehabilitation as an example, during a planning discussion in one state agency, the subject of standards came up. How many rehabs was a counselor expected to complete in a year? Several of the participants (all line supervisors) indicated that the agency had no formal standard. Yet they stated that they were able to assess the performance of subordinates without difficulty.

The director of field services listened to this discussion for a few minutes, then interjected, "By golly, I know what the standard is! It's 25 rehabs per year!" There was a general nodding of heads in agreement. One supervisor who had previously professed ignorance of any standard now stated, "That's about what I thought it was."

In short, a production standard existed, and people understood and used the standard while publicly disavowing any knowledge of it. Without second-guessing the motives of executives in the agency for not formalizing the standard, we can observe that it would be much better for rehab counselors if they clearly understood what the minimum standard was.

In addition to clarifying expectations, the reassessment of performance standards can provide a useful framework for reinvigorating employee dedication to the mission of the agency and help build a consensus for fairly assessing individual performances.

Elsewhere, we have identified four types of standards: historical standards, comparative standards, industry standards, and engineered standards.[9] Historical standards are arrived at through assessing previous output, or they may merely evolve as organization norms. The closure expectation noted previously is an example of a historical standard that evolved. The agency might check the standard with comparable organizations to assess its reasonableness. Accrediting agencies, by contrast, often set industry standards. Public hospitals use industry standards to set staffing levels relative to workflows. Performance standards for individual professionals can also use industry standards as a starting point.

Potentially, the most dynamic method for developing standards is to engineer them. As agencies flatten their hierarchies and remove whole tiers of managers in favor of self-governing work teams, it only makes sense for them to establish performance standards for the group and individual members.

EMPLOYEE COUNSELING AND DISCIPLINE

A well-defined set of performance standards facilitates the employee counseling process. Once employees are aware of agency performance standards, substandard performers can increase their efforts to match the productivity of their peers. Others may realize that they need assistance to meet the standard. Ideally, low performers will seek the advice and assistance of their immediate supervisors; normally, however, the supervisor must take the initiative.

Supervisors, in most cases, are the feedback source for poor performers. Feedback should take two forms. When a worker's productivity slips, it is the responsibility of the supervisor to counsel him or her immediately. At first, this counseling should be informal; indeed, informal ongoing counseling of all employees is central to good supervision. If the message is not received, however, the supervisor must formalize the counseling process in one-to-one counseling sessions in which the employee's performance is the only item on the agenda.

CONSTRUCTIVE CRITICISM.   Perhaps no other responsibility weighs so heavily on the first-line supervisor as the duty to counsel substandard performers. Consequently, these sessions are often postponed as long as possible. In some cases, managers are so anxious to avoid conflict that they will accept inferior performance. Other supervisors have every intention of counseling poor performers but do so only when they become personally angry. As a result, what could have been a productive counseling session turns into a shouting match that often ends with the employee's resignation.

Insofar as managers wish to rid themselves of poor performers, a resignation is not all bad. If, however, the manager wishes to salvage a potentially productive worker, the counseling session must take an entirely different tack.

A number of books are available on how to handle problem employees.[10] Suffice it to say here that the supervisor must confine criticisms to the actual job performance of the subordinate. Care must be taken to state specifically the areas in which the employee's performance is deficient. The supervisor should also state specifically what steps should be taken to improve that performance. For most employees, these discussions can be confined to the quality, quantity, timeliness, and accuracy of the employee's work.

There are times, however, when the issue is one of cooperation with fellow workers, appropriate behavior, or appropriate language. If, for example, the employee is given to outbursts in meetings that are demeaning to other workers or disruptive of the flow of work in groups, counseling may be more complicated. Overbearing people are frequently unaware of their impact on others. Counseling them can also lead to an outburst directed at the supervisor. These persons must be told that their behavior is unprofessional and in need of correction. Further, the supervisor may suggest that the employee undertake training in interpersonal skills.[11]

Employees who use inappropriate language or who engage in conduct that is fraught with sexism or otherwise offensive to coworkers can be a bigger problem than bellicosity. If left unchecked, such conduct can result in a lawsuit against the agency on the grounds that management knowingly permitted it on the premises. If the language is sexually explicit, allowing it to continue unchecked may constitute type two sexual harassment: an offensive working environment (see Chapter 4).[12]

Such offensive conduct goes beyond failure to perform one's own duties. It degrades and offends coworkers and creates an environment in which they cannot adequately perform their duties. Offending employees must be told in no uncertain terms that their conduct violates agency and societal norms, and the supervisor must document that formal corrective action was taken immediately.

CORRECTIVE ACTION.   Disciplinary action might take the form of a letter of reprimand in the personnel file of the offender for such relatively minor offenses as the first occurrence of offensive sexual comments to or about other employees. Management has a responsibility to investigate and punish such behavior. If an employee is unjustly censured, the worst that can happen to the agency is a letter from the merit protection authority admonishing the agency to cease and desist, and possibly a reversal of any disciplinary action against the alleged offender. Failure to take corrective action can cost the agency many thousands of dollars in legal fees and court awards or out-of-court settlements.

In extreme cases, it may be necessary to transfer, suspend, demote, or discharge the offender. The last three remedies are normally subject to review by the merit protection system, which means that management action must be justified and well documented.

DOCUMENTATION.   No manager, regardless of how well intentioned, can hope to prevail in an adverse action against an employee without documentation that substantiates the need for the action. In disciplinary matters, this involves constructing an adequate paper trail to justify one's actions in the postdisciplinary appeals process, inside and outside of the agency (see Chapter 11).

POSITIVE COUNSELING.   By far the greatest potential of appraisal systems lies in their use for establishing mentoring relationships with staff members.[13] A supervisor can create an environment of mutual respect and support by negotiating realistic goals, objectives, and work plans with employees. Employees can then feel free to approach their supervisors, not only with problems and projects but also with career aspirations. Supervisors can encourage subordinates to test their abilities and raise their aspirations. Supervisors can also advise employees on strategies for self-development, including the acquisition of new skills and training to prepare them for advancement to the next echelon.[14]

REWARD DISTRIBUTION.   The most frequent use of performance appraisal systems is as a basis for distributing organization rewards. Each year, thousands of employers assess the performance of each of their employees, then use the results to justify or deny pay increases.[15] Valued employees are rewarded while the nonperformers, at best, are counseled to improve their performance. Frequently, however, nonperformers receive only a written assessment of their substandard performance. Often they are not advised as to how they can improve.

The irony of appraisal systems is that the more they are used for purposes of justifying rewards, the less valuable they become as mechanisms for employee counseling and development. Workers may be reluctant to report problems and mistakes for fear that doing so may adversely affect the size of their raises. And the benefits of the counseling process may diminish as employees become absorbed with learning just how large a raise they will receive.

Conversely, if there is no linkage between an organization's appraisal and reward systems, employees may become cynical regarding the process. The linkage to the reward system, however, need not be directly pecuniary in order to be meaningful. The military services, for example, go to great lengths to regularly appraise and counsel troops. Rewards in the military come in the form of timely promotion to the next rank rather than immediate pay increases. Substandard performers are encouraged to improve or separate from the service. However, they are not penalized economically in relation to their peers, as are civilian managers in the federal service.

WHO SHOULD EVALUATE. Tradition holds that the most appropriate person to conduct performance appraisal is the immediate supervisor. He or she is responsible for setting organization expectations and normally is the principal actor in socializing subordinates regarding behavioral norms of attendance, civility, and so forth.

With flattened hierarchies and self-directing teams, the supervisor may not be the most knowledgeable regarding the contribution of team members. A new system is known as *360 evaluation* and seeks input from everyone with whom the worker has contact. These include work group peers, customers, and members of other agency departments with whom the employee has regular contact. Each of these is a potential participant in the appraisal process, with the possible exception of customers. Not all members of government have direct contact with the public, and those who do often do not have the sort of repeated contact with clients that would make assessment feasible. Nevertheless, assessments from one's subordinates and peers can provide valuable insights into one's work habits.[16]

INSTRUMENTS OF EVALUATION

Many evaluation instruments now in use are testaments to the triumph of process over purpose. So many workers have to be evaluated and compared that the evaluation instrument can rarely be precisely applicable to the duties and responsibilities of individual employees.

Evaluation instruments do not reflect the purpose of the evaluation as envisioned by the executives who order their use. Instead, the instruments reflect the needs of the personnel administrators who must oversee their use. Instruments are also sometimes altered to accommodate managers' reluctance to write lengthy justifications in their assessment of subordinates. Documentation is traded off for simplicity of use.

Another factor in instrument design is the bureaucratic tendency to homogenize the process for ease of comparison. The push for generic evaluation may come from senior managers who are most interested in justifying merit pay increases (or lack thereof). The human resource division may also recommend homogenization to facilitate analysis of the evaluations. Precise graphs and charts can only be constructed if uniform criteria are used and employees are rated on identical scales of, say, 1 to 5.

Concern for comparisons often results in highly generic instruments that are used to evaluate a broad range of employees based on uniform criteria that may or may not have value for employee development and counseling. The most compelling examples of uniformity are rating systems that rely as much on employees' traits as on their behavior.

MATRIX RATING SYSTEMS

A common type of rating system lists a number of traits and performance criteria followed by a set of boxes that the rater can check (see Figure 10.1). These boxes represent a scale of 1 to 4, 5, or even 10. On the 5-point rating scale illustrated in Figure 10.1, 1 means unsatisfactory, 2 means needs improvement, 3 means satisfactory, 4 means above average, and 5 means outstanding.

To arrive at an employee's score, the supervisor simply adds up the ratings on all the items and divides the result by the number of items in the scale. In our example, the scores add up to 33; dividing by 10 produces an overall rating of 3.3. Because a score of 3.3 out of 5 has little meaning for most people, ratings are often standardized by means of a multiplier and a constant. With a multiplier of 10 and a constant of 50, the 3.3 rating becomes 83 out of a possible 100 ($3.3 \times 10 + 50 = 83$). In academic terms, this would make the employee a B student.

■ **FIGURE 10-1**

SAMPLE MATRIX RATING INSTRUMENT

	1	2	3	4	5
1. Quality of work					X
2. Quantity of work				X	
3. Timeliness of work completion				X	
4. Accuracy of work				X	
5. Cooperativeness		X			
6. Communications skills			X		
7. Attendance				X	
8. Appearance		X			
9. Attitude		X			
10. Loyalty			X		

TOTALS

$$\text{Rating} = \frac{\text{Points}}{10}$$

PROBLEMS WITH MATRIX RATINGS.   Proponents of matrix rating systems point to their standardized format and ease of application. These systems, however, are flawed in several ways.

First, such homogenization lumps everyone together and measures them against some idealized employee. In the process, virtually all value of evaluation in work planning and employee development is lost.

Second, these rating instruments do not distinguish between performance that is critical and traits that are desirable. In our example, the quality of the employee's work is outstanding. The quantity of work, its timeliness and accuracy, and the employee's attendance record are all superior. The employee's shortcomings are in the areas of cooperativeness, appearance, and attitude. These trait ratings reflect the subjective perceptions of the rater and may be the product of bias.

Suppose, for example, that the employee in question is a female member of an ethnic group that discourages women from assertive speech. Her lack of forth-right responsiveness could be interpreted by the manager as an attitude problem or a lack of cooperation. Her dress, moreover, may reflect the standards of appropriateness in her own community rather than those of the supervisor. If appearance codes are to be enforced, they must be based on well-conceived, universally applied standards that are systematically communicated to rank-and-file workers.

Our imaginary employee has received a rating of 83 out of 100 despite her supervisor's concerns. Organization decision makers might thus argue that the system did no real damage to the employee. Nevertheless, a rating of 83 certainly would not entitle her to merit pay or bonuses.

Third, the use of homogenized rating criteria that involve subjective evaluations of personality traits may at times be illegal. If those adversely affected by the rating criteria and their weights are members of ethnic minorities, the potential exists for lawsuits based on civil rights violations.

Finally, because employee evaluations are frequently taken into consideration in promotion decisions, the criteria used in the evaluation must be validated. This means that there must be a direct relationship between those criteria and the employee's duties and responsibilities.

WEIGHTING THE ITEMS.   At a practical level, it makes no sense to weight all criteria equally. In our example, more importance could be given to the four performance criteria than to the traits simply by weighting them differently. Suppose performance is to count as 70 percent of the evaluation and traits only 30 percent. The first step is to total the four performance ratings, divide by 4, then multiply the composite by .70 (5 + 4 + 4 + 4 = 17 ÷ 4 = 4.25; 4.25 × .70 = 2.98). The process is then repeated with the six trait ratings, which add up to 16 (16 ÷ 6 = 2.67; 2.67 × .30 = .80). Finally, the employee's performance and trait scores are added together and converted to the standardized appraisal score (2.98 + .80 = 3.78; 3.78 × 10 = 37.8; 37.8 + 50 = 87.8). Rounding up, the rating is 88 out of a possible 100. When differential weighting is used, our B employee becomes a B+, which more accurately reflects her superior performance and contributions to the organization. Nevertheless, the issues surrounding potential rater bias remain when traits are included in the matrix.

MANAGEMENT-BY-OBJECTIVE SYSTEMS

Attributed originally to Peter Drucker, management by objective involves negotiating goals and objectives with each employee, then holding workers to the attainment of those goals.[17] MBO can be an effective method for coordinating worker efforts and achieving desired outcomes. During the 1960s and 1970s, the MBO movement generated systems for the comprehensive management of organizations. In some organizations, unfortunately, these systems became ends in themselves. That is, employees and managers sometimes became overly concerned with appearing to comply with the system and appearing to have achieved their negotiated goals. MBO thus became a matter of making the record as opposed to achieving organizational ends.

The actual MBO appraisal instrument may be as simple or complex as management requires. Management may elect to structure the instrument around organizational outcomes or to leave it open-ended. In the public sector, however, many programs are largely routine, with a few specialized projects assigned to various individuals. The appraisal instrument needs to reflect this mixture.

MIXED SYSTEMS

Public managers need an evaluation instrument designed to accommodate routine tasks and special projects as well. A county probation office, for example, may wish to undertake a major community outreach effort. This might include the development of small-group counseling sessions for troubled youths as a six-month goal for an inner-city branch office. Working with parents and school authorities to get the program running might be assigned as a secondary duty to one or more probation officers.

Other components of the officers' evaluations might include case service to clients (such as developing job placements and monitoring compliance with conditions of probation or parole), court liaison, and cooperation with law enforcement agencies and prison officials. The appraisal instrument for such an agency is illustrated in Figure 10.2.

Notice that the routine tasks are printed on the form under normal duties, while the small-group program is written in under special projects. The spaces between the normal duties are provided so that management can negotiate with individuals the expectations within each area. These negotiations might include needed improvements in work quantity, quality, and so forth. On the other hand, fully satisfactory employees must be permitted to maintain current production levels without being penalized for nonimprovement. Otherwise, a satisfactory rating is tenuous at best.

Unrealistic expectations on the part of management that workers must continually improve, regardless of the level of previous performance, have been the undoing of many MBO systems. Problems occur when line managers or executives decide that MBO success levels are high because expectations are too low. Expectations are then raised again and again as the employees work harder and harder to hit an ever-moving target of performance expectations.

■ FIGURE 10-2

SAMPLE MBO EVALUATION FORM FOR A HYPOTHETICAL PROBATION DEPARTMENT

	Rating (1–5)
Normal Duties	
1. Case services (job development, client monitoring) Expectations:	☐
2. Court liaison Expectations:	☐
3. Cooperation with law enforcement agencies Expectations:	☐
4. Appropriate application of laws and regulations Expectations:	☐
Special Projects	
5. Small-group counseling program Expectations:	☐
Overall Evaluation	☐
Comments:	

The downside of establishing specific standards that are adhered to over time is that the dynamic qualities of MBO systems may be underutilized. Some sort of balance can be struck by combining standardized performance criteria with the open-ended negotiation features of an MBO system.

Figure 10.3 illustrates a two-tiered evaluation instrument designed for assessing the performance of managers. At the top of the form are listed ten criteria germane to the performance of government managers.[18] Space is provided between criteria so that notations of specific expectations can be made by the supervisor.

Below this standardized list is the discretionary special projects section. Finally, the commentary section at the bottom of the page can be expanded to as many pages as necessary to profile the worker's performance. This section is necessary to clarify expectations and document specific behavior. Documentation, in turn, can be used to support recommendations for merit pay increases or to support adverse personnel actions as necessary.

The column marked E represents the evaluation of the manager's performance on a scale of 1 to 5, where 5 is exceptional, 4 is superior, 3 is fully satisfactory, 2 is needs improvement, and 1 is unsatisfactory. This column is filled in by the supervisor at the end of the rating period.

A SAMPLE TWO-TIERED EVALUATION FORM FOR PUBLIC MANAGERS

	E	R	S
Managerial Criteria			
1. Work planning	5	5	25
2. Problem solving	3	5	15
3. Productivity of work unit	4	5	20
4. Effectiveness of work coordination	5	3	15
5. Intergroup coordination	3	3	9
6. Development of subordinates	3	1	3
7. Delegation	2	1	2
8. Communication	1	1	1
9. EEO affirmative action efforts	5	2	10
10. OSHA compliance	5	1	5
Special Projects			
TOTALS		27	105

$$\text{Evaluation} = \frac{105}{27} = 3.89$$

Commentary

The R (for relatedness) column is used to indicate, also on a scale of 1 to 5, how relevant a criterion is to the manager's performance during a given rating period. A 5 means that the criterion is critical to job performance, 4 means it is highly related, 3 means it is somewhat important, 2 indicates marginal relevance, and a 1 indicates little or no relevance. The relatedness of the various criteria are negotiated between employees and their superiors at the beginning of the rating period. Thus, the relatedness of a given item may vary from worker to worker and from one rating period to the next.

Item 9 (EEO), for example, is a necessary component of every government manager's responsibilities, but its specific relatedness may vary. For a manager who supervises park rangers at a remote site and is not anticipating any employee turnover or promotional openings, EEO might have a relatedness of 2. This indicates that he or she is responsible for providing a harmonious work environment free from religious or ethnic discrimination or sexual harassment.

If the same manager were in the process of recruitment or serving on a selection task force to pick a new director of personnel services, the relatedness of the EEO criterion might increase dramatically. For a director of personnel, of course, the relatedness of this criterion would be consistently high.

The actual rating received by a manager is calculated by multiplying his or her rating on the evaluation scale by the importance attached to that criterion in the relatedness column. The hypothetical manager in Figure 10.3 was evaluated as outstanding (5) on the criterion of work planning. The relatedness of work planning was set at 5. The manager, therefore, achieved the maximum score of 25 for planning in the S (for score) column.

A manager's overall evaluation is arrived at by dividing the total score by the total of the relatedness column. Because our sample manager had no special projects during the rating period, the overall performance score is 105 divided by 27, or 3.89 (out of a possible 5).

This type of evaluation form seeks to combine the standardization available in matrix systems with the open-endedness of MBO. The ability to adjust the weights allocated to the various criteria adds further flexibility. By adopting a mixed system, agencies can add the benefits of MBO for managing special projects to standard evaluations of employees' performances on routine tasks.

CRITICAL-INCIDENT SYSTEMS

Critical-incident systems are the ultimate in open-endedness. They can begin with negotiation of goals and performance expectations between managers and those they evaluate, although this step is not necessary for a critical-incident system to work. Managers must, however, maintain careful records on each employee throughout the rating period. In short, the manager makes a note for the employee's file of each significant performance factor. These notations may be positive or negative.

At the end of the rating period, the manager has documentation on each worker's performance well beyond that found in matrix or MBO systems. Documentation notwithstanding, the principal shortcoming of the critical-incident approach is its emphasis on extreme examples. One must either perform in a superior manner or do something untoward in order to warrant the manager's notice. Solid, steady performers have little in their files on which the supervisor can base an assessment.

A second flaw is the possibility that ambitious employees will seek to draw attention to those elements of their performance that will garner a positive rating. By the same token, they will be extremely reluctant to share negative information with their supervisors. As a result, the ambitious vie with one another to capture the positive notice of the manager while solid, steady performers may go unrewarded.

Critical-incident record keeping can be used in conjunction with other systems to bolster the manager's memory of events and the performances of subordinates (especially those that occur early in the review period). The potential for competition among the ambitious still exists when the critical incidents are merely supplemental, however, so managers who use them would do well to keep their note-taking practices private.[19]

BEHAVIORALLY ANCHORED RATING SYSTEMS

Behaviorally anchored rating systems (BARS) use standardized evaluation criteria and an evaluation scale that is linked to actual behavior through the use of statements.

The object is to eliminate the halo effect of giving an employee a uniformly outstanding or negative rating when he or she is only truly superior or truly unsatisfactory in one or two categories. A generic version of the scale might read as follows:

5. The employee exceeds and sometimes greatly exceeds the performance standards for this criterion.

4. The employee normally meets and sometimes exceeds the performance standards for this criterion.

3. The employee fully meets the performance standards for this criterion.

2. The employee normally meets but sometimes falls below the performance standards for this criterion.

1. The employee does not meet the minimally acceptable performance standards for this criterion.[20]

A behaviorally anchored rating scale can be used in conjunction with generic rating criteria (such as those listed in Figure 10.1), or it can be used with more open-ended criteria such as are found in MBO. The intent is to link ratings as closely as possible to specific elements of the employee's job performance rather than the manager's generalized impression of the worker as an individual.

CHECKLIST SYSTEMS

Checklist systems ask the rater to select a statement that best describes the employee in question from among several seemingly unrelated statements (see Figure 10.4).[21] Like BARS, the primary object of this approach is to cut down on the halo effect. The strength of forced distributions is also their primary weakness because the rater has no idea what effect he or she is having on the employee when selecting one statement over another.

A checklist evaluation form may contain as many as fifty groups of statements. The statements are prepared and grouped by psychometric experts, who are the

■ FIGURE 10-4

SAMPLE CHECKLIST-STYLE FORCED-CHOICE ITEMS

Most	Least	
( )	( )	Does not work to limit of ability
( )	( )	Reads materials before filing them
( )	( )	Always complaining
( )	( )	Rarely needs prodding
( )	( )	Aggressive without causing resentment
( )	( )	Work is rarely interrupted by personal business
( )	( )	A very clear thinker
( )	( )	Not always punctual

only ones who know the real impact of selecting one statement over another. By indicating the most descriptive and the least descriptive statement in each group, the manager provides those who analyze the appraisal with a supposedly objective profile of the person under review.

The benefits of a completely objective assessment of workers by rank-and-file managers (using criteria selected by upper management) must be traded off against the loss of evaluation as either a counseling tool or a system of managing for results. Insofar as the latter are important, using the checklist system is a triumph of process over purpose.

Regardless of the system used, performance appraisal is only worth doing when it is an integral part of the managerial system of the organization. As we have seen, the most sophisticated systems can be used for planning and monitoring programs. At the very least, however, appraisal systems must utilize objective criteria that are directly related to the duties and responsibilities of the employee being rated. Doing less diminishes the value of the appraisal system and may constitute a violation of civil rights statutes.

SUMMARY AND CONCLUSION

Performance appraisal systems are value neutral they are only as effective as the managers and supervisors who operate them and the ends the agency is trying to achieve. Too often in the past, appraisal systems were a residual from some long ago administration. Managers and supervisors consider the process a hassle and enjoy it less than the people receiving the evaluation. One response is to let the appraisal process slide in favor of more pressing issues. Another is to merely rate everybody satisfactory and thereby avoid having to provide written justifications of the raters' conclusions. It need not be so.

Appraisal systems can be an excellent tool for imparting organization goals and performance expectations to individual employees. They also have been put to good use as an instrument of employee development and counseling. If appraisals are used, they become a part of the employee's permanent record. The ratings employees receive, therefore, should square with management's view of the employees. Many a manager has found his or her efforts to discipline substandard employees overridden by civil service hearing examiners or labor arbitrators because the employee was able to produce years of positive performance reviews.

BOUNDARY LIMITS AND EMPLOYEE COUNSELING

The Redevelopment Agency of Cerdo Gordo California is a freestanding organization that operates outside the city's civil service system. The agency was established in 1986 through a special act of the state legislature and revision of the city charter that passed with a 73 percent voter support. The charter amendment created a special tax district that included the city's industrial center (filled with high-tech companies) and the downtown area that desperately needed renovation. In the ensuing years, the downtown has undergone a complete makeover, with theaters, shops, libraries, and museums replacing rundown neighborhoods.

Having substantially completed its initial mission, the agency director is casting about for new projects to spend its hundreds of millions of dollars of tax revenue. If viable projects are not developed, the city council may propose a ballot initiative to abolish the agency and place its resources in the city's general fund. Should that happen, the county and local school districts would also receive a revenue windfall in added tax revenues.

All employees are at-will and can be removed at any time for any legitimate reason. They are also exempt from the city's retirement and health-care benefits systems. Each employee is paid a generous salary (normally 20 percent higher than regular city employees) and they receive a benefits stipend equal to an additional 25 percent of their salaries. Work in the agency is interesting and morale is high.

The agency operates in a project management mode in which planning and development specialists form teams to carry out specific projects. When a project is complete, the team dissolves and members are assigned to new projects or their contracts with the agency are severed.

Billy Janson is a 44-year-old division chief in the Redevelopment Agency. She oversees five project teams and manages the team leaders directly. She is responsible for the performance appraisals of the five team leaders. The agency operates an elaborate pay structure to reward employees through raises and one-time bonuses. These are largely determined by the appraisal and salary recommendation of the immediate supervisor.

Larry Christensen, age 34, has been a team manager for 18 months. His current project is upgrading the storefronts of businesses and installing decorative trees and new streetlights along the city's main street, Chupa Pierdes. Technically, much of the project was outside the area specified in the agency's mandate. Nonetheless, the renovations were desperately needed, and the council revised the agency's mandate by adding a two-block-wide three-mile-long strip to the mandate of the agency. The project is almost complete, and citizen groups and the council seem well satisfied with the aesthetics of the project.

Janson is troubled, however, because Christensen substituted very expensive palm trees for native plants as called for in the project proposal at a cost add-on of $750,000. The money was available in the agency budget, nevertheless. Christensen took it upon himself to order trees and to plant them before seeking approval from Janson. Christensen claims it was an oversight and promises never to repeat the mistake. Janson remains unconvinced. She believes that Christensen took his cue from the agency director, whose approach to the city council is characterized by the adage, "It's easier to get forgiveness than permission."

Janson is perplexed. She admires Christensen's initiative but fears that it may border on recklessness. She could very well justify withholding his bonus for a project completed on time on the basis of the $750,000 cost overrun. At the same time, she does not wish to squelch Christensen's enthusiasm. The appraisal conference with Christensen begins in two hours, and she has still not reached a decision. She decides to wait until after the conference to decide on a bonus recommendation.

Assignment One

Form small groups and discuss the facts in the case and decide what should be done.

1. If you were Janson, what would you do?
2. Is there ever a legitimate excuse for exceeding one's authority?
3. Should Christensen receive a bonus? If yes, should it be 10, 15, or 20 percent of his annual base salary? Should the bonus be given and a step increase withheld? Or, vice versa?

Assignment Two

The instructor will assign two class members to play Janson and Christensen. The class may be formed into a circle for ease of observation.

1. The student playing Janson should tell Christensen what the group has decided regarding his performance and the reward that he is to receive.
2. The student playing Christensen should respond to the information as naturally as possible.
3. Other class members will observe the simulated meeting and take notes on what was done well and what was done poorly.
4. The instructor then leads a discussion of appropriate counseling, and class observations will be shared with the actors.

Notes and Resources

1. On the planning benefits of appraisal systems, see Henry R. Migliore, *An MBO Approach to Long-Range Planning* (Englewood Cliffs, NJ: Prentice-Hall, 1983).

2. Readers interested in public-sector applications of planning principles should see John M. Bryson, *Strategic Planning for Public and Nonprofit Organizations* (San Francisco: Jossey-Bass, 1988); and Jack Koteen, *Strategic Management in Public and Nonprofit Organizations* (New York: Praeger, 1989).

3. See Richard Beckhard and Ruben T. Harris, *Organizational Transition: Managing Complex Change* (Reading, MA: Addison-Wesley, 1977).

4. For a fuller discussion, see Ronald D. Sylvia, Kathleen M. Sylvia, and Elizabeth M. Gunn, *Program Planning and Evaluation for Public Managers*, 2nd ed. (Prospect Heights, IL: Waveland Press, 1997): 27–64.

5. A classic in the field is George S. Ordione, *Management by Objective: A System of Managerial Leadership* (New York: Pitman, 1965). For updated treatments, see George Ordione, *MBO II: A System of Managerial Leadership for the 80s* (Belmont, CA: Fearon Pitman, 1979); and Paul Mali, *MBO Updated: A Handbook of Practices and Techniques for Managing by Objectives* (New York: Wiley, 1986).

6. For a fuller discussion of setting community standards and holding agencies accountable, see David M. Ammons, *Municipal Benchmarking: Assessing Local Performance and Establishing Community Standards* (Thousand Oaks, CA: Sage, 1996).

7. See Dennis M. Daley, "Designing Effective Performance Appraisal Systems," in Stephen E. Condrey, ed., *Handbook of Human Resource Management in Local Government* (San Francisco: Jossey-Bass, 1998), 223–45.

8. See Robert D. Brown, *Performance Appraisal as a Tool for Staff Development* (San Francisco: Jossey-Bass, 1988).

9. See Ronald D. Sylvia, Kathleen M. Sylvia, and Elizabeth M. Gunn, *Program Planning and Evaluation for Public Managers,* 2nd ed. (Prospect Heights, IL: Waveland Press, 1997): 68–72.

10. See, for example, Lawrence L. Steinmetz, *Managing the Marginal and Unsatisfactory Performer,* 2nd ed. (Reading, MA: Addison-Wesley, 1985); see also Donald W. Myers, ed., *Employee Problems Prevention and Counseling: A Guide for Professionals* (Westport, CT: Quorum Books, 1985).

11. Perhaps no more difficult task faces the manager than effective performance appraisals. For assistance, see William S. Swan and Phillip Margulies, *How to Do a Superior Performance Appraisal* (New York: Wiley, 1991); or Robert G. Johnson, *The Appraisal Interview Guide* (New York: Amacom, 1979).

12. See S. P. Burchett and K. De Meuse, "Performance Appraisal and the Law," *Personnel* 48 (July 1988): 29–37.

13. See Donald L. Kirkpatrick, *How to Improve Performance Through Appraisal and Coaching* (New York: Amacon, 1982).

14. See Robert D. Brown, *Performance Appraisal as a Tool for Staff Development* (San Francisco: Jossey-Bass, 1988).

15. See D. Mitchell and R. Broderick, "Flexible Pay Systems in the American Context: History, Policy, Research and Implications," in D. Lewin, K. Lipski, and K. Sockell, eds., *Advances in Industrial and Labor Relations* (Greenwich, CT: JAI Press, 1991).

16. Jayart Kirksey, "Companies Evaluate Employees from All Perspectives," *Personnel Journal* at <http://www.quality.org/tqmbbs/tools-techs/360pa.txt> downloaded 10/10/2000.

17. See Weinz Weihrich, *Management Excellence: Productivity Through MBO* (New York: McGraw-Hill, 1985).

18. The managerial criteria were developed by the author by means of a Delphi survey of 25 aerospace managers and 25 support managers at the NASA Langley Research Center, in cooperation with James Meyer. "The Status of WPPR," an unpublished research report to NASA, 1978.

19. One of the earliest reports of the technique was James Flanagan, "The Critical Incident Technique," *Psychological Bulletin* 51 (1954): 327–58.

20. See James Berkshire and Richard W. Highland, "Forced Choice Performance Rating—A Methodological Study," *Personnel Psychology* 6 (1953): 355–78; and H. John Bernardin, "Behavior Expectation Scales Versus Summated Scales: A Fairer Comparison," *Journal of Applied Psychology* 63 (1977): 422–27.

21. Figure 10.4 abstracted from Robert I. Lazer and Walter S. Wikstrom, *Appraising Managerial Performance: Current Practices and Future Directions* (New York: The Conference Board, 1977), p. 117.

EMPLOYEE TRAINING AND DEVELOPMENT

Futurist studies claim that the characteristics of the workplace in the twenty-first century will be vastly different from what most employees find today. These differences will be based, in part, on the continued growth of job specialization; the spin-off effects of basic science and research that will result in new technologies; and an increase in the growth of employment in the service sector, including health care, transportation, retail sales, and government employment. Forecasts predict that between 40 and 60 percent of the jobs people will hold in the next 20 years have not yet been created. These trends underscore the need for lifelong acquisition of new information, knowledge and skill development through in-service training programs, continuing adult education, internships, on-the-job training, and self-education, as well as traditional forms of education.

Training and development are key elements in modern personnel systems. A commitment to training at all levels of government is expressed in public policy pronouncements and resource allocations. Perhaps no other human resource activity so directly influences career advancement within organizations.[1] Indeed, systematic training efforts have become part and parcel of the strategies used for organizational change and adaptation.

The term *training* has come to encompass a variety of activities in addition to the acquisition of technical and managerial problem-solving skills. Other training activities include organization adaptations to demands from the environment; systematic efforts to adapt to long-range change; and activities aimed at problem solving, team building, conflict management, and changing employee attitudes and behavior.[2]

The discussion that follows treats training as a valued aspect of public personnel management. Training is discussed in the context of organization size and resource availability. Various training activities are then described in relation to organization functions. Finally, some of the problems surrounding current training strategies are considered, and an alternative approach is offered in which training is tied directly to organization needs and integrated with other organization activities.

TRAINING IN THE PUBLIC SECTOR

Training, especially program-specific training, has become an important activity of government that is valued by program managers as well as by personnel administrators. For example, federal programs of assistance to state and local governments require that the programs be operated within clearly defined limits. Achieving program compliance requires a good deal of inter-governmental communication that includes training related to program standards and requirements. In addition, federal funding of various categorical programs requires that state governments operate merit-based, nonpartisan personnel systems for persons employed in these programs. Merit has also come to mean using up-to-date management systems that require a good deal of attention to training.

At the federal level, the Government Employees' Training Act of 1958 required heads of federal agencies to become more involved in personnel management by using both external and internal facilities for employee training. Nearly a decade later, President Lyndon B. Johnson issued Executive Order 11348, which instructed the U.S. Civil Service Commission to conduct yearly reviews of training needs and to evaluate their effectiveness. Subsequently, the U.S. Bureau of Training was created to facilitate interagency training through its regional centers. Since its creation in 1978, the Office of Personnel Management has operated a variety of training programs through its regional offices on such topics as statistical methods, equal employment opportunity, and computer programming. The federal government also operates management training centers at Denver, Colorado, and Shepherdstown, West Virginia. Executives are trained at the Federal Executive Institute at Charlottesville, Virginia. The Clinton administration has recognized the critical nature of ongoing training by authorizing a program of Individual Learning Accounts (ILA). The goal is to enhance training of individual employees with a special emphasis on technology-mediated instruction. Each federal employee is to have a fund to pay for training and skills development. Agencies are to have autonomy in designing and delivering their own specialized programs. OPM has authorized pilot programs in a number of agencies.[3] The agencies have adopted a variety of training sponsorship models. Thus far, however, only the General Services Administration has followed the technology-mediation component of the mandate by creating a virtual university where its employees can take a variety of courses on-line regardless of the location of their duty stations.[4]

In addition to OPM-sponsored training, many agencies use programs aimed at their own specialized needs. For example, the U.S. Postal Service operates technical centers to train employees in various mail-handling technologies, and the State Department offers specialized instruction to its foreign service officers. Generally speaking, agencies provide the preponderance of training for their employees through in-house programs.

State and local governments are also committed to the development of their personnel. Many operate in-house units that offer a variety of training. The type and magnitude of training vary according to resource availability and managerial preferences. Organizations that do not possess sufficient financial resources or staff size to warrant investment in a training unit have other options available to them. Some agencies dispatch their personnel to the training seminars operated by the regional offices of OPM. Others choose to enter into training consortiums that can vary the training context according to the size of the government unit and the type and complexity of its operations.[5] Some managers of small municipalities engage in independent programmed instruction ' t is carried out on the job.[6] The Federal Executive Institute has initiated a new training program in which executives participate in training seminars, but they spend most of the time applying the seminar skills to problems in their own agencies. In effect, it is a mix of on-the-job and off-site training.

THE PROFESSIONALIZATION OF PUBLIC SERVICE

The public-service emphasis on training generally, and managerial training specifically, has resulted in a nationwide proliferation of advanced-degree programs in public administration. The National Association of Schools of Public Affairs and Administration (NASPAA) has more than 246 member institutions. It has developed curriculum standards that provide considerable latitude to member institutions seeking accreditation—a status granted to only 135 master's of public administration (MPA) degree programs nationally as of 2000.[7]

Persons engaged in continuing education for the public sector debate the relative emphasis that such programs should place on ethics and values, managerial skills, and holistic efforts at developing the complete individual.[8] MPA programs located in political science departments tend to emphasize the environment in which public programs operate and the need to instill a sense of public accountability in public servants. Programs located in schools of management or administration place greater emphasis on management as a technology that is equally applicable in public and private organizations.[9] Some observers argue that continuing education should shift away from the academic emphasis on learning that is to be applied only after graduation toward an emphasis on learning that the practitioner-student can apply immediately.[10] Others maintain that a theoretical emphasis and the on-the-job needs of students are not mutually exclusive and that an accommodation can be achieved between the two without sacrificing program content or quality.[11]

Recognition of the special needs of students pursuing public-service careers has resulted in innovative program delivery systems that depart from the traditional academic semester. Several schools, including the University of Oklahoma and the University of Southern California, operate programs on an intensive-semester basis. The intensive-semester format requires students to engage in advance preparation for seminars and utilizes lengthy instructional contact hours in a condensed period. These innovative delivery systems have made continued learning possible for persons who lack access to traditional university facilities, especially at the graduate level.

Government has traditionally been the principal employer of certain professionals, such as teachers and social workers. Governments at all levels also use the services of doctors, lawyers, engineers, planners, nurses, chemists, and computer technicians. Unfortunately, the curricula of most professional schools lack a public-service orientation and place little emphasis on the acquisition of supervisory or managerial skills. As a result, government must supplement the training of many professionals to equip them with managerial skills and to resocialize them away from their professional frames of reference toward a broader organizational perspective.[12]

Advanced training in public administration constitutes the newest form of professionalization in the public service. The problems associated with other professions in the public service should be much less evident among public administration professionals because the curricula of public administration programs are specifically managerial. The NASPAA guidelines emphasize the public-sector context of decisions and stress ethics and accountability—an emphasis that is coterminous with agency values.

Of course not all government positions require a master's degree. Training and development are as important for those entering at the bottom of the hierarchy, as well as for those who enter at midlevel. In fact, federal agencies are at times the recipients as well as the instruments of policy changes. Federal agencies were encouraged to actively participate in the Clinton administration's Welfare-to-Work program. Over 14,000 former welfare recipients were hired by federal agencies during the first two years. Such an influx of employees with little or no work experience must have strained agency resources.[13]

AN ORGANIZATIONAL PERSPECTIVE ON TYPES OF TRAINING

Training in the public sector encompasses far more than the development of management skills. It includes a broad range of activities related directly to the delivery of services, planned change in the organization, socialization of employees to organization values, and the management of conflict.[14]

Commonly cited virtues of training include the following:

1. It improves the level of worker productivity (quantity of work produced).
2. It improves the quality of the work produced.
3. It reduces or prevents employee obsolescence.
4. It increases job satisfaction.
5. It reduces the number and cost of work-related accidents.
6. It reduces the cost of equipment repair and maintenance.

For all these reasons, training is believed to be important.

Once the decision to train has been made, an appropriate training method must be selected.[15] It may be as traditional as on-the-job interactions between employees and supervisors, or it may be highly specialized. The type of training used depends on the nature and complexity of the theories, concepts, attitudes, knowledge, and skills to be developed.

In on-the-job training (OJT), the worker interacts with the supervisor or with experienced and competent peers while actually performing the tasks associated with the job. OJT is a centerpiece of Deming's principles of quality improvement, discussed later in this chapter.[16]

Alternatively, a worker can gain basic job skills or learn new methods using programmed instruction in which the trainee is systematically exposed to increments of job knowledge. Trainees use programmed books, computer software, or machines that enable them to learn one component of the job at a time. Each new skill that is learned is additive, so workers do not progress until all necessary information has been learned and tested. The latest version of programmed learning is computer-assisted instruction (CAI), in which the trainee interacts with a computer program designed to provide and test appropriate knowledge and job-related skills. Subject matter ranging from mathematics to languages, computer programming, collective bargaining, and public budgeting have been effectively taught through computer-assisted instruction.

Role playing, management games, and simulations are also used in training programs. With these methods, workers assume assigned roles or respond to simulated working conditions and make managerial or job-related decisions. Other, more traditional methods of training involve lectures, seminars, and topical workshops. These may take place at the agency, in an external training center, or at an institution of higher education.

To be meaningful, all training should be designed and implemented with a special concern for mission relevance. All organizations, from the nuclear family to the largest government agency, can be analyzed using a functional framework. The analysis that follows utilizes four basic macro functions of organizations, a typology developed by Katz and Kahn.[17] These four functions are production, adaptation, socialization, and coordination.

PRODUCTION

Production refers to the principal activity of the organization. In the case of General Motors, it is the manufacturing of automobiles. In the case of the Social Security Administration, it is the delivery of social security, Medicare, and other benefits to eligible clientele. In the case of General Motors, production involves high technology and large capital investments in machinery and equipment. In the case of the Social Security Administration, it involves interaction among individuals, various work units, and agency clientele. In all organizations, new employees learn the expectations of their positions through training. Such training normally involves the acquisition of specific job skills and provides an orientation to the rules and procedures of the organization.

The delivery system of skills and orientation training for production frequently involves the line supervisor and the work group. Many organizations, unfortunately, do not recognize that this OJT format also constitutes the principal values training activity of the organization. It cannot be assumed that supervisors possess the interpersonal and communication skills necessary to socialize new employees, yet it is these supervisors to whom the organization entrusts its most critical training activity. Only through systematic training of supervisors can organizations be certain that proper operation of organization technology is taught and that organization values and regulations will be internalized.

Skills training for managers and supervisors traditionally receives greater emphasis in government agencies than the training of rank-and-file employees. Skills training for supervisors involves working through and with others rather than doing it oneself. Skills training for managers may also involve budgeting and financial analysis, controlling, planning, quantitative decision making, leadership development, and so on. Frequently, however, organizations partake of such training irregularly in response to announcements from external training sources such as the OPM regional offices or private vendors.

ADAPTATION

Adaptation refers to an organization's need to deal effectively with changing demands from its environment. Adaptation is particularly important for public organizations that are accountable to external authorities. At the federal level, for example, an agency is accountable to Congress, the president, and the congressional and presidential auditing agencies—the General Accounting Office and the Office of Management and Budget, respectively. In addition, government organizations must deal with other agencies engaged in related activities, private-sector competitors, and organized groups that use the agency's services. Legislative changes in social policy or the organization of auxiliary agencies that provide services to line agencies may also require systemic adaptation.[18]

ORGANIZATIONAL DEVELOPMENT. Organization adaptations do not occur solely in reaction to mandates from the environment. A growing number of public and private organizations engage in systematic assessments of themselves and their environments to achieve organizational goals more effectively. These self-assessments produce strategies for planned changes in the organization that can be categorized broadly under the heading of organizational development (OD). OD can be defined as change that is "(1) planned, (2) organization-wide, and (3) managed from the top to (4) increase organization effectiveness and health through (5) planned interventions in the organization's 'process' using behavioral science knowledge."[19]

Traditionally, OD is conducted with the assistance of an external change agent drawn from the ranks of university faculties or private consulting companies. Recently, public agencies have developed their own organizational development units. Persons assigned to these units generally act as consultants to line managers and as trainers in team-building and conflict-resolution programs. They do not perform line management duties.

Among the specific methods associated with OD is the managerial grid, which is used as an analytical technique for defining organizational climate as a prelude to systematic change efforts.[20] Another, associated with Warren Bennis, is the systematic assessment of an organization's resources and actors, as a prelude to specific strategies for change.[21] Finally, team-building exercises aimed at developing a consensus among organization actors are frequently a part of OD strategies.[22]

Strategies such as planning exercises and grid analysis of the organization place a great deal of emphasis on defining where the organization is going but often neglect what the organization must do to get there.[23] The transition phase, in which new operating procedures are put in place, requires carefully planned task assignments and a clear delineation of the supports that various units must contribute to the effort.[24] Neglecting the management of the change process can doom the best-laid plans to failure.

SOCIALIZATION

Organizations also engage in training aimed at shaping the attitudes, values, and perceptions of members. New members often enter the organization with no preconceived notions about the proper roles and functions of government bureaucracies. Or they may enter with a set of reference points acquired during their professional training, or with attitudes and reference points developed in other organizations. Finally, persons may be promoted into positions of supervision or management that require a new set of organization reference points.

To effectively transmit their work rules and values, organizations frequently provide extensive orientation to new employees before allowing them to assume their assigned duties and responsibilities. In its most intensive form, this type of socialization training is mixed with basic skills training in induction facilities for military recruits. In the case of commissioned officers, each service branch operates an academy in which the academic curriculum is combined with a military lifestyle designed to perform the socialization function.[25] The academies are supplemented by Reserve Officer Training Corps (ROTC) programs, which provide military training within the context of the general university.

Civilian organizations that use professionally trained employees (social workers, teachers, rehabilitation counselors, public administrators) would do well to borrow a leaf from the military's ROTC book. All too frequently, professionally trained recruits enter the bureaucracy with unrealistic expectations regarding workloads and resource availability. Public managers at all levels of government can ease this cultural shock by becoming involved with university faculties in the design of curricula and by providing the opportunity for students to gain practical experience as part of their training. The latter occurs, to some degree, in internship programs and student teaching assignments. Unfortunately, this real-world experience, where it exists, comes rather late in the educational experience, sometimes after professional expectations are well formed in the minds of students.

Systematic socialization is particularly important for public employees whose previous experience has been limited to private industry. Private organizations emphasize productivity, market share, and profit margins. In contrast, government agencies frequently engage in ongoing service activities whose productivity is difficult to quantify. Market position is generally irrelevant as an agency reference point, as is profit. The emphasis is more likely to be on efficiency, equity, and effectiveness. Socialization in government, therefore, should emphasize a client-service orientation coupled with the maintenance of the highest personal and professional standards in one's work. Finally, the socialization of government employees should focus on accountability to elected officials and an overall public-service orientation.

The socialization of newly promoted supervisors and managers is important because, along with the development of new skills, they must undergo a change of perspective. Many managerial development programs seek to supplement decision-making and problem-solving training with socialization aimed at inculcating in the trainee a human-relations orientation or outlook.

The human-relations (HR) approach postulates that individual employees can and will accept responsibilities, are capable of and seek to engage in independent thought, and can and will internalize organization goals as their own.[26] In HR organizations, supervisors and managers are willing to delegate authority as well as responsibility, share decision making, and commit themselves to the nurturing and development of their subordinates.[27]

Other training approaches focus on the development of the manager as a person, believing that if he or she develops a healthier personality, the organization will benefit. The T-group (T stands for training) is one example.[28] A variant of the T-group involves sending the manager to a site away from the organization where trainees interact with persons from other organizations regarding their own behavior and the nature of group processes. The participants are supposed to learn to interact in an open, straightforward fashion without depending on symbols of power or the manipulation of others.

Critics of T-groups point out that when such training occurs detached from the organization, only the individual participants acquire the ability to respond openly and spontaneously. The organization continues to operate in its traditional fashion. The returning participant (unless in a position of power sufficient to impose the new perspective on the organization) will suffer culture shock or find it necessary to reconstruct his or her own defenses to survive. T-group training is most effective when integrated into a long-term effort at systematic interventions using the OD planned-change model.[29]

TOTAL QUALITY MANAGEMENT.   The most recent organizationwide intervention is total quality management (TQM).[30] TQM programs first and foremost seek a constancy of purpose toward quality improvement. The process begins with a comprehensive analysis of various aspects of the organization's mission. Relations with suppliers, organization processes, and relations with consumers of organization products are scrutinized for patterns of suboptimal performance. TQM uses trend analysis to identify and alter problem spots. Finally, TQM uses quantitative measures to determine progress in quality improvements.

Based on the teaching of W. Edwards Deming, TQM production methods are credited with the phenomenal productivity improvements of modern Japanese industry. Deming's system places responsibility for quality control on line workers rather than mass-based inspections. Workers are encouraged to come forward with suggestions for improvement and to engage in collective problem solving. As noted in Chapter 9 on compensation, workers share collectively in the savings from quality improvements; as noted in Chapter 10 on appraisal, TQM discourages individual performance standards in favor of overall unit productivity. TQM uses on-the-job training and cross-training of workers to increase mutual assistance and cooperation as well as enrich the jobs of workers.

TQM has been widely adopted in government. Most notably, the United States military is currently undertaking comprehensive TQM efforts. Another federal agency reporting TQM success is the Environmental Protection Agency.[31] State and local governments are also using TQM principles to upgrade service quality.[32]

By letting workers define quality and engineer their own production standards, TQM reduces costs through reducing errors. Enhanced quality and error reduction, in turn, lead to enhanced profits. Critics point to the absence of profits in government and the difficulty of finding other ways to measure quality improvements. This focus on output is overly narrow and is fundamentally unfair to government and TQM. TQM emphasizes relationships with customers and suppliers and improving internal processes. Public applications of TQM must pay close attention to the definitions of customers and clients. The former are overhead authorities and the community served. Clients are the members of the public with which the agency deals directly. This is particularly important when applying TQM in law enforcement agencies. Furthermore, TQM and its employee involvement in improving internal processes has brought huge savings in government supply costs, and it has reduced the paperwork attached to service delivery.[33]

COORDINATION

Coordination is generally thought of as a critical management activity, especially in modern organizations characterized by a high degree of task differentiation and subunit loyalty.[34] Because mission complexity dictates a division of labor, there is a high probability that the goals of subunits will displace the macro goals of the organization in the minds of their members, which may result in conflicts among task groups.

Interunit conflict frequently occurs when staff units, such as personnel or accounting, impose time demands on line managers. Personnel, for example, may demand significant amounts of the line manager's time to assure compliance with equal employment opportunity requirements. The personnel administrator may perceive the requirements as legitimate and necessary to meet external requirements. The line managers may perceive these demands as unwarranted consumption of time and energy that should be channeled into production.

A common response to such problems is to bring in an outside consultant to analyze the problem and suggest solutions. The consultant may prescribe activities aimed at reasserting the macro goals of the organization and achieving a commitment to them by those in various subunits of the organization. Specific interventions involve conflict management, which is designed to improve intergroup processes by making various units aware of the mission and time perspective of other, interdependent units.[35]

The importance of work-unit coordination is also reflected in the skills training available in various government training programs. Such programs emphasize decision-making models, technologies such as matrix management, operations research, and planning—all of which stress the necessity of coordination among work units.

Training coordination is also critical at the organization level. In Chapter 6 we discussed the importance of succession planning. Identifying employees with the potential for leadership is only the first step. Second, the organization should assess their deficits as well as strengths as their duties and responsibilities are expanded. A common approach is to study the organization to identify the skill mix needed, then provide aspiring managers with the training and mentoring necessary to succeed.

Similarly, we noted diversity realities of the twenty-first-century workforce in Chapter 3 and Chapter 5. Supervisors and managers must be in tune with agency diversity goals, and they must be trained to watch for and guard against discrimination in the workplace. They should be given the human relations skills needed for dealing with victims of discrimination. And, they must be trained in the appropriate way to proceed with complaint investigations in a manner designed to protect the rights of the accused as well as the alleged victim.

As organizations strive to enhance the quality and efficiency of their operations and to break down barriers between departments and work units, employees must be cross-trained on the various duties of their expanding positions. Technology, too, will require adaptive training so that workers can operate equipment correctly and efficiently and so that they will work smarter rather than harder.

All the above pose training problems for the organization. Few agencies have the in-house resources to provide a wide variety of training. Training directors and human resources managers, moreover, rarely have the organization clout to impose a training regimen on line managers who are often swamped with day-to-day activities. The organization's executive leadership must therefore elevate training and development from an obscure staff function to an organization priority. One theory suggests turning the organization into a "learning organization." Workers and work units strive to understand the workings of other units and strive to coordinate and cooperate. Staff and managers are urged to turn learning into an organization priority.[36]

SUMMARY AND CONCLUSION

Training is expensive; therefore, its effectiveness must be carefully weighed. The cost of training includes both the actual expenses of training programs and the time lost to the organization as a result of participant absences. The benefits of training are more difficult to calculate, particularly when one is attempting to assess the aggregate value of all available training. Direct and consistent improvements in the delivery of state and local government services that have resulted from the expenditure of training funds are virtually impossible to demonstrate.

Critics have questioned the benefits of various types of training at the organization level. Some advocates of change in government programs argue that educational training has little influence upon agencies because these programs are individual in focus, are delivered outside the organizational context, and reinforce existing structures.[37]

The bureaucratic structure of organizations is another possible impediment to training effectiveness. Critics cite rigid classification systems, reward systems that are not tied to skill acquisition or the development of subordinates, an overemphasis on technical rather than managerial qualifications for advancement, and pension systems that discourage the movement of uniformed personnel into civilian management positions.[38]

The charge that training efforts have not lived up to their advance billing applies equally to organizational development efforts aimed at self-analysis and modifications in organization culture. Unfortunately, funding limitations, a lack of executive commitment, or both have often precluded the creation of ongoing training programs to implement the desired changes. Other organizations that dispatch "available" personnel to training seminars that may or may not be related directly to the needs of the organization may also experience limited organizational benefits.

Many of the foregoing problems can be dealt with if the organization's leadership is willing to fund training programs based on careful self-analysis of the organization's goals and integration with other management systems. The first step is for management to decide where the organization is and where it should be in the foreseeable future. Next, the appropriate mix of technical, clerical, and managerial skills necessary to achieve the desired ends should be determined. Only then should the organization turn its attention to the design of training programs. Resource limitations, of course, may necessitate ordering the priorities of training plans. Training and development programs should then be integrated into the operating procedures of the organization.

MADISON COUNTY'S ZERO-TOLERANCE FOR HARASSMENT AND DISCRIMINATION DIRECTIVE*

Maggie Jones mused over the statistics she had just read concerning the attitudes of military members toward gays and lesbians. She wondered if the "don't ask, don't tell, don't pursue" policy that was put into place in 1993 by President Clinton's administration would stand the resistance it was receiving, especially from male soldiers. In any event, the data had been gathered, the analysis made, and the Department of Defense acknowledged it had a problem.

As human resources training specialist, she had literally heard and seen it all when it came to discussing and valuing differences. The treatment of African Americans, Asians, and Hispanics always raised questions about the legacy of racism, segregation, and separation, and most recently, the issues of "one nation, one people, one language," were on the front burner. She dealt with the stereotypical attitudes about women—that they were too emotional "because of their special kind of hormones"; that they preferred male "bosses" over their female counterparts; that it was common knowledge that women are only in the workplace as "babes," "gals," or "girls," and were primarily interested in getting a man

---

*Prepared by C. Kenneth Meyer and Lance Noe, Drake University.

who would be, in the final analysis, the real breadwinner and family provider. Yes, she had heard it all! And to complicate things even further, she now had to deal with the biases of age, religion, and appearance.

Now, the brutal murder of a young male soldier in the 101st Airborne Division at Fort Campbell, Kentucky, who was thought to be gay, raised new questions. The media had reported that gays were often harassed at Fort Campbell and taunted verbally and by body language—gestures, movement of hands, eyes, and general physical demeanor. The graffiti in the barracks and other public places left no doubt that some soldiers hated those whom they perceived to have a different sexual orientation than their own. Some soldiers felt that political correctness (PC) had gone awry with the differentiation that was made in their diversity training between sexual preference and sexual orientation. They were sure that gay soldiers actually preferred being homosexual—it was that simple and that easy to understand, and "that was that." Discrimination and harassment of homosexuals was rampant at Fort Campbell, and the high discharge rate of gays and lesbians there, in contrast to other military installations of similar size, pointed to an overall organizational climate of intolerance and rejection that reached a low point at the installation when the young soldier was slain. Of course, the DoD had sent in its inspectors and interviewed several thousand soldiers and civilians in an attempt to assess the magnitude of antigay attitudes and behavior. Jones recounted in her mind that they had found harassment to be commonplace and that it was often manifested in terms of comments and gestures and other forms of mistreatment and abuse.

Maggie Jones wondered how she would develop an antiharassment training plan for her own county—a county that was largely urban with a diverse population. She found the expression of negative attitudes as revealed in recent local newspaper and media editorials about the influx of Somalians, Haitians, Bosnians, and Guatemalans to add further evidence that there really existed a culture of intolerance in America. She knew these attitudes and beliefs had to be addressed, but how was she to do it without turning off a group of employees that by most conventional standards were considered caring and compassionate people. Would she take a strident, aggressive approach to the needed training? Would she lay it all on the line in terms of what she personally felt—ideas that were mostly supported by the academic literature? There was no room to set this complex set of issues aside, for she had to deal with the directive she recently received from Carolyn Fong, the county manager for Madison County.

The directive said that Madison County had "a zero-tolerance for all forms of harassment, violence, and discrimination. Supervisors will be held accountable for the actions of their subordinates who engage in intimidating, hostile, abusive, or violent behavior against other employees, clients, customers, or vendors." The directive left no room to wiggle; it was a tall order and Jones knew that her own professional reputation would clearly be placed on the firing line.

QUESTIONS AND INSTRUCTIONS

1. If you were Maggie Jones, what would comprise the key elements in your antiharassment action plan? Please list in the order that these important elements would appear in your comprehensive action plan.

2. Do you believe the employees of Madison County should be queried about their attitudes toward gays and lesbians? What about the complementary issues of race, age, gender, religion, national origin, and socioeconomic status or class? Is this information needed for the development of your comprehensive action plan? Please elaborate.

3. In the final analysis, do you believe that discriminatory attitudes and behavior directed against gays and lesbians can be changed? What key issues do you expect the trainees to raise? List some of them. Especially, how would you personally deal with the belief some hold that homosexuality is unnatural, immoral, and that homosexual people can be transformed into healthy heterosexuals? Please discuss.

4. Does a zero-tolerance policy against intolerance violate the premise of tolerance in American civic culture? Please elaborate and give examples.

NOTES AND RESOURCES

1. Peter F. Drucker, *The New Realities: In Government and Politics/In Economics and Business/In Society and World View* (New York: Harper & Row, 1989), pp. 242–52.

2. Robert L. Craig, ed., *Training and Development Handbook* (New York: McGraw-Hill, 1987). The training specialists of the federal government identify team leadership, visioning, problem solving, conflict resolution, and decisiveness as a few of the skills that go into a quality federal executive; see OPM, "Great Leaders for Great Government," The Federal Executive Institute and Management Development Centers at <http://www.leadership.opm.gov/programs.html> downloaded 10/22/00.

3. Executive Order 13111, "Using Technology to Improve Training Opportunities for Federal Government Employees" (January 1999). The pilot programs are in the Department of Commerce, the Department of Defense/Air Force, the Environmental Protection Agency, the General Services Administration, the Department of Health and Human Services, the Department of Housing, the Department of the Interior, the Department of Labor, the Occupational Safety and Health Review Committee, OPM, the Social Security Administration, the Department of Transportation/Federal Highway Administration, and the Department of the Treasury, at <http://www.opm.gov/HRD/Lead/ILASIDE.HTM>.

4. See General Services Administration, "Online University ILA Pilot," at <http://www.opm.gov/HRD/desila7.htm>. The program is open to all GSA employees and has an initial funding of $140,000.

5. Robert Mowitz, "Training Model for State and Local Governmental Personnel," *Public Personnel Management* 3 (1974): 451–53.

6. Winston Crouch, *Local Government Personnel Administration* (Washington, DC: International City Management Association, 1976).

7. National Association of Schools of Public Affairs and Administration, *2000 Directory of Programs* (Washington, DC: NASPAA, 2000).

8. O. White, ed., "Symposium: Towards a Grounded Approach to Public Administration Training," *Southern Review of Public Administration* 3 (1979): 244–308.

9. Howard E. McCurdy, "Selecting and Training Public Managers: Business Skills vs. Public Administration," *Public Administration Review* 38 (1978): 571–78.

10. Frederick Fischer, "Give a Damn About Continuing Adult Education in Public Administration," *Public Administration Review* 33 (1973): 488–98; see also Robert B. Denhardt,

"On the Management of Public Service Education," *Southern Review of Public Administration* 3 (1979): 273–83.

11. L. A. Wolf, "In Defense of the Ivory Tower," *Southern Review of Public Administration* 3 (1979): 264–72.

12. J. A. Bayton and R. L. Chapman, *Transformation of Scientists and Engineers into Managers* (Washington, DC: NASA, 1972).

13. OPM reports that the federal government's Welfare-to-Work initiatives have produced good results. Welfare-to-Work participants have a one-year retention rate of 69 percent; more than double that of grade-comparable peers. OPM Director Janice R. Lachance, "Open Letter to Employers," at <http://www.opm.gov/wtw/html/openlet.htm>.

14. John Schermanerhorn, "Does Mentoring Breed Success?" *Training and Development Journal* 40, no. 11 (November 1986): 38–43; see also Linda Ackerman, "Change Management: Basics for Training," *Training and Development Journal* 40, no. 4 (April 1986): 67–70; and Arthur B. Van Gundy, *Creative Problem Solving: A Guide for Trainers and Management* (New York: Quorum Books, 1987).

15. See Gerald T. Gabris, "Implementing More Productive Management Training Programs," *Public Productivity Review* 12 (1989): 437–45.

16. See Mary Walton, *Deming Management at Work* (New York: G. P. Putnam's Sons, 1990).

17. See Daniel Katz and Robert L. Kahn, *The Social Psychology of Organizations* (New York: Wiley, 1966).

18. Ronald D. Sylvia, Kathleen M. Sylvia, and Elizabeth Gunn, 2nd ed., *Program Planning and Evaluation for Public Managers* (Prospect Heights, IL: Waveland Press, 1997): 65–90.

19. Richard Beckhard, *Organization Development: Strategies and Models* (Reading, MA: Addison-Wesley, 1969), p. 9.

20. See Robert R. Blake and Jane S. Mouton, *The Managerial Grid* (Houston: Gulf, 1964).

21. Warren G. Bennis, *Organization Development: Its Nature, Origins and Prospects* (Reading, MA: Addison-Wesley, 1969).

22. Douglas McGregor, *The Professional Manager* (New York: McGraw-Hill, 1976).

23. Linda Ackerman, "Change Management: Basics for Training," *Training and Development Journal* 40, no. 4 (April 1986): 67–70.

24. Richard Beckhard and Ruben J. Harris, *Organizational Transition: Managing Complex Change* (Reading, MA: Addison-Wesley, 1977).

25. Samford M. Dornbush, "The Military Academy as an Assimilation Institution," *Social Forces* 33 (1955): 316–21.

26. Douglas McGregor, *The Human Side of Enterprise* (New York: McGraw-Hill, 1960).

27. Jerry Willbur, "Does Mentoring Bring Success?" *Training and Development Journal* 41, no. 11 (November 1987): 38–41.

28. Robert Golembiewski, "The Laboratory Approach to Organizational Development," *Public Administration Review* 27 (1967): 215–17.

29. Richard Beckhard, "The Appropriate Use of T-Groups in Organizations," in B. Blackwell, ed., *ATN Occasional Papers: 2. T-Group Training: Group Dynamics in Management Education* (New York: Oxford University Press, 1965).

30. For a comprehensive look at TQM, see Yoji Akao, *Hoshin Kanri: Policy Deployment for Successful TQM* (Cambridge, MA: Productivity Press, 1991); see also Mary Walton, *Deming Management at Work* (New York: G. P. Putnam's Sons, 1990).

31. Steven Cohen and Ronald Brand, "Total Quality Management in the U.S. Environmental Protection Agency," *Public Productivity and Management Review* 14 (1990): 99–114.

32. For a discussion of TQM and its adoption in government agencies, see James E. Swiss, "Adapting Total Quality Management to Government," *Public Administration Review* 52 (1992): 356–62.

33. The National Performance Review is a prime example of process improvement, rethinking regulations, and a reduced burden of paperwork. It was undertaken with task forces and project teams made up of federal employees. See Office of Management and Budget, *A Report to the President on the Third Anniversary of Executive Order 12866: More Benefits, Fewer Burdens,* at <http://www.whitehouse.gov/search?NS-search-page=documents&NS-rel-doc-name=/OMB/in> posted December 1996.

34. Max Weber, *The Theory of Social and Economic Organizations* (New York: Oxford University Press, 1974).

35. Paul R. Lawrence and Jay W. Lorsch, *New Direction for Organizations* (Cambridge, MA: Harvard University Graduate School of Business Administration, 1967).

36. Janice A. Cooke, et al., *Learning Organizations in the Public Service* (Brookfield, VT: Gower, Ashgate, 1997).

37. Roy B. Gregg and John Van Maanen, "The Realities of Education as a Prescription for Organization Change," *Public Administration Review* 33 (1973): 522–33.

38. W. D. Heisel, "A Non-Bureaucratic View of Management Development," *Public Personnel Management* 9 (1980): 95–98.

PUBLIC-SECTOR COLLECTIVE BARGAINING

THE HISTORICAL CONTEXT OF LABOR RELATIONS IN THE UNITED STATES

Early on, leaders of the American labor movement decided to let the principle of pragmatism guide their choice of allies and enemies. When labor leader Samuel Gompers was asked what the unions wanted, he replied, "More, more, more— now!"[1] He was expressing both his dedication to improving the lot of working people and his conscious choice to reject ideological movements and all their trappings.[2] In effect, the unions endorsed the American capitalist system. The significance of this choice can be illustrated by comparing the course of American unions with that of their European counterparts.

American labor leaders struggled to legitimize collective bargaining, and their involvement in politics was directed at securing legislation conducive to that end. Labor leaders also supported change in areas such as child labor, social security, and minimum wage provisions. Of course, European labor leaders also have sponsored the passage of similar legislation; however, they have frequently sought those ends as part of a larger effort to reorder their societies along Marxist lines. The pragmatic approach to achieving worker benefits within existing structures taken in the United States stands in contrast to European mergers of ideological movements and labor unions. A notable exception to the pragmatic approach were the "Wobblies" (Industrial Workers of the World), who believed the labor movement to be part of a larger class struggle between exploited workers and their bosses.[3] The forces of government were also turned against union leaders with leftist leanings. Various states passed laws against anarchists and criminal syndicalists who advocated the overthrow of government or engaged in or advocated industrial sabotage. The most famous case was the imprisonment of a New York union official for such advocacy that encouraged bad tendencies.[4]

THE EARLY YEARS

Prior to the passage of the National Labor Relations Act in 1935, progress toward organizing workers and securing collective bargaining agreements was made fitfully in a free-market society whose rules favored management. Labor experienced some of its greatest early successes during World War I, when the government was willing to lend its support to labor unions in exchange for no-strike pledges.[5] Not all unions cooperated. A prominent representative of the railroad workers and leftist presidential candidate Eugene V. Debs was imprisoned for advocating draft resistance.[6]

At the time, entering into collective bargaining agreements with workers was anathema to most American capitalists, who believed that dealing with workers' interests collectively would drive up production costs and make the companies' products less competitive. Few anticipated the new industries and markets to be generated by increasing the disposable income of workers and thereby increasing the demand for consumer goods.

This period was characterized by sweatshop working conditions in most industries and by "yellow-dog contracts," which required that workers pledge that they were not members of any union or that they withdraw their membership and promise never to join another union. Of course, all workers were forced to swear as a condition of employment that they would never subsequently join a union, regardless of their previous associations.[7] Yellow-dog contracts were outlawed in 1932 as part of the Norris–La Guardia Anti-Injunction Act.

In the absence of national legislation regulating labor relations, organizing had been a matter of approaching the workers of a given employer and convincing them that they could benefit from forming a common front. Organizers then convinced the employer to enter into a collective bargaining agreement with the designated representative of the workers. The principal weapon of the unions was the withholding of services in the form of strikes. Unions also pressured their adversaries by using secondary boycotts—that is, by persuading consumers of the company's products to do business elsewhere. Frequently, the consumers were other companies that were already unionized. The targets of such boycotts frequently sought injunctive relief in the courts.[8]

The injunction tactic involved an employer's convincing a magistrate that the disruption of work constituted a criminal conspiracy, threatened the public safety, or menaced the public interest through adverse effects on the economy. The courts were generally sympathetic to these appeals, even though providing injunctive relief often required feats of judicial legerdemain, given various precedents of Anglo-American common law that permitted all sorts of alliances and conspiratorial activities to businesses in order to gain advantage over their competitors.

The Sherman Anti-Trust Act of 1890 provided a substantial rule change in terms of how commerce was to be conducted; it also provided federal judges with statutory justification for issuing injunctions against union activities.[9] Congress sought to overturn the use of the injunction to prevent strikes with the passage of the Clayton Act of 1914, which specified the nonenjoinability of legitimate actions between employers and employees under the Sherman Act. The Supreme Court, however, chose to define "legitimate actions" narrowly, prohibiting the use of nonemployee picketers and secondary boycotts. Real anti-injunctive legislation was not forthcoming until 1932, with the passage of the Norris–La Guardia Act.

FEDERAL LEGISLATION

THE NATIONAL LABOR RELATIONS ACT. The legislative zenith of organized labor's gains was achieved in 1935 with the passage of the National Labor Relations Act, sometimes referred to as the Wagner Act, which brought all private-sector labor relations under the authority of the federal government. The act also created the National Labor Relations Board (NLRB) to oversee those relations, certify union elections, and investigate and punish unfair labor practices. The magnitude of the victory can best be appreciated against the backdrop of American political values, which normally resist government regulation—especially of commerce—and jealously guard the sanctity of state and local government prerogatives.

Labor's successes in the 1930s and 1940s have not since been equaled. At the time, Congress was receptive to labor's agenda because labor unions were the bedrock upon which the Roosevelt coalition erected its presidential majorities.[10] The courts, too, had become less and less receptive to the appeals of management, as 20 years of Democratic appointments took effect. The situation balanced out somewhat in 1946 with the coming of the first Republican majority in 16 years and the subsequent passage of the Labor Management Relations Act of 1947, better known as the Taft-Hartley Act.

THE TAFT-HARTLEY ACT. The most widely known feature of the Taft-Hartley Act was the establishment of a National Emergency Impasse Procedure that authorized the president to take steps resulting in an 80-day "cooling-off" procedure when a labor dispute was thought to endanger the national safety or health.[11] Other features of the act were less controversial but have had a greater impact on routine relations between employers and employee groups.

Taft-Hartley prohibited closed shops; thus, union membership may not be made a precondition of employment. The act also provided that states may pass right-to-work legislation to prevent union contracts from compelling union membership upon employment (a union shop). The act also protects the employer from being jostled about by competing unions, allowing employers to petition the NLRB to conduct a representative election when more than one union is attempting to represent its workers. The employer's ability to manage is strengthened in the act by excluding supervisors from the definition of *employee.* In other words, when workers become supervisors, they forfeit their rights to inclusion in the collective bargaining unit.[12] Finally, Taft-Hartley specified a list of union practices that were defined as unfair (the original Wagner Act only dealt with unfair management practices).[13]

THE LANDUM-GRIFFIN ACT. By the 1950s, collective bargaining in the private sector had ceased to be a public policy controversy. Subsequent legislation regarding private-sector unions focused instead on their internal activities. The Landum-Griffin Act of 1959 provided certain guarantees of rank-and-file participation in union elections and made union officials accountable for how organization funds were spent. The same act also forbade union office to persons convicted of any one of a variety of felonies, ranging from embezzlement and bribery to robbery and assault.

COLLECTIVE BARGAINING IN THE POSTINDUSTRIAL SOCIETY

Collective bargaining in the current era is characterized by an acceptance of the rules by all parties. The National Labor Relations Board administers a process in the private sector that is, by and large, institutionalized. Cases that reach the NLRB generally result in fine-tuning the process rather than in wholesale change. Unions, however, continue their efforts to advance their self-interest through the national legislative process. They also resist the continuing efforts of antiunion groups to secure right-to-work legislation at the state level.

Institutionalization of the process notwithstanding, the percentage of the workforce that is unionized is on the decline. The greatest single cause of this decline is that the traditional base of union strength was in manufacturing and the skilled trades. The postindustrial society from the 1960s on has been characterized by the growth of economic enterprises that do not involve product manufacturing. These so-called service industries include such specialties as insurance, hotels and leisure, and food services. Unions have not had the organizing success in service industries that they enjoyed with manufacturing workers.

A second possible reason for the decline of unionization is the very success unions have achieved in advancing the lot of American workers through changes in government policy. The incentives for workers to organize are reduced by such existing policies as minimum wage standards, social security, safety regulations, workers' compensation systems, and unemployment insurance. Collectively, these all contribute to the general well-being of working people.

Unions whose rank-and-file membership base is in manufacturing must also assume a portion of the responsibility for the declining percentage of unionized workers. Union leaders with institutionalized power based on one group of workers have had little incentive to attempt expansion into other industries. Established unions, of course, have supported expansionist efforts into service industries indirectly through their contributions to the American Federation of Labor and Congress of Industrial Organizations (AFL-CIO).[14] Indirect support, however, cannot substitute for a dedicated cadre of affected workers diligently striving to organize their fellows. Heretofore, expansion into white-collar and service industries has had scant success—with the glowing exception of the public sector, where mounting discontent among workers has resulted in an astounding growth in unionization.

In recent years, the leadership of the AFL-CIO has shifted its organizing efforts to target traditionally nonunionized workers in service industries like fast foods, janitorial services, and so forth. The AFL-CIO has also embraced the rights of immigrant workers, affirmative action, and equal pay for women.[15]

UNIONIZATION IN THE PUBLIC SECTOR

GROWTH OF PUBLIC-SECTOR UNIONS

Labor leaders initially were reluctant to expend limited resources in attempting to organize the public service. To paraphrase George Meany, the late past president of the AFL-CIO, the public sector can never be organized because the government will never grant public employees permission to strike. Meany believed that without labor's ability to strike and disrupt services, there can be no good-faith bargaining on the part of management.[16] Meany, of course, was wrong. The ratio of unionized to nonunionized public employees has grown, while the percentage of unionized workers in the total economy remains relatively constant. In 1961, unionized workers in the national workforce totaled 22 percent; in 1999, 13.9 percent. Wisconsin became the first state to allow bargaining for public employees in 1960. Table 12.1 illustrates the percentage of state and local public employees that were unionized in the two succeeding decades, when 36 of the 50 states and the District of Columbia granted public employees some form of collective bargaining.[17]

The proportion of organized public employees is now four times that in the private sector. The highest percentages are found among public-safety workers and teachers. Local employees, in general, are much more organized than state and federal employees.

Labor's success in gaining collective bargaining rights for public employees is due in part to the involvement of unions in the political process. Part of the change must also be attributed to an evolution in the attitudes of the public and politicians. Acceptance of collective bargaining for public employees has also been facilitated by the development of impasse resolution mechanisms such as mediation, fact finding, and arbitration, which are thought to reduce the threat of strikes by public-service employees.

MOTIVATIONS TO ORGANIZE

Economic, solidarity, and purposive motivations underlie the decision to organize and seek collective bargaining rights. The first two are relevant to unionization in the private as well as the public sector; purposive motivation is, by and large, a public-sector phenomenon.

ECONOMICS.   Wishing to improve one's economic situation is the most easily understood of the three motivations. The fact that one's compensation is inadequate to meet basic living needs is readily grasped. Deciding that the best way to advance one's economic interests is through collective action is less obvious to most workers. The task of the union organizer, therefore, is to instill a sense of solidarity in workers. "Workers of the world unite!" was the rallying cry of early union organizers as well as of ideological movements.

■ TABLE 12-1

PERCENTAGE OF UNIONIZATION GOVERNMENT AND THE PRIVATE SECTOR IN 1999

All Workers	Private	Federal	State	Local
13.9	9.4	33.8	27.8	43.8

SOLIDARITY. Instilling a sense of solidarity is particularly difficult when organizing public employees, because so many are white-collar workers who traditionally identify with management. This identification with management began to decline, along with the earning power of public employees relative to private-sector workers, beginning in the late 1960s and continued into the 1980s. The economic decline was due to shrinking resources caused by inflation: as the inflation rate went up, the real spending power of public agencies declined. Politicians were reluctant to seek tax increases in austere times, so public managers were forced to make program cutbacks. Large-scale cuts had to come from salaries and benefits or through the outright elimination of positions, because salaries make up a preponderance of the public expenditures that can be cut. These realities did much to raise the collective consciousness of public employees. As noted in Chapter 9, average public-sector wages and benefits have surged ahead of their private-sector counterparts, which may be due in large part to the organizing successes of public-sector unions.

The solidarity that public workers felt with their fellows was further enhanced by their perception of the cumbersomeness and partiality of the civil service system, which frequently supported management actions against individual employees.[18] Union organizers pointed out that fairness could be assured only by making outside arbitration of grievances a condition of the contract.

Most recently, public-sector unions have made inroads into the ranks of clerical workers by advocating comparable worth to determine the relative value of clerical positions and other job categories. Thus, stressing an economic issue (pay equity) has allowed the unions to make common cause (solidarity) with the previously hard-to-organize clerical workers.

PURPOSIVE MOTIVATION. In the United States, purposive motivation is a phenomenon unique to the public sector. As it is used here, the term refers to an ideological or values framework that motivates the tactics of the union negotiator to bring about changes in public policy. Some public-sector unions initially grew out of the professional values framework of their membership.

The unionization of teachers, social workers, and nurses, for instance, grew out of professional organizations that were created to advance those professions through sharing theoretical and applied knowledge. These organizations also sought to influence the course of public policy insofar as it affected their particular field of expertise.[19] Professionalization also enhanced solidarity, which in turn facilitated the development of a collective consciousness with regard to declining wages and benefits.

Purposive concerns, such as the kind of texts that should be adopted, classroom size, or caseloads of social workers, are public policy questions that go beyond the scope of most labor contracts, which are usually limited to wages, fringe benefits, and working conditions. Teachers, social workers, and nurses are professionals who could be included as individual professionals in such organization decisions as textbook adoptions and client ratios—whether the "clients" are students, welfare recipients, or hospital patients. Once such matters are included in labor contracts, they cannot be easily negotiated out. Public-sector managers must therefore take pains to ensure that such matters do not become bargainable topics.

Making public policy by means of the collective bargaining process can be a threat to popular sovereignty. In the United States, sovereignty rests in the people and is supposed to be exercised by their elected representatives. Union contracts, by contrast, are frequently negotiated by career managers and employee representatives. If those contracts incorporate substantive policy decisions, legislative participation could dwindle to pro forma ratification rather than reflecting thoughtful legislative consideration and choice, thereby vesting enormous power in a few individuals.

PUBLIC- VERSUS PRIVATE-SECTOR UNIONS

Public officials sometimes oppose public-sector collective bargaining based on a negative image of private unions and the strike tactic, equating public unions with such giants as the Teamsters and Steelworkers. The reality, however, is quite different. The two largest federal employees' unions are the American Federation of Government Employees and the Postal Workers Union. State and local unions are generally local units of confederations such as the American Federation of State, County, and Municipal Employees (AFSCME), the largest single union. The Fraternal Order of Police (FOP) and the International Fire Fighters Association (IFFA) are other confederations that serve highly specialized constituencies. All of these confederations are made up of relatively small local unions that lack the negotiating and organizational expertise of their private-sector cousins. They also conspicuously lack the financial reserves needed to provide legal assistance to members during disputes or to finance work stoppages. The American Association of University Professors, the American Federation of Teachers, the National Education Association, and the American Nursing Association are professional associations that have evolved from advancing their professions to bargaining over contracts. Not only are these organizations smaller than private-sector unions, they have certain other limitations on their power.

Public employees normally lack the resources of their private-sector counterparts to carry out tactics designed to disrupt the productivity of their employers. The strike weapon is legally forbidden to many public employees. More important, even when strikes are undertaken, public unions do not have the economic resources to sustain their members through protracted disputes. Local unions also may not enjoy the support of similar unions. Police officers in city A are not likely to strike in sympathy with the police officers in city B, nor can they boycott the products of city B. It is far more likely that they will be dispatched to provide police services to the city in question under a mutual assistance agreement. Finally, management negotiators in the public sector may be elected officials, which may politicize the bargaining process.

COLLECTIVE BARGAINING AT THE STATE AND LOCAL LEVEL

The activities that state and local employee unions undertake reflect the political cultures of individual states and the legislation that governs the activities of public employees. In some states, public employees have the right to engage in collective bargaining and the right to strike in the event of an impasse. Other states allow collective bargaining for some employees, such as teachers, police, and firefighters, but provide elaborate impasse resolution procedures to ensure that strikes will not occur.

Some states provide for meet-and-confer sessions in which public-sector managers are required to meet with employee representatives and consider their concerns. What is permissible under meet-and-confer legislation is a matter of interpretation. One city might take the legislation at face value, while another in the same state might enter into a full-blown collective bargaining agreement.

Finally, some states specifically forbid collective bargaining or make no mention of it one way or the other. In states without a law, there is no real pattern to collective bargaining. Employees in one municipality may persuade the city council to grant them bargaining rights under the city's "charter city" authority, while other cities may refuse to discuss issues, much less bargain. The result is a hodgepodge of employer-employee relations that defies rationality and frequently leads to illegal work stoppages.

One of the arguments against public-employee unionization is that essential services, especially police and fire protection, could be disrupted. Ironically, the uniformed services are the groups who have been most successful in securing the right to bargain. This success is due as much to the militancy of police and firefighters and their willingness to work at organization as it is to the public's fear of disruption of essential services.

State-level employees have been the slowest to organize and to achieve bargaining rights. Apparently, the merits of orderly negotiations at the local level are more readily apparent to legislators than are the benefits of collective bargaining for state employees. In states where bargaining is not permitted, public employees have formed associations that lobby legislators and governors in the interest of state employees. These associations generally exhibit an interest in self-survival equal to that of the unions. One of the first items on their legislative agendas is securing dues-checkoff privileges, meaning that the state payroll office deducts membership dues from members' paychecks and forwards it to the association. Thus freed from the mundane necessity of collecting membership dues, the associations can focus their energies on the legislature.

Clearly, public-sector unionization is a reality of modern government. States that have accepted unionization have passed legislation that explicitly defines the nature of their recognition and the range of issues that will be subject to bargaining. They have also provided for well-staffed administrative structures to oversee the process. Finally, legislatures have prescribed impasse resolution procedures to safeguard against the disruption of essential services, and some have passed legislation that even grants employees a limited right to strike.

THE RIGHT TO BARGAIN

As noted previously, local uniformed services' unions have achieved widespread recognition; other public employees should be entitled to the same rights, privileges, and protections. Certainly the impact on society of a potential work stoppage by city clerical workers is far less threatening than one by the uniformed services. So why the delay?

For one thing, the number of employees involved at the state level and the variety of job categories complicate the decisions faced by legislatures wishing to grant state employees the right to bargain. For example, should a state enter into one agreement covering all employees? Or should the faculties of state universities—or members of the state police—be covered by separate contracts? Should all bargaining be conducted by a single office of employee relations, or should agencies be allowed to bargain with their employees over their specific issues of concern? Finally, should professional employees of a given agency be included in the same bargaining units as its clerical workers and truck drivers?

The complexity of the factors involved in public-sector labor relations demands well-reasoned answers to these questions. The process by which public policies are made, however, is not amenable to the formation of comprehensive policies. In a typical scenario, the uniformed services lobby to secure bargaining rights, followed by the teachers, and so on. Each successive group finds the legislature more receptive to its demands, partly because the policy climate is increasingly conducive to the issue and partly because established groups support the goals of those who come after. Existing statutes are amended to cover the new groups, or new legislation specific to them is drafted. The process is piecemeal. However, policymakers in some states have developed comprehensive legislation through a reevaluation of interrelated statutes. Such legislation should provide for an adequate administrative structure to oversee the process, provide for bargaining unit certification, assist in the resolution of bargaining impasses, and investigate unfair labor practices.

COLLECTIVE BARGAINING ADMINISTRATION

ADMINISTRATIVE STRUCTURES. The most impressive feature of labor relations in the private sector is the orderly administration of the process provided by the National Labor Relations Board. Orderly administration is no less important to collective bargaining at the state and local level. When they exist, these administrative structures are frequently known as Public Employee Relations Boards (PERBs). Appropriate responsibilities for a PERB include the certification of bargaining units, the promulgation of rules regarding the conduct of bargaining relations, the proscribing of unfair labor practices, and the determination of whether an issue is within the scope of bargaining or is subject to resolution by legally prescribed impasse resolution procedures.

BARGAINING UNIT CERTIFICATION. When a bargaining unit wishes certification, the PERB conducts representation elections in which the interests of all parties are protected. A PERB election rule might require that petitions signed by 30 percent of the workers in the proposed bargaining unit be collected before holding an election. In the election, eligible workers vote on whether they wish a particular union to represent them. A vote of 50 percent plus one member is normally required for certification by a PERB. Sometimes, however, more than one union seeks to represent workers in a given organization. In such cases, the voting choices are no union, union A, or union B. Majorities are required in these elections, just as they are when the choice is union or no union; there are no plurality unions.

Prior to conducting an election, the PERB must determine what constitutes an appropriate bargaining unit. The criterion for this determination is whether a group of workers constitutes a sufficient community of interest to warrant inclusion in a bargaining unit. Professional employees, such as social workers and nurses at a state mental hospital, may not wish to be included in a bargaining unit with clerical workers, groundskeepers, mental health aides, and kitchen staff. Fairness dictates that a union seeking recognition at a hospital secure majorities of each of these subgroups in order to represent them.

BARGAINING STATUS OF SUPERVISORS. The inclusion of supervisors in a bargaining unit is a problem unique to public-sector protective workers. Private-sector employers have been judged to be entitled to a cadre of workers who protect the management's interest, and the Taft-Hartley Act's exclusion of private-sector supervisors from the bargaining unit has been deemed appropriate by the courts.[20] In the public sector, by contrast, the community-of-interest test has sometimes allowed the inclusion of supervisors in police and fire department bargaining units. Police and firefighters have made the case that the relationship of workers and supervisors among their ranks is unique and warrants inclusion of supervisors in the bargaining unit. Firefighters base their argument on the fact that supervisors and workers literally live together while on duty. Both police and firefighters argue that their work frequently involves life-threatening situations requiring cooperative levels not necessary elsewhere.

The foregoing contention is probably valid with regard to first-line supervisors such as fire lieutenants, who act more as lead persons than managers. However, mid-level supervisors who are involved in the making and administration of departmental policy may also be included in the bargaining unit. As a result, the administration of city policy and the interpretation of management rights and prerogatives under the contract is placed in the hands of members of the bargaining unit. The inclusion of mid-level supervisors in the bargaining unit, therefore, may run contrary to the public interest insofar as that is defined as the orderly administration of public programs.

When labor relations statutes fail to specify the bargaining status of supervisors, the matter is left to the bargaining table or to interpretation in the courts. In the absence of legislative guidance, judges are as apt to expand as they are to constrain bargaining unit participation by supervisors. In Oklahoma, for example, the state supreme court extended bargaining unit membership to all police and fire-fighting personnel, with the exception of the chief and one deputy. The test used there was whether the individual made policy.[21] Such interpretations may be overly narrow, because on second and third shifts, the ranking officer frequently is a police or fire captain who must interpret and apply departmental policy over a range of issues. Policymakers may also seek input from mid-level managers in policy formulation.

The inclusion of uniformed supervisors in bargaining units with rank-and-file workers may have worked, in part, because of the paramilitary nature of these organizations. Police and fire supervisors simply do not take their union membership into consideration when enforcing discipline. Nevertheless, instances can occur in which cities find it necessary to defend themselves against both sides in an adverse action. First, the rank-and-file union member files a grievance against a supervisor and wins in arbitration. Subsequently, the senior uniformed officials might discipline the supervisor in question for failure to comply with departmental policy. The supervisor, in turn, might then file a grievance and be represented by the same union that filed the grievance against the supervisor in the first place. Conversely, first-line supervisors are often officers in the union. When their own subordinates are the subjects of investigations for wrongdoing, the union recourse is closed to them because their supervisor/accuser is also the union president, steward, or other officer. The interests of all concerned might be better served if supervisors were in a different bargaining unit.

SCOPE OF BARGAINING AND MANAGEMENT RIGHTS

In the private sector, appropriate bargaining issues include wages and salaries, fringe benefits, and working conditions. Organizational policies should be outside the scope of bargaining. When private-sector managers have consented to include in the contract issues that would otherwise be management prerogatives, they have been stuck with the necessity of bargaining them out. For example, an employer who agrees to specify the size of work crews in the contract will have to negotiate the impact of changes in technology on the work crews. If a new machine is purchased that makes fewer workers necessary, layoffs will have to be justified and negotiated. Unions representing the uniformed services may wish to prescribe contractually the number of firefighters that must be assigned to a given shift or the number of police officers assigned to a given car or area of the city. A union may also attempt to define by contract the ratio of workers to supervisors, arguing that these staffing issues are working conditions because staffing levels have a direct relationship to safety, especially among the police. From management's perspective, however, safeguarding the public demands the maximum possible scheduling flexibility to deal with contingencies such as natural disasters, industrial accidents, and civil uprisings.

DEFINING MANAGEMENT RIGHTS BY STATUTE.　Public employers can ward off assaults on the rights of management by taking shelter in state legislation guaranteeing those rights. Such statutes also reinforce the sovereignty rights of local government. The strongest management rights statutes are in force in New York and Nevada, where government management exercises exclusive rights to determine the nature and delivery of services, and to hire, fire, promote, discipline, assign work, determine workloads, and classify employees. Civil service regulations are also exempted from contract negotiations.[22]

Such legislation provides management with bargaining insurance, because even if such matters are included in a contract, their inclusion is voluntary and may be removed at will by management.[23] In the private sector, by contrast, an issue voluntarily included in a contract must be negotiated out, usually at a heavy cost to management.

DEFINING MANAGEMENT RIGHTS BY CONTRACT. Failing to define bargainable topics by statute or provide a PERB with enforcement powers results in interpretations by arbitrators as well as by judges. At best, a case-by-case interpretation approach results in a patchwork of public policy. At worst, these interpretations may lead to usurpations of management's policy-making authority by arbitrators with a vested interest in the arbitration process. For example, suppose a city manager learned that each day two firefighters took three hours to shop for and prepare the noon meal of each duty crew. The manager might issue an order specifying that lunch preparation would be limited to one worker, who was to take no more than two hours for it. The union might take the city into arbitration on the grounds that the lunch preparation, although not specified in the contract, constituted an established practice. Management would take the position that work assignments were a management prerogative not subject to negotiation.

Public-sector labor contracts often specify that *personnel policies and procedures in place at the time of the contract shall remain in place for the duration of the contract.* Public-sector managers who want the discretion to alter work rules without fear of being overturned in the arbitration process should spell out their unilateral authority over such matters in the contract. Interestingly, the notion of an established practice is a public-sector phenomenon. Private employers can change work rules at will (unless they have specified otherwise in the contract).

UNFAIR LABOR PRACTICES

Management-labor relations are adversarial affairs, in which each side presses for an advantage. Given this simple truth, state legislatures have found it necessary to pass legislation that clearly specifies what constitutes an unfair labor practice. Some statutes empower the PERB to investigate unfair practices, issue cease and desist orders, and, if necessary, file suit against the offending party. Other states leave interpretation to arbitrators.

To define unfair labor practices, public policymakers have looked for guidance to the rules governing the private sector. The NLRB has the authority to investigate unfair labor practices on the part of management and labor and to issue cease and desist orders. If an offending party refuses to follow its ruling, the NLRB can seek enforcement by the appropriate federal court. By not granting the NLRB the power to enforce its own orders, the legislature placed a check upon the activities of the board.

Following is a list of unfair labor practices monitored by the NLRB; individual states have developed their own variations.

UNFAIR LABOR PRACTICES BY MANAGEMENT IN THE PRIVATE SECTOR

1. Interference with employees exercising their right to organization or nonorganization

2. Encouragement or discouragement of membership in organizations by discrimination in regard to hiring, tenure, promotion, or other conditions of employment

3. Control or domination of employee organizations or contribution of financial or other support to employee organizations

4. Discipline of or discrimination against any person who files charges of an unfair labor practice

5. Refusal to bargain in good faith with a certified employee organization

Unfair Labor Practices by Unions in the Private Sector

1. Restraint or coercion of employees in their attempts to exercise their rights to organization or nonorganization, or in their selection of a bargaining representative

2. Participation in secondary boycotts

3. Attempts to cause an employer to discriminate against an employee for nonmembership in a labor organization (unless an agreement is in place and the employee refuses to pay dues or membership fees)

4. Refusal to bargain in good faith

5. Attempts to induce an organization or its agent to engage in an unfair labor practice

6. Other unfair practices named under the Taft-Hartley Act, involving unfair uses of work stoppages[24]

Not all unfair practices are equally applicable in the public and private sectors. Secondary boycotts, for example, are not applicable to the public sector. What follows are some examples of the more common public-sector problems.

Bargaining in Good Faith. An unfair practice encountered often in the public sector is the refusal to bargain in good faith. Good-faith bargaining means meeting with the opposition, listening to its demands and concerns, and making concrete proposals regarding the new contract. This does not mean that an employer or union representative must make a counterproposal to every issue raised, but rather that a bargaining team must give an explanation for its refusal to bargain on an issue. Understanding what can or must be bargained is important, because topics that might be negotiated voluntarily in the private sector may, in the public sector, involve making and implementing public policy and, therefore, be beyond the scope of the contract.

A number of topics that the union might raise are valid concerns of the rank-and-file membership. Such demands as increased scheduling flexibility could affect the city's capacity to deal with emergencies. A refusal by management to even consider such issues can undermine morale, making workers less willing to cooperate on matters not specifically defined in the contract.

Some of these problems can be avoided if management will listen to the concerns of workers even when those concerns are not to be included in the contract.

Thus, in the scheduling example, a city could agree to review its scheduling practices to secure sufficient coverage without unduly disrupting scheduled days off or forcing workers to accept erratic work schedules.[25]

DISCRIMINATION AGAINST UNION MEMBERS. Selecting supervisors and managers from among the members of the bargaining unit is much more prevalent in the public sector than in private industry. Management might therefore be tempted to induce people to leave the bargaining unit by letting it be known that union membership would be a negative factor in promotional decisions. Workers' knowledge of such a policy (whether formal or informal) might reduce union participation among ambitious members of the bargaining unit. Without a PERB and clearly defined unfair practices, only the courts remain as a solution to the union's dilemma.

Public employees who are not covered by a collective bargaining law have little or no recourse if management engages in practices considered unfair by the general society. In the absence of state-level regulatory legislation, state employees could be subject to management harassment for joining public employee associations. These employees have little recourse, because their association memberships are not protected by state merit rules. Of course, an individual's right to join any organization is constitutionally guaranteed by the First Amendment; seeking redress in the federal courts, however, is a costly and time-consuming process that few would undertake just to gain the right to join and pay dues to an organization that can do no more than lobby the legislature.[26] At a minimum, then, state legislatures should make the freedom to join such associations a right protected under state civil service law.

UNFAIR USE OF WORK STOPPAGES. The Supreme Court ruled long ago that workers could not disrupt workflow by such tactics as calling unscheduled union meetings whenever management left the floor of the plant.[27] In the public sector, such tactics as the blue flu and work slowdowns have been used. In the *blue flu* (so named for its popularity among police and fire unions), workers call in sick in order to disrupt the flow of work without the loss of wages that would occur if they struck. The tactic is particularly effective where workers do not have the right to strike. Work slowdowns can be achieved either through laconic efforts by workers or through strict observation of procedures. The latter tactic was popular with the now-defunct Professional Air Traffic Controllers Organization, discussed later in this chapter. By rigidly adhering to every rule in the manual, controllers could back up air traffic all over the country.

COLLECTIVE BARGAINING AT THE FEDERAL LEVEL

THE RIGHT TO ORGANIZE

Federal employees enjoyed the statutory right to join unions long before state and local workers did. The Lloyd-LaFollette Act of 1913 gave federal employees the right to join employee associations, thereby giving them a means of articulating their interests before Congress. Over the years, a number of groups were successful in their dealings with Congress, but none was more effective than the postal workers.

The postal workers were instrumental in electing a number of members to Congress despite the Hatch Act's prohibition against partisan political actions by federal employees.[28] Much of the strength of the letter carriers lay in their ability to supply volunteer workers for favored candidates who, in turn, served on the House Government Affairs Committee.

The right to organize and lobby, of course, is not the same as the right to bargain collectively with representatives of federal agencies. In granting the former, the Congress did not wish to forego its own control over the wages of federal employees or to risk the disruption of vital national services. Students of federal labor relations must also bear in mind that federal employees had been granted job security rights and civil service protections against adverse actions that far exceeded those enjoyed by private workers. The fact that these protections were granted to insulate the implementation of public policy from the vagaries of politics does not lessen the reality of their existence. Granting federal employees the right to bargain collectively, furthermore, posed a potential threat to institutions charged with protecting the rights of workers.

THE RIGHT TO BARGAIN

Federal employees first gained the right to engage in collective bargaining in 1962 under President Kennedy's Executive Order 10988. This order allowed for several classes of union recognition but let the agencies decide on the appropriateness of bargaining issues and retained the right of Congress to determine the pay of federal employees.

The Kennedy order established three categories of recognition. Exclusive recognition would be granted to a union if it could garner the votes of 50 percent plus one of the workers in an agency. Formal recognition, including the right to negotiate contracts, would be granted to a union that could gain the support of 10 percent of the workers. And informal recognition was possible for unions with less than a 10 percent membership. The order clearly intended to encourage union organization activities, because the three categories of recognition allowed a fledgling union access to management before majority status was obtained. By contrast, a clear majority must precede all negotiations in the private sector.

The gains made by labor unions under the Kennedy administration were augmented by two executive orders issued by President Nixon. Executive Order 11491 created the Federal Labor Relations Council to administer the program, but the council exercised no real authority over such matters as bargaining-unit certification or the prosecution of unfair labor practices. The order also created a federal service impasse panel to resolve impasses in the bargaining process. Executive Order 11616, issued in 1971, required agencies to negotiate grievance procedures and strengthened the rights of employees in the grievance process.

What an agency must negotiate was expanded in 1975 by President Ford's Executive Order 11838, which required agencies to negotiate their regulations affecting employee relations and personnel policy. For example, civilian employees of the Defense Department could challenge its right to deploy them in remote sites for extended periods of time or on very short notice. Under the terms of the order, an agency had to show "just cause" why a regulation should not be negotiated. But an agency could argue that a particular regulation was a matter of its internal security, necessary to preserving the national defense, and therefore nonnegotiable.

The foregoing discussion of executive orders illustrates the incremental nature of policymaking in the United States. While the movement was clearly toward granting federal employees full bargaining rights, the climate remained hostile. Political conservatives and those interested in preserving the existing civil service system resisted the trend.

In the early 1970s, two groups of federal workers engaged in highly effective actions that resulted in their gaining bargaining advantages not shared by other federal employees. The special bargaining status of postal workers and air traffic controllers thus came to be defined by special legislation.

POSTAL WORKERS. The widespread walkout by postal workers in 1970 brought the nation its first significant work stoppage by federal employees. The fragility of federal antistrike statutes was clearly demonstrated by the actions of the postal workers, who remained out even in the face of a court order.

As the result of their actions, postal workers gained significant pay increases and the right to bargain over much the same issues negotiated by private-sector employees. The Postal Reorganization Act of 1970 conferred this special status on postal employees and provided them with impasse resolution procedures. The difference in bargaining status can be justified on the grounds that the act made the postal service a government corporation; thus, postal workers are technically no longer employed by a government agency.

The postal workers were successful, in part, because they were able to secure public sympathy for their demands and because they were able to disrupt the flow of commerce as well as the mail. The strike began in New York, whose financial centers could not operate efficiently without mail service. A similar strike in the current era would not have the same effect because of the widespread use of electronic transmission of messages and funds.

AIR TRAFFIC CONTROLLERS. Unlike the postal workers, who struck, the air traffic controllers gained their special-status legislation by a literal interpretation of air traffic control regulations, which slowed the air transportation industry to a crawl in 1970. As a result of their actions, the Professional Air Traffic Controllers Organization (PATCO) received the right to bargain on a whole range of issues in exchange for a pledge not to strike.

The success of these two federal work stoppages must be assessed in the context of the factors that surrounded them. In the case of the postal workers, President Nixon never took action to discharge the illegally striking workers, although he did send in military troops to provide interim mail service. He seems to have exchanged amnesty for the striking workers for their support for his postal reorganization plan pending before the Congress. Neither did the president take an assertive position against the air traffic controllers in 1970; had he done so, the 1981 strike might have been averted, because the controllers might not have challenged the no-strike statute so readily. When they did strike in 1981, President Reagan signed a back-to-work order that eventually led to decertification of PATCO by the Federal Labor Relations Authority.[29]

THE CIVIL SERVICE REFORM ACT OF 1978

The rules that govern labor relations for most federal workers underwent a major overhaul as part of the 1978 Civil Service Reform Act. The provisions of the act retained some of the features spelled out in the earlier executive orders and drew upon the National Labor Relations Act to define administrative structures and unfair labor practices. The act also specified the rights of management, the status of managerial and supervisory personnel, and impasse resolution procedures. Despite all this, however, federal employees still do not enjoy the quintessential right to bargain over wages.

THE FEDERAL LABOR RELATIONS AUTHORITY.   The reform act created a Federal Labor Relations Authority to oversee relations between federal agencies and the elected representatives of federal employees. The duties and responsibilities of the FLRA are much like those of the National Labor Relations Board for the private sector. The act specifies that the FLRA shall have three members, one of whom is to serve as the chairperson. These members are appointed for fixed terms by the president. The legislation also provides for a general counsel, who serves at the will of the president and is responsible for assisting the FLRA in the monitoring and interdiction of unfair labor practices. The FLRA also contains the Federal Service Impasse Panel, responsible for the resolution of disputes in the negotiation process.

The FLRA has the authority to investigate and prosecute unfair labor practices that are spelled out in the act. It also has the authority to designate appropriate bargaining units, conduct elections, and resolve controversies over whether one side or the other is refusing to bargain in good faith. Finally, it is authorized to rule on exceptions to the decisions of arbitrators. An arbitrator's ruling can be overturned if it can be shown that the decision is "contrary to any law, rule or regulation" or "on other grounds similar to those applied by Federal courts in private sector labor management relations."

MANAGEMENT RIGHTS.   Section 7106 of the reform act is a clear statement of management rights. Management is to have unilateral authority to determine the mission of the agency and its organization, to make budgetary decisions, to determine the number of employees, and to define the internal security practices of the agency.

Regarding personnel matters, the act gives management exclusive authority to hire, assign, and direct employees. Management also has the authority to lay off or retain employees, to suspend them or reduce their rate of pay, or to take disciplinary action against them. Management also enjoys the exclusive right to assign work, to contract out work, and to determine by whom work shall be carried out. However, management may *voluntarily* choose to negotiate with workers the number and types of employees assigned to a project. Management may also choose to bargain over technical methods and means of performing work.

WORKING CONDITIONS. The security of management rights, as defined in the reform act, is somewhat diminished by a definition of working conditions that includes personnel policies. Under the act, "'conditions of employment' means personnel policies, practices and matters, whether established by rule, regulation, or otherwise, affecting working conditions." The definition does exempt policies dealing with political activities, classification, or matters prescribed by law. Working conditions, under the act, are defined with sufficient vagueness to result in numerous resorts to arbitration and appeals to the FLRA over the operative part of the statute or the contract clause that is to be applied in a particular instance.

IMPASSE RESOLUTION. Resolution of impasses in the negotiation process is the province of the Federal Service Impasse Panel. When impasses develop, disputants are first encouraged to seek the assistance of the Federal Mediation and Conciliation Service, or they may agree to seek the assistance of an outside mediator. If the resort to mediation does not resolve the impasse, either party may request the impasse panel to step in. Alternatively, the parties may agree to settle the issue by arbitration, in which the arbitrator's ruling is absolute and final. The agreed-upon arbitration process, however, is subject to approval by the panel.

Once it receives an appeal, the impasse panel may provide fact-finding and mediation services to the parties. If resolution is not forthcoming, the panel may hold formal hearings, then make a determination that is binding on both parties for the duration of the agreement.

GRIEVANCE PROCEDURES. Section 7121 of the reform act specifies that all labor agreements will contain a procedure for the simple and timely resolution of grievances. The act further provides that the final step in the process is to be binding arbitration. The aggrieved employee has the right to appeal either under the negotiated process or on the basis that the action in question violates statutory provisions, such as discrimination because of age, sex, race, or handicap, or because an agency has violated the prohibition against political coercion of employees. Aggrieved employees must decide at the outset whether to use the negotiated or the statutory process; they may not choose both. The act does provide, however, that using the negotiated process does not preclude appeals of the final outcome to either the Merit System Protection Board or the Equal Employment Opportunity Commission.

FEDERAL LABOR RELATIONS UNDER THE 1978 ACT. The labor relations aspects of the 1978 reform act provide for the orderly conduct of management-labor relations in the federal service and for timely and appropriate procedures for the investigation of unfair labor practices. The authority and responsibilities of the FLRA in these regards are modeled on the best features of the NLRB. Impasse resolution procedures under the act may be cumbersome or simple, depending on the route chosen by the parties to the dispute. In general, however, the means whereby disputants come to the impasse panel seem cumbersome when compared to similar procedures at the state and local level and in the private sector.

What is most significant about the labor relations provisions of the act is their statutory existence. Bargaining privileges that were initiated by executive order and limited in scope are now institutionalized by statute and cover a wide range of topics. The current state of affairs has come about slowly and incrementally: fully 16 years elapsed between the initial presidential order and the statutory mandating of bargaining and administrative oversight mechanisms.

STRIKES

The traditional response of private-sector unions to bargaining impasses or contract disputes is to withhold services from the employer, or strike. The advantage of strikes is that they disrupt the employer's capacity to produce and thereby to conduct a profit-making business. Such work stoppages have been deemed unacceptable in the public sector because the public service has been viewed by society as a public trust, and more important, because work stoppages by public employees result in the disruption of services deemed essential by many: police and fire protection, garbage removal, and air traffic control, to name just a few.

An old union adage is that meaningful negotiations are possible only when the union is capable of carrying out a successful work stoppage. The key word is successful—not necessarily legal. And in fact, striking workers have been able to secure such things as recognition of the bargaining unit and significant wage increases because of their ability to disrupt services, legally or not. In the public sector, strikes are particularly threatening. Critics of public employee strikes argue that they place unfair pressure on public managers to settle disputes by triggering public fear of losing protective services or public revulsion at uncollected garbage. Strikes by public-sector clerical workers, of course, pose more of a threat to the orderly conduct of city business than to public health.

On the other hand, public-sector strike activities sometimes backfire, because taxpayers may revolt against the increased taxes brought on by union demands. Local protective services, moreover, rarely have a monopoly on their services; in the case of a police strike, state troopers or, in extreme cases, the National Guard can provide police protection. Similarly, cooperative arrangements among neighboring cities can ensure fire protection. Even refuse collection can be contracted out or, if necessary, be carried out by the National Guard. Such factors make successful strikes all the more remarkable. Whether they are legally conducted, successful strikes by public employees have several components.[30]

FACTORS IN SUCCESSFUL STRIKES

Successful public-sector strikers usually have a short list of realistic demands. Short lists are necessary so that they can be readily understood by the general public, whose support is necessary. Reasonable demands are necessary in order to have any hope of winning. When, for example, the local economy is in a down cycle and substantial unemployment exists, wage-hike demands by public workers will be unlikely to enlist widespread support.

Successful strikes usually exhibit substantial solidarity, in that most members of the bargaining unit participate. Management's resistance is strengthened when a substantial minority of employees refuses to join the strike. Finally, successful strikes are usually well planned and effectively led. Persuading employees to walk out, then convincing them to remain out, is the stuff of which strong labor leaders are made. Regardless of union members' commitment to the issues, they are not likely to walk out or to remain out without organization and leadership on the part of union officials. Conversely, strong union leadership may entail persuading angry employees to remain on the job when a strike is liable to work against their best interests.

The foregoing positive factors usually result in strikes of limited duration. Long-term strikes tend to erode public support and weaken the union's position. Quick settlements are also in the interest of individual workers, because local public-sector unions usually lack the resources to sustain their members during prolonged work stoppages.

PATCO's Failure

The disastrous outcome of the 1981 strike by members of the Professional Air Traffic Controllers Organization illustrates what can happen when union leaders overlook the factors essential to a successful strike. In the first place, the leadership of PATCO appears to have been out of touch with the wishes of rank-and-file air traffic controllers. It had agreed to a contract with the Department of Transportation that the membership subsequently rejected overwhelmingly. The leaders then had to return to the bargaining table with a new list of demands not covered in the first contract.

For its part, the Reagan administration made clear its willingness to work toward a resolution of the impasse but its intolerance of a strike. The secretary of transportation was meeting personally with PATCO and a mediator in an effort to reach a compromise, and there is evidence to suggest that progress had been made on a number of issues prior to the strike.

PATCO was unsuccessful in gaining public support for its demands for three reasons. First, a popular president had taken a position squarely against PATCO. President Reagan was not only opposed to the strike but willingly used his authority under the Taft-Hartley Act to fire striking controllers. Private-sector employers enjoy no such authority. Second, its list of demands was so long that it could not hope to sustain widespread public interest or support. Finally, and perhaps most important, PATCO was unable to substantially disrupt the flow of air traffic. By using military air traffic controllers, the government was able to keep operations at major airports 90 percent effective, although slower than usual—and significantly, the flow of traffic was maintained without accidents.[31]

SERVICE DISRUPTIONS

Some public workers have opted for activities short of long-term strikes to make their grievances known to management. One- or two-day strikes to focus public attention on a short list of demands can be useful if carefully orchestrated for the media. They are also more acceptable to rank-and-file workers who are reluctant to walk out indefinitely.

Other types of service disruptions include abuse of sick leave and overzealousness in the performance of one's duties. The blue flu has been mentioned: police officers (or other public employees) call in sick in large numbers, making it impossible for the department to function normally. Another police tactic is no-tolerance enforcement of traffic laws. This tactic gets the attention of the citizenry, who must pay the fines, and also strains the judicial system and takes officers away from routine patrol duties. In 1970, the air traffic controllers used absolute adherence to prescribed procedures to cause flight delays and thereby make their demands felt by the transportation industry. Interns and residents employed by Los Angeles County hospitals brought attention to their demands for wage adjustments by holding a "heal-in." During the heal-in, every patient who came to the hospital was immediately admitted. When the corridors were filled, county officials were ready to talk.

ALTERNATIVES TO STRIKES

The development of alternative impasse resolution procedures in some jurisdictions has made it possible for public unions and employers to fairly advance their interests without the adverse effects that accompany strikes or other job actions. These alternatives include mediation, fact finding, and arbitration. Mediation and fact finding will be described briefly here; arbitration has so many forms that it will require a separate, somewhat lengthier discussion.

MEDIATION

A good mediator is like a good marriage counselor, possessing the ability to bring disputes to a mutually satisfactory resolution. Also like the marriage counselor, the mediator possesses no authority to compel compliance; reason and persuasion are the mediator's only strengths. Mediation is required by law in the federal government and in some states. In other cases, the parties may voluntarily agree to seek the assistance of a mediator to resolve their impasse. Pennsylvania public employees enjoy a limited right to strike only after they seek the services of a mediator, which are paid for by the state.[32]

FACT FINDING

The fact finder, like the mediator, is an unbiased third party called upon to help resolve an impasse. However, unlike the mediator, who is supposed to work quietly behind the scenes to resolve an impasse, the fact finder produces a public report in which he or she reviews the dispute and affixes responsibility for the impasse. Of course, many fact finders conduct themselves like mediators and try to bring the two sides together. If a settlement cannot be reached, the fact finder's report is published in the local media so that citizens know who is responsible for continuing the dispute. In a recent case, a Northern California school board rejected a fact finder's report that called for substantial wage increases for public school teachers. Angry parents turned out in large numbers in the following year's election to turn out two members in favor of members supportive of teachers. Public pressure notwithstanding, disputant acceptance of the fact finder's recommendations is voluntary.

Fact finding and mediation have met with varying degrees of success in the public sector, because cooperation with the mediator or compliance with the fact finder is voluntary. When fact finding or mediation is only the first step in an impasse resolution process paid for by the state, moreover, there is little incentive to accept recommendations that are contrary to the interests of one side or the other. By contrast, the findings of arbitrators are generally binding on both parties, which encourages them to seek a resolution of their differences at the bargaining table before placing their fate in the hands of a stranger.

ARBITRATION

Submitting impasses to an independent arbitrator whose decision in the matter is final and binding on both parties is the strongest method of providing public employees with the right to engage in collective bargaining while avoiding the disruption of essential services. The resolution of disputes arising out of contracts without resorting to work stoppage is in the interests of both management and labor. Management benefits through a continuation of productive work while the issue is being resolved, and the workers benefit from the continuity of wages during impasse resolution.

Arbitration takes many forms. It may be compulsory (required by law) or mandatory (required by the terms of the contract). The findings of the arbitrator may be binding on both parties or only on the union—or they may be merely advisory in nature. A distinction must also be made between arbitration of issues that will go into a contract under negotiation (interest arbitration) and arbitration of disputes growing out of the contract (grievance arbitration). A further distinction is between arbitration in which the arbitrator may choose to rule for one side on some issues and for the opposite side on others (line-item arbitration) and arbitration that requires the arbitrator to choose between the final offers of the disputants. Finally, arbitration, which was heralded as the solution to litigation in labor disputes, has itself become bogged down in legalities, causing some to question its current value for expeditious impasse resolution. These critics call for a new form, known as expedited arbitration.

The term *arbitration* describes two distinct processes: interest arbitration and grievance arbitration. *Interest arbitration* refers to contract negotiations or what will go into the contract. Interest arbitration is normally confined to wages, salaries, and fringe benefits, but it may also deal with proposed changes in the status quo known as established practices. The cost of interest arbitration is normally split between the parties. Interest arbitration is rarely used in the private sector and then only by mutual consent of the two parties. It is often required by law in the public sector. Major league baseball also uses interest arbitration to resolve disputes over individual players' contracts.

Grievance arbitration deals with interpreting the contract and has been used to great success in the public and private sector. Grievance arbitrators are called upon to interpret contracts with regard to policies and procedures, especially when the city seeks to alter them between contract rounds. Grievance arbitrators are also called upon in individual disciplinary cases. State law or city charter may call for grievance arbitration in the public sector, or the two parties may write it into the contract.

COMPULSORY ARBITRATION

Compulsory arbitration is required by statute. A legislature may require that, upon declaring themselves at an impasse, the parties submit their dispute to arbitration. Each side is then required by law to accept and implement the terms of the arbitrator's decision. Compulsory arbitration over the contents of contracts (whether binding on both parties or not) is a public-sector phenomenon. There is no national labor relations statute either requiring or prohibiting arbitration of bargaining impasses in the private sector.

Arbitration, however, may be compulsory for both sides without making the decision binding on both parties. For example, the state of Oklahoma provided for collective bargaining for police and firefighters. Impasses in the bargaining process submitted to a panel of three arbitrators, one selected by the city, one by the union, and a third, neutral arbitrator. The findings of the panel were binding on the union, but only advisory to the city; Oklahoma cities were free to accept or reject the arbitrators' findings. The Oklahoma State Supreme Court ruled that if the law were binding on cities, it would conflict with the charter city provisions of the state constitution. This way there is no conflict between the collective bargaining statute and the constitution. Police and firefighters unions fought against the fundamental unfairness of advisory arbitration for the cities. The result was a new procedure that requires cities that reject the arbitrator's decision to submit their decisions to a vote of the people. Given the cost of running special elections, Oklahoma's uniformed services have substantially achieved binding arbitration.[33]

MANDATORY ARBITRATION

Arbitration is possible without a statute if the two parties agree to it under the terms of the current contract. The most celebrated example of mandatory arbitration is the relationship between the United Steelworkers and the steel industry. The steelworkers agreed not to strike over disputes involving contract interpretation in exchange for management's agreement to submit all such disputes to binding arbitration. Arbitration as a means of dispute resolution short of litigation was legitimized in three 1960 Supreme Court cases involving the steelworkers, often referred to as the steelworkers trilogy.[34]

UNITED STEELWORKERS V. AMERICAN MANUFACTURING CO.   In this case, the Court held that the parties had contractually agreed to submit all interpretation disputes to binding arbitration. The company had argued that an employee who had previously received a workers' compensation judgment against the company was not entitled to return to work under seniority provisions of the contract. The company had refused to consider reinstatement because it believed that, having accepted the judgment, the employee was no longer subject to the seniority clause. The Court held that the test of arbitrability that courts must employ was whether arbitration was required by the language of the contract, and that a judicial interpretation of the merits of a given case was not warranted if such arbitration was provided for. Thus, when the no-strike clause is exchanged for arbitration, neither side can seek to avoid that process through appeals to the courts.

UNITED STEELWORKERS V. WARRIOR AND GULF NAVIGATION CO.   Here the Court ruled that what is subject to arbitration should be interpreted broadly. The issue in this case was whether the company had the right to contract out certain activities that had previously been performed by members of the bargaining unit. The case was complicated by the contract's management rights clause, which stated in part, "Issues ... which are strictly a function of management shall not be subject to arbitration under this section."[35] The Court applied an industry standard, in which contracting out is normally a subject for arbitration, and held that if the company meant to exclude contracting out, it should have been made explicit in the language of the contract.

UNITED STEELWORKERS V. ENTERPRISE WHEEL AND CAR CORP.   The final case in the trilogy addressed the extent to which the courts should examine the decision of the arbitrator. The Court held that lower courts should not question the correctness of an arbitrator's decision any more than they should rule on the arbitrability of an issue based on the merits of the grievance.[36]

IMPACT OF THE STEELWORKERS TRILOGY.   More recently, the logic of the steelworkers trilogy was applied to the company's right to determine the need for layoffs in *AT&T Technologies* v. *Communication Workers* (1986).[37] The company argued unsuccessfully that an article in the contract gave it the right to determine layoffs unilaterally. Here again, the Supreme Court ruled that disputes arising out of interpretations of the contract must be submitted to arbitration when arbitration is called for in the contract.

The steelworkers trilogy established the parameters within which court reviews of arbitration decisions must operate. Review must be limited to the question of whether arbitration is provided for in the contract, rather than address the merits of the individual case. Nor may the loser in the arbitration process appeal the arbitrator's award to the courts on the basis of unfairness. The courts normally only refuse to enforce an arbitrator's decision when the court finds that the arbitrator exceeded the provisions of the contract in making his or her decision.[38] For all intents and purposes, when the parties are committed to the arbitration process, whether by statute or by mutual consent, the arbitrator's decision has the force of law.

INTEREST ARBITRATION VARIATIONS

Interest arbitration addresses impasses over what shall be contained in a contract; grievance arbitration, to be discussed later, deals with disputes that grow out of interpretations of contract language. Interest arbitration, in turn, has two forms: line item and final offer. The discretionary authority of the arbitrator is significantly different in the two processes.

LINE-ITEM ARBITRATION. The arbitrator exercises maximum discretion under line-item [arbit]ration. Suppose, for example, that a number of issues are before an [arbitrator, inclu]ding the amount of sick leave, the cost of uniform cleaning, and [t]he wage increase for the upcoming contract. Under line-item arbitrator conceivably could grant the sick-leave demands of the [union, split] ayment for cleaning costs, and rule for management on the wage [issue. . . .] must normally choose between the final offers of management [and labor on each giv]en issue; they are not free to split the difference. The flexibility [of line-item arbitra]tion allows the arbitrator to exercise his or her best judgment, [but is also criticiz]ed as a disincentive to bargain in good faith and as a threat to [the soverei]gnty rights of elected government officials.

Line-item arbitration discourages good-faith bargaining because the number of issues that are likely to be resolved at the bargaining table declines precipitously once either side becomes substantially convinced that arbitration will eventually be necessary. The problem is particularly acute in jurisdictions that have histories of bargaining impasses. Disputants who develop impasse mind-sets may tend to plan their bargaining strategies with an eye toward arbitration. Those who have previously gained concessions from arbitrators that they could not win at the bargaining table may be particularly inclined to arbitration.

The sovereignty of elected government officials may be diminished by line-item arbitration because the decision of the arbitrator carries the force of law and must be implemented by the jurisdiction regardless of available resources. The arbitrator may pick and choose then depart the vicinity, leaving the disputants to implement the decision. The potential negative impacts of arbitration upon sovereignty are reduced when final-offer arbitration is used. In a democracy, sovereignty resides in the people and is exercised through their elected officials. Thus, the final, complete offer of one side or the other that must face the community is thought to be more democratic than a hodgepodge decision by an outsider whose decision is not subject to review.

FINAL-OFFER ARBITRATION. In this system, management and labor must negotiate the issues until both sides are willing to declare themselves at an impasse, having conceded all that they can. Before going to arbitration, however, each side must present the other with its last, best offer. The bargaining parties may accept their opponent's last offer or go on to arbitration. If a final offer is substantially different from a side's previous position, it may lead to further negotiations. Once arbitration is sought, however, the arbitrator must decide to accept one or the other's final offer in its entirety, regardless of the merits of specific items in the offer.

Final-offer arbitration provides an incentive for both sides to bargain in good faith, because they must place everything at risk before the arbitrator. For example, in the course of negotiations a city might have tentatively agreed to a union demand that the city pay a greater share of employees' health insurance costs but refused to budge on its offer of a 4 percent wage increase. Suppose that the union demanded a 6 percent increase in addition to the gain in insurance benefits. The city might make a final offer of a 4.25 percent hike but reduce the amount to be paid out for insurance. This final offer might result in a net loss to employees, after taxes, compared to what would have been gained under the original proposal. The union could continue to hold out for the increased insurance benefit and 6 percent. In other words, the two parties may choose to gamble on the arbitrator's ruling or to accept the other side's last offer. The logical thing to do, however, is to remain at the table and continue to bargain in good faith until a mutually acceptable package emerges.

Final-offer arbitration has the added advantage of a lesser impact upon local sovereignty. When arbitration is undertaken, whether line item or final offer, elected government officials lose their approval authority over the economic features of the contract. Under the final-offer system, however, the arbitrator chooses between the preferences of one side or the other. The winning side can then be held accountable to its fellow citizens for the effects of the contract.

The one disadvantage of final-offer arbitration is that it must be limited to economic issues in order to be viable in the public sector. Disputes over shift schedules, civil service protections, and the rights of management cannot be settled fairly by the final-offer arbitration process. To do so could allow union bargainers to gain steps toward the determination of public policy by grouping an objectionable policy issue with a reasonable set of economic demands and having the whole package ratified by an arbitrator. As noted earlier, determination of whether an issue is negotiable under statute or is a managerial right should be the province of the Public Employee Relations Board.

MEDIATION ARBITRATION. One other variation on interest arbitration is mediation arbitration. When the parties reach an impasse, a mediator/arbitrator is appointed to seek a compromise. If the parties cannot arrive at a mutually satisfactory solution with the aid of the mediator, he or she becomes an arbitrator and imposes a solution.

GRIEVANCE ARBITRATION

The most carefully constructed contract cannot hope to cover every contingency. The grievance arbitration process provides a mechanism for resolving impasses over interpretations of the contract that affect the bargaining unit as a whole. The process also provides for the redress of grievances of individual members of the bargaining unit. Even in Oklahoma, when interest arbitration was compulsory for both parties but binding only on the union, the decisions of grievance arbitrators were binding on both parties.[39]

Setting up an effective grievance arbitration process in the public sector is more complex than in private industry because of civil service protection statutes. Many states and municipalities have carefully prescribed appeals processes to safeguard the rights of individual employees. Obviously, when the appeals process is legally defined it cannot be superseded by a labor contract. Public employees in these jurisdictions, therefore, are doubly protected. They may seek redress of an adverse personnel action both through the civil service system and under the grievance arbitration process defined in the contract. Safeguarding merit rules while maintaining the integrity of the contract requires careful designing of the organization's internal grievance processes, which precede the submission of differences either to the merit protection system or to outside arbitration. The initial steps of the process can be constructed so as to meet the due-process requirements of either a merit appeal or an external arbitration hearing.

THE GRIEVANCE PROCESS. Processing an individual grievance normally begins when a supervisor seeks to discipline a subordinate. The initial encounter may be only an oral reprimand for alleged misconduct. Normally, unions do not become formally involved in the process until an adverse action is undertaken against an employee covered by the contract. An adverse action may simply be placing a letter in the employee's file that documents the occurrence of counseling. The letter remains in the file for a specified time (usually three months), after which it is removed. If a repetition occurs during the specified time or another offense is committed, the counseling letter becomes documentation for stronger adverse actions, which may include suspension without pay, demotion, transfer, or discharge.

When management undertakes an adverse action, it starts the clock on the appeals process. The aggrieved employee has a specified amount of time (frequently ten working days) to initiate an appeal to the next higher echelon. An employee who does not file within the specified time waives his or her right to appeal. The appeals process can be repeated through several levels of the organization before an external review of the action either by the civil service system or a labor arbitrator.

A properly constructed appeals process will provide employees with the right to representation of their own choice during each step of the process. This representative might be an attorney or a representative of the union. In most jurisdictions, the union is responsible for representing aggrieved employees regardless of whether they are members of the bargaining unit.

The choice of whether to pursue a grievance to the civil service protection board or to external arbitration is up to the individual employee, although seeking redress by one avenue may not preclude an appeal to the other. Seasoned union officials, however, may advise employees to take their grievances to the civil service protection board unless the decision will have significant implications for other members of the bargaining unit.

THE CIVIL SERVICE OPTION.   This option is attractive because the services of the commission's hearing examiners are free. The costs of outside arbitrators, in contrast, normally are divided between the city and the union or are handled on a loser-pays basis. Because public unions usually lack the resources of their private-sector counterparts, they will tend to limit use of the arbitration process to issues of contract interpretation that have implications beyond the case in question. The unions' preference for the civil service appeals process is ironic in light of union organization efforts that argue the inadequacies of the civil service protections and the consequent need for unions. Some jurisdictions have chosen a third path, where arbitration is used to resolve issues impacting all members of the bargaining unit, and the civil service system addresses adverse actions against individual employees.

THE ARBITRATION OPTION.   Arbitration may be used to appeal adverse personnel actions even when personnel policies are exempt from contract negotiations by statute or when the contract contains no specific language regarding the offense in question. The mechanism that makes this possible is a contract clause that states that the jurisdiction's personnel policies shall be considered a part of the contract. Thus, management cannot unilaterally change its personnel policies without seeking union concurrence. For example, a union could seek arbitration if, for safety reasons, a city chose to change its grooming code for firefighters by forbidding beards or hairstyles that protruded from beneath the helmet. The union could seek arbitration on the grounds that the city's action constituted a unilateral change of personnel policy and a violation of the contract. The contract, however, might also contain language allowing the city to set safety policy without union consultation. The arbitrator would be asked to decide which of the contract clauses took precedence. An individual worker might become involved in the dispute by refusing to shave off a beard or get a haircut. If the refusal resulted in disciplinary action, the worker would have the right to appeal either through arbitration or through the civil service process.

OTHER OPTIONS.   Union grievance processes are sometimes complicated by the availability of other processes. For instance, state agencies sometimes have their own internal grievance processes that operate separately from the union grievance process. The process prescribed by the contract may be further complicated if the conflict involves civil rights issues, such as racial discrimination or sexual harassment. In such a case, the grievant might file a court suit under either state or federal civil rights statutes.

EXPEDITED ARBITRATION

The greatest potential benefit foreseen by arbitration advocates was the unburdening of the court system from the weight of myriad labor disputes. Arbitration began to realize its potential when the Supreme Court decisions in the steelworkers trilogy invested the arbitrator's decisions with the force of law. Another anticipated virtue of arbitration was the timely resolution of issues, which was to benefit both management and labor. Finally, freeing arbitration from the judicial system was also supposed to free it from legal formalities and the paper engorgement that comes with transcribing hearings, taking depositions, and so forth.

The legalistic nature of arbitration, however, attracted a preponderance of attorneys to the arbitration process. Formality and legalism ensued, so that arbitration hearings, especially in the public sector, now resemble formal court proceedings. The arbitration process has been further complicated by taking depositions, rendering transcripts, requiring written briefs, the perceived need for the involvement of legal counsel, and the cross-examination of witnesses. As a result, arbitration has become nearly as cumbersome as the judicial remedies it was supposed to replace.

Reformers now call for a system that provides a more timely resolution of contract disputes through a process known as expedited arbitration.[40] In an expedited process, only oral arguments are presented, and no transcript is kept of the proceedings. Most important, the arbitrator issues an oral decision. Given the speed with which disputes can be settled, a number of cases can be resolved on a given date. Rather than a revolutionary idea, expedited arbitration is really a return to the original intent of arbitration.

Maintaining an adequate list of arbitrators is indispensable to the expedited arbitration process, but this can prove particularly difficult in nonmetropolitan areas, where fewer persons are trained in the nuances of arbitration. Given the intent of the process, however, a knowledge of personnel policies and practices is probably more useful than a knowledge of legal precedents. Thus, a state legislature seeking to institute expedited arbitration might do well to instruct its PERB to create a list of expediting arbitrators that includes personnel experts as well as attorneys.

SUMMARY AND CONCLUSION

During much of the twentieth century, collective bargaining for public employees was anathema to the concept of good government. The specter of work stoppage was the principal stumbling block to putting public employees on an equal footing with their private-sector counterparts. The notion of strikes by police and firefighters was most troubling to the public. Beginning in the 1960s, however, states began to grant collective bargaining rights to state and local employees. The fear of work stoppage was allayed by the creation of alternative impasse procedures coupled with nonstrike legislation. A number of states, however, still do not permit bargaining with employees although the number is shrinking, and the rate of public-sector unionization is much higher than in the private sector.

Unlike the private sector, where there is one set of labor laws and one administrative authority overseeing the entire process, state and local laws are a hodgepodge of permissible bargaining subjects and impasse resolution procedures. Where strikes are permitted, they are used sparingly because unions as well as management prefer to continue working without a contract to strikes. When public-sector strikes do occur, they are normally short-lived. One-day strikes to capture public attention are more frequent than longer-term stoppages that annoy the public, disrupt work flow, and damage the household budgets of individual workers.

Federal employees still do not enjoy the right to bargain over salary issues because of the unwillingness of Congress to give up its control over wage determination in the federal service. Ceding such authority would undermine congressional and presidential control of the federal budgetary process. It would also require the support of legislative majorities in both houses as well as presidential support, which is unlikely in the current era of divided government.

NOTES AND RESOURCES

1. Quoted in David A. Dilts and Clarence R. Deitsch, *Labor Relations* (New York: Macmillan, 1983), p. 164.

2. Under the leadership of Gompers, the American labor movement turned from party politics and ideology to "bread-and-butter" issues. See Harold C. Livesay, *Samuel Gompers and Organized Labor* (New York: Little, Brown, 1978).

3. For a detailed discussion of the labor movement of the early 1900s, see Selig Perlman and Phillip Taft, *History of Labor in the United States, 1896–1932,* Vol. 4 (New York: Macmillan, 1935).

4. See *Gitlow* v. *People,* 268 U.S. 652 (1925).

5. See Dilts and Deitsch, *Labor Relations,* pp. 39–40.

6. See *Debs* v. *U.S.,* 244 U.S. 211 (1919). Debs's statements were made at public rallies against the war. He had been a presidential candidate and gotten 6 percent of the vote. Nevertheless, his antidraft, antiwar statements led to a conviction upheld by the Supreme Court.

7. For a detailed discussion of yellow-dog contracts, see Charles O. Gregory and Harold A. Katz, *Labor and the Law,* 3rd ed. (New York: Norton, 1979), pp. 174–84.

8. Ibid., pp. 83–104. The issue of secondary boycotts became extremely complex with the passage of the 1948 Taft-Hartley Act and subsequent court interpretations of the act. See also Douglas L. Leslie, *Labor Law,* 2nd ed. (St. Paul, MN: West, 1986), pp. 125–84.

9. Judges were normally members of the propertied class, which goes a long way toward explaining their seeming favoritism toward management, both in equity courts and in granting antitrust injunctions under the Sherman Anti-Trust Act. Benjamin J. Taylor and Fred Witney, *Labor Relations Law,* 2nd ed. (Englewood Cliffs, NJ: Prentice-Hall, 1975), pp. 52–64; Charles O. Gregory and Harold A. Katz, *Labor and the Law,* pp. 31–52, 158–200.

10. The Roosevelt coalition comprised, in addition to labor, big-city political machines, farmers, the South, and civil rights groups. For a comprehensive study of American political parties, see Frank Sorauf, *Party Politics in America,* 3rd ed. (Boston: Little, Brown, 1970).

11. For a discussion of the steps in the National Emergency Impasse Procedure, see Dilts and Deitsch, *Labor Relations,* pp. 73–74.

12. Only foremen were excluded from bargaining units under the Taft-Hartley Act. The exclusion was later extended to all management employees in *NLRB* v. *Bell Aerospace Co.,* 466 U.S. 267 (1974).

13. For a detailed discussion of unfair labor practices under the terms of the Wagner and Taft-Hartley acts, see Dilts and Deitsch, *Labor Relations,* pp. 67, 72–73.

14. Originally, the American Federation of Labor was mostly concerned with advancing the interests of craft unions. The Congress of Industrial Organizations came into existence in 1935 to advance the rights of unskilled workers, such as manufacturing workers. The groups competed until 1955, when they were united into a single association for advancing the interests of member unions.

15. The Web page of the AFL-CIO resembles a collection of social causes. In addition, the AFL-CIO has begun actively recruiting a new generation of labor organizers through paid training and a job placement program. This effort includes bilingual and non-English speakers. See <http://www.aflcio.org/home.htm>.

16. Cited in Leo Kramer, *Labor's Paradox—The American Federation of State, County and Municipal Employees* (New York: Wiley, 1962), p. 41. Meany's remarks were made in 1955; the AFL-CIO passed a resolution supporting collective bargaining for public employees in 1959. For a fuller discussion, see Jack Stieber, *Public Employee Unionism* (Washington, DC: The Brookings Institution, 1973), pp. 114–19.

17. Bureau of Labor Statistics, *Union Members in 1999,* at <ftp://146.142.4.23/pub/news.release/union2.txt>.

18. Worker mistrust of civil service commission tools of management is exemplified by the remarks of a past president of AFSCME, Jerry Wurf, who characterized the civil service system as "the managerial system of the boss—he owns it." Jack Stieber, *Public Employee Unionism,* p. 116.

19. Public employee unions, like their private-sector counterparts, lobby legislatures on a number of issues. AFSCME, for example, has lobbied state and national legislatures on issues as broad as national health care and comprehensive welfare reform. Most frequently, however, union lobbyists have sought changes in labor statutes such as antistrike provisions and in the use of public employee retirement funds. Alan E. Bent and T. Zane Reeves, *Collective Bargaining in the Public Sector* (Menlo Park, CA: Benjamin Cummings, 1978), pp. 168–78.

20. Supervisors have argued that they were being denied union membership without just cause or the right to a hearing or appeal. The courts have rejected this argument. See *Shelofsky* v. *Helsby,* 295 2d 744 (1973). The Supreme Court refused to review a lower court ruling that denied union membership to a supervisor who argued that he was denied freedom of assembly. See *National Labor Relations Board* v. *Edward G. Budd Mfg. Co.,* 169 F2d 571 (1948).

21. The Oklahoma Supreme Court rendered its decision in *Oliver* v. *Turner* in October of 1982. Subsequently, a police captain successfully appealed a wrongful demotion under the terms of the contract and was reinstated. Prior to the Oliver decision, he would have had no protection.

22. Hard-line management rights statutes such as those of New York and Nevada are difficult to make operational in the give-and-take of the negotiation process. More reasonable intermediate approaches that respect the legitimate interests of all parties are much more desirable. For a detailed discussion, see Don Vial, "The Scope of Bargaining Controversy: Substantive Issues vs. Procedural Hangups," in *Trends in Public Sector Labor Relations: An Information Guide for the Future: Vol. 1. 1972–1973,* Arvid Anderson and Hugh N. Jascourt, eds. (Chicago: International Personnel Management Association, 1975), pp. 79–99.

23. The New York City Office of Collective Bargaining ruled that when an issue was bargained voluntarily, its continued presence on the negotiating table required the agreement of both parties. *Communication Workers of America and City of New York,* OCB Decision No. B-7-72. The NLRB would most likely rule the opposite way in a private-sector dispute over contract content; that is, if bargaining over the issue was undertaken by mutual consent, both parties would have to agree to eliminate the issue from the contract.

24. The NLRB rules are reported in Dilts and Deitsch, *Labor Relations,* pp. 70–74.

25. See Don Vial, "The Scope of Bargaining Controversy," pp. 87–89.

26. In those states that have modified the at-will doctrine, the courts might be receptive to a challenge to the practice on the grounds that such actions constitute a violation of public policy. See Chapter 7.

27. See *U.A.W. Local 332* v. *Wisconsin Employee Relations Board*, 336 U.S. 245 (1949).

28. The Supreme Court upheld the 1939 prohibition in *United States Civil Service Commission* v. *National Association of Letter Carriers*, 93 S. Ct. 2880 (1973).

29. For a fuller discussion, see U.S. Congress, House Committee on Public Works and Transportation: Subcommittee on Investigation and Oversight, *Aviation Safety, Air Traffic Control (PATCO Walkout)* (Washington, DC: U.S. Government Printing Office, 1982).

30. For an insightful analysis of the complexities of an effective public-sector strike, see Alan E. Bent and T. Zane Reeves, *Collective Bargaining in the Public Sector* (Menlo Park, CA: Benjamin Cummings, 1978), pp. 212–61.

31. For a detailed discussion, see H. R. Northrup, "The Rise and Demise of PATCO," *Industrial and Labor Relations Review* 37 (1984): 167–84.

32. Limited right-to-strike rules are limited in their potential effectiveness because they are open to judicial interpretation of the potential impact of the strike on the public welfare. For a multifaceted look at such a strike, see Hugh D. Jascourt, "Limited Right to Strike Laws: Can They Work When Applied to Public Education?" in *Trends in Public Sector Labor Relations*, Arvid Anderson and Hugh D. Jascourt, eds. (Chicago: International Personnel Management Association, 1975), pp. 145–78.

33. *City of Midwest City* v. *Gobel Cravens et al.*, 312 OK S. Ct. 47552. See Public Law 11–51–111, Oklahoma Attorney General's Office, Oklahoma Public Legal Research System, at <http://oklegal.onenet/oklegal-cgi/ifetch?Oklahoma_Statutes.99+18233834083+F>.

34. *United Steelworkers of America* v. *American Manufacturing Co.*, 363 U.S. 564 (1960); *United Steelworkers of America* v. *Warrior and Gulf Navigation Co.*, 363 U.S. 574 (1960); *United Steelworkers of America* v. *Enterprise Wheel and Car Corporation*, 363 U.S. 593 (1960).

35. Quoted in Douglas L. Leslie, *Labor Law*, 2nd ed. (St. Paul, MN: West, 1986), p. 277.

36. For a discussion of the exceptions to the trilogy rulings, see Dennis R. Nolan, *Labor Arbitration Law and Practice* (St. Paul, MN: West, 1979), pp. 79–103.

37. *AT&T Technologies, Inc.* v. *Communication Workers*, 106 S. Ct. 1415 (1986).

38. See Douglas L. Leslie, *Labor Law*, pp. 283–86.

39. *City of Midwest City* v. *Carmon Harris et al.*, 50 OK S. Ct. 225 (1977).

40. Dennis R. Nolan, *Labor Arbitration Law and Practice*, pp. 212–16.

MANAGEMENT IN A UNION ENVIRONMENT

The previous chapter presented the historical and legal context of union-management relations in the public sector. The one certainty that can be drawn from the diversity of union circumstances is that managers must adapt their personal managerial styles, as well as their human resource management systems, to the reality of collective bargaining. This chapter begins with a discussion of the constraints that union contracts place on managerial policymaking in such areas as contracting-out and affirmative action. The chapter then discusses the importance of establishing workable relations with union representatives.

UNION CONTRACTS AS CONSTRAINTS ON MANAGEMENT

The choices that public managers make are constrained, first and foremost, by the reality of third-party dispute resolution.[1] Whether by mutual agreement or by statute, many government entities are inhibited by a requirement that disputes growing out of contract interpretation must be submitted to a neutral third party. This is done to avoid costly litigation over contract language, which can take months or even years to resolve.

What managers sometimes fail to realize is just how much of a limitation this requirement can put on their managerial discretion.[2] Union contracts are binding on both parties for the duration of the contract. And neither side possesses sufficient prescience to anticipate every contingency that may arise in the course of the contract. The best the two sides can hope for is that their immediate concerns can be met in the limited time available for negotiations. By mutual consent, therefore, many contracts contain a clause that specifies that the personnel policy manual of the agency that is in place at the time the contract goes into effect "shall be deemed to be a part of this contract." In other words, management cannot change personnel policies and procedures within the time frame of the contract without consulting the union. Managers, therefore, are well advised to consult with the union whenever they believe there is need to alter a managerial practice that may affect the union's interest.

Consulting with the union, in this context, means that management must secure union consent to proposed changes. If there is substantial disagreement between the parties, management should forego the change until the next round of negotiations. Failure to properly consult can cause a major union dispute, as the following example illustrates.

Management of a large midwestern city decided to review its personnel policies a short time after signing a one-year contract with the local chapter of the International Fire Fighters Association. Management made dozens of changes over the course of the next several months. Each time, the union was sent a copy of the change for its records.

One item, however, proposed to change the city's payment system by building a two-week delay into the biweekly payroll system. Management intended the change as a cost-saving measure. Hundreds of worker hours per year were spent correcting time-card errors that resulted from submitting pay warrants for employees in anticipation of the hours they would work. Oftentimes, illness caused schedule changes, or firefighters had to work overtime. By changing the system, the city would always be two weeks behind, thereby allowing it to pay workers only for the hours that they actually worked. Management proposed to phase-in the system, gradually adjusting the day that employees were paid by one day a week for fourteen weeks until the full adjustment had been made. The first week employees would be paid on the following Monday instead of Friday, the second week they would be paid on Tuesday, and so forth until they could be paid for two-weeks' work per pay period with a two-week delay.

The union protest was quick and vociferous. Why, if management was losing money, had they not raised the issue in the last round of negotiations? The union protested, moreover, that the net effect of the transition system would be to postpone payment of a portion of negotiated raises.

Management's position was that the change was within the purview of the city manager to make in the interest of good government. Furthermore, the inconvenience to workers would be minor.

The case ultimately went to arbitration, where the union secured a return to the old system on the following grounds: First, the personnel manual was deemed a part of the contract for its duration, and the manual clearly specified a biweekly payment system without a delay. Second, the arbitrator ruled that management had the duty to secure the consent of the union before making such a change. Finally, if the agreement to the change could not be secured through consultation, the proposal should be placed on the table at the next round of contract talks.

The arbitrator's ruling gave no weight to management's argument that all the other changes in the manual had been made without union protest or consultation. The fact that workers see no harm in one or two or a dozen changes in procedures does not constitute union acquiescence in all changes that management might wish to make unilaterally.

Conflicts such as these use up the time, energy, and financial resources of both parties. The losing side's anger, moreover, is usually matched by that of the winners, who may feel vindicated but wary and distrustful of their antagonists. The next round of contract talks after an arbitration dispute is often protracted and bitter, as each side seeks to ferret out the other's real intent. The antagonists may take strong positions against the proposals of the other side, not because the proposals require sacrifice but because the other side wants them.

ESTABLISHED PRACTICES

Public managers who are required by state law to submit all disputes to third-party settlement may have additional limitations placed on their discretionary authority by the state legislature to which management never agreed.[3] Issues that are covered neither by the contract nor in the personnel manual may nonetheless fall under the principle of established practices. This principle holds that if a practice is in place at the time the contract is signed, it must remain in place for the duration of the contract—regardless of whether it is spelled out in the contract. This is far different from managerial discretion in the private sector, where management can change work rules at will unless specifically prohibited by the language of the contract. The principle can be illustrated by means of contrasting private- and public-sector incidents.

A floor supervisor at a tire manufacturing plant saw an employee remove a shoulder holster and pistol and put them in his locker before donning his coveralls for the start of his shift. The supervisor sent the employee home on a suspension without pay pending a final disciplinary decision. The manager based his action on the principle that any civilized person should know that guns are not permitted in the workplace. The union filed a grievance and won reinstatement for the employee on the grounds that there was no policy specifically prohibiting bringing guns to work. The arbitrator ruled that if management wished to initiate such a policy, then employees must be informed of the change before any adverse actions could be taken.

Notice that the arbitrator questioned only the way in which management implemented the policy. Nothing was said about management's right to make the change. This is very different from the experiences of public managers.

An assistant city manager of a small city was driving past a local supermarket when he noticed a fire truck parked in the lot. His curiosity piqued, the manager entered the store to see if there was some sort of emergency. Instead of a fire, the manager found the three-member truck crew shopping (they explained) for foodstuffs with which to prepare the noon and evening meals for the entire crew at the firehouse.

Upon returning to the office, the assistant reported the encounter to his boss. The city manager phoned the fire chief demanding to know why it took three people to purchase and prepare a meal for a crew of 10. The chief explained that a fully staffed truck was always dispatched in case a fire or other emergency requiring an immediate response were to occur while the shopping was in progress. By sending the truck and crew, the dispatcher could save valuable minutes if it became necessary to dispatch the unit.

Probing further, the manager learned that not only were the purchases made on city time but the crew responsible for cooking that day would take two-and-one-half hours to prepare and serve each meal. The disbelieving manager verbally ordered an immediate cessation to the practice. It seemed to her that one firefighter could prepare the meal without assistance while the other two returned to their regular assigned duties.

The union filed a grievance immediately upon receipt of the manager's new order. In the course of the arbitration hearing, the fire chief testified that the practice had been going on for at least as long as he could remember, because of the unique nature of the 24-hour shifts that the firefighters worked. City representatives argued that had they known about the practice sooner, it would have been stopped. The arbitrator ruled that the practice was an established one, and therefore, could not be altered during the course of the current contract. Management was free, however, to raise the issue at the next bargaining session.

PRIVATIZATION

The delivery of public programs through private rather than public agencies became a cause célèbre during the presidency of Ronald Reagan.[4] President Reagan established the Grace Commission (named for its chair, J. Peter Grace) to study how government programs could benefit from adoption of the techniques of management and economy practiced in the world of business. The savings that the commission claimed could be achieved have since been questioned by scholars of public administration.[5] But the commission's report was a catalyst for a national debate on government efficiency and the contracting-out of services.

The contracting-out of services currently delivered by public employees who are union members can cause considerable unrest. Management may hold to the position that the union need not be consulted based on management's traditional authority to decide matters of policy and staffing levels. A court fight may be in store for managers who seek to ignore the unions, however, because contracts or the enabling legislation may require the submission of all matters of contract interpretation to arbitration.[6]

Consulting the union before contracting-out will not always prevent a court fight, but it might. At a minimum, union input is necessary to the establishment of an orderly layoff procedure.[7] Although seniority normally must be observed, it may not be completely clear whether affected employees are entitled to bump-back privileges across department lines. That is, truck drivers in the sanitation department might be more senior than truck drivers in the parks department. Management must be careful to observe civil service seniority provisions as well as the letter of the contract layoff provisions.

Even when bump-backs across departments are not required, satisfactory employees whose positions are being abolished are entitled to consideration by their employer for positions in other departments for which they qualify. A mechanic in the sanitation department might be transferred to the motor pool or to the police or fire department, laborers in the sanitation department might be reassigned to maintenance crews, and so forth. The flexibility of reassignments is limited, of course, by the extent to which privatization is pursued across departments and the union contracts that are in place.

In addition to cooperative efforts to find positions for employees within the organization, agencies can assist employees by providing them with job-search training in resume writing and interview skills and employment referrals to other government and private-sector employers.[8]

AFFIRMATIVE ACTION

A recurring theme of contention between unions and government managers is the issue of affirmative action.[9] Management often finds itself caught between civil rights groups and federal compliance officials on the one hand, and employee unions interested in protecting the interests of their members on the other.

Suppose, for example, the United States Department of Labor examines a county government's employment practices and finds that in the sheriff's department only 12 percent of the deputies and none of the supervisors are minorities, even though 25 percent of the county's residents are members of minority groups. The Department of Labor would likely press the county to step up its recruitment efforts in the minority community and increase promotion of minorities. The former could probably be accomplished through an aggressive outreach recruitment program. Altering the promotion rate of minorities might begin with a review of the selection process. It could be that minorities perform satisfactorily on the written examination but do not fare well before promotion boards made up of senior white officers. The situation might call for training senior officers to sensitize them to the possibility that their ethnic stereotypes (whether conscious or not) are resulting in lower ratings of minorities in the interview process.[10]

A good-faith compliance effort by the county, however, could result in union resistance and even legal challenges from the union representing the deputies. This union response might be grounded in the belief that all supervisors obtained their positions strictly on the basis of merit and that tinkering with the system now would amount to preferential treatment for minorities. Particularly strong challenges could be expected to any effort to change the selection procedures that were in place at the time the current contract was signed.

Should either county management or the sheriff's office resist federal efforts, the matter could result in a lawsuit from the Justice Department, or a civil suit by civil rights groups representing the interest of the minority sheriff's deputies, or both. If a prima facie case of discrimination is established, the county management may be pressured by elected officials and the courts to enter into a consent decree to solve the problem as quickly as possible. (See the discussion of consent decrees in Chapter 3).

Consultation with unions should be a part of management's affirmative action efforts. When training is required to deal with supervisors' attitudes, union consultation can enhance employee acceptance. When a consent decree is in the offing, union consultation can bring the matter to conclusion with a minimum of litigation. Failure to consult with unions at the time the program is being developed can result in court challenges years after the fact, as occurred in *Martin* v. *Wilks* (1989).[11]

More generally, the best strategy for management in a union environment should include careful preparation for contract talks, mechanisms for ongoing consultation between contract cycles, and a disciplined effort on the part of all managers to recognize and respect the requirements of the contract.[12]

GAINSHARING

As noted in Chapter 9, some governments have undertaken programs to reward workers collectively. The program, known as gainsharing, rewards workers collectively for reducing cost or increasing productivity. For gainsharing to be successful, the program and its compensation rates should be formulated in close consultation with the union. To do otherwise is to invite costly and time-consuming grievances and noncooperation on the part of union members. When gainsharing is undertaken, its goals and timetables should be carefully spelled out in the contract or in a memorandum of understanding with the union. Otherwise, management may find it difficult to end a gainsharing effort that has achieved its purpose or that has failed utterly.

Unions have been surprisingly accepting of group rewards. Unlike individual merit pay, which is antithetical to the concept of a single bargaining unit with a single rate of compensation for all, gainsharing equally divides a portion of cost saving among bargaining-unit members, and the reward is not added to salary bases.

PREPARING FOR NEGOTIATIONS

RECORD KEEPING

Getting ready for the next round of negotiations should begin as soon as a contract is in place. Those responsible for labor relations (these may include the city manager or a single assistant, the director of personnel, or a division of specialists within the agency, city, county, or state government) must develop a file on problems growing out of the contract.

The file may be as simple as a monthly reporting of issues in controversy from each supervisor in a particular division. The file can then be organized by the primary labor relations specialist according to type of complaint. Appropriate subfiles might include such interpretation issues as employee discipline and personnel policies. Other issues might include working out of one's classification without being paid for it, the method whereby overtime is awarded, or whether management can compel emergency personnel to work beyond their regularly scheduled shifts. Maintaining such a file serves two purposes. First, it helps management organize its priorities for the next round of bargaining. Second, the file can also help management identify training needs among supervisory employees.

SUPERVISORY INVOLVEMENT

Effective management in a union environment also requires the intelligent involvement of supervisors. Supervisors need to understand and follow the contract, and they must implement a common collective-bargaining philosophy.

As noted previously, management and the union frequently differ over the precise meaning of contract provisions. Management cannot reasonably expect supervisors to comb through the contract looking for changes in contract language that may require them to alter the way they operate their units.[13] Instead, management should hold contract briefings for supervisors as soon as possible after the contract is printed. During these sessions, management should also take note of supervisors' concerns regarding problems that they envision growing out of the contract. Managers should take care to identify supervisors who disagree with elements in the new contract. These dissenters must be made aware that the contract language is binding on them and that good-faith compliance with the contract is one of their professional duties.

Two supervisory perspectives on labor relations can cause problems. First, some supervisors believe that union contracts only deal with money, insurance, retirement, and vacations. The contract is thus seen as irrelevant to the supervisor's personal managerial style. The supervisor may ask workers to perform tasks that are not in their job description or ask them to work overtime without compensation, on the assumption that whatever the supervisor asks should be done if it is for the good of the organization. On the same reasoning, a supervisor may discipline workers for a perceived violation of policy and refuse to discuss the matter with the union representative, believing that the supervisor is under no obligation to speak with the union. Such assumptions are incorrect because supervisors are agents of the organization, which will be held responsible for any mistakes they may make.

Such attitudes often exist among supervisors in police and fire departments. Ironically, uniformed supervisors are often members of the union and are covered by the same contract. As a result, a city can find itself before an arbitrator because it disciplined a supervisor for violating the terms of the union contract in his or her treatment of subordinates who are protected by the same contract.

A second potential source of problems is that front-line supervisors may not really consider themselves to be part of management. Supervisors promoted from the ranks, in particular, may identify more with subordinates and the union than with management. And working supervisors who perform much the same duties as those they supervise may have difficulty developing a management perspective.

Problems can arise if, for example, a supervisor allows workers in the unit to leave early on a regular basis on evenings when they have night classes. Extending such favors, when one is in a supervisory position, can result in an established practice that entitles others in the unit to the shorter working day. In short, managing in a union environment requires uniform adherence to the terms and conditions of the contract.

DEVELOPING A POSITIVE APPROACH

Collective bargaining in the public sector is a relatively new phenomenon when compared with the private-sector experience. Public unions developed when public employees found their wages falling behind those paid in the private sector and came to the conclusion that the civil service system did not provide them with adequate protection from management actions (see Chapter 12).

From a management perspective, the advent of unions further complicated the role of public managers, who were struggling to meet program needs in the face of shrinking resources. And, for many managers, unionization represented a lapse of professionalism among public employees.

These views sometimes led to an adversarial relationship between unions and management. For some managers, the mission was to obstruct, resist, and defeat the emerging unions. More moderate managers found themselves in conflict with union representatives bound and determined to advance the interests of their constituents, regardless of the impact on services.

Shrinking resources turned negotiating economic issues into a zero-sum game, in which one side could only advance its interests at the expense of the other. Union wage and benefit demands, for example, often could only be met by raising taxes. Dedicated rank-and-file public employees had no desire to eviscerate public services, but they had families to feed, and the double-digit inflation of the 1970s was eroding their incomes. The resulting combination of labor disputes, salary freezes, work stoppages, and arbitration hearings did little to reduce the adversarial relationship between management and unions.[14]

The range of issues on which management and labor representatives readily cooperate is limited. Nevertheless, management should proceed on the premise that public employee unions are a fact of doing business in government. Public managers should work toward developing a professional relationship based on mutual trust and cooperation with union officials.[15] Among the key elements in such a relationship are the following:

1. Treating union representatives as professionals with a legitimate interest in matters affecting their members

2. A forthright presentation of management's position on various aspects of the contract

3. Establishing a system of routine consultation with union leaders over matters of mutual concern

4. Creating a fair and equitable grievance process that resolves grievances at the lowest possible level

How these elements can best be achieved depends on the current state of relations between the two parties. In the best case, the chief executive officer (CEO) and his or her division heads will have approached labor relations with a positive attitude throughout their dealings. When this occurs, most if not all of the above will have been accomplished. Unfortunately, this is rarely the case.

TREATING UNION REPRESENTATIVES AS PROFESSIONALS

START-UP CONSTRAINTS. When dealing with a new union or a turnover in union leadership, management must realize that the union leaders have limited discretion in making bargaining concessions. Newly elected union leaders, like politicians, must adhere to the agenda that got them elected. Unlike politicians, however, union representatives know that their performance is directly and closely scrutinized by their constituents. Novice union leaders, therefore, may have to take a hard line regardless of the reasonableness of management's position or the agency's ability to pay.

ONGOING UNION-MANAGEMENT RELATIONS. Wages and benefits are perennial subjects on the union agenda. After union leaders have established credibility with their constituents, however, they can be more flexible and accommodating to management's positions. As matters continue, moreover, union negotiators will turn their attention to working conditions, grievance procedures, and other issues.

Once union interests have broadened, and if management has consistently treated union representatives with respect and professionalism, relations can move into a system of bilateralism. Bilateralism means that management no longer reacts to union demands. Instead, managers come to the table with their own agenda covering such items as contracting-out, productivity improvements, and management's rights. The preconditions of bilateralism are a recognition of the union reality, a commitment by management to operate within a union environment, and the establishment of mutually respectful professional relationships with union leaders. Managers who have established good bilateral relations with union leaders may find their tasks eased somewhat in subsequent years when economic issues and employee job security again dominate public-sector negotiations.

Managers often find themselves caught squarely in between city councils and state legislatures bent on limiting spending and militant unionists bent on raising their salaries. The manager in this situation cannot expect the automatic trust and cooperation of the union leaders. Nevertheless, managers must conduct themselves in a professional, forthright manner, even when union-management relations are strained.

In times of stress, professionalism means that the managers will state agency positions honestly. Should layoffs be necessary, managers should seek to cooperate with the union to minimize the damage to workers. Rancor-free relationships also entail listening to the substance of union positions without reacting to the anger that may characterize the union presentation. The worst thing management can do is to personalize the process by interpreting union criticisms as personal attacks. Indeed, even when the media report that the union has accused the manager of insensitivity to worker needs (or worse), managers should not respond in kind. Only by maintaining the highest level of professionalism can managers hope to salvage anything from the situation.

CONSULTATION. When cutbacks and layoffs become necessary, unions should be consulted rather than notified. The specific wording of the contract may require only that management notify the union of the necessity of the layoffs and that seniority be strictly observed. Normally, civil service procedures (and the contract) will require that appropriate notification be sent to each affected employee and to the union.

Through consultation, however, management might work with the union leadership to persuade more senior members of the bargaining unit to take early retirement. If enough senior employees retire, and vacancies that occur through normal turnover are left unfilled, layoffs of less senior employees can be minimized. This approach offers some added bonuses. By persuading more senior employees to retire, a greater cost saving can be achieved than if less senior, lower-paid workers are laid off. Cooperation can also help minimize union attempts to bring political pressure to bear on management through direct appeals to the board, council, or legislature.

FORTHRIGHT PRESENTATION OF MANAGEMENT'S POSITION

Of the various bargaining strategies available to management, the most productive in the long run is to be open and forthright. Some managers believe that the best way to get what one wants is to hammer away at the opposition on other, less important issues until their resistance is worn down—then switch to the real priority, seemingly as an afterthought. Others refuse to state a position (at least not their real position) on any item until they have heard the opposition's complete list of demands. By holding back or releasing smoke screens, these negotiators claim they can best formulate a strategy for maximum gain.

As noted previously, union-management relations are usually adversarial. Of the bargaining strategies just described, only forthright presentation of management's positions can lessen tensions. The other is to start from the premise that management-labor relations are a contest from which one side or the other will emerge as a winner in each round of negotiations.

The forthright strategy starts from the premise that dealing with unions is a fact of life in managing government programs. By stating positions, reaching accords with one's bargaining counterparts, then following through on commitments, managers can begin to break down union distrust and resentment that in the past have thrown up barriers to professional relationships.

The foregoing should not be construed to mean that management ought to begin negotiations by stating its final positions on economic matters. Appointed public managers are the surrogate of elected officials and, by extension, the people. In this surrogate role, public managers must act in the public interest which, in this case, involves the provision of quality government services at reasonable costs.

When applied to the wages of public employees, the term *reasonable* should mean the payment of a wage that is competitive with comparable government entities and the prevailing wage in the area being served. Reasonable does not mean paying public employees the lowest amount possible, thereby discouraging able people from undertaking careers in the public service. By the same token, managers must also be guided by the resources available in a given contract year. When the economy is in recession and unemployment is on the rise, tax revenues must surely decline. The ability to effectively balance the needs of public employees and the interests of the taxpaying public is a distinguishing feature of professionalism in public-sector collective bargaining.

ESTABLISHING A SYSTEM OF ROUTINE CONSULTATION

Managers who do not like unions do not enjoy talking with them. Like them or not, however, managers cannot avoid union contact, nor should they attempt to do so. Instead, managers should set up a program of regular consultations to discuss issues arising from contract interpretation or policies and programs that management might wish to undertake that have potential impact on members of a particular bargaining unit.

Contract interpretations are frequently a matter of amazement to newcomers to the realm of collective bargaining. "How could they possibly interpret this clause that way?" is a lament heard on both sides of the process. Such variations in viewpoint are not surprising, given the complexity of the issues involved and the potential impact of one interpretation over another upon the interests of the parties.

The best way to deal with differences is in regular sessions that meet on a monthly basis, or more often as necessary. At these sessions, each side should be free to raise issues of interpretation and have the opportunity to persuade the other side. Upon clarification of issues, the two sides may draft and sign a memorandum. This practice of clarifying contract clauses with side memos has become so popular in some jurisdictions that the clarification documents are as long as the actual contract.

The consultation sessions are also an appropriate vehicle for management to propose changes in operating procedures that may affect union members. The example of altering the biweekly pay system described earlier is a good case in point for the types of issues that can be dealt with by consultation. Had the city in question followed a policy of regular consultation with the union, it might never have found itself in front of an arbitrator. Resolving the issue by consultation or during the contract negotiation process is preferable to a cavalier attitude on the part of management regarding the union's right to participate in management decision making.

CREATING A FAIR AND EQUITABLE GRIEVANCE PROCESS

A number of variations are possible in the grievance process.[16] Generically, the process involves a timely appeal of a dispute to each subsequent echelon in the organization, with a final appeal possible to an external, third-party decision maker. What constitutes a justifiable grievance, the definition of a timely appeal, and who the third-party neutral shall be vary from jurisdiction to jurisdiction. Management must also decide how it will treat grievances as a matter of policy.

NATURE OF THE GRIEVANCE. Some agency grievance procedures are so open-ended that they allow any employee to complain about any issue regardless of its contract relevance. Such open access to upper management allows expression of worker concerns regarding various policy issues and should, therefore, be via a process that is separate from contract matters.[17] The separation is necessary if for no other reason than the authority of labor arbitrators is found within the four corners of the contract. A good rule of thumb is if an issue may ultimately be resolved by arbitration, then it must be based in the language of the contract.

A contractual base to a grievance means that the employee must spell out the action of management to which he or she is objecting and the contract clause or clauses that have allegedly been violated. Issues that are readily linked to the contract include unfair disciplinary actions, working out of one's classification without extra compensation, overtime pay for work beyond eight hours on a holiday, and the like.

Matters that are more appropriate for regular communication channels include questions of agency policy or the amount of consultation to which individual employees are entitled regarding service procedures. Unless contract-related grievances are clearly spelled out, noncontract matters may take up inordinate amounts of agency time and resources.

TIMELY GRIEVANCES.   Grievance time limits are normally prescribed in the contract. The clause may specify that the grievance clock starts the moment that the incident in question occurs. Suppose, for example, that a supervisor instructs a clerical worker to get a ladder from the storage closet and wash all the overhead light fixtures in the office. The worker may object that such work is the responsibility of maintenance. If the manager insists that the worker perform the task, a grievance would be in order. How much time the contract allows workers to file a grievance might be 5, 10, or 30 days. Failure to file in a timely manner constitutes a forfeiture of grievance rights.

Care should be taken to ensure that contract language specifies whether the number of days in question are calendar or working days. Calendar days can be a problem, especially when a grievance occurs near a holiday. Suppose, for example, that a municipality has a 10-calendar-day grievance process. An incident occurring on July 1 would require that a grievance be filed by July 11 (10 calendar days). If, however, the Fourth of July holiday fell on a Thursday, the city offices would probably be closed on July 5 as well as for the weekend of July 6 and 7. The employee would then have only 6 days in which to file a timely grievance. If an organization is sincere about correcting injustices, a 10-working-day grievance process is highly preferable.

The timing of grievances is not cut-and-dried. When an employee is unaware that a violation of the contract has occurred until after the filing period, the arbitrator may first rule on the timeliness of the grievance as a threshold issue before deciding its actual merits.

Supervisors should be required to inform employees of the time frame for filing a grievance whenever an adverse action is undertaken. Of course, if the grievance grows out of whether the supervisor has the authority to order the employee to perform a task, it is up to the employee (in consultation with union representatives) to determine whether to pursue the matter.

THIRD-PARTY RESOLUTION.   Not every grievance procedure calls for third-party resolution of disputes as the final step (see the discussion of grievance arbitration in Chapter 12). The contract, in fact, may call for a final decision by the appointing authority (that is, the chief executive officer of the agency). Sometimes this is a department head, the city manager, or the director of a state or county agency.

As a practical matter, civil service rules require that employees are entitled to have such adverse actions as suspension, demotion, or discharge heard by a third-party neutral. Thus, even without an arbitration provision in the contract, a union may actively defend workers in the merit appeals process.

DUAL SYSTEMS.   In some jurisdictions, employees have access to contract-based arbitration and also retain their civil service protections. Where dual systems exist, management should negotiate language that allows the employee to pursue only one of the two options. To do otherwise is to invite duplicative appeals of the same grievance to different forums.

Grievances involving adverse actions against individual employees may be heard by an arbitrator under the just-cause provisions of the contract, or they may be appealed to the merit protection agency. Which forum will handle a grievance depends partly on the nature of the grievance and partly on the strategy selected by the employee in conjunction with the union.

If the adverse action grew out of contract language, then an arbitrator may be most appropriate. Suppose, for example, that a firefighter is suspended for failing to keep his hair cut short enough to meet departmental safety standards. The firefighter might contend that the hairstyle is an expression of his ethnic heritage. The city might contend that this is a safety issue because long hair protruding from under the helmet could catch fire. As a safety issue, management might believe that the decision regarding hair length is a unilateral management prerogative. The union, however, might regard the controversy as an example of management throwing its weight around as well as stretching the interpretation of the management-rights clause. The union, therefore, might counsel the employee to take the matter to arbitration to narrow the definition of managerial prerogatives.

Suppose, on the other hand, that an employee is discharged for repeated failure to perform the duties of his or her position. The union would have the responsibility of attempting to get the employee reinstated under the just-cause provisions of the contract, even though other members of the bargaining unit are not directly affected. In such a case, the union might advise the employee to appeal the discharge to the merit protection agency rather than an arbitrator.

Pursuing a merit-based appeal has three advantages. First, the union can keep faith with the employee by paying for his or her legal representation without getting into matters of contract interpretation. Second, a merit protection appeal can be pursued without the cost of an arbitrator; the cost of the hearing is absorbed by the merit agency. Finally, if the employee should lose with the hearing examiner, normally he or she can appeal to the merit board on procedural grounds and subsequently pursue the matter in district court. Decisions made by arbitrators, on the other hand, are generally final.[18]

The finality of an arbitrator's decision may be particularly attractive, however, to agencies and unions whose primary goal is speedy grievance resolution, especially if the contract calls for expedited arbitration with no written opinions.

RESOLUTION AT THE LOWEST LEVEL.   The purpose of a grievance procedure is (or ought to be) to resolve the controversy at the lowest possible level of the organization. Thus, the procedure might call for employees to attempt first to rectify grievances via conferences with their supervisors. If the matter is not resolved, the next step might be a written grievance filed within 10 working days with the next echelon of the organization, and so forth up to the agency head. If the matter is still not resolved to the satisfaction of the grievant, the contract may call for a hearing by an independent third party.

Recognizing the legitimacy of the grievance process means not only a recognition of the employee's right to grieve but a willingness on the part of management to reverse incorrect decisions without going to arbitration. When a lower-level supervisor has erred, the manager should have the strength of character to reverse the decision. There is little to be gained by compounding the error in the interest of presenting a united front. In fact, if management never intends to reverse itself, then the arbitrator should become the first as well as final point of appeal.

When a reversal becomes necessary, it should be announced through the chain of command. That is, the manager should tell his or her immediate subordinate, who can pass the decision down to the next lower level, until the grievant is informed personally by his or her own supervisor. Failure to observe the chain of command undermines the authority of subordinate managers and can give the grievant or the union the false impression that they have special access in the system. Passing decisions down through channels preserves the integrity and dignity of the organizational structure.

SUMMARY AND CONCLUSION

To summarize, management in a unionized environment is complex and challenging. Public managers, far more than their private-sector counterparts, must take union interests into account when making a broad range of decisions. When negotiating contracts, public managers are structuring the context within which public policy will be implemented. When negotiating wages and benefits, they are allocating public resources. As such, management is exercising a public trust that will undergo closer scrutiny than practically any of their other endeavors. This scrutiny comes from the media and public interest groups as well as the leadership of the union and elected officials. Managers must be guided by the highest professional standards when conducting union relations.

NOTES AND RESOURCES

1. See Dennis R. Nolan, *Labor Arbitration Law and Practice* (St. Paul, MN: West, 1979). For current trends in labor relations, see Katharine G. Abraham and Robert B. McKersie, eds., *New Developments in the Labor Market: Toward a New Institutional Paradigm* (Cambridge, MA: MIT Press, 1990); and Jeanette A. Davy and George W. Bohlander, "Recent Findings and Practices in Grievance Arbitration Procedures," *Labor Law Journal* 43 (1992): 184–91.

2. See David A. Dilts and Edwin C. Leonard, Jr., "Win-Loss Rates in Public Sector Grievance Arbitration Cases: Implication for the Selection of Arbitrators," *Journal of Collective Negotiations in the Public Sector* 18 (1989): 337–44.

3. Public-sector arbitration that is prescribed by law is quite different from voluntary private agreements to grievance arbitration. See Ann C. Hodges, "The Steelworkers Trilogy in the Public Sector," *Chicago-Kent Law Review* 66 (1990): 631–84.

4. See Robert H. Carver, "Examining the Premises of Contracting Out," *Public Productivity and Management Review* 13 (1989): 27–40; and Stanley C. Wisniewski, "A Framework for Considering the Contracting Out of Government Services," *Public Personnel Management* 21 (1992): 101–18.

5. *Report on Privatization* (Washington, DC: U.S. Government Printing Office, 1983). First among the critics was Charles T. Goodsell, "The Grace Commission: Seeking Efficiency for the Whole People," *Public Administration Review* 44 (1984): 196–205. The most serious questioning of the commission's cost-savings projections was by the Congressional Budget Office, *Contracting-Out: Potential for Reducing Federal Costs* (Washington, DC: U.S. Government Printing Office, 1987).

6. The most recent Supreme Court reaffirmation of this concept was set forth in *AT&T Technologies, Inc.* v. *Communication Workers,* 106 S. Ct. 1415 (1986).

7. For a discussion of current job security issues, see Robert J. Colon, "Job Security Issues in Grievance Arbitration—What Do They Tell Us?" *Journal of Collective Negotiations in the Public Sector* 19 (1990): 243–52.

8. See Robert Schneider, Neil B. Colan, and Bradley Googins, "Supervisor Training in Employee Assistance Programs: Current Practices and Future Trends," *Employee Assistance Quarterly* 6, no. 2 (Summer 1990): 41–57.

9. See Russel Nieli, ed., *Racial Preference and Racial Justice: The New Affirmative Action Controversy* (Washington, DC: Ethics and Public Policy Center, 1991); Jonathan S. Leonard, *Unions and Equal Employment Opportunity* (Cambridge, MA: National Bureau of Economic Research, 1984); and Don Jaegal and N. Joseph Cayer, "Public Personnel Administration by Lawsuit: The Impact of Supreme Court Decisions on Public Employee Litigiousness," *Public Administration Review* 51 (1991): 211–32.

10. For a treatment of stereotyping, see Melinda Jones, "Stereotyping Hispanics and Whites: Perceived Differences in Social Roles as a Determinant of Ethnic Stereotypes," *Journal of Social Psychology* 131 (1991): 469–76.

11. *Martin* v. *Wilks* 109 S. Ct. 2180 (1989). The decision was limited to those whose interests were not protected in the original suit by the 1991 Civil Rights Act (see Chapter 3).

12. See David Coursey and Hal G. Rainey, "Perceptions of Personnel Systems Constraints in Public, Private, and Hybrid Organizations," *Review of Public Personnel Management* 10 (1990): 54–71.

13. See Mollie H. Bowers, *Contract Administration in the Public Sector* (Chicago: International City Managers Association, 1976).

14. See Alan E. Bent and T. Zane Reeves, *Collective Bargaining in the Public Sector* (Menlo Park, CA: Benjamin Cummings, 1978).

15. See Roger M. Schwarz, "Participative Decision Making and Union Management Cooperative Efforts: Attitudes of Managers, Union Officials and Employees," *Review of Public Personnel Administration* 11 (1990): 38–54; Thomas J. Quin, Mark Rosenbaum, and Donald S. McPherson, "Grievance Mediation and Grievance Negotiation Skills: Building Collaborative Relationships," *Labor Law Journal* 41 (1990): 762–71; and Robert N. White, "Positive Negotiations Tactics," *School Business Affairs* 56, no. 2 (February 1990): 28–35.

16. See Lee T. Paterson and Reginald T. Murphy, *The Public Administrator's Grievance Arbitration Handbook* (New York: Longman, 1983); and Donald S. McPherson and Kevin N. Rogers, *Resolving Grievances: A Practical Approach* (Reston, VA: Reston Publishing, 1983).

17. See Douglas M. McCabe and David Lewin, "Employee Voice: A Human Resource Management Perspective," *California Management Review* 34, no. 3 (Spring 1992): 112–23; and Matthew T. Roberts, Roger S. Wolters, and William H. Holley, Jr., "Grievance Mediation: A Management Perspective," *The Arbitration Journal* 45, no. 3 (September 1990): 15–23.

18. This has been the case since the steelworkers trilogy, although the courts have accepted appeals from time to time; see Dennis R. Nolan, *Labor Arbitration Law and Practice* (St. Paul, MN: West, 1979), pp. 43–54.

Employee Discipline and Conflict Resolution Systems

Employee discipline and conflict resolution systems are essential components of any well-run human resource program. As in most areas, however, public agencies are limited by various external policies and procedures. These may be legislative enactments or the policies of such human resource regulatory agencies as federal and state equal employment opportunity commissions and federal, state, and local government personnel agencies. Despite these constraints, however, agencies exercise some latitude as to the internal procedures and programs they establish to operationalize these external policies. Internal systems are important to the good-faith protection of the rights of individual employees, as well as the timely and just resolution of disciplinary problems and conflicts between employees and their supervisors.

In many jurisdictions, employee and supervisor disputes are an issue between the agency and the designated bargaining unit that represents the individual employee. Thus, how a grievance is resolved affects all workers in the unit. As we shall see, moreover, the authority of the manager does not stop at the parking lot exit. The private behavior of public employees may also impact their work and is therefore subject to the disciplinary system.

EEO CONSTRAINTS

Congress has enacted various pieces of civil rights legislation that are incumbent upon all government agencies as a matter of law and as a condition of federal funding of programs. Chapter 3 outlined the barriers to selection and promotion against which agencies must be ever vigilant to ensure fairness and equality of opportunity. To avoid litigation, agencies must establish processes that allow resolution of EEO complaints at the lowest echelon and in the shortest possible time. First, agencies are required to achieve a minimum level of compliance by drafting a clear statement of agency EEO policies and by maintaining a work atmosphere free of bias. Second, agencies must designate a person who is responsible for overseeing the policy and processing grievances. Finally, agencies must tell employees whom to contact regarding complaints. Considerable latitude exists within these parameters for public managers to establish the level of priority that EEO shall have in the agency.

EEO GRIEVANCE SYSTEMS

EEO grievances do not necessarily follow the chain of command, because they frequently involve charges against the employee's immediate coworkers or supervisor. Charges against coworkers involving racial, ethnic, or sexual harassment normally begin with a complaint to the employee's immediate supervisor. In some cases, however, the complainant may be uncomfortable reporting to his or her supervisor because of that person's perceived insensitivity or because the employee would be uncomfortable revealing the details of a sexual harassment complaint to a person of a different gender or sexual orientation.

The agency must establish an EEO grievance process outside the chain of command.[1] In a small, single-site agency, the process would involve reporting directly to the EEO/affirmative action officer. The name, office location, and telephone number of this person should be posted conspicuously so that everybody knows how to contact him or her. Larger agencies with multiple branch offices should see to it that at least one employee representative at each location is available to assist employees in filing specific complaints. These persons need not be equal-employment specialists; equal employment can be an additional duty. However, they should be knowledgeable about the appeals system and know where to refer aggrieved employees for expert assistance. They need not have investigative authority nor the power to resolve issues. Rather, they should be equal-employment advocates who are available to facilitate the timely filing of grievances and to assist grievants with the necessary paperwork.

The establishment of a readily accessible advocacy grievance system expedites the resolution of complaints. At times, the advocate may be able to resolve the problem by counseling the complainant. In other instances, the system serves to bring the matter quickly to the attention of management.

GRIEVANCE COUNSELING

EEO advocates should undergo training regarding the law, agency policy, and the techniques of counseling. In some cases, the advocate may find it necessary to refer overwrought victims of discrimination to psychological counseling.[2] In others, the advocate may only have to supply the employee with appropriate complaint forms. Normally, the advocate's role is somewhere between these two extremes, requiring some counseling and assistance with filing the grievance.

Suppose, for example, that a Mexican-American employee is the butt of office horseplay involving reference to his heritage. Suppose that his coworkers have dubbed him "the Frito Bandito" or "Speedy Gonzales" or have hung signs on his work cubicle such as "Do not disturb, siesta in progress" and "It's no my yob." Suppose, further, that the employee has reported these incidents to his supervisor, who has told him not to take things so seriously, that the coworkers' jokes mean they like him. Without an advocacy grievance system, the employee has few options. He can pursue the complaint to the next echelon, take the supervisor's advice, or resign.

With an advocacy system, the advocate who receives the complaint (1) documents in writing that a complaint has been filed; (2) immediately reports the matter to the accused employees, their superiors, and the central EEO office for investigation; and (3) assures the victim of the agency's commitment to an EEO work environment and that the agency will investigate and resolve the problem. Advocates should not be responsible for investigating incidents or counseling supervisors. These activities are the responsibility of line management and central EEO personnel.

Maintaining a separation between the advocate system and the grievance process accomplishes several things. First, the advocates can maintain their objectivity and perspective as advocates for the agency's EEO policies. The ability of these advocates to discern precisely the seriousness of the problem and to decide on an appropriate corrective action is questionable. A mistake by a duly authorized agent of the organization can have the effect of making an in-house remedy impossible, thereby forcing the matter into the courts. Second, if advocates are given investigative and enforcement power, their ability to perform their regular duties may be compromised, and their relations with other employees may suffer. Finally, giving advocates enforcement authority can jeopardize their relationships with managers to whom they are supposedly subordinate. The most important reason for not empowering the advocates, however, is that doing so absolves line managers of the responsibility for maintaining a bias-free work environment.

When the advocate reports to a line manager that a complaint has been filed, the manager is put on notice that a problem exists that must be dealt with in a timely fashion. In agencies that are truly EEO affirmative action employers, vigorous enforcement of antibias policy is an accepted responsibility of line managers. When line managers are not given that responsibility, equal employment opportunity is unlikely to be a reality, and those who enforce the policies are likely to be viewed as enemies by line managers, whether or not they personally are under scrutiny.

COUNSELING AS SCREENING.   The counseling function of advocates may serve as a screening device, thus preventing unwarranted complaints from being pursued. Suppose, for example, that an employee who is a member of a minority group is counseled by her supervisor regarding unsatisfactory work attendance. The employee (out of anger and fear) might go to the advocate to complain of supervisory racism. In this instance, the advocate might take pains to explain to the employee what constitutes a racially biased adverse action as opposed to an acceptable form of employee discipline. If the employee remains unconvinced, however, the advocate would be responsible for assisting with the filing of appropriate forms.

Counseling may also result in quick resolution of a grievance, such as when the employee is reluctant to register an initial complaint with his or her supervisor regarding the conduct of coworkers. Suppose, for example, that a female firefighter is the object of unwelcome sexual overtures from her male coworkers. Suppose, further, that her rejection of them has resulted in jokes, innuendos, and other behavior that she finds offensive.[3] In this instance, the victim may not wish to appear prudish or unable to take a joke. She may also fear that going to her supervisor could cause an escalation of the harassment to the point where she could no longer be effective as a firefighter. She may even fear that her coworkers might not come to her aid in an emergency.

Advocacy counseling might persuade her to go to her supervisor. In fact, the advocate could go with her as moral support, if need be. The supervisor might then respond promptly and affirmatively by immediately putting those responsible on notice that sexual harassment will not be tolerated in the department. By monitoring through both the victim and the supervisor, the advocate could ensure satisfactory resolution of the situation. If not, central office action and a response from higher up might become necessary.

Of course, if the supervisor was the harasser, the role of the advocate would be to assist the grievant in pressing the complaint up through the chain of command.

AVOIDING LITIGATION

The advocacy system can have the additional benefit of helping the agency avoid litigation.[4] Before the federal EEOC will issue an individual employee a certification to file suit in federal district court, he or she must have exhausted all lower remedies. Furthermore, state and local agencies that do not provide a means for satisfactory resolution of EEO grievances may find themselves in state court defending suits filed under state EEO statutes. Such statutes often have provisions for the awarding of punitive damages as well as actual damages. A California jury, for example, recently awarded three female deputy sheriffs a total of $2.7 million in a sexual harassment case because jury members believed that the sheriff's department did not take adequate measures to protect the women from subsequent harassment by fellow officers. The damages were awarded even though the offending supervisor had been disciplined for his conduct.[5]

An advocacy system has the advantage of allowing victims to report their complaints without adhering to the chain of command. This is particularly important if the victim is subordinate to the victimizer. As reported in Chapter 4, in the case of *Meritor Savings Bank* v. *Mechelle Vinson et al.* (1986),[6] the Supreme Court unanimously held that the employer was liable for damages stemming from the conduct of a supervisor because the company failed to provide a reporting system outside the chain of command.

MERIT SYSTEM CONSTRAINTS

Congress, state legislatures, and the courts have seen fit to grant nonprobationary merit employees protection from discharge other than for economic necessity or just cause. Just cause is defined as misfeasance (doing the job incorrectly), malfeasance (violations of law or policy), or nonfeasance (failure to perform). In lay terms, merit employees have a property interest in their jobs and cannot be deprived of them without due process of law. At a minimum, prior to discharge, an employee must be told the reason for the proposed discharge (orally or in writing), be given notice of the anticipated date of the discharge, and be given the opportunity to respond (orally or in writing).[7]

Employees who are separated by discharge are entitled to a hearing before an impartial examiner, who has the authority to determine whether the discharge was for just cause.[8] At this hearing, the discharged employee may present his or her own case or be represented by counsel. The employee and counsel for the agency may call witnesses, cross-examine hostile witnesses, and submit written documentation to the hearing officer. In small jurisdictions, the appeal of the discharge may be heard directly by the merit protection board or civil service commission. As the legal issues become more complex and the number of cases grows, however, more and more jurisdictions have adopted the use of hearing examiners who are experts in personnel law and administrative procedures. They may or may not be members of the legal profession.

The hearing officer, in most jurisdictions, has the authority to uphold the discharge or to order that the employee be reinstated if just cause for the discharge is lacking. Some jurisdictions allow hearing officers to reduce the penalty to suspension or demotion if they feel that discharge is unwarranted. The losing party has the right to have the decision of the examiner reviewed by a merit review board made up of distinguished citizens appointed by elected officials, such as the governor, mayor, or president, and leaders of the legislature, board, or council. These boards review the decision for procedural errors or violations of policies. A decision may be appealed because the hearing officer excluded relevant testimony that directly bore upon the case and supported the appellant's position. Sometimes appeals are made on public-interest grounds; that is, the examiner made no procedural error but reached a conclusion not supported by the facts that, if allowed to stand, would set an improper precedent.[9]

Rarely do merit boards conduct full-blown hearings of the case under appeal. Instead, they may have a different examiner review the transcripts or tapes of the first hearing to determine if the alleged error occurred. Alternatively, the board may order a complete new hearing. Some boards can reverse the hearing examiner, based on the briefs filed by the appellee, but this rarely occurs because it undermines the system. If the board finds that reversible error occurred in the first hearing, it should order a new hearing with a different examiner.

Normally, the losing party has the option of filing suit in the appropriate state or federal court. Obviously, the appeals process is technical and complex. The number of possible appeals, moreover, makes it imperative that agencies establish procedures that protect the rights of employees as well as the agency's interest in maintaining an honest and productive workforce.

Even though the appeals process may be rigorous, an agency still has considerable latitude in determining the content and procedures in its disciplinary process. Considerable discretion exists, moreover, regarding how strictly it chooses to enforce discipline.

DISCIPLINARY SYSTEMS

The disciplinary process may be prescribed by a central personnel authority.[10] What is more likely, however, is that the central authority will establish guidelines for agencies. The principal instrument of disciplinary procedures is the first-line supervisor. How rigorously such work rules as attendance and performance standards are enforced varies from supervisor to supervisor. Although most public employees are hardworking, dedicated professionals, some are not. Whether the latter are compelled to correct their behavior depends on the individual supervisor. The supervisor's response, in turn, may depend on the degree of support that supervisors feel they can anticipate from higher-ups in the organization.

Agency managers who want a topnotch professional organization must initiate and follow through on clear-cut and reasonable disciplinary procedures. Management also must provide agency supervisors with the skills training necessary to navigate the system. And, most important, management must be willing to expend the time and resources necessary to support supervisors through the appeals process. Jurisdictions with union contracts in place must adhere to the terms and conditions set forth in the union contract. Some contracts call for a review of grievances by an external arbitrator. Others specify that disciplinary action against an individual in the bargaining unit will be adjudicated using the civil service system. When, however, the issue is a matter of contract interpretation that impacts the entire work unit, the union may want to have the issue resolved by an arbitrator. Most union contracts specify that the personnel rules in place at the time the contract was signed are deemed to be a part of the contract and may not be unilaterally altered by management. Individual employees, moreover, are entitled to legal representation paid for by the bargaining unit regardless of whether the grievance is heard in the civil service system or before an arbitrator.

Adverse actions against tenured public employees must be for *just cause,* which is defined as misfeasance, malfeasance, nonfeasance, or a combination thereof.

Misfeasance: Doing one's job incorrectly, such as making multiple errors or misinterpreting rules and regulations.

Malfeasance: Violating agency policies or rules, or violations of civil or criminal law.

Nonfeasance: Failure to comply with a direct and lawful order of a supervisor, known as gross insubordination; work performance that falls substantially below acceptable quantity standards; chronic lateness or frequent unexplained and unauthorized absences from the duty station or abuse of sick leave.

DOCUMENTATION

The agency must establish documentation as its number-one priority in the disciplinary process. All personnel actions, whether positive or negative, must be based on clear-cut agency policies and be documented in writing. Thus, for example, a school principal who wants to not reappoint a teacher based on inadequate teaching must follow district rules to the letter. The principal should be able to document inadequate teaching based on student test scores, classroom disciplinary records, formal student complaints, peer review, and so forth. The decision should not be based on hearsay reports from other teachers as reported to them by anonymous students.

Without adequate documentation, a good teacher might be wrongly discharged. Conversely, lack of documentation may lead to the reinstatement of a truly bad teacher, who is then in the position to resist subsequent attempts at removal on the grounds that the action is in retaliation for the previously successful appeal. The same holds true, to a lesser extent, regarding compliance with district notification rules. Failure to notify the individual in a timely fashion can result in a reinstatement.

Written documentation provides managers and hearing examiners with a paper trail of incidents that precipitated the disciplinary action, and it can assist the agency to recall events that may have occurred months or years earlier. Suppose, for example, that an aide in a children's psychiatric hospital is accused of using excessive force while breaking up a fight between children. Suppose that, as a result of the incident, one child suffered a broken nose. At issue would be whether the injury was inflicted by the other child or by the aide while restraining the injured child. Before taking action against the aide, the supervisor must also determine if the aide was using prescribed procedures in restraining the child.

Even if the supervisor was present at the incident, he or she should secure written statements from all employees who were also present. These statements should be written as soon after the incident as possible but, in any case, before the end of work that day. Statements should be written without consultation among employees, and they should be dated and signed. By having witnesses reduce their views of an incident to writing immediately, the manager is assured of fresh recollections. Furthermore, the presence of one's written statement in the hands of management might discourage a reluctant witness from later relating the event in terms more favorable to the accused at a disciplinary hearing. And, if need be, the statement can form the basis of a disciplinary action against witnesses who subsequently alter their statements or if their testimony is proven to be false. Perhaps the most important reason for reducing everything to writing immediately is the slowness of the grievance process. Management may initiate an adverse action as soon as they feel it is warranted. The employee then has several days to prepare for the hearing. In the interim, the manager is likely to forget who was present, and the details may become fuzzy in the manager's own mind.

The supervisor should also interview the children involved in the incident as soon as possible. These interviews should be conducted in the presence of another adult who was not present at the time of the injury. An oral interview would be necessary in this case because emotionally disturbed children cannot be expected to reduce their statements to writing. A witness is necessary to corroborate what the supervisor heard from the children, because disturbed children may also be plagued with cloudy memories.

After gathering data by these means, the supervisor is prepared to document the incident as a permanent part of the patient's record and to comply with external reporting requirements, such as to a children's protection agency.

Before taking an adverse action against the employee, the supervisor must be reasonably sure that agency procedures for correctly restraining children were not followed. The supervisor must also be sure that the employee in question was instructed in the procedures for restraining a child in this circumstance. Finally, if more than a written reprimand is intended, the supervisor should be confident in his or her own mind that the employee meant to injure the child and that the written evidence substantiates this belief.

APPROPRIATE DISCIPLINE

In every disciplinary case, the supervisor must be guided by agency policy.[11] Agency policy, in turn, must balance the interest of the agency in maintaining an efficient and honest workforce against the rights of the individual employee. The rules of the merit system also constrain the agency. The disciplinary options that an agency allows its supervisory employees should reflect these constraints.

PROGRESSIVE DISCIPLINES. A well-designed disciplinary system will allow supervisors to apply a sanction that is appropriate to the offense in question. Progressive discipline systems prescribe that manager's first try to correct the behavior of errant employees and apply sanctions only when it appears that the employee has not improved his or her performance. The first step in the process is the presumed ongoing counseling that is part and parcel of the supervisory function. When an employee makes a mistake, the supervisor's first reaction should be that of a teacher who corrects the employee and instructs him or her in the appropriate agency procedure.[12]

The supervisor's reaction would be similar if a worker begins taking extra-long lunches or breaks, comes in late, or seems to be abusing sick leave. The employee should first be counseled as to the agency rules regarding attendance and be given the chance to correct his or her behavior before sanctions are taken.

The next step in the process is a letter of reprimand that documents a formal counseling session informing the individual of the unacceptability of his or her conduct. The letter also advises the employee that should another formal counseling become necessary within a specified time, the next level of sanction—suspension without pay—will be imposed.

The letter becomes a part of the employee's personnel file for a specified length of time that varies from jurisdiction to jurisdiction. The period may range from six months to as much as two years or longer if subsequent disciplinary action is taken. In instances of an employee's inability to correctly perform his or her duties, management may find it more appropriate to reassign the employee before imposing a suspension.

If the issue is performance, the agency may wish to consider demoting the employee to a position at a more appropriate skill level. Of course, the demotion option is not available for employees at the bottom of the hierarchy. Demotion is a more extreme form of discipline than suspension, because it reduces an employee's pay level as well as altering his or her job duties. Demotion also reduces an employee's status and authority in the organization.

Demotions are traumatic for workers and should not be pursued lightly by supervisors. Nevertheless, there are instances in which employees have been placed in positions above their competency levels. In such cases, a supervisor may (in consultation with higher-ups) seek to negotiate a voluntary demotion with the employee.

When all else fails, the agency has the discharge option. Before exercising it, however, the agency must be able to demonstrate that the employee was counseled about his or her inadequate performance and was given the opportunity to correct unacceptable behavior. Furthermore, the agency should possess documented proof that less severe forms of punishment were attempted without success.

This documentation should include formal letters of reprimand, suspension documents, and so forth. Most human resource management systems allow employees to appeal the adverse actions of suspension, demotion, and discharge to a merit protection agency. When an agency undertakes an adverse action against a nonprobationary employee, the documentation should also be included in the individual's performance appraisal record. More than one demoted, suspended, or discharged employee has persuaded a hearing examiner that his or her treatment was unjust based upon contradictory evidence in the performance appraisal record. Simply put, a supervisor cannot rate an individual satisfactory in performance categories (sometimes for several years) and expect to be upheld for an adverse action based only on performance for a short time. If an employee's performance is inadequate, he or she has the right to be counseled about it at every phase of the review process. To do less is to invite questions as to the real motive of the supervisor.[13]

APPROPRIATE PUNISHMENT.   The disciplinary action should fit the offense in question. There is no requirement that an agency act with restraint when it has compelling evidence of fraud, gross mismanagement, or serious violations of agency policies, such as abuse of clients or theft of agency property. Offenses such as these require more immediate and extreme sanctions to protect the public interest. Especially in cases of suspected fraud, theft, or abuse of trust, the agency should consider immediate removal of the employee through suspension with pay until a thorough investigation can be completed. Doing less can result in loss of evidence, further abuses, and agency liability exposure for the conduct of the employee.

Malfeasance—doing something illegal or that violates agency policy—may involve a single incident. Malfeasance, moreover, can involve criminal procedures as well as job discipline. The incident described previously involving a child injured in state custody is a case in point.

Many states require that any suspected abuse of children be investigated by the child protection division of the department of human services. The law may also require that such instances be reported to the district attorney's office for possible prosecution. Such layering of accountability is designed to protect children in institutions. However, it can also compound the difficulties of supervisors who wish to insulate their agencies from potential threats to the children.

As noted previously, supervisors must gather as much written documentation as possible concerning the incident. Then, regardless of whether the district attorney believes there is enough evidence to warrant a prosecution, the agency can proceed with discharge procedures, bearing in mind that the standard of proof for a criminal assault conviction is much higher than the standard for pursuing an adverse job action. Regardless of the ultimate outcome, when a supervisor is convinced that physical abuse has occurred, the appropriate immediate action is suspension with pay pending the outcome of the investigation.

Managers who do not take disciplinary action when necessary do a disservice to the agency, the public at large, the coworkers of the nonperformer, and themselves. In many instances, a diligent manager can correct the behavior of nonperformers before extreme disciplinary actions become necessary. When appropriate action is taken early on, moreover, the groundwork is laid for subsequent severe actions if they should become necessary.

JOB RIGHTS OF CLASSIFIED EMPLOYEES

One of the most salient features of public employment is job security. This security was part and parcel of the decision to limit the political rights of public employees. Classified employees were given a "property interest" in their jobs that cannot be withdrawn without "due process of law," thus putting them beyond the reach of partisan political retaliation.

Not all public employees are covered by civil service merit systems, however. Those not covered ("unclassified" employees) have been shielded from removal for partisan reasons by recent Supreme Court decisions; otherwise, however, they serve at the will and pleasure of the appointing authority and can be dismissed for a variety of reasons unrelated to job performance or the employer's economic need for an employee in the position in question. Of course, whether classified or unclassified, public or private, employees cannot be dismissed for reasons that public policy has proscribed; all have recourse to the courts if they believe that an adverse personnel action was motivated by ethnic discrimination or other violations of the 1964 Civil Rights Act, such as unwelcome sexual advances, or by violations of the Americans with Disabilities Act. Classified employees can seek redress through civil service remedies; unclassified employees must turn immediately to the judicial system.

RIGHTS OF CLASSIFIED EMPLOYEES

The appointment and retention of public employees in the earliest days of the republic were contingent upon partisan affiliation and satisfactory performance. In 1883, Congress passed the Pendleton Act, which "provided for the creation of a classified Civil Service, and required competitive examination for entry to the service."[14] In 1897, Civil Service Rule II provided that classified employees could not be removed except for "just cause."[15] Enforceable protections of federal employees from wrongful discharge, however, did not come about until passage of the Lloyd-LaFollette Act of 1913.[16] State merit statutes also make provision for postdischarge appeals rights for classified public employees. Most of these statutes, however, do not specify as clearly as did the Lloyd-LaFollette Act the predischarge rights of public employees. A number of court cases over the years have spelled out the rights to which tenured, or classified, public employees are entitled.

PROPERTY INTEREST.   Statutes such as the Lloyd-LaFollette Act invest nonprobationary classified public employees with a property interest in their jobs. The property interest of tenured public employees was established by the Supreme Court in the 1972 case of *Board of Regents* v. *Roth,* in which the Court stated,

> Property interests, of course, are not created by the Constitution. Rather, they are created and their dimensions are defined by existing rules or understandings that stem from an independent source such as state law—rules or understandings that secure certain benefits and that support claims of entitlements to those benefits.[17]

In the *Roth* case, an instructor employed under a year-to-year contract was found to have no such entitlement to the renewal of his contract, but the case was important in establishing the Court's acceptance of entitlement when "existing rules or understandings" *have* validated it.

A property interest can also grow out of agency understandings about continued employment, as the Court ruled on the same day as the *Roth* case in *Perry* v. *Sinderman.*[18] In the *Sinderman* case, the judgment hinged on whether a state-supported college had a de facto tenure system. Such a system would establish a property interest even if it were not provided by statute. As the faculty handbook of the college stipulated that an instructor could expect continued employment for satisfactory job performance, the Court ruled that the plaintiff must be given the opportunity to demonstrate that such a system in fact existed. The matter was eventually settled out of court with a financial payment and an offer of reemployment, which was declined.

DUE PROCESS.   The Lloyd-LaFollette Act specified the procedures whereby federal employees could be deprived of their jobs. Removal under the Lloyd-LaFollette Act was possible only after the classified employee had received a written copy of the charges against him or her. The employee must also have been given a reasonable time to respond to the charges in writing and to provide affidavits addressing the charges.

These due-process provisions were challenged in the 1973 case of *Arnett* v. *Kennedy.*[19] Kennedy, an employee of the Office of Economic Opportunity (OEO), was discharged on the grounds of misconduct for allegedly making false and defamatory statements about other OEO employees. Kennedy maintained that he was denied his constitutional rights of due process because neither the Lloyd-LaFollette Act nor the OEO and civil service procedures provided for a full evidentiary proceeding—in which all relevant information would have been considered, witnesses called and cross-examined, and Kennedy represented by counsel—before discharge.

The *Kennedy* case addressed two issues. The first was whether a tenured public employee possessed a property interest in continued employment. Second, if a property interest were established, the Court then had to determine whether the procedural rights of the employee were protected by statute or by constitutional guarantee.

Applying the reasoning set forth in *Roth*, the Court ruled that Kennedy's property interest was defined in the Lloyd-LaFollette Act. However, it could not agree on the source of Kennedy's procedural rights. Writing for a plurality of the Court, Justice Rehnquist rejected the notion that the statutorily granted property rights of classified employees in their jobs must meet constitutional due-process tests beyond those specified in the statute: "where the grant of a substantive right is inextricably intertwined with the procedures which are to be employed in determining that right, a litigant in the position of the appellee [Kennedy] must take the *bitter with the sweet*" [emphasis added].[20] In other words, one may not rely on a portion of a statute that provides a right yet reject another portion of the same statute that prescribes the due process.

Other members of the Court agreed on the statutory origins of Kennedy's property rights; however, they believed that once a property interest is established, the procedures for removal must meet constitutional due-process requirements. The Court noted that the private interest of the employee must be balanced against the government's interest in the removal of unsatisfactory employees. A majority of the Court upheld the constitutional adequacy of the procedures extended to Kennedy under the provisions of the Lloyd-LaFollette Act.

PREDISCHARGE RIGHTS. The bitter-with-the-sweet doctrine enunciated in *Arnett* v. *Kennedy* was subsequently rejected by a margin of 8 to 1 in the 1985 case of *Cleveland Board of Education* v. *Loudermill*.[21] In that case, the Court held that James Loudermill had not been granted constitutionally sufficient due process prior to his discharge as a security guard for the Cleveland public school system.

Loudermill was terminated when it was learned that he had lied about having been convicted of a felony on his preemployment application. Loudermill appealed through the appropriate civil service process on the grounds that he thought the conviction was a misdemeanor and that he could have explained had he been given an opportunity to do so prior to being dismissed. A hearing examiner's ruling that Loudermill should be reinstated was overturned by the full board. Loudermill's subsequent suit in the district court was dismissed for failure to state a claim upon which relief could be granted. The lower court reasoned that the Ohio statute that provided property rights also specified removal procedures and that Loudermill had been granted those procedures (the bitter-with-the-sweet doctrine).

The Supreme Court disagreed, holding that the right to due process "is conferred not by legislative grace, but by constitutional guarantee. While the legislature may elect not to confer a property interest in [public] employment, it may not constitutionally authorize the deprivation of such interest, once conferred, without appropriate procedural safeguards."[22] As to what constituted constitutionally sufficient due process prior to dismissal, the Court declared that "the tenured public employee is entitled to oral or written notice of the charges against him, an explanation of the employer's evidence, and an opportunity to present his side of the story."[23] The Court specified that something less than a full evidentiary hearing was necessary. "It [the hearing] should be an initial check against mistaken decisions—essentially, a determination of whether there are reasonable grounds to believe that the charges against the employee are true and support the proposed action."[24] Finally, the Court specified that in those cases "where the employer perceives a significant hazard in keeping the employee on the job, it can avoid the problem by a suspension with pay."[25] The foregoing, then, are the safeguards that the appointing authority must provide prior to discharge. The Court also found that the Ohio civil service appeals procedures provided sufficient post-discharge protection, even though the process took nine months to complete.[26]

For all of the straightforwardness of its language, the *Loudermill* case is still subject to interpretation because the Court specified that an employee be given notice, a statement of the charges, and an opportunity to respond, but it failed to define "sufficient notice." The judgment did cite the *Kennedy* opinion, in which 30-days' notice was found to be sufficient. What has not been determined is whether 30 days would be amply or minimally sufficient. State and local merit protection agencies must interpret what sufficient notice is. Surely 5 working days would not place too great a burden on the system, especially if the charges that the employee were called upon to answer were complex. What is required at this point is that merit protection agencies take steps to ensure that a uniform minimum of predischarge notice be provided to all employees under their aegis.[27]

APPEALS

Appeals of adverse personnel actions to the merit system are a fact of life in public management. The prospect of preparing for such hearings takes time away from other activities, and the fear of being reversed by the hearing examiner can cause otherwise dedicated managers to forgo adverse actions against employees who truly deserve removal. The prospect of review need not be exceptionally daunting to managers if they will but lay the proper foundation to support their actions. To maximize their chances of winning, managers must put themselves in the position of the hearing examiner, securing their own case before going forward. The hearing examiner will publicly examine the case from three perspectives: the substance of the case, the behavior of the principals, and the procedures followed.

SUBSTANTIVE ISSUES. The most important element management must consider is whether the agency will be able to convince the hearing examiner that its actions against the employee are due to malfeasance, misfeasance, or nonfeasance. The last two are the most difficult to demonstrate.

To demonstrate misfeasance, the agency must prove that the employee performed his or her tasks incorrectly despite guidance from management, and that the errors reduced agency efficiency sufficiently to warrant discharge. Nonfeasance is perhaps even more difficult to demonstrate because the issue is work volume rather than accuracy. Volume (especially among white-collar professionals) is highly subjective. Social workers, for example, normally do not punch a time clock and may be out of the office serving clients for hours at a time. The amount of time needed by each client also varies.

PREPONDERANCE OF EVIDENCE. The standard of proof used by hearing examiners is known as the preponderance of evidence.[28] The agency must be prepared to produce sufficient evidence to win. This does not mean that the agency must prove its case beyond a shadow of a doubt or to a moral certitude. Rather, *the agency must persuade the hearing officer that its actions were justified by evidence that is more compelling than the appellee's.*

Convincing the examiner in misfeasance and nonfeasance cases can be accomplished by demonstrating that the employee was not performing to agency standards. Documentation might include producing a written set of standards or copies of relevant policies and procedures. Further useful evidence includes the letters of reprimand and memos documenting that the supervisor had counseled the employee. The standards that the agency must meet are generally uniform across jurisdictions, especially when the grievance is to be heard by a labor arbitrator.[29]

TESTS OF A GRIEVANCE

Following is a review of issues likely to be considered by a labor arbitrator or other examiner in any disciplinary grievance procedure.

1. IS THE GRIEVANCE IN QUESTION RELATED TO THE POLICY CITED? In other words, was the offense for which the employee was disciplined covered by the personnel policies of the employer and/or the terms and conditions of the contract in place at the time of the grievance? The arbitrator must first decide whether he or she has jurisdiction to decide the issue.

Normally, the arbitrator will attempt to achieve an agreement between the parties about exactly which articles of the contract are in dispute. If the parties cannot agree, they may ask the arbitrator to define the limits of the dispute. Public-sector disputes frequently involve management's contention that it can make unilateral changes in work rules under the provisions of the management rights clause. The union may counter that the "previous practice" clause guarantees that rules in place at the beginning of the contract must remain unchanged for the duration of the contract. The unions further contend that any changes during the contract period require the consent of both parties. Previous practice clauses usually result from legislative prescriptions that may allow unions to limit public managers' discretion in changing work rules. Private-sector contracts usually do not contain previous practice clauses.

2. DOES SUFFICIENT EVIDENCE EXIST TO SUBSTANTIATE THAT THE ALLEGED OFFENSE OCCURRED? This standard is most carefully applied in just-cause discharge actions. Management must first demonstrate with a preponderance of evidence that the offense occurred. Once this test has been satisfied, the remaining criteria come into play. The preponderance-of-evidence standard is much less stringent than the beyond-a-reasonable-doubt standard that is used in criminal cases. The preponderance standard means that the weight of the evidence tends to support the claims of one side or the other.

3. WAS THE POLICY REASONABLE? In this test, the arbitrator uses an industry standard to determine whether the policy was reasonable. For example, to discharge a permanent public employee for being late twice in one pay period might be judged unreasonable even if the jurisdiction's personnel policies specifically stated that tardiness could be grounds for dismissal. One industry standard coming into vogue in the public sector is the use of progressive discipline. It first calls for oral counseling, followed by a written reprimand, suspension without pay, and ultimately discharge. An arbitrator might find that firing a person for tardiness without first resorting to lesser forms of discipline violated the principles of progressive discipline.

4. IS THE POLICY TOO BROAD OR VAGUE? If a grievant can demonstrate that a policy is overly broad or so vague as to allow for different interpretations, he or she has a good chance of having the adverse action overturned by the arbitrator. Many public-sector job descriptions, for example, contain the phrase "other duties as assigned." Such a statement is obviously broad and may lead to legitimate differences in interpretation. For example, a police officer might be instructed to clean the rest rooms of the police station while working the booking desk of the precinct. From management's perspective, refusal to clean the rest rooms could lead to disciplinary action, because nothing in the position description specifically prohibits such an assignment. On the other hand, the union might take the position that such an order exceeded the duties normally associated with professional police work (an industry standard). In such cases, an arbitrator might rule that management's interpretation of the "other duties as assigned" phrase was overly broad. At the same time, the arbitrator might uphold the disciplinary action on the grounds that the officer should have obeyed the order under protest and then filed a grievance.

A union axiom is "Work now, grieve later." Unless a management order involves something dangerous, illegal, or unethical, it is to the grievant's advantage to perform—and then grieve. To do otherwise can result in discipline for failure to obey a direct order or for insubordination. Both of these charges are serious and put the grievant in the position of appealing an adverse action against himself or herself. On the other hand, a grievance of having been forced to perform a task outside one's job classification results in a union grievance against management. The latter does not place one's job in jeopardy.

5. IS THE POLICY APPLICATION DISCRIMINATORY OR INCONSISTENT? Not only must a punishment be called for in the agency's personnel policies but the policy must be applied uniformly. For example, a computer operator accused of abusing his break time allowance might be demoted under a policy that allowed for letters of reprimand, demotion, or discharge. In his defense, the employee might call as witnesses other employees who routinely engaged in the same practice (with the knowledge of management) without being punished or without being punished as severely.

Frequently, such grievances arise from the same incident. Suppose, for example, that a two-person city ambulance crew transported a patient from the local public hospital to a private facility. Suppose that upon their arrival at the private hospital, the receiving room physician asked the drivers to transport a charity patient back to the public hospital. Suppose, however, that the crew had planned to stop for lunch on the return run and, therefore, refused to transport the patient. They might justify their action on the grounds that they had no authorization from their supervisors to provide the transportation.

Such behavior could result in a complaint to the administration of the public hospital and ultimately in disciplinary action against the two employees. Suppose, however, that the driver were suspended for the action, while the attendant was merely reprimanded. The hospital administration could defend its seemingly disparate treatment if it could demonstrate that the driver had previously been disciplined for the same offense, whereas it was the attendant's first offense.

6. WAS THE GRIEVANT AWARE OF THE POLICY AND/OR GIVEN THE OPPORTUNITY TO CORRECT HIS OR HER BEHAVIOR? If an employee did not know about the policy, he or she is entitled to be counseled and given a chance to change. Such cases often result from recent policy changes that are not widely disseminated. For example, suppose a city manager learns that meter readers are routinely carrying firearms to defend themselves from attacks by dogs. Merely posting an edict against firearms on the personnel bulletin board would not be sufficient to assure that all employees are aware of the order. To be certain, all employees should be notified in writing, and to be absolutely certain, supervisors would have to explain the new rule to all employees. Management should not assume that any reasonable person, including an arbitrator, would agree that the bearing of firearms at work is or should be against city policy, especially in those states that permit carrying concealed weapons.

7. WERE THERE EXTENUATING CIRCUMSTANCES? Arbitrators assess situations in their entirety to determine if the employee's behavior was excusable. Suppose, for example, that the appeal involved an employee who had been repeatedly counseled about chronic tardiness and had been warned that the next incident would result in a suspension. An arbitrator might overrule the suspension if the employee could demonstrate that the tardiness on the occasion in question was due to a traffic accident.

8. WAS THE PUNISHMENT REASONABLE, GIVEN THE VIOLATION? This test is often used in conjunction with the fourth criterion regarding policy broadness or vagueness and the fifth regarding discriminatory or inconsistent application of the policy. For example, a jurisdiction may have a policy stating that an employee can be disciplined, even discharged, for behavior unbecoming a public servant. Suppose for example, that a police officer, in a phone conversation with a friend, charges another officer with dishonest conduct. Suppose that their supervisor learns of the conversation through the rumor mill and confronts the gossiping employee. Suppose, further, that the accuser has no proof of the charges and indicates that he was merely repeating a rumor. If the agency were to discharge the officer for "conduct unbecoming a police officer," it could expect to have its actions overturned by an arbitrator, especially if the employee's record is otherwise satisfactory.

SEXUAL BEHAVIOR AND THE RIGHTS OF PUBLIC EMPLOYEES

NATIONAL SECURITY IMPLICATIONS

The most widely known case of disciplinary action against an employee for private behavior is the case of Air Force Sergeant Leonard Matlovich, who was discharged from the service because he was a self-proclaimed homosexual. The sergeant argued that his personal sexual orientation had no bearing on his job performance. The Air Force argued that Matlovich was potentially subject to blackmail because of his sexual orientation. This potential was believed to be a threat to national security because of the sergeant's access to sensitive secret data. The sergeant's career of superior service to the nation ended in an out-of-court settlement in which the sergeant agreed to drop his suit for reinstatement.[30] As the case never reached trial, the question of how a foreign power could blackmail an avowed homosexual with threats of public disclosure never came up.

President Clinton initiated action to lift the ban on military service by homosexuals. Congressional hearings were held, and the military leadership expressed the belief that having gays serve openly would undermine good order and discipline in the ranks and thereby damage unit cohesion and fighting readiness. What emerged from the debate was U.S. Code, Title 10§654, that adopted virtually verbatim the position of the generals:

> The presence in the Armed Forces of persons who demonstrate a propensity or intent to engage in homosexual acts would create an unacceptable risk to the high standards of morale, good order and discipline, and unit cohesion that are the essence of military capability.[31]

Implementation of the law was a compromise to placate the administration called "Don't Ask, Don't Tell." Under the policy, military authorities may not inquire into a service person's sexual orientation (Don't Ask). Gays and lesbians may serve provided they do not disclose their sexual orientation or act on it (Don't Tell). Under the policy, the military is prohibited from investigating suspected gays and lesbians, and the services must protect them from harassment from their military peers.

Critics of the policy charge that the rate of discharge for gays and lesbians is higher now than before the policy went into effect. Furthermore, critics charge that those who violate the policy go unpunished and that the military has proceeded against gays and lesbians based on information that was obtained in a manner prohibited by the policy.[32]

Gays and lesbians in civilian government service have not undergone the oppositionality directed against their peers in the uniformed services. Nevertheless, there is no national civil rights protection based on sexual orientation. On the other hand, a number of state and local governments have included sexual orientation in their employment discrimination statutes. The Supreme Court struck down an amendment to the Colorado state constitution that would have prevented gays and lesbians from seeking such legislative protection. The court held that the prohibition was a constitutionally impermissible restraint on the First Amendment rights of gays and lesbians (*Romer* v. *Evans*, 1996).[33] Whether homosexuals are welcomed, ignored, or scourged in local government service is a function of community standards.

COMMUNITY STANDARDS

Government officials often hold public employees to a different standard of personal conduct than that applied to society as a whole. At the local level, unmarried police officers have been disciplined for cohabitation, and schoolteachers have been discharged or asked to resign because their private conduct ran counter to the values of the appointing authority. An Oklahoma City teacher, for example, was summarily discharged when he was stopped for a traffic violation and police officers discovered pornographic materials (involving children) in his vehicle trunk. Criminal charges were not pursued because the authorities believed that the search violated Fourth Amendment protections. The teacher initially resigned, then retracted his resignation, at which point the school district began termination procedures. After two years of fighting the dismissal, the teacher decided to resign.

Had the teacher been employed in the private sector, the facts of the arrest would not have been reported to his employer, and certainly would not have received substantial coverage in the media.

GUIDELINES FOR OFF-DUTY CONDUCT OF PUBLIC EMPLOYEES

The best current guidelines for the off-duty conduct of public employees are the decisions of labor arbitrators. In the course of interpreting union contracts, arbitrators have delimited the parameters of employer-employee rights and developed criteria to assess the job relevance of the off-duty conduct of public employees and the actions their employers are entitled to undertake. Other public employees, not covered by labor contracts, do have appeals rights to civil service systems, whose hearing examiners can be expected to use the same sorts of standards in weighing the offense in question against the established policies and procedures of the organization. The standards are presented here as a guide for current and potential public-sector managers who may be faced with the problem of assessing the impact of the off-duty conduct of subordinates on their job performance and the general well-being of the agency.

Labor arbitrators have determined that

> the jurisdictional line which separates the cases with which the employer may be concerned from those with which he may not, is not always the physical line which bounds his property on which his plant is located. . . . The point is that the jurisdictional line which limits the company's power of discipline is a functional, not a physical line. It has power to discipline for misconduct directly related to the employment. It has no power to discipline for misconduct not related to the employment.[34]

The criterion, then, is job relatedness. To guide their efforts, arbitrators have developed six guidelines to determine whether the off-duty conduct is related to employment.

1. Does the behavior affect the employee's job performance?
2. Does the behavior affect the efficiency of fellow workers or management?
3. Does the behavior directly hurt the employer?
4. Does the behavior indirectly hurt the employer?
5. Is there clear and convincing proof of the negative impact of the employee's behavior on the employer?
6. In the case of an employee's off-duty criminal activity, does it affect job performance?

Although these standards seem straightforward and reasonable, they are only applicable where union contracts are in effect that require the arbitration of grievances. And, of course, the standards are subject to interpretation by individual arbitrators. Some examples may help to clarify the trends in interpretation.

STANDARD 1: EFFECTS ON JOB PERFORMANCE

Arbitrators have chosen to define narrowly the effects on job performance of off-duty behavior. An off-duty employee arrested for possession of marijuana, therefore, would probably win reinstatement unless the employer could demonstrate that possession or use of the drug had impaired the employee's performance.

STANDARD 2: EFFECTS ON THE EFFICIENCY OF FELLOW WORKERS OR MANAGEMENT

The most obvious example of an impact on the efficiency of others is a crime of violence, such as an off-duty assault on a supervisor. An arbitrator might also sustain the discharge of an employee convicted of a heinously violent off-duty crime against persons not connected with the organization.[35]

STANDARD 3: DIRECT INJURY TO THE EMPLOYER

This standard has the least relevance for the public sector, because it is most often applied to cases in which an employee uses off-duty time to engage in a business that competes directly with the employer. Because public employers are not engaged in profit-making activities, the standard generally would not apply.

STANDARD 4: INDIRECT INJURY TO THE EMPLOYER

This standard is frequently applied to the disciplining of public employees. Agency personnel manuals and the merit laws frequently contain provisions for discipline or dismissal based upon such behavior as "conduct unbecoming" or "moral turpitude" or behavior that "casts a stain on the public service." Police officers and schoolteachers are frequently the objects of discipline based upon such passages.

A police officer, for example, who engaged in an act of petty theft punishable only by a fine or probation might be disciplined or even discharged by the department.[36] A private citizen would be answerable only to the courts. Schoolteachers arrested on drug charges or morals charges involving children can expect immediate disciplinary action against them. In the case of a drug conviction, indirect injury to the work situation might be argued because the teacher's position as a role model undermined school substance-abuse prevention programs for students.

Morals charges involving children might be construed to have a devastating effect upon the community standing of a school system that employed a child molester. Of course, an arrest and conviction for morals charges involving children would probably also entail the first and second standards involving job performance and the efficiency of fellow workers (in this case, students in the workplace). By contrast, conviction on a morals charge involving children probably would not be sufficient reason for discharge if the place of employment or the job duties of the worker did not require contact with children.[37]

STANDARD 5: THE STANDARD OF PROOF

Arbitrators have greatest discretionary latitude in applying the standard of proof. An arbitrator whose judgment has been finely honed by legal training may apply a vigorous standard requiring "clear and convincing proof." Another may apply a lesser standard calling for a "preponderance of the evidence." This latitude is possible because arbitration hearings are not courts of law; the rules of evidence are not the same as they would be in a full-blown criminal procedure.

STANDARD 6: CRIMINAL ACTIVITY

This standard overlaps significantly with the others because so many off-duty cases involve violations of the law. But it bears repeating that arbitrators generally consider criminal activity only insofar as it affects job performance as determined by the other standards. An arbitrator, for example, might order the reinstatement of a truck driver who had been convicted of writing bad checks and placed on probation. The same arbitrator might sustain the dismissal of an employee in the finance division who was convicted of the same charge.

The issue becomes cloudier when it involves violations of federal law by state and local employees. An Oklahoma state trooper was discharged, ostensibly for having pleaded no contest to filing a false income tax return. The officer claimed, first before the hearing examiner, later to the Oklahoma Merit Protection Commission, and finally to the courts, that he had merely signed the return his wife prepared and was not aware of the undeclared income on it. The Oklahoma Department of Public Safety pointed out that the income was paid to the officer from the Oklahoma motor vehicle registration agency that his wife operated. Further, the payments were made for janitorial and security services that others were providing. Therefore, the funds were paid to him for services that he had not provided. The money otherwise would have gone toward the operating costs of Oklahoma schools, as provided for in the legislation creating the tag agencies. The Merit Protection Commission refused to review whether the no-contest plea in federal court was sufficient to sustain a discharge by the state. Instead, it ruled that the circumstances of the payments constituted conduct unbecoming an officer. That is, the commission applied standard four rather than standard six.[38]

Finally, when a public employee must serve a prison sentence for an off-duty criminal action, discharge can occur. An incarcerated person cannot show up for work; imprisonment, then, may have a secondary effect of job abandonment.

The issue of the off-duty conduct of employees is further clouded when the off-duty conduct involves job-related activities. Schoolteachers, for instance, are frequently expected to attend such after-hours functions as Parent-Teacher Association (PTA) meetings and school social activities. The standards for conduct on such occasions are the same as for regular working hours. Teachers may not, for example, physically or verbally abuse their supervisors, students, board members, or fellow workers. In short, the on-duty versus off-duty distinction is not always clear for teachers.

DRUG TESTING AND THE RIGHTS OF PUBLIC EMPLOYEES

The goal of a drug-free society has become a cause célèbre.[39] Contract negotiators between team owners and professional athletic associations continue to struggle over the leagues' interest in maintaining a corps of athletes free of recreational drugs and the athletes' interest in avoiding overly intrusive searches. Many private-sector employers have come to recognize that drug use on and off the job causes accidents, reduces efficiency, and frequently leads to absenteeism and abuse of sick leave. These employers may elect to make submission to drug testing a condition of continued employment. Government employers, however, are not so free to compel drug testing of employees, because public employers are also the state.

The Fourth and Fourteenth Amendments to the Constitution protect United States citizens from unreasonable search and seizure by agents of the state. These amendments do not provide absolute protection; each case must be weighed on its own merits, considering the circumstances of the search and the degree of privacy the person in question can legitimately expect. Thus, in the military, where the right to privacy has long been qualified, random drug testing has been approved by judicial authorities. In the civilian sector of government employment, a number of court rulings have addressed the need to balance the interests of the state against the rights of individual employees. The courts have established standards regarding who or what can be searched and for what reason. Most recently, the courts have outlined qualified rights to privacy of public employees that affect the way searches can be conducted and that monitor the overall reasonableness of drug-testing programs. Random or comprehensive tests of the workforce for drug use predicated on no more justification than the need for a drug-free government workforce have been challenged as unconstitutional.

DRUG TESTING IN THE MILITARY

The military services make submission to drug testing a condition of retention. The military reasons that drug use impairs the user's ability to perform the mission regardless of whether the use is on or off duty, because active duty personnel are technically on duty 24 hours a day, 7 days a week.

Drug testing in the military dates back to 1969, when President Richard Nixon ordered testing of all persons returning from Vietnam. These tests, designed to identify heroin addicts before their return to society, did not go unchallenged. However, in the 1975 case of *Committee for GI Rights* v. *Callaway*,[40] an appeals court upheld warrantless drug searches of military personnel as part of routine inspections.[41] The reality was, however, that the primary drug being abused was marijuana, for which no testing procedure existed in the 1970s. Once testing for marijuana became legally and technically possible, the military instituted administrative procedures to ensure a drug-free workforce.

Uniformed personnel must now submit to legally ordered drug tests under penalty of court martial according to Article 92 of the Uniform Code of Military Justice. The range of circumstances that make an order legal is much broader than that permissible in civilian agencies. The practical applications in the army illustrate the options available to military authorities.

INSPECTIONS. Routine inspections for mission readiness can include random drug testing of an entire unit or base. Those to be tested are usually selected by using the last two digits of their social security numbers. A positive test may result in administrative action, including discharge.

PROBABLE CAUSE. A commander may order a drug test if he or she has "probable cause" to believe that drug use has occurred. An order for a urinalysis based upon the probable-cause standard must meet carefully defined legal criteria, usually involving the suspicion of drug intoxication or participation in a drug-related crime. A positive test performed under the probable-cause standard can be used as evidence in a criminal prosecution.

REASONABLE SUSPICION. A commander has much broader latitude to order a drug test based on "reasonable suspicion" because of "unauthorized absence, disobedience of direct orders, apprehension for drunk driving or drug related offenses, crimes of violence or repeated serious misconduct."[42] Commanders may prefer to order drug tests under the reasonable-suspicion standard, because they are not as vulnerable to legal challenges as are searches based on probable cause. If such a test is positive, however, it may not be used in a disciplinary action; the findings can only be used to support administrative actions, which can include discharge for honorable reasons. The intensity of drug scrutiny on a base depends on the attitudes of the base commander. At Fort Lee Virginia, for example, any soldier who is there for a class of longer than two weeks can expect to be tested. All personnel permanently assigned to the base can anticipate testing twice a year. Any service member, regardless of rank, with more than three years service who tests positive will be separated from the service. Persons with less than three years may be separated.[43]

If the commander's goal is to separate the drug user from the service, he or she will probably choose the reasonable-suspicion standard. If the desired end is punishment, however, the more rigorous probable-cause standard should be used. As the following discussion of civilian drug testing will illustrate, the federal judiciary also permits the application of the reasonable-suspicion standard.

DRUG TESTING OF CIVILIAN GOVERNMENT EMPLOYEES

President Ronald Reagan launched his administration's offensive against the use of illegal drugs by federal employees with Executive Order 12564. The order prohibited drug use by federal employees, specified testing policies, and ordered an employee assistance plan for those who tested positive. Testing for drugs is required when there is reasonable suspicion that an employee is using drugs or when drug use is suspected in conjunction with an accident or unsafe act. Testing may also be required as part of counseling and rehabilitation programs and is required of new employees.

Agency heads were also directed to establish guidelines for the testing of employees in sensitive positions. What constitutes a sensitive position is ill defined, but may include those working in areas of national security, health specialties, hazardous occupations, or law enforcement.

The most controversial feature of the Reagan order was its call for employees not included in any of these categories to undergo voluntary testing to demonstrate that they were drug free. Many employees viewed this feature of the program as degrading and insulting to their individual honor, not to mention an unnecessary intrusion on their privacy.

TESTING FOR PUBLIC SAFETY. One of the earliest rulings regarding blood and urine testing of public employees was the 1976 case of *Amalgamated Transit Union (AFL-CIO)* v. *Suscy.*[44] Here the court of appeals upheld the right of the Chicago Transit Authority (CTA) to require blood and urine tests of employees involved in serious traffic accidents. In balancing the interest of the state against the rights of individual employees, the court held that

> the CTA has a paramount interest in protecting the public by insuring that bus and train operators are fit to perform their jobs. In view of this interest, members of plaintiff

Union can have no reasonable expectation of privacy with regard to submitting to blood and urine tests. Further, the conditions under which the intrusion is made and the manner of taking of the samples are reasonable.[45]

The procedures whereby the testing could be initiated under CTA guidelines were found to be reasonable because standards for employee conduct and the procedures to be followed when drug or alcohol use was suspected had been clarified in writing in the agency manual. The tests were to be conducted after a serious accident, in a hospital, and only after two supervisors deemed them necessary.

The Supreme Court came to much the same conclusion in *Skinner* v. *Railway Labor Executives Association* (1989).[46] In this case, the Federal Railroad Administration had issued standards calling for blood and urine tests of train crews involved in major accidents. The regulation was challenged on the grounds that an individualized suspicion was necessary to warrant such a search. The Court, by a 7-to-2 majority, upheld the regulation. Because the railroads are a regulated industry, the Fourth Amendment did apply in such cases. But the Court felt bound to balance the government's interest in public safety against the individual rights of the railroad workers, and it found the government's interest compelling.

The foregoing transportation examples illustrate the willingness of the courts to grant agencies considerable latitude in order to protect the public safety. The clear intent of the Reagan order, however, was to prevent drug use. Preventive testing is supposed to detect illegal drug use and deter employees from such use. Prevention poses a more serious challenge to constitutional rights than does testing in the aftermath of an accident.

PREVENTIVE DRUG TESTING. Let us suppose that a corrections department wishes to interdict illegal drug traffic into the prison system. To this end, its drug-related policies might involve searches of automobiles and strip searches of individuals, as well as blood and urine tests. A federal district judge in Iowa has set forth the guidelines whereby the state's Department of Corrections can prevent both the introduction of drugs into the prison and drug use by corrections employees. In the case of *McDonnell* v. *Hunter*, the judge ruled that normal pat-downs and the use of electronic equipment to prevent the introduction of weapons or contraband were within the scope of the Fourteenth Amendment.[47] Furthermore, searches of employee automobiles were permissible if the autos were parked in an area accessible to prisoners, regardless of whether they were on state property. But strip searches and chemical tests of blood and urine were deemed to require a more rigorous justification.

These tests must be "based on reasonable suspicion, based on specific objective facts and rational inferences that may be drawn from those facts in light of experience."[48] In other words, in order to justify a strip search, the authority must have good reason to believe that the employee is, at the time of the search, engaged in smuggling contraband. Vague suspicion is constitutionally insufficient. Blood and urine tests must meet the same test of reasonableness. Further, tests can be ordered only on the authority of the highest officer in the institution at the time, and "the specific objective facts shall be disclosed to the employee at the time the demand is made and shall be reduced to writing and preserved."[49] Those in authority must have reasonable suspicion that the employee is under the influence of alcohol or a controlled substance at the time the test is ordered. Tests cannot be ordered on the suspicion that an employee has previously used drugs.

In another challenge, the Appeals Court of the District of Columbia ruled that the procedure for testing police officers for suspected drug use was constitutionally permissible. Unlike the Iowa court, which allowed testing only on the highest authority in the institution, the policy of the District of Columbia Police Department permits testing on the reasonable suspicion of any department official. In the case of *Turner* v. *Fraternal Order of Police,* the court held that the public has a compelling interest in ensuring that its police officers are free of drug use.[50]

> Without a doubt, drug abuse can have an adverse effect upon a police officer's ability to execute his duties. Given the nature of the work and the fact that not only his life, but the lives of the public, rest upon his alertness, the necessity of rational action and a clear head unbefuddled by narcotics become self-evident. Thus, the use of controlled substances by police officers creates a situation fraught with serious consequences to the public.[51]

The court did rule that there must be a reasonable suspicion that the test "will produce evidence of an illegal drug use."[52]

RANDOM DRUG TESTING. What is most controversial is the use of random or comprehensive drug testing to determine illegal drug use. For years, lower federal courts ruled that such testing should be based on reasonable suspicion.[53] The view of those who would insist on reasonable suspicion is illustrated in this ruling by a District Court judge in *Capua et al.* v. *City of Plainfield* (1986).

> The invidious effect of such mass, round-up urinalysis is that it casually sweeps up the innocent with the guilty and willingly sacrifices each individual's Fourth Amendment rights in the name of some larger public interest. The City of Plainfield essentially presumed the guilt of each person tested. The burden was shifted onto each firefighter to submit to a highly intrusive urine test in order to vindicate his or her innocence. Such an unfounded presumption of guilt is contrary to the protections against arbitrary and intrusive government interference set forth in the Constitution.[54]

The opposite view is that certain categories of workers can and should be held to a higher standard, especially those employed in law enforcement because they carry firearms and those engaged in drug enforcement because they are the public's line of defense. It is believed that the individual rights of these employees must be balanced against the public interest. In the 1989 case of *National Treasury Employees Union and Argent Acosta* v. *Von Raab,*[55] the Supreme Court ruled 5 to 4 that it was not unreasonable to require drug testing for employees seeking promotion into positions where they would be directly involved in drug interdiction activities or required to carry firearms.

Since the *Von Raab* decision, the Supreme Court has let stand an appeals court ruling allowing the Boston Police Department to randomly test officers who carry firearms or who handle illegal drugs.[56] The net effect of these decisions is an expansion of administrators' discretion in their efforts to ensure a drug-free public workforce. Ironically, law enforcement officers sworn to uphold the law are afforded fewer constitutional protections against invasion of their privacy than are the criminal suspects society asks them to apprehend.

SUMMARY AND CONCLUSION

When faced with the complexities of the civil service system, union contracts, and the Constitution, it is little wonder that public managers throw up their hands in frustration or, worse, allow problems with employees to go unchecked rather than learn the system. A second downside to these complexities is that line managers may come to view the personnel department as the "employee police" who must be obeyed in all such matters. The alternative is to rationalize the discipline system. When union contracts are in place, negotiations should be undertaken to remove overlapping and redundant appeals systems. Furthermore, a training priority should be the education of line managers on the content of union contracts and the civil service rules regarding discipline. Personnel can also schedule training in employee counseling as a component of their basic supervisory training curriculum.

The protections that public employees enjoy, such as a property interest in their jobs, a higher standard of due process before discharge, and constitutionally protected rights against unwarranted search and seizure are all the result of public policy decisions. As such, they are part of doing business in government. Managers who chafe at constraints on their authority may wish to seek careers in the private sector. Alternatively, managers can learn the rules and follow them scrupulously. When they do, they will find personnel professionals, hearing examiners, and arbitrators quite supportive.

TEACHER DISCIPLINE

Professor Janet Stubbs was employed on a part-time basis by the economics department of a California State University (CSU) branch located in the Central Valley of California. She had worked there for seven years on a non-tenure track appointment that varied from year to year according to the department's needs. Her appointment ranged from .40 to .60 (two or three classes) per semester. On three separate occasions two different chairs had found it necessary to counsel Stubbs. The first was for arbitrary grading practices. Another was for charges from male students that she treated them different from women students. She was also cautioned on another occasion regarding her low scores on the student evaluation form. She attended a workshop on effective teaching, and her overall evaluations rose to near the average of the department. Students continued, however, to rate her low on fairness and approachability.

In January 1998, Billy Rae Ricardo became chair of the economics department. In his first evaluation of Stubbs, Ricardo indicated that she was a good scholar and a serious, caring teacher. This positive assessment was submitted based on her Fall 1997 evaluations only. The following year, Ricardo noticed that Stubbs's evaluations in some classes were substantially below the previous year, and he was approached by several students wishing to complain about her teaching style.

In Spring 1999, Ricardo notified Stubbs that her performance in the large-section general education class was substandard. Stubbs blamed her team teacher for a lack of grading standards and attention to detail. Ricardo indicated that he would not schedule Stubbs for any further team-taught classes. He scheduled her for two classes for the upcoming fall semester. All assignments, however, are subject to budget availability, enrollments, and department needs. Faculty appointments, moreover, are tentative until an official appointment is forthcoming from the dean's office.

During the last week of the semester, a Chicana student approached Ricardo and leveled charges against Stubbs for racial insensitivity and condescension. Ricardo advised the student that she must put the complaint in writing before action could be taken. He further advised her that she should wait to complain until after she received her grade in the class. The student did so in June 1999.

In July 1999, student evaluations for the previous semester were issued to the departments. Stubbs's evaluations were extremely weak. A review of her grade sheets revealed that the majority of students in one of her courses had withdrawn or did not complete the course, choosing to take a grade of U (calculated as an F on the transcript) rather than complete the course. The large team-taught section also had a 40 percent drop rate.

Ricardo found this an unacceptable level of performance, especially, in a cutback year when students could not get classes. He consulted with the associate academic vice president (AAVP) as to whether he could merely not renew Stubbs's contract for the upcoming year. She indicated that he was within his authority but that the nonrenewal must be based strictly on the current performance. Older matters could not be cited.

Because it was summer and the university was not in session, Ricardo attempted to contact members of the department's personnel committee by phone to consult with them regarding his desire to not renew Stubbs. Ricardo could reach only two of the committee members, both former chairs who supported the decision. (The total committee consisted of five faculty including Ricardo.) He also consulted with the dean of social sciences by phone, who agreed to support the decision.

Ricardo notified Stubbs by mail that she was not being renewed for the fall. She subsequently phoned Ricardo in the belief that her nonrenewal was based solely on budgetary cutbacks. Ricardo indicated that her continuance would not be in the best interest of students, and he had therefore decided not to reappoint. Stubbs demanded a face-to-face meeting, which was scheduled for two days later.

Stubbs showed up at the meeting with a representative of the California Faculty Association, Benjamin LeBold. LeBold asked a number of questions regarding the level of consultation that was undertaken and why the decision was not made until summer.

A written grievance was filed with Faculty Affairs the following week. The grievance charged that:

1. Ricardo had failed to adequately consult with colleagues before the decision.
2. Stubbs was not given adequate notice.
3. The letter from the Chicana student that was used against Stubbs was a surprise and had not been part of the official personnel file (kept in faculty affairs) and could not therefore be used.
4. Ricardo's actions were punitive and motivated, in part, by gender discrimination.

The first level of the grievance process is Faculty Affairs, where a new AAVP tried to settle the matter by asking that the personnel committee convene to review Ricardo's actions and any response that Stubbs had to them. The grievance clock was suspended until the committee could meet. Stubbs did not appear at the meeting and submitted a request for payment of a year's wages, benefits, and the unemployment she lost by not being notified sooner. Her total claim was for $38,000.

Ricardo presented the committee with the data on which he based his decision and asked that the committee support his recommendations to separate Stubbs. However, he acknowledged that had he acted sooner, the financial impact on Stubbs might have been less. He proposed that the economics department pay Stubbs for the four weeks of lost unemployment benefits and that the department pay her health care benefits for the upcoming semester, for a total of $3500. The money would come from departmental discretionary funds received from the continuing education program.

The committee unanimously supported Ricardo.

Faculty Affairs upheld the department's decision. The new AAVP, however, asked that the department report on Stubbs's previous disciplinary problems, to assist him in the appeals and arbitration process. (After the level-one grievance step is passed, the faculty affairs office takes over the case.)

Level two of the grievance process occurs at the chancellor's office in Long Beach; the chancellor reviewed the case and sustained the decision not to rehire. It was sustained, in part, on the additional information regarding Stubbs's prior performance problems. If the matter goes to arbitration, the chancellor's office represents the university.

QUESTIONS AND INSTRUCTIONS

1. Suppose that the matter has been brought to arbitration. What are relevant facts that you would use if you were the arbitrator hearing this case?
2. If you were the arbitrator, in whose favor would you rule?
3. Did Ricardo adequately consult before reaching a decision?
4. Is there evidence of gender bias?
5. Was Stubbs given adequate notice?
6. Was the department's offer to pay Stubbs her unemployment benefits and insurance costs a collegial gesture, or should the arbitrator interpret the offer as an admission of wrongdoing by the university?

OPOSSUMS AND OTHER EXCUSES*

During the years 1998 and 1999, the city of Silicon Ridge experienced severe financial difficulties. Departments experiencing reduced general-fund operating budgets proposed cuts in both personnel and equipment to balance shrinking budgets. Some departments proposed cuts by means of a method to retain only productive employees with less seniority than nonproductive and troublesome, longer-term staff.

The department of street overhead-signs and sidewalks (SOS) was one of those creative departments that used the city budget mandates of 10 percent staff cuts to weed out what they considered department deadwood. Cut staff were transferred to other city vacancies or bumped to other lower-seniority department staff. Among those forced to move was Freddie Spike, who had worked for the city for 10 years. Freddie had worked his way up in the engineering technician series of the departments of design and construction (D&C) and SOS, where he was promoted in 1995 to a senior engineering technician. Freddie was considered difficult to deal with, having a history of bad dealings with supervisors. Freddie was often openly critical of their management skills and work ethics. However, he did have good customer service skills. In October 1999, Freddie was cut from his SOS department position and directed to report to the department of D&C.

Spike's new section planned to make every effort to assimilate him. Spike immediately met the director of the construction section of the D&C department, Fred Bienvenides. Bienvenides set up immediate training and work assignment goals for Spike. Spike's reputation was well known by the department of D&C, but they decided to attempt to accept him and to forget past issues because there was nothing that could be done to avoid the transfer to their department.

Extensive training for Spike began immediately. The challenge of the training process was compounded by the fact that Spike had to be trained by one of the employees he had bumped during his transfer. Spike's assimilation was made more difficult because his new work would be more detailed and technical than his past role in the department of SOS. Also, he would have to work with computers, software spreadsheets, and complex testing and inspection reports for his new section's clients.

For the first six months, Spike was cooperative with his new department's management. As the months went on, his attendance began to slip, and it began to affect his quality and quantity of work. So bad was the absenteeism that by the twelfth month of Mr. Spike's transfer, he was seriously behind in all aspects of his work. In an effort to straighten out his performance, section managers provided daily, weekly, and monthly verbal and written guidance on needed work performance.

The constructive criticism was not well received by Spike. He began missing Mondays and Fridays. Over the next four months he was absent over 50 percent of all Mondays. Excuse after excuse was used. The excuses were documented and accepted for illness and only with a doctor's excuse. Spike also asked for and was given leave for such problems as dealing with ants in his house, then needing time

---

*Prepared by Richard Coco, San Jose State University

at home for the exterminator, then later getting ill from the poison used to get rid of the ants.

Documentation of verbal counseling and written direction to Spike filled a folder four inches thick and consumed many management hours by the summer of 2000. Fearing that Spike might be having psychological or chemical dependency problems, his supervisor referred him to the city's employee assistance program.

After two more months of this unacceptable performance and continued absenteeism, progressive discipline was increased in the form of a written reprimand and a pay deduction for lost hours due to unexcused absences. Spike didn't respond to this written and verbal discipline; in fact, he sank deeper into even worse performance and more lost time from his duties. Excuses from Spike for missing work went beyond reason during the fall of 1993. One morning Spike called in to report that he could not work because an opossum had moved in under his house and was leaving opossum poop. He indicated he couldn't work because the smell was so intense that he could not sleep. That was the last straw for the managers.

With all efforts exhausted to motivate and assimilate Spike, section management sought the help of the city's employee relations manager. This coordinated effort was good timing, because Spike's situation got even more complex when he filed for workers' compensation, claiming that he had hurt his back on the job. The city's risk manager handled the claim over the next two months and granted Spike three weeks disability and paid wages for lost time. The three weeks of paid disability were not enough for Spike, who claimed many more weeks of lost time due to the injury. He refused to return to work but was told to return by a November 1, 2000, deadline or lose his job. He reluctantly returned.

Under the guidance of the employee relations manager, Spike was given a special performance review. It included documentation of his poor quality and quantity of work. It also set up a timetable for Spike to improve his work quality. Management warned him that if he continued with his lack of attendance and substandard performance, further discipline would follow. The review was kept confidential, and the discipline counseling he received was delivered in a professional manner. Spike refused to sign the review, rejecting outright the notion that his performance was substandard. In fact, he demanded union representation on any further meetings with management. The day of the review was the last day Spike came to work. He refused to return, claiming harassment.

The matter was moved to the attorney's office when Spike filed a suit. Several months went by, and the construction section managers went about their business without Spike. The workload of the section began to increase with the improving economy, and his position was filled by a provisional appointment a few weeks later. In January 2001, the city attorney's office contacted the construction section regarding Spike's harassment claims. His claim indicated that the management was "out to get him!"

Two months later, the construction section was informed that Spike had reached an out-of-court settlement with the city. The attorney's office further informed management that Spike was to return to work in two weeks, and under no circumstances was he to be supervised by the same managers who had initiated the discipline against him.

QUESTIONS AND INSTRUCTIONS

1. Were Spike's original supervisors at fault for pushing him out of their division under the guise of the lay-off policy?

2. Did Spike's new supervisors conduct themselves professionally? Was there anything else they might have done to salvage him as an employee in light of their drug use suspicion?

3. Did the city attorney's office act in the city's best interest by settling the case? Alternatively, they might have asked the court for a summary judgment remanding the case to the city's civil service board.

4. If the city attorney's office were going to settle the matter, should they have protected the city's interest by insisting that Spike not be allowed to return to city employment as a condition of the settlement?

5. Were the managers in Spike's last division given the support they needed by upper management, including the city manager, who had to approve the terms of the settlement?

SUPERVISING GOD*

Roscoe Jones was by all accounts a religious person who applied his beliefs to all aspects of his life. However, it was the expression of his religious views in the office that began the drama that resulted in his termination and subsequent lawsuit. When Jones was hired to direct the department of assessment for Regency County, he made no secret of the fact that religion was the most essential element of his life. It was a core commitment and value! During the interview, Jones wore a small religious pin on his lapel and referred to his Christian religious beliefs when asked questions about how he would approach administrative problems. Jim Radick, Regency's county manager thought it was slightly unusual, if not peculiar, that Jones' referred so often to his beliefs; in fact, it made him personally uncomfortable. However, because the previous director of assessment was fired for dishonest practices, he thought the change to a leader with strong religious principles would be refreshing for the department, and so a letter was sent to Jones offering him the position, which he immediately accepted.

Three months into the job, Radick began to receive complaints from some long-time members of the department of assessment. They complained that Jones allowed employees who shared his fundamental faith to read religious literature at their work stations during office hours. Other employees claimed he encouraged donations to various sectarian causes by supporting the distribution and routing of contribution envelopes for certain charitable programs in the office. It was noted that the envelope-routing path always seemed to end in the director's office, and this caused some employees to become suspicious that he was "playing book" on who did and did not contribute. Still others claimed that Jones would

---

*Prepared by Lance Noe and C. Kenneth Meyer, Drake University

spend countless hours in his office talking with anyone willing to discuss their religious faith, provided, of course, it matched his own beliefs. No one claimed that he had purposively attempted to convert employees during working hours to his brand of religion or that he had harassed employees who didn't share his beliefs. Several employees complained, however, that they felt alienated and shunned by their director and that attitude was largely a result of religious disposition rather than performance or productivity.

When county manager Radick stopped by Jones's office to discuss the issues of potential religious discrimination, he was surprised to see a large framed picture of the "House of Faith and Works Center" dominating the space directly behind his chair. The center of the picture portrayed an enormous glass, stone, and steel architectural wonder that Jones was quick to point out, that had "recently won an international design award." Playing loudly on the speakers of his personal computer were live religious teachings and music from the House of Faith and Works Center. After the volume was turned down to allow conversation, Jim asked Roscoe, "Doesn't the picture and preaching create an inappropriate environment for a public department?" Roscoe replied, "I don't see how the picture is any different from photos of Rome, Paris, London, and Berlin that hang in your office. It tells me we both enjoy architectural wonders that happen to be religious buildings." Regarding the live teaching and music from the Center, Roscoe noted that of course he turns it down when meeting with his coworkers, but he emphasized that the teaching contributes to his good and honest job performance. "Many of my employees have told me that the teaching and music from the House of Faith and Works inspires them to do honest and quality work. It certainly is better that the shouting talk radio shows that I hear in other city departments," he opined.

When asked about the other complaints that had been registered by employees, Roscoe said he couldn't recall every conversation he has ever had with coworkers, nor did he remember every donation envelope that got passed around the office. And as for allowing employees to read religious publications or material while on the job, he said he assumed that the employees were reading the material during their personal and regular breaks. "Who am I to censor what people read? Maybe taking God out of the workplace is what got this department into trouble before you hired me!" Jones fired back. The meeting confirmed for Radick that Roscoe Jones was not going to modify his practices and would consider it a violation of his religious rights if either asked or pressed to do otherwise.

Manager Radick retreated to his office and began to consult with the county attorney. The county attorney warned Jim that he was exposing the county to considerable risk by allowing such a religiously charged atmosphere to continue in a department of county government. "There is the matter of separation of church and state, you know," he said. Based on the legal advice, Roscoe Jones was next ordered to cease all "religious activity" at work or face disciplinary action that could include termination. As expected, he did not modify his practices, and after consulting with the county commission, Roscoe Jones was given a notice of termination.

Ten months later, a federal court brought back their decision in *Jones* v. *County of Regency.* Roscoe Jones was awarded $500,000 in damages for the "unwarranted and heavy-handed order and subsequent action" that the court saw as excessively infringing on the right to free religious expression.

QUESTIONS AND INSTRUCTIONS

1. To what extent can a person's religious beliefs be expressed in a public workplace? Does it matter if a person is in a supervisory position?
2. Evaluate the perspective that the county manager brought to the first meeting with Roscoe Jones in his office?
3. Should a person be required to leave her or his religious beliefs "at the door" when seeking public-sector employment?
4. What does this court decision tell the public sector regarding the role religion should play, if any, in the workplace?

THE SWEET SMELL OF A GOOD APPEARANCE POLICY*

John Kimmer, director of personnel, didn't look forward to dealing with the complaint he received about Chris Drapeir, the newest trainer to join the Department of Parks and Recreation's training center. Earlier in the year, the department had received a special appropriation to provide local citizens with computer skills. Computer instructors were difficult to hire and nearly impossible to retain in an economy desperate for these job skills. Kimmer was understandably delighted when he was able to recruit Drapeir, a knowledgeable and enthusiastic trainer. His enthusiasm was short-lived.

The first site assigned to Chris was a community center for retired persons—many who had retained their membership for a long time in a local community-based social club. The more active social club members also regularly attended many of the city council meetings and prided themselves on having the "ear of local elected officials." Kimmel thought that the center would be a good place for Drapeir to get his feet wet. Within two days, however, the head of the community center called to report, "This hippie you sent to us wears an earring the size of Christmas and he smells funny. We don't like it, send somebody else!" Kimmel apologized and said he would speak to Chris the next day.

The next day Kimmel met with Drapeir and immediately noticed that his cologne was strong and unique. Kimmel also noticed that Drapeir was wearing a large earring, which he had not worn at the initial interview. The normal pleasantries were passed and eventually Kimmel transitioned into explaining the appearance policy. Chris sat nervously through the counseling session and wondered why the appearance issue was being singled out for special attention. After all, his previous high-tech employers had never brought up his style and dress.

Kimmel recognized Chris' nervousness and after several minutes had elapsed finally told Chris of the specific complaints. Chris responded with astonishment and disbelief. His first reaction was embarrassment, then he became angry. "The

*Prepared by Lance Noe and C. Kenneth Meyer

fragrance I have on is especially designed to promote a professional atmosphere. It is not only expensive but is imported from France. Besides, smell is something that is very personal, and I find the fragrance you are wearing today to be rather strong." Kimmel, now angered by the response to what he thought was a rational statement, sharply responded, "We at the Parks Department demand that you promote a little more professionalism and a whole lot less atmosphere! And while you are at it, lose the earring. This isn't San Francisco or New York."

An angry Chris Drapeir stormed out of Kimmel's office and out of the building. Kimmel was left to wonder where he could recruit a computer trainer with Chris' credentials but without his sense of fashion.

QUESTIONS AND INSTRUCTIONS

1. Should there be a different expectation for appearance policies based on "representing the firm" versus working in-house? If so, why? If not, why not? Elaborate.

2. Most appearance policies do not specifically refer to fragrance. How would you write a policy to deal with this subject? Why have policies dealing with cosmetics, deodorants and fragrance, etc., recently drawn more attention? Who may be adversely affected by what fragrance, if any, employees choose to wear? Please explain.

3. Should the standard for jewelry as well as fragrance differ for men and women?

4. Would you have handled this situation differently? Be specific.

NOTES AND RESOURCES

1. For instructions on compliance, see Prentice-Hall, Inc., *Equal Employment Opportunity Compliance Manual* (Englewood Cliffs, NJ: Prentice Hall, 1992); the manual is updated regularly. On state and local government, see U.S. Equal Employment Opportunity Commission, State and Local Reporting Committee, *EEOC Form 164, State and Local Government information (EEO-4): Instruction Booklet* (Washington, DC: EEOC, 1987). For a report on the processing of EEO complaints in the federal government, see U.S. Congress, House Committee on Government Operations, *Processing EEO Complaints in the Federal Sector: Problems and Solutions,* Committee Hearings 99th Congress (Washington, DC: U.S. Government Printing Office, 1985). For a discussion of the constraints on government contractors, see U.S. Department of Labor, Office of Contract Compliance, *Making EEO and Affirmative Action Work* (Washington, DC: Office of Federal Contract Compliance, 1987).

2. See Kathryn Quina, *Rape, Incest and Sexual Harassment: A Guide for Helping Survivors* (New York: Praeger, 1989). For an example of EEO counseling in the federal government, see U.S. Department of Agriculture, Employee Appeals Staff, *EEO Counseling, Mediation and Complaint Program* (Washington, DC: U.S. Department of Agriculture, 1989).

3. For a treatment of the types of activities that are offensive and might constitute harassment, see Nancy D. McCann, *100 Women Define Inappropriate Behavior in the Workplace* (Homewood, IL: Business One/Irwin, 1992); Michele A. Paludi, *Academic and Workplace Sexual Harassment: A Resource Manual* (Albany: State University of New York Press, 1991); and Ellen Bravo, *The 9 to 5 Guide to Combating Sexual Harassment: Candid Advice From 9 to 5, the National Association of Working Women* (New York: Wiley, 1992).

4. See David P. Twomey, *A Concise Guide to Employment Law: EEO and OSHA* (Cincinnati: South-Western, 1986).

5. The case of *Cynthia Bates et al.* v. *County of Santa Clara,* C892328 CAL (1989), was tried in a federal court, but the suit was filed under both Title VII of the Federal Civil Rights Act and the California Fair Housing Act. Most of the damages were for emotional damages under the California act.

6. *Meritor Savings Bank* v. *Mechelle Vinson et al.,* 54 L.W. 4703 (1986).

7. These rights were set forth in *Cleveland Board of Education v. Loudermill,* 105 S. Ct. 1487 (1985).

8. See Adolph M. Koven and Susan L. Smith, *Just Cause: The Seven Tests* (San Francisco: Coloracre, 1985).

9. For a discussion of the federal appeals systems, see General Accounting Office, *Survey of Appeal and Grievance Systems Available to Federal Employees: Report to the Chairwoman, Subcommittee on Civil Service* (Washington, DC: U.S. Government Printing Office, 1983).

10. See James R. Redeker, *Employee Discipline: Policies and Practices* (Washington, DC: Bureau of National Affairs, 1989); and Bureau of National Affairs, *Employee Discipline and Discharge* (Washington, DC: Bureau of National Affairs, 1985).

11. Louis V. Imundo, *Employee Discipline: How to Do It Right* (Belmont, CA: Wadsworth, 1985).

12. See A. B. Chimezie and Y. G. Osigweh, eds., *Communicating Employee Responsibilities and Rights: A Modern Management Mandate* (New York: Quorum Books, 1987).

13. See Steven M. Sack, *The Employee Rights Handbook: Answers to Legal Questions—From Interview to Pink Slip* (New York: Facts on File, 1991).

14. Associate Justice William Rehnquist, writing for the plurality in *Arnett* v. *Kennedy,* 416 U.S. 134 (1973), p. 135.

15. *Fifteenth Report of the United States Civil Service Commission (1897–1898)* (Washington, DC: U.S. Government Printing Office, 1899), p. 70.

16. The processes specified in the Lloyd-LaFollette Act were incorporated into the 1978 Civil Service Reform Act, Title II, Section 75b.

17. *Board of Regents* v. *Roth,* 408 U.S. 564 (1972), p. 577.

18. *Perry* v. *Sinderman,* 408 U.S. 593 (1972).

19. *Arnett* v. *Kennedy,* 416 U.S. 134 (1973).

20. Ibid., pp. 153–54.

21. *Cleveland Board of Education* v. *Loudermill,* 105 S. Ct. 1487 (1985), p. 1493.

22. Ibid., p. 1493.

23. Ibid., p. 1495.

24. Ibid., p. 1495.

25. Ibid., p. 1495.

26. The Court found the nine-month delay in final resolution not to be excessive on its face. In other words, if nine months was the usual elapsed time, Loudermill had no complaint.

27. Requiring both notice and an opportunity to respond might lead agencies to infer that an employee on the verge of discharge should be given some time to prepare for the hearing. Such a conclusion is not unreasonable given the Court's suggestion that where a danger is perceived, the appointing authority has the option of suspension with pay pending a hearing. Further litigation may result from the Court's failure to prescribe the period of time that must elapse between the notice and the hearing. In Oklahoma, for example, some administrators

have gone so far as to initiate a predischarge hearing in the middle of a counseling session. As a result, the state's Ethics and Merit Commission has prescribed five working days as adequate notice.

28. See Daniel Oran, *Oran's Dictionary of the Law* (New York: West, 1983), p. 326

29. See Adolph M. Koven and Susan L. Smith, *Just Cause: The Seven Tests.*

30. For a fuller discussion, see Donald E. Klingner and John Nalbandian, *Public Personnel Management: Contexts and Strategies,* 2nd ed. (Englewood Cliffs, NJ: Prentice-Hall, 1985), pp. 362–63.

31. Quoted in "U.S. Army Homosexual Conduct Policy Don't Ask, Don't Tell," at <http://www.se.suar.army.mil/332medbde/homosexual%20conduct%policy%20slides/outlin> posted 2/10/00.

32. Stacey L. Sobel, Kathi S. Westcott, Michelle M. Benecke, C. Dixon Osburn, and Jefferey M. Cleghorn, *Conduct Unbecoming: Sixth Annual Report on "Don't Ask, Don't Tell, Don't Pursue, Don't Harass,"* Service Members Legal Defense Network at <http://www.sldn.org/reports/sixth.htm> posted March 9, 2000. The report alleges that there were 968 incidents of antigay harassment, including a murder, assaults, death threats, and verbal gay bashing between February 15, 1999 and February 15, 2000, an increase of 148 percent. In addition, 1,034 service members were discharged in fiscal year 1999.

33. *Romer, Governor of Colorado et al.* v. *Evans et al.,* 517 U.S. 620 (1996). See Army Substance Abuse Program (ASAP) at <http://www.lee.army.mil/adco/Mlitary_Testing.htm>.

34. Quoted in Michael Marno, *Arbitration and the Off-Duty Conduct of Employees* (Washington, DC: International Personnel Management Association, 1985), p. 23.

35. Ibid., p. 25.

36. Ibid., p. 44. In this case, the officer was reinstated because the theft was considered an aberration that would not affect job performance.

37. Ibid., pp. 23–24.

38. Oklahoma Merit Protection Commission Case Number 87–27, *Tomlin* v. *Department of Public Safety* (1987).

39. A 1986 survey found that 69 percent of respondents favored drug testing in the companies in which they were employed. "Drawing the Battlelines," *Time,* September 22, 1986, p. 26.

40. *Committee for GI Rights* v. *Callaway,* 174 U.S. App. D.C. 73 (1975).

41. Military personnel have fewer rights to privacy than are enjoyed by citizens in general under the First Amendment. See *Parker* v. *Levy,* 417 U.S. 733, 94 S. Ct. 2547 (1974).

42. Robert D. Smith, "Air Force Drug Testing in the Pacific" (unpublished master's thesis, University of Oklahoma, Norman, 1987), p. 27.

43. See Army Substance Abuse Program (ASAP) at <http://www.lee.army.mil/adco/Mlitary_Testing.htm>.

44. *Amalgamated Transit Union (AFL-CIO)* v. *Suscy,* 538 F.2d 1264 (1976).

45. Ibid., p. 1267.

46. *William Skinner, Secretary of Transportation* v. *Railway Labor Executives Association,* 109 S. Ct. 1402 (1989).

47. *McDonnell* v. *Hunter,* 612 F. Supp. 1122 S.D. Iowa (1985).

48. Ibid., p. 1129.

49. Ibid., p. 1132.

50. *Turner* v. *Fraternal Order of Police,* 500 A.2d 1005 C.D.C. App. (1985).

51. Ibid., p. 1008.

52. Ibid., p. 1009.

53. See, for example, *Capua et al.* v. *City of Plainfield,* 643 F. Supp. 1507, N. N.J. (1986) regarding firefighters; *City of Palm Bay* v. *Bauman,* 475 S. 2d 1322 Fla. App. 5 Dist. (1985) regarding police and firefighters; *McDonnell* v. *Hunter,* 612 F. Supp. 1122 S.D. Iowa (1985) regarding corrections officers; *Allen* v. *City of Marietta,* 601 F. Supp. 482 N.D. Ga. (1985) regarding employees working around dangerous equipment; *Jones* v. *McKinzie,* 628 F. Supp. 1500 D.D.C. (1986) regarding schoolbus drivers.

54. *Capua et al.* v. *City of Plainfield,* 643 F. Supp. 1507 N. N.J. (1986), p. 1512.

55. *National Treasury Employees Union and Argent Acosta* v. *Von Raab,* 109 S. Ct. 1384 (1989).

56. *Guiney* v. *Roache,* 873 F. 2d 1557 (First Circuit 1989), certiorari denied.

Predicting the future, especially regarding government programs, is risky. Who would have thought that after the 1980s, government would ever again deal with anything but cut-back management and making due. In the words of Yogi Berra: "The future ain't what it used to be." Elected leaders are now fighting over how to spend anticipated surpluses. Nevertheless, the field of public personnel management continues to adapt to the changes in its mandate that have occurred over the last twenty years. For the time being, there is no reason to suspect that the reform and reengineering trends that have been put in place over the last two decades will not continue. The entire raison d'être for civil service has been called into question. Government is expected to work better, smarter, and faster—generally with less. The specialization of human resource management must also adapt to the changing trends. Finally, technology will continue to impact various operations of human resource management in the public sector.

THE NEW CIVIL SERVICE

In the 1970s, would-be reformers began to question whether patronage posed the same threat to the nation that Lincoln, Pendleton, and company feared in the nineteenth century. Even if it was still necessary to shield employees from discharge for partisan reasons, was the centralization of all personnel functions within a single entity the only, or even the best, way to recruit, classify, discipline, and protect government employees?

The 1978 Civil Service Reform Act began an attack on red tape and rules-for-rules' sake that the National Performance Review (NPR) continued in the 1990s. As a result of the NPR, the Federal Personnel Manual was abolished. Agencies must still adhere to the principles of merit set forth in Title 5, which defines merit, but much decentralization has occurred in the areas of recruitment, classification, training, and discipline. In fact, nearly one-half of federal employees work in agencies that are partially or wholly exempt from Title 5.[1] Of course, the U.S. Postal Service and its 800,000 employees account for most of those employees. These agencies need not, for example, adhere to the rule of three in hiring nor must they give veterans' preference points. Most notably, they may negotiate wages with their employees' designated representative.

A review of the Title 5–exempt agencies determined that, by-and-large, they have kept the merit principles, although some have developed internal protection processes in lieu of third-party dispute resolutions. The factor that most characterizes these agencies is flexibility: flexibility in the drafting of job specifications and significant participation of line managers in the recruitment process, including screening resumes, interviewing, and selecting candidates. Some have departed from the rank-in-position classification system for rank-in-person. This allows them flexibility in determining compensation packages and to develop salaries based on market competitiveness.

State and local governments, too, have adopted more flexible employment systems. The most extreme initiative was the state of Georgia's abolition of Civil Service. Less dramatic but equally important is the trend towards removing high-level positions from the protection of merit. Instead, they now serve at the will and pleasure of the City Manager, Governor, or agency head as the case may be. State and local governments have also expanded their use of contractors and temporary workers, especially for projects that are not ongoing.

THE NEW PERSONNEL MANAGER

The Office of Personnel Management reports that reinventing government initiatives has resulted in an overall reduction in number of human resource management employees. In total in the decade from 1988 to 1998, 17.5 percent of personnel positions in the federal government were abolished. The Department of Defense was disproportionately impacted by the change, with a reduction of approximately 25 percent. The rest of the civil workforce personnelists were reduced by 11 percent.[2] Much of the reduction was achieved through the retirement of senior personnelists. With them went a great deal of institutional memory and plain old knowledge of how to get things done. On the other hand, they also took with them much of the potential opposition to changes in the status quo. In the wake of these retirements, we find a personnel workforce that is more generalist rather than specialist. This shift is significant in light of the increased responsibility that line managers play in the process.

The new personnel generalist, as envisioned by OPM, will serve more as a consultant and facilitator than a gatekeeper. The new personnelist will also be an active partner in developing program strategies and working through human resource needs. The new personnelists will be expected to take on a customer service orientation towards line personnel. He or she will troubleshoot and problem solve rather than monitor and judge. All in all, the new personnelists will be organization assets rather than a necessary evil imposed by external rules devised by a daunting central authority. The OPM bases its recommendations on adaptations in the personnel function in the private sector.[3]

THE NEW PERSONNEL TECHNOLOGY

Technological advances have impacted government in ways most of us never imagined. The automation of the Social Security payment system has turned a bookkeeping nightmare into an agency lauded for its customer service. Similar technology potentials exist for human resource managers as well. As noted in Chapter 7 on recruitment, electronic application procedures and computer scanning of resumes can free up large numbers of workers who may now focus on customer service. This is but the beginning. On the horizon are integrated recruitment, retention, and promotion systems in government. The technology now exists that integrates these functions using an intranet rather than the Internet. These systems are particularly appropriate to very large organizations that engage in multiple job searches in a given year. The system is based on a philosophy of looking inside before going outside. Employees who know they are first in line for new and exciting assignments and promotional opportunities are likely to stay with the organization.

Businesses and governments who adopt this technology will be able to post all job openings at a central location accessible to all current employees. Employees post their resumes at the same site. They can electronically update their posted resumes whenever they acquire a new job skill, attend a training seminar, or complete a college class. More importantly, the intranet will cross-match resumes and job listings. It will automatically scan and rank in-house candidates for open positions. When deemed appropriate by the organization, electronically submitted resumes from outside the agency can also be integrated into the list. Finally, the intranet notifies the predetermined interview committee of the time and place of scheduled interviews, as well as providing them with the electronic resumes of the candidates.

Little imagination is necessary to conceive of further integration of the various human resource systems. Programs can be written that routinely scan current employment records by agency, division, or work unit then notify management when prospective retirements and other turnover variables reach a specified threshold. Management can then begin its succession planning activities. A little more integration and the system could help identify employees in the database with the potential for skill development. The personnelist, moreover, can use the data contained in the resumes to plan and project training needs.

More and more, it seems, public managers are recognizing that far from an auxiliary function, personnel is a critical line activity that must be at the top of each manager's agenda. Personnel offices, moreover, will no longer be a collection of EEO, classification, recruitment, planning, and training specialists. Instead, they will be smaller operations staffed by generalists who problem solve and provide customer service to line managers in personnel matters. These generalists will need, however, extensive training in the application of human resources software programs and electronic databases. This streamlining can occur without sacrificing the principles of merit that are the hallmark of the public service.

NOTES AND RESOURCES

1. U.S. Office of Personnel Management, Office of Merit Systems Oversight and Effectiveness, *HRM Policies and Practices in Title 5–Exempt Organizations* (Washington, DC: Office of Personnel Management, 1998): p. 3.

2. U.S. Office of Personnel Management, *Looking to the Future: Human Resources Competencies: An Occupation in Transition, Part 2,* (Washington, DC: Office of Personnel Management, 1999).

3. U.S. Office of Personnel Management, *The HR Workforce: Meeting the Challenge of Change: An Occupation in Transition, Part 3,* (Washington, DC: Office of Personnel Management, 2000).

Any attempt to be exhaustive in listing the thousands of Web sites that are available in the area of public personnel management would be inadequate. The following Web sites represent a highly select number that the authors have found useful in their own research and consulting and ones that have been recommended by practicing public personnelists. The Web sites that follow are listed by area of interest, accompanied by a brief description of each Web site's salient feature(s). They are provided in an attempt to get managers to go on-line. Our experience instructs us that the more we use these sites in preparing for class and conducting research, the more they get incorporated into our everyday world of management. The Web sites referenced here are listed in the following order:

1. Performance Appraisal and Work Quality
2. Pay/Compensation/Benefits
3. Recruitment
4. Unions
5. Collective Bargaining
6. Equal Employment
7. Affirmative Action
8. Federal Personnel Systems
9. Gender Issues
10. General Personnel Issues
11. Legal Aspects (EEOC and Antidiscrimination)
12. Disabilities
13. State, Regional, County, and Municipal Organizations
14. Productivity
15. Reinvention and Reengineering of Government
16. Jobs and Careers
17. Comprehensive Access for Government

1. PERFORMANCE APPRAISAL AND WORK QUALITY

<http://www.mapnp.org/library/perf_mng/perf_mng.htm> This Web site specifically addresses performance management and includes activities to ensure that organizational goals are consistently met in an effective and efficient manner. Performance management also focuses on performance of the organization, a department, or process to build a product or service, and on employees. This Web site provides some of the overall activities involved in performance management. Your understanding of performance appraisals can be enhanced by reviewing closely related library topics referenced on this Web site.

<http://www.zigonperf.com> Zigon Performance Group specializes in performance appraisal, performance management, and performance measurement systems for hard-to-measure work and teams. They offer on-line resources, books, how-to workshops, and custom consulting services to assist in measuring, managing, and improving employee performance.

<http://performance-appraisal.8m.com/index.htm> This site is dedicated to educating managers, supervisors, human resource professionals, and staff so they can maximize the value they gain from performance management and performance appraisal.

<http://www.escape.ca/~rbacal/main.htm> A Web site specially designed to help the administrator find books dealing with human resources and performance appraisal.

<http://www.jalmc.org/> A Web site that offers newsletters and up-to-date information about performance management.

<http://www.skyenet.net/~leg/tqm.htm> A Web site for the manager that is working with total quality management (TQM). It will help pinpoint problems and give answers to fix the problems. There is additional information on measuring quality that will be useful to the manager.

<http://www.mcb.co.uk/tqm.htm> The TQM Magazine illustrates how organizations build quality into every department and process within their operational structure in order to be successful. It describes the various techniques used to select the best type of training and demonstrates how it can be delivered with the best results.

<http://ix.db.dk/Lise/index.htm> This Web site provides a comprehensive resource guide to total quality management.

<http://members.aol.com/hrmbasics/index.htm> This site contains information and many links on the basics of human resource management: compensation and benefits, diversity, human resource management on the Internet, job analysis, organizational development, performance management, recruiting, and training.

<http://www.aqp.org> Association for Quality and Participation

<http://www.workteams.unt.edu/> The Center for the Study of Work Teams is based at the University of North Texas and was created for the purpose of education and research in all areas of collaborative work systems. The Center was officially incorporated as a nonprofit organization in 1992, although the first conference took place in 1990.

<http://www.peoplemanagement.co.uk/Index.html> People Management from the United Kingdom

<http://www.pmn.net/> The Performance Management Network, Inc. is an incorporated Canadian company focusing on management consulting, education, and the exchange of ideas in all areas of performance improvement, including resource management, organizational design and development, and outcomes management.

<http://www.ispi.org/> Founded in 1962, the International Society for Performance Improvement (ISPI) is the leading international association dedicated to improving productivity and performance in the workplace.

<http://www.siop.org/> Society for Industrial and Organizational Psychology

<http://www.essential.org/> Congressional Accountability Page

<http://www.excelgov.org/> The Council for Excellence in Government

2. Pay/Compensation/Benefits

Compensation

<http://management.about.com/smallbusiness /management/library/weekly/aa041498. htm?pid > 2737&cob = home> This site is listed as an article; however, it has several links to other compensation and benefits sites that managers will find useful.

<http://www.worldatwork.org/worldatwork. html> A professional association with information about compensation, benefits, and total rewards.

<http://www.eci-us.com/Resources-Home.html> Effective Compensation Incorporated (ECI) has prepared various articles and white papers on a wide range of compensation topics.

<http://www.dutch.nl/bart/reward.htm> Performance Management Reward is a site that lists links relevant to the general topic of performance management.

Benefits

<http://www.benefitslink.com/topics.html> This site is the King Kong of benefits listing and references. Lots of material pertaining to a wide variety of benefits.

<http://www.compensationlink.com> Compensation Link is the global on-line service that unites principal Internet-based compensation resources from the United States, Canada, Europe, Asia, and Latin America with compensation and human resource professionals around the world.

<http://www.benefitnews.com> Benefitnews.com, the Internet's most comprehensive resource for benefits professionals, is now a free, members-only site, but registration is required.

<http://www.opm.gov/lmr/html/flexible .htm> U.S. Office of Personnel and Management—The Federal Employees Flexible and Compressed Work Schedules Act of 1982, codified at 5 U.S.C. § 6120 et seq. (the F&CWS law), authorizes a versatile and innovative work-scheduling program for

use in the federal government. In recent years, the importance of flexible and compressed work schedules has been enhanced by the emergence of work and family issues.

<http://www.usda.gov/da/employ/ffwg .htm> Department of Agriculture: Family Friendly Guide. Provides many examples of a federal agency addressing family-friendly issues, such as flextime, child care, eldercare, domestic violence, adoption, fatherhood support, domestic partners, and nursing mothers.

<http://www.opm.gov/oca/leave/index.htm> U.S. Office of Personnel and Management provides the law, regulations, and forms for such family-friendly leave policies as the Family Medical Leave Act (FMLA), organ donor leave, and sick leave to care for a family member.

<http://www.opm.gov/family/wrkfam/index .html> U.S. Office of Personnel and Management/Family Friendly Workplace Advocacy.

3. Recruitment

These are difficult sites to find, especially if the searcher is not interested in the advertisements that many consultant, executive placement, and other temporary agencies have placed on the Web.

<http://www.erexchange.com/> A great site for articles on selection, retention, training, interviewing and screening, metrics, employment law, and general employee referral programs. It also has information on college recruiting, Internet recruiting, and

orientation and assimilation. Click on "Jobs" and the senior executive recruiter, manager recruiter, technical recruiter, and recruiter consultant world unfolds before your eyes.

<http://www.hr-guide.com> This is a huge Web site for human resources information

and Internet guidance within the comprehensive field of human resources management. If you can't find it here, you aren't looking!

<http://www.best-in-class.com/> This Web site is for Best Practices, LLC. It has a link for information regarding human resources. Best Practices, LLC, is a recognized leader in the field of human resources benchmarking and process improvement.

<http://www.interbiznet.com/eeri/index .html> Internet recruiting sites.

<http://www.shrm.org> The Society for Human Resource Management. A must for any serious student or professional in the field of personnel management.

4. UNIONS

<http://www.aflcio.org> The official Web site for the American Federation of Labor and Congress of Industrial Organizations (AFL-CIO).

<http://www.nlma.org> The National Labor Management Association (NLMA) is a national membership organization devoted to helping management and labor work together for constructive change.

<http://www.nlrb.gov/> The National Labor Relations Board is an independent federal agency created by Congress to administer the National Labor Relations Act, the primary law governing relations between unions and employers in the private sector.

5. COLLECTIVE BARGAINING

<http://homepages.uhwo.hawaii.edu/clear/ CB-FAQ.html://

<http://www.opm.gov/cplmr/html/labrmgmt html-ssi> The U.S. Office of Personnel Management—Labor-Management Relations Guidance Bulletin

<http://www.law.cornell.edu/topics/collective _bargaining.html> A legal discussion about collective bargaining and labor arbitration.

<http://www.fmcs.gov/> The Federal Mediation and Conciliation Service (FMCS) was created by Congress in 1947 as an independent agency to promote sound and stable labor-management relations. FMCS offers services in the following areas: dispute mediation, preventative mediation, alternative dispute mediation, arbitration services, and labor-management grants.

6. EQUAL EMPLOYMENT

<http://www.eeoc.gov> The official Web site for the U.S. Equal Employment Opportunity Commission (EEOC).

<http://disabilities.about.com/health/disabili­ ties/library/weekly/aa092500a.htm> This link is a thorough site about.com and is in an article form. There is some additional information listed for further reference, such as court cases and other material that would be useful in courses that discuss current issues of personnel management.

<http://classiclit.about.com/cs/gendertheory/ index.htm> A listing of related HR material.

7. AFFIRMATIVE ACTION

<http://www.racerelations.com/> UConsultUs is home to sixty Web sites that feature management consultants, conferences, specialty e-mail addresses, and resources.

<http://www.auaa.org/> Americans United for Affirmative Action

<http://www.washingtonpost.com/wp­ :srv/politics/special/affirm/affirm.htm> An affirmative action Web site that lists key stories, editorials, and other stories from the *Washington Post*.

<http://aad.english.ucsb.edu/> This site presents diverse opinions regarding affirmative action topics. Rather than taking a pro or con position, it is designed to help lend many different voices to the debates surrounding the issues of affirmative action. This site is an academic resource and it provides scholars, students, and the interested public with on-site articles and theoretical analyses, policy documents, current legislative updates, and an annotated bibliography of research and teaching materials.

<http://www.now.org/issues/affirm/> A National Organization of Women and affirmative action Web site.

<http://www.affirmativeaction.org/> The American Association for Affirmative Action is the association of professionals managing affirmative action, equal opportunity, diversity, and other human resource programs.

<http://www.ss.ca.gov/Vote96/html/BP/209.htm> Prohibition against discrimination or preferential treatment by state and other public entities.

1. Prohibits the state, local governments, districts, public universities, colleges and schools, and other government instrumentalities from discriminating against or giving preferential treatment to any individual or group in public employment, public education, or public contracting on the basis of race, sex, color, ethnicity, or national origin.

2. Does not prohibit reasonably necessary, bona fide occupational qualifications (BFOQ) based on sex and actions necessary for receipt of federal funds.

3. Mandates enforcement to extent permitted by federal law.

4. Requires uniform remedies for violations. Provides for severability of provisions if invalid.

<http://www.naacp.org/> Founded in 1909 in New York City by a group of black and white citizens committed to social justice, the National Association for the Advancement of Colored People (NAACP) is the nation's largest and strongest civil rights organization.

<http://www.apa.org/ppo/aa.html> American Psychological Association: Affirmative Action, Who Benefits?

8. Federal Personnel Systems

<http://www.fedguide.com/> The Federal Personnel Guide Home Page

<http://www.ustreas.gov/jobs/ses.html> The U.S. Senior Executive Service Web site.

<http://www.usajobs.opm.gov/a.htm> Current job listings for the federal government. Get on-line and see what is available in your chosen area of interest.

<http://www.opm.gov/oca/payrates/> United States Office of Personnel Management: Salaries and Payrates

<http://www.fpmi.com/> Federal Personnel Management Institute (FPMI) Communications offers consulting and technical assistance services to federal agencies in all aspects of human resources, management, and EEO. They can assist your agency by providing experienced professionals to perform specific tasks in virtually any human resources field—from labor relations to position classification.

<http://www.whitehouse.gov/WH/Services> The official White House Web site.

<http://www.library.vanderbilt.edu/central/staff/fdtf.html> This is a large, multilisting for federal government Web sites.

<http://www.firstgov.gov/> This is a large, multilisting for the federal government of the United States and should be one of the first stops on your way to accessing what is available in cyberspace.

<http://www.doleta.gov/> The Department of Employment and Training Administration for the United States

<http://www.ipma-hr.org/> International Personnel Management Page

<http://www.mspb.gov/> U.S. Merit System Protections Board—Established by the Civil Service Reform Act of 1978, the board serves as guardian of the federal government's merit-based system of employment, principally by hearing and deciding appeals from federal employees of removals and other major personnel actions. The board also hears and decides other types of civil service cases, reviews significant actions and

regulations of the Office of Personnel Management, and conducts studies of the merit systems.

<http://fedbbs.access.gpo.gov/mspb01.htm> The U.S. Merit Systems Protection Board (MSPB) protects the integrity of the federal merit systems and the rights of federal employees working in the systems. The MSPB distributes information in five file libraries on the Federal Bulletin Board.

<http://www.osc.gov/> U.S. Office of Special Counsel—OSC's primary mission is to safeguard the merit system by protecting federal employees and applicants from prohibited personnel practices, especially reprisal for whistle-blowing.

<http://www.opm.gov/studies/> U.S. Office of Personnel Management—Special Studies on the Federal Civil Service. Provides studies on human resource management issues and policies that have a critical effect on the federal civil service. These studies are

prompted by analyses of personnel trends, the findings from oversight reviews of agencies, and by such stakeholders as the Congress and other interested parties.

<http://www.opm.gov/feddata/factbook/index.htm> The Fact Book: Federal Workforce Statistics—From the Office of Personnel Management, The Fact Book contains statistics on employee demographics; compensation, payroll, and work years; performance management and the Senior Executive Service (SES); retirement and insurance programs; and student employment programs.

<http://www.opm.gov/ovrsight/index.htm> U.S. Office of Personnel Management: Merit Systems Oversight and Protection—Mission to ensure that personnel practices are carried out in accordance with merit system principles.

<http://www.opm.gov/ses/index.htm> Office of Personnel Management: Senior Executive Service

9. Gender Issues

<http://www.workplacesolutions.org/> Women in the workplace.

<http://www.ilr.cornell.edu/library/e_archive/gov_reports/glassceiling/default.html?page=home> Glass ceilings and how they impact women.

<http://www.dol.gov/dol/wb/> U.S. Department of Labor: A Voice For Working Women

<http://www.womenswire.com/glass/>

<http://www.diversityinc.com/>

<http://www.nationalpartnership.org/workandfamily/workplace/pregdiscrim/pregdiscrimmain.htm> Pregnancy in the workplace.

<http://www.now.org>: National Association for Women is a good resource for all women-in-the-workplace issues.

<http://www.parentsoup.com/calendar/rights.html> Parental workplace rights.

<http://www.transitionsinc.com/Corporate/Corporate.html> Lactation issues that assist in making the workplace more employee friendly.

<http://www.storknet.org/> Good place to look for topics related to pregnancy issues.

<http://www.uakron.edu/lawrev/robert1.html> Sexual harassment issues.

<http://www.borealis.net/lawbooks/> Sexual harassment.

<http://www.nolo.com/encyclopedia/emp_ency.html> Provides a plethora of material on topics as diverse as sexual harassment, health and safety, fair pay and time off, and discrimination.

<http://www.workingmother.com> *Working Mother* magazine Web site.

<http://www.eoc.org.uk/html/parental_leave.html#plwhatisit> Paternity leave Web page.

<http://www.aflcio.org/women/equalpay.html> Equal work for equal pay. You can find out what the lack of equal pay costs you each year and during your professional career.

<http://www.advancingwomen.com/> Web site devoted to women and the many issues they face in the workplace.

<http://www.lwv.org/> The League of Women Voters, a nonpartisan political organization, encourages the informed and active participation of citizens in government, works to increase understanding of major public policy issues, and influences public policy through education and advocacy.

<http://www.wesg.org/> Women Executives in State Government (WESG) is a national nonprofit membership organization committed to excellence in state government—through innovation, creative public-private

partnerships, and the development of future leaders. It was founded in 1983 by a group of women from around the country to exchange practical information about successful strategies in state government. Today, WESG members are among the leaders who are making a difference in public service. High-quality management and leadership training; peer-to-peer exchange and networking opportunities; partnerships with public- and private-sector leaders; and issues education are all part of WESG.

<http://compnetworking.about.com/cs/networkgender/index.htm> A comprehensive listing of gender-related sites and articles.

10. GENERAL PERSONNEL ISSUES

<http://www.mapnp.org/library/topics.htm> This site has it all, everything you could possibly imagine in relation to human resource management and administration. It has superb links to advertising and promotion, benefits and compensation, career development, communication, crisis management, customer service and satisfaction, E-commerce, creativity and innovation, evaluations, employee performance management, ethics, financial management, group performance management, interviewing, legal information, leadership development, organizational change, training and development, staffing, and social entrepreneurship, and quality management.

<http://www.aspanet.org/> With a diverse membership composed of thousands of practitioners, scholars, teachers, and students, the American Society for Public Administration (ASPA) is the largest and most prominent professional association in the field of public administration. As students in public administration, you will access this site frequently. It also provides many excellent links to governmental agencies and other professional associations.

<http://www.napawash.org/napa/index.html> The National Academy of Public Administration is an independent, nonpartisan organization chartered by Congress to assist federal, state, and local governments in improving their effectiveness, efficiency, and accountability. For more than 30 years the academy has met the challenge of cultivating excellence in public management and administration.

<http://www.dot.gov/ost/dapc/> U.S. Department of Transportation: The Office of Drug and Alcohol Policy and Compliance. Its mission is to provide expert advice to industry representatives regarding implementation of the controlled substances and alcohol testing rules. And, where possible, they have attempted to simplify and standardize testing operations across the United States.

<http://www.kepner-tregoe.com/> Kepner-Tregoe, a worldwide management consulting firm, helps integrate an organization's knowledge base and critical thinking skills with its strategy, its structure and systems, and the processes by which goals are accomplished.

<http://www.public-policy.org/> National Center for Policy Analysis

<http://www.ipma-hr.org> International Personnel Management Association

<http://www.nlma.org> The National Labor Management Association (NLMA) is a national membership organization devoted to helping management and labor work together for constructive change.

<http://www.shrm.org> Society for Human Resource Management home page.

<http://www.workforce.com/> This Web site is for business leaders in human resources. It includes a variety of practical human resources management (HRM) information that is useful to the personnel administrator on a day-to-day basis.

<http://www.mcb.co.uk/> The Human Resource Network provides Internet services for subscribers to MCB human resources and training journals.

<http://www.hrlive.com/> A monthly digest of news, views, tips, and trends.

<http://www.hrworld.com/> A quarterly magazine on using informational technology effectively in human resources.

<http://www.fpmi.com/> This U.S. site has a listing of HR publications, a daily government news feature, and two HR lists on general personnel and training for government agencies.

<http://www.hrstrategy.com/> This is the source for information about the

Performance Model of Human Resources, a state-of-the-art innovation that is changing the way people hire and manage employees. According to the Web site, "The Performance Model is reshaping the industry and filling organizations with highly productive top performers. Best of all, it significantly lowers human resource program costs and saves valuable time."

<http://www.bcsolutionsmag.com/> U.S. magazine with featured articles on human resources management.

<http://www.humanresourcesinfo.com/> A Canadian newsletter focusing on the issues of compensation, productivity, restructuring, performances management, and managing change.

11. LEGAL ASPECTS

This section includes sites dealing with EEOC and other antidiscrimination measures.

<http://www.eeoc.gov/> This site is a clearinghouse for all issues relevant to the Equal Employment Opportunity Commission (EEOC).

<http://www.corporateinformation.com/> A place to find corporate information by state and country. It also has links to other sites such as the state supreme court archives and decisions.

<http://www.epa.gov/epahome/lawreg.htm> The U.S. Environmental Protection Agency (EPA) Web site relevant to environmental laws and regulations. If you are concerned about employee exposure to hazardous substances and how such substances can be properly disposed of in a safe and environmentally friendly manner, this site will be most valuable.

<http://www.whistleblowers.org/> The National Whistleblower Center is a nonprofit, tax-exempt educational and advocacy organization committed to environmental protection, nuclear safety, civil rights, government accountability, and protecting the rights of employee whistle-blowers. Established in 1988, the center has successfully established many of the most important precedents protecting employee whistle-blowers throughout the United States and has revolutionized the protection afforded them. If you want to study what happens to whistle-blowers, this site is a must.

<http://www.ahipubs.com/> Good resource for legal information pertaining to all phases of employment.

<http://www.osc.gov/discl.htm> U.S. Office of Special Counsel Whistleblower Disclosure Section—The OSC provides a safe channel through which current and former federal employees, and applicants for employment, may disclose information that they believe shows a violation of law, rule, or regulation; gross mismanagement; gross waste of funds; abuse of authority or a substantial and specific danger to public health or safety.

<http://fedlaw.gsa.gov/> FedLaw was developed to see if legal resources on the Internet could be a useful and cost-effective research tool for federal lawyers and other federal employees. FedLaw has assembled references of use to people doing federal legal research and that can be accessed directly through "point and click" hypertext connections.

<http://www.naspaa.org/> The National Association of Schools of Public Affairs and Administration (NASPAA) is an institutional membership organization that exists to promote excellence in public-service education. The membership includes 245 U.S. university programs in public affairs, public policy, public administration, and nonprofit management. Visit this site and see what the issue of program accreditation is all about and whether your MPA program is accredited.

12. DISABILITIES

<http://www.aarp.org/> This site is dedicated to the American Association of Retired Persons (AARP).

<http://www.ahipubs.com> This is a good site to use if looking for information about employing persons with disabilities. In addi-

tion, this site also has legal information regarding a full range of employment issues.

<http://www.dredf.org/> Founded in 1979 by people with disabilities and parents of children with disabilities, the Disability Rights Education and Defense Fund, Inc. (DREDF) is a national law and policy center dedicated to protecting and advancing the civil rights of people with disabilities through legislation, litigation, advocacy, technical assistance, and education and training of attorneys, advocates, persons with disabilities, and parents of children with disabilities.

<http://www.eeoc.gov/> U.S. Equal Employment Opportunity Commission (EEOC)

<http://www.dol.gov/dol/esa/public/regs /compliance/whd/1421.htm> U.S. Department of Labor FLMA Compliance Guide—The Family and Medical Leave Act (FMLA) provides certain employees with up to 12 workweeks of unpaid, job-protected leave a year, and requires group health benefits to be maintained during the leave as if employees continued to work instead of taking leave. This Compliance Guide summarizes the FMLA provisions and regulations, and provides answers to the most frequently asked questions.

<http://www.opm.gov/oca/leave/index.htm> U.S. Office of Personnel Management: Family Leave—The Office of Personnel

Management provides governmentwide leadership on federal leave policies and programs. This is accomplished by developing and maintaining governmentwide regulations and policies on the administration of leave, including the Family and Medical Leave Act, family-friendly leave policies, federal leave-sharing programs, annual leave, sick leave, and time off for special circumstances—e.g., early dismissal or closure for weather emergencies. However, each federal agency is responsible for administering leave policies and programs for its own employees.

<http://www.access-board.gov/> The Access Board of the Federal Government—The Access Board is an independent federal agency devoted to accessibility for people with disabilities. It operates with about 30 staff and a governing board of representatives from federal departments and public members appointed by the president. Key responsibilities of the board include developing and maintaining accessibility requirements for the built environment, transit vehicles, telecommunications equipment, and for electronic and information technology; providing technical assistance and training on these guidelines and standards; and enforcing accessibility standards for federally funded facilities.

13. STATE, REGIONAL, COUNTY, AND MUNICIPAL ORGANIZATIONS

<http://www.naco.org/> The National Association of Counties (NACo) Web site. This is the only national organization that represents county governments in the United States. If the county-level of government is your interest, then this Web site will be a high priority on your browsing list.

<http://www.geocities.com/CapitolHill /1389/> This Web site serves as a collection of city-related URLs from throughout the United States.

<http://www.lgi.org/> The Local Government Institute (LGI) is an independent nonprofit organization dedicated to improving the quality of local government.

<http://www.statelocal.gov/> A state and local government link.

<http://www.statesnews.org/> Site contains links to regional and state information.

<http://www.icma.org/> The International City/County Management Association (ICMA) is the professional and educational organization representing appointed managers and administrators in local governments throughout the world. If your interest is in the area of county management, this is the capstone Web site.

<http://www.nga.org/> National Governors' Association (NGA) is the only bipartisan national organization of, by, and for the nation's governors. Its members are the governors of the fifty states, the commonwealths of the Northern Mariana Islands and Puerto Rico, and the territories of American Samoa, Guam, and the Virgin Islands. Through NGA, the governors identify priority issues and deal collectively with issues of public

policy and governance at both the national and state levels.

<http://www.nlc.org/> The mission of the National League of Cities (NLC) is to strengthen and promote cities as centers of opportunity, leadership, and governance. NLC was established in 1924 by and for reform-minded state municipal leagues. NLC now represents 49 leagues, more than 1,700 member cities, and, through the membership of the state municipal leagues, NLC represents more than 18,000 cities and towns of all sizes in total.

<http://www.usmayors.org/> The United States Conference of Mayors is the official nonpartisan organization of cities with populations of 30,000 or more. There are about 1,100 such cities in the country today.

Each city's chief elected official, the mayor, represents the city in the conference.

<http://www.statesnews.org/> Council of State Governments

<http://www.civic.net/> Local government network.

<http://www.natat.org/> The purpose of the National Association of Towns and Townships (NATaT) is to strengthen the effectiveness of town and township government. It does so by educating lawmakers and public policy officials about how small-town governments operate and by advocating policies on their behalf in Washington, D.C.

<http://www.narc.org/> The National Association of Regional Councils (NARC) is a nonprofit membership organization serving the interests of regional councils nationwide.

14. PRODUCTIVITY

<http://www.nlma.org/> The National Labor Management Association (NLMA) is a national membership organization devoted to helping management and labor work together for constructive change.

<http://www.astd.org> American Society for Training and Development. Anything and everything you need to know if training is your forte.

15. REINVENTION AND REENGINEERING OF GOVERNMENT

<http://www.npr.gov/> An informational source about federal executive agency reinvention and reengineering. This site says it all on the reinvention of government movement that is stalking the halls of government at all levels. The works of Peters, Osborne, and Gaebler come to life in the National Performance Review. This Web site provides a wealth of information on how to reinvent, reinvention accomplishments, awards, partnerships, etc., and all of this information is presented in plain language. Also, a great source for best practices information and on government kiosks that continue to dot the country, including views on E-government. It links to Access America and Access America E-Gov E-Zine. The NPR initiatives, such as Budget-Net and AfterSchool, and many awards that have been given for innovation and excellence are reported on this site.

<http://www.alliance.napawash.org/alliance/index.html> The Alliance for Redesigning Government was established at the National Academy of Public Administration in 1993

in response to the groundswell of public-sector innovation in state and local governments. The alliance is the center of a national network and clearinghouse for state, local, and federal innovators; nonprofit and corporate leaders; and scholars who advocate performance-based, results-driven governance.

<http://www.icma.org> International City/County Management Association (ICMA). This Web site is your essential source for information on managing the municipality or the county. Also, a great source for international management initiatives that help break down our own ethnocentric biases concerning how a large number of problems might be remedied.

<http://www.afscme.org/private/index.html> American Federation of State, County, and Municipal Employees (AFSCME) is a comprehensive Web site for those who wish to learn the union perspective on topics such as privatization and contracting-out. This site's special feature and strength is found in the many links to labor unions, both

domestic and international, and the traditional listing of topics: classification, compensation, bargaining, diversity, testing, gay and lesbian issues, health care, labor studies and resources, women's issues, and workers' compensation.

16. JOBS AND CAREERS

<http://www.jobsingovernment.com/> A Web site devoted to jobs and employment in the public sector.

<http://www.opajobs.com/> Find job opportunities in public affairs on this Web site.

<http://www.usajobs.opm.gov/> The U.S. Government's official site for jobs and employment information provided by the United States Office of Personnel Management.

<http://www.usajobs.opm.gov/b1f.htm> Senior Executive Service current job openings.

<http://www.doi.gov/indexj.html> The Web site for the Department of the Interior has listing for jobs within the department.

<http://www.jobsfed.com> A place to look for government job listings.

17. COMPREHENSIVE ACCESS FOR GOVERNMENT:

The following provide comprehensive materials on selected institutions and organizations of government and provide many valuable links to topics associated with modern personnel management practices.

<http://www.lcweb.loc.gov/> Library of Congress—Need we say more?

<http://www.si.edu/> Smithsonian Institute

<http://www.whitehouse.gov/> White House Web site. Valuable links to other federal executive agencies and congressional organizations.

<http://www.firstgov.gov/> A comprehensive site that can link to almost all government sites, which are easily listed as executive, legislative, and judicial branches and offices. This is the "real McCoy" of federal government Web sites and is touted as the one single best source for information on the U.S. government.

<http://www.epa.gov/> The Environmental Protection Agency (EPA) Web site keeps up-to-date information about environmental programs and Superfund site clean-ups.

<http://www.wto.org/> The World Trade Organization Web site.

<http://www.searchgov.com/> An in-depth site for links to federal and state governmental programs and agencies.

<http://www.census.gov/> The U.S. Census Bureau site provides information about recent census data, people, business, geography, news, and additional topics. A top notch site for demographic, social, and economic data compiled nationally, by state, and by locale.

<http://www.supremecourtus.gov/> The official Web site for the U.S. Supreme Court.

<http://www.dhhs.gov/> The Department of Health and Human Services is the United States government's principal agency for protecting the health of all Americans and providing essential human services, especially for those who are least able to help themselves.

<http://www.va.gov/> The Department of Veteran Affairs Web site contains information about health, compensation, education, insurance, and special services, and links to state and local sites.

<http://www.fda.gov/> Food and Drug Administration's official Web site.

<http://www.doi.gov/indexj.html> The official Web site for the Department of the Interior.

The authors wish to acknowledge the helpful assistance of Brian Hanft in compiling this listing of useful Web sites.

Adams, John, 2
Adaptation, 232–233
Adarand v. *Pena* (1995), 86
Administrative accountability, 5
Administrative Careers With America (ACWA)
 exam, 14–15
Adverse actions, 296
 appeals, 303–304
Advocacy grievance systems, 292–294
Affirmative action (AA), 279
 courts and, 73–78
 federal implementation of, 62–64
 four-fifths rule, 75–76
 history of, 58–62
 layoffs and, 126
 remedial, 78–86
 as social policy, 148–149
 three degrees of, 69–71
AFSCME v. *The State of Washington* (1985), 98
Agency planning. *See also* Human resource
 planning
 bumping back and, 125–126
 for change, 122–123
 for cutbacks, 124–125
 for succession, 123–124
 systematic, 121–122
Albamarle Paper Co. v. *Moody et al.* (1975),
 76–77
Amalgamated Transit Union v. *Suscy* (1976),
 313–314
American Federation of Labor and Congress of
 Industrial Organizations (AFL-CIO),
 246
Americans with Disabilities Act (ADA), 45,
 71–73
Annual leave benefits, 202
Appeals, to adverse actions, 303–304
Appraisal systems. *See* Performance appraisal
 systems
Arbitration, 264–271
 compulsory, 265
 expedited, 270–271

final-offer, 267–268
grievance, 265, 268–270
interest, 264–265
line-item, 267–268
mandatory, 265–267
mediation, 268
Arnett v. *Kennedy* (1973), 301–302
At-will employment, 52–53

Bakke, Alan, 78–79
Bargaining. *See* Collective bargaining
Beard politics era, 3
Behaviorally anchored rating systems (BARS),
 221–222
Benchmark factor systems, 98, 167–170
Benchmark-position method, for pay scales,
 172–174
Benefit packages, 201–203
Blue flu, 256
"Blue sky" agreements, 7
Board of Regents v. Roth (1972), 301
Bottom-up method, for pay scales, 170–172
Bradwell v. *State of Illinois* (1873), 95
Branti v. *Finkel* (1980), 8–9
Brennan, William, Jr., 83
Breyer, Stephen, 69
Brown v. *Board of Education* (1954), 58, 60
Brownlow Commission, 17
Bumping back, 125–126
Burger, Warren, 80
Burlington Industries, Inc. v. *Ellerth* (1998), 100
Bush, George H. W., 11, 22, 25, 68
Business Work-Life Study (BWLS), 108, 110

Cameron, Simon, 4
Capua et al. v. *City of Plainfield* (1986), 315
Carter, Jimmy, 18, 65–66
Change, planning for, 122–123
Churchill v. *Waters* (1994), 12
City managers, 50–52
City of Richmond v. *J.A. Croson Co.* (1989), 86
Civil Rights Act of 1964, 45, 57, 60, 97

Civil Rights Act of 1991, 68–69, 84, 100
Civil rights movement, 57–58
Civil Service Act of 1883, 5, 10, 13
Civil Service Commission (CSC), 10–11, 62,
    63–64
    personnel management role of, 16–17
Civil Service Reform Act of 1978 (CSRA), 10,
    18–19, 22, 199, 259–261
Classification, techniques of, 166–170
Classification Act of 1923, 15, 163
Classification Act of 1949, 15, 163–164
Classification systems
    employee compensation and, 15–16
    in federal civilian service, 163–164
    rank in the corps, 161–162
    rank in person, 159–161
    rank in position, 162–163
    reclassification and, 164–165
    state merit systems and, 46
Classified employees, job rights of, 300–303. See
        also Public employees
Clayton Act of 1914, 244
Cleveland Board of Education v. Loudermill (1985),
        302–303
Clinton, Bill, 11, 22, 307
Closed candidate lists, 144–145
Collective bargaining, 246
    administration, 251–253
    developing positive approach to, 281–288
    at federal level, 256–261
    management rights and, 253–254
    preparing for, 280–281
    at state and local level, 249–251
Community standards, 308
Comparable worth methodology, 98
Compensation
    as motivation, 196–203
    private-sector vs. public sector, 195–196
Compliance planning, 207
Compulsory arbitration, 265
Computer-assisted instruction (CAI), 231
Conflict resolution
    arbitration, 264–271
    fact finding, 263–264
    mediation, 263
Connecticut v. Teal (1982), 77
Constructive criticism, 213–214
Constructive discharge standard, 100
Contract compliance, 64, 65–66
Corruption, 4–5
Council-manager systems, 51–52
Counseling
    employee, 212–213
    as screening, 293–294

County governments, personnel systems in, 53
Critical-incident systems, 221
Criticism, constructive, 213–214
Cutbacks, planning for, 124–125

Daley, Dennis M., 210
Day care, 106–107
Demotions, 298–299
Developmental appraisal systems, 210
Disciplinary systems
    determining appropriate disciplines and,
        298–300
    documentation and, 296–298
Disparate impact, 77
Disparate treatment, 77
Dixiecrats, 60
Documentation
    for disciplinary systems, 296–298
    employee discipline and, 214
    for labor negotiations, 280
Domestic partners registration, 105–106
"Don't Ask, Don't Tell" policy, 307–308
Drug testing, of public employees, 311–316
Dual grievance systems, 287
Due process, for classified employees,
        301–302

Eisenhower, Dwight D., 59, 60
Eldercare, 107–108
Electronic recruitment, 141–142
Elrod v. Burns (1976), 8
Employee counseling, 212–213
Employee development, 210–212
Employee discipline, 214, 296–300
Employee rights, 85
Employees. See Classified employees; Military
        employees; Public employees
Equal employment opportunity (EEO)
    advocacy grievance systems for, 292–294
    Carter administration and, 65–66
    constraints, 291
    courts and, 73–78
    grievance process for, 292–294
    merit systems and, 63–64
    Reagan administration and, 66–68
    at state level, 48–49
Equal Employment Opportunity Commission
        (EEOC), 26–27, 57, 63–64, 65
Equal Pay Act of 1963, 97–99
Established practices, 277–278
Evaluation instruments, 215–223. See also Perfor-
        mance appraisal systems
    behaviorally anchored rating systems,
        221–222

checklist systems, 222–223
critical-incident systems, 221
management by objective, 217
matrix rating, 216–217
mixed systems for, 218–221
Examinations, 14, 142–143. *See also* PACE
(Professional Administrative Career
Exam)
Executive Order 1183, 257
Executive Order 8587, 59
Executive Order 9981, 59
Executive Order 10925, 17, 26, 60–61
Executive Order 10988, 27, 257
Executive Order 11246, 63
Executive Order 11348, 228
Executive Order 11375, 61
Executive Order 11478, 61
Executive Order 11491, 257
Executive Order 11616, 257
Executive Order 12086, 64
Executive Order 12320, 66
Executive Order 12564, 313
Expectancy theory, 197–198
Expert estimates, 128

Fact finding, 263–264
Factionalism, 2–3
Fair Employment Practices Commission, 59,
62–63
Family and Medical Leave Act of 1993, 105,
110
Faragher v. *City of Boca Raton* (1998), 100–101
Federal Employee Retirement System (FERS),
21, 201
Federal employees. *See* Military employees;
Public employees
Federal Employees Leave Sharing Amendments
Act, 105
Federal Employees Part-Time Career
Employment Act of 1978, 109
Federal Employees Political Activities Act of
1993, 11
Federal Labor Relations Authority (FLRA),
27–28, 259
Final-offer arbitration, 267–268
Firefighters' Local 1784 v. *Stotts* (1984), 84, 85,
126
First Amendment, public employees rights and,
11–13
Fisher v. *Walker* (1972), 12
Flexible leave, 110
Flexible staffing, 109–110
Flexiplace, 110–111
Flextime, 108–109

Ford, Gerald R., 257
Forecasting
complexity of, 127–128
computer-assisted, 128
for human resource planning, 126–127
for new operations, 128–129
Four-fifths rule, 75–76
Fullilove v. *Klutznick* (1980), 64

Gainsharing, 280
Garfield, James, 5
Gays/lesbians
domestic partners registration of, 105–106
military rights of, 307–308
Ginsberg, Ruth Bader, 69
Glass Ceiling Commission, 69, 99
Good-faith bargaining, 255–256
Gore, Al, 22
Government employees. *See* Public employees
Government Employees' Training Act of 1958,
228
Governors, state
personnel management and, 45–47
personnel reform as management control
for, 47–50
Grace Commission, 278
Grievance arbitration, 265, 268–270
Grievance processes
developing, 285–288
EEO, 292–294
Grievance systems, advocacy, 292–294
Grievance tests, 304–307
Griggs v. *Duke Power and Light Co.* (1971), 27,
74–76
Group reward programs, 199–200

Hamilton, Alexander, 1–2
Harris v. *Forklift Systems, Inc.* (1993), 100
Hatch Act of 1939, 11, 13
Health care benefits, 201–202
Herzberg, Frederick, 197
Historical analysis, 127
Homosexuals
domestic partners registration of, 105–106
military rights of, 307–308
Honest graft, 4–5
Human-relations approach, training and, 234
Human relations theory, 196–197
Human resource planning. *See also* Agency
planning; Planning
as forecasting, 126–129
skills inventories and, 129–131
state merit systems and, 46–47
Humphrey, Hubert, 60

Impasse resolution, 260
Incentive systems, 197–198
    governments and, 198–199
    group, 199–200
Individual Learning Accounts (ILA), 228
Innocent individuals, rights of, 85
Interest arbitration, 264–265, 267–268
Internships, 141
Interviews, 144

Jefferson, Thomas, 1–2
Jeffries v. *Harleston* (1995), 12–13
"Jim Crow" laws, 58
Job evaluation, 166
Job sharing, 109
Johnson, Lyndon B., 57, 60–61, 228
Johnson v. *Transportation Agency, Santa Clara
    County* (1987), 81–82
Judgmental appraisal systems, 210

Kaiser Aluminum and Chemical Corp. v. *Weber*
    (1979), 80–81
Kennedy, Anthony, 68
Kennedy, John F., 26, 27, 60–61, 257

Labor Management Relations Act of 1947. *See*
    Taft-Hartley Act of 1947
Labor practices. *See* Unfair labor practices
Labor relations
    collective bargaining and, 246
    early history of, 243–244
    federal legislation, 245
Landum-Griffin Act of 1959, 245
Layoffs, dark side of, 126
Lesbians/gays
    domestic partners registration of, 105–106
    military rights of, 307–308
Life insurance benefits, 202
Lincoln, Abraham, 4
Line-item arbitration, 267
List certification, 70
Lloyd-Lafollette Act of 1913, 11, 13, 256–257,
    301–302
*Local 28, Sheet Metal Workers' International
    Association et al.* v. *Equal Employment
    Opportunity Commission et al.* (1986),
    83–84
Local 93, International Association of Firefighters v.
    Cleveland (1986), 62–63
Local government employees. *See* Public
    employees
Local governments, personnel systems in,
    50–53
Longevity, rewarding, 166, 200

McDonnel v. *Hunter*, 314
Malek Manual, 17
Malfeasance, 296, 299
Management
    affirmative action and, 279
    developing positive approach to unions by,
        281–288
    established practices and, 277–278
    gainsharing and, 280
    privatization and, 278–279
    union contracts as constraints on, 275–277
Management by objective (MBO) systems, 48,
    217
Management rights
    Civil Service Reform Act of 1978 and,
        259–260
    collective bargaining and, 253–254
Mandatory arbitration, 265–267
Marbury v. *Madison* (1803), 2–3
Marshall, John, 3
Martin v. *Wilks* (1989), 82, 279
Master's of public administration (MPA)
    programs, 229–230
Matlovich, Leonard, 307
Matrix rating instruments, 216–217
Mediation, 263, 268
Mentoring, 214
Merit award programs, 199
Meritor Savings Bank v. *Mechelle Vinson et al.*
    (1986), 99–100, 294
Merit pay, 28
Merit System Protection Board (MSPB), 14–15,
    24, 147
Merit systems, 13–15
    constraints, 294–295
    equal employment opportunity and, 63–64
    personnel management under, 149–151
    recruitment in, 137–146
    social equity and, 146–149
    state-level trends, 43–45
Military employees. *See also* Public employees
    drug testing of, 312–313
    sexual behavior and rights of, 307–308
Misfeasance, 296
MPA programs, 229–230
Muller v. *Oregon* (1908), 96

National Association for the Advancement of
    Colored People (NAACP), 58
National Association of Schools of Public
    Affairs and Administration
    (NASPAA), 229–230
National Labor Relations Act of 1935, 243,
    245

National Organization for Women (NOW), 97
National Performance Review (NPR), 22, 329
National Treasury Employees Union and Argent Acosta v. *Von Raab*, 315–316
Negotiations. *See* Collective bargaining
Nixon, Richard M., 61, 257
Nonfeasance, 296
Nonmonetary award systems, 203
Norris-La Guardia Anti-Injunction Act of 1932, 244

O'Connor, Sandra, 67, 69
Off-duty conduct, public employees and, 308–311
Office of Contract Compliance, 64
Office of Personnel Management (OPM), 19–22, 228
    reinventing government initiatives of, 330
Office of Special Counsel (OSC), 25–26
O'Hare et al. v. *City of Northlake* (1996), 9
Oncale v. *Sundowner* (1998), 101
On-the-job training, 230–231
Open candidate lists, 144–145
Organizational development (OD), 232–233
Outreach recruitment, 140–141

PACE (Professional Administrative Career Exam), 5, 14. *See also* Examinations
Patronage systems
    advantages of, 3–4
    beard politics era of, 3
    at county level, 6–7
    disadvantages of, 4
    Lincoln and, 4
    methodology of, 6
    recruitment in, 135–137
    solutions to, 7–8
    Supreme Court decisions limiting, 8–9
Pay scales, constructing
    benchmark-position method, 172–174
    bottom-up method, 170–172
Pendleton Act. *See* Civil Service Act of 1883
Performance appraisal systems. *See also* Evaluation instruments
    developmental *vs.* judgmental, 210
    employee counseling/disciplining and, 214–215
    employee development and, 210–212
    evaluation instruments for, 215–223
    organization outcomes and, 207–210
Performance Management and Recognition System (PMRS), 28, 199
Personnel Administrator v. *Feeney* (1979), 146
Philadelphia Plan, 64

Pickering v. *Board of Education* (1968), 12
Piecework, 197–198
Planning. *See also* Human resource planning
    for change, 122–123
    for cutbacks, 124–125
    public sector types of, 207–208
    succession, 123–124
    textbook way of, 121–122
Plessy v. *Ferguson* (1896), 57–58
Point factor classification systems, 173–175
Political participation, and public employees, 11, 13
Position analysis, 137–138
Position classification systems, 166–167
Position control audits, 47–48
Positive state, 43
Postal Reorganization Act of 1970, 258
Predischarge rights, of classified employees, 302–303
Pregnancy Discrimination Act of 1978, 110
Preponderance of evidence, 304
Presidential Rank Award, 199
Prewitt v. *The United States Postal Service* (1981), 66
Privatization, 278–279
Production, 231–232
Professional Air Traffic Controllers Organization (PATCO), 256, 258–259, 262
Programed instruction, 231
Program planning, 208
Progressive disciplinary systems, 298–299
Promotion quotas, 84
Property interests, of classified employees, 301
Public Employee Relations Boards (PERBs), 251–252
Public employees. *See also* Classified employees; Military employees
    drug testing and rights of, 311–316
    First Amendment rights of, 11–13
    off-duty conduct guidelines, 308–311
    political participation and, 11, 13
    sexual behavior and rights of, 307–308
Public service, professionalization of, 229–230

Quotas, 68, 70
    court-sanctioned, 82–84
    promotion, 84

Ramspeck Act, 59
Randolph, Philip, 59
Rank-in-the-corps classification, 161–162
Rank-in-person classification, 159–161
    reclassification and, 164–165

Rank-in-position classification, 162–163
Reagan, Ronald, 25, 66–68, 259, 278, 313
Reasonable person standard, 100
Reclassification, 164–165
Recruitment
    candidate selection and, 145–146
    electronic, 141–142
    internships and, 141
    under merit systems, 137–146
    outreach, 140–141
    under patronage systems, 135–137
    process of, 138–142
    screening process and, 142–145
    state merit systems and, 46
The Regents of the University of California v. *Bakke*
        (1978), 78–79, 148
Rehnquist, William, 67, 80–81, 302
Retirement benefits, 201
Roosevelt, Franklin D., 59
Roosevelt, Theodore, 10
Rule of three, 15, 70, 145
Rutan v. *Republican Party of Illinois* (1990), 9

Salaries. *See* Compensation
Salary surveys, 172–173
Same-sex harassment, 101
Same-sex relationships, 105–106
Scalia, Antonin, 8
Screening process, and recruitment, 142–145
Senior Executive Service (SES), 22–24
Set-aside programs. *See* Quotas
Sexual harassment, 99–101
Sherman Anti-Trust Act of 1890, 244
Sick leave benefits, 202
Skilled trades, 64, 79–82
Skill pay, 200–201
Skills inventories, 129–131
Skills training, 231–232
Skinner v. *Railway Labor Executives Association*
        (1989), 314
Socialization, organization, 233–235
Souter, David, 59
Sovereign factors, 127, 128–129
Spreader factor, 170–172
Standards of performance, 211–212
State government employees. *See* Public
        employees
State governments
    merit systems in, 43–45
    personnel management changes in, 45–47
    personnel reform as management control in,
        47–50
Step increases, 165–166
Strategic planning, 207–208

Strict scrutiny, parameters of, 86
Strikes
    alternatives to, 263–264
    factors in successful, 261–262
    service disruptions and, 263
Succession planning, 123–124
Supervisors
    bargaining status of public sector, 252–253
    collective bargaining involvement of, 280–281
Supreme Court
    decisions limiting patronage, 8–9
    quotas and, 82–84
    Reagan appointments to, 67–68

Taft-Hartley Act of 1947, 245
Taylor, Frederick, 197
Tenured employees. *See* Classified employees
Testing systems, 14–15
T-groups, training and, 234
Thomas, Clarence, 69
360 evaluation, 215
Thurmond, Strom, 60
Title 5, 329–330
Total quality management (TQM), 234–235
Training, public sector, 227–229
    adaptation and, 232–233
    coordination and, 235–236
    mission relevance and, 231
    of professionalism, 229–230
    socialization and, 233–235
    for supervisor skills, 232
    types of, 230–231
    virtues of, 230
Truman, Harry S., 59
Trustee period, 1–2
Turner v. *Fraternal Order of Police,* 315
Turnover analysis, 127
Two-tiered evaluation system, 219–221

Unfair labor practices
    by management in private sector, 254–255
    by unions in private sector, 255–256
Union contracts, as constraints on management,
        275–280
Unionization
    motivations for, 247–249
    public- *vs.* private-sector, 249
    public-sector, 246–247
United States v. *Paradise et al.* (1987), 84

Veterans' preference, 145–146
Vickery v. *Jones* (1996), 9
Volker Commission, 22
Voting Rights Act of 1965, 57, 60

Wagner Act, 243, 245
Wallace, Henry, 60
Wards Cove Packing Co., Inc. v. *Antonio* (1989), 76
Washington, George, 1–2
Washington Co. Oregon v. *Gunther* (1981), 97–98
Weber, Brian, 80–81
Weber, Max, 195
Whistleblower Protection Act of 1988, 25–26
Whistleblowers, 5, 25–26

Whole-job evaluation, 166
Wobblies (Industrial Workers of the World), 243
Women
    equal pay and, 97–99
    glass ceiling and, 99
    in work force, 95–97
Wygant v. *The Jackson Board of Education* (1986), 85–86, 126

Yellow-dog contracts, 244